Tabernacle OF HATE

Seduction Into Right-Wing Extremism

SECOND EDITION

KERRY NOBLE

With an Introduction
by Jean Rosenfeld

Syracuse University Press

Second Edition 2010
10 11 12 13 14 15   6 5 4 3 2 1

First edition published as *Tabernacle of Hate: Why They Bombed Oklahoma City* by Kerry Noble (Prescott, Ontario: Voyageur Publishing / Voyageur North America, 1998)

For a listing of books published and distributed by Syracuse University Press, visit our Web site at SyracuseUniversityPress.syr.edu.

ISBN: 978-0-8156-3247-4 (cloth)
          978-0-8156-3248-1 (paperback)

Library of Congress Cataloging-in-Publication Data
Noble, Kerry, 1952–
   Tabernacle of hate : seduction into right-wing extremism / Kerry Noble ; with an introduction by Jean Rosenfeld. — 2nd ed.
      p. cm. — (Religion and politics)
   Includes bibliographical references (p.   ) and index.
   ISBN 978-0-8156-3247-4 (cloth : alk. paper) — ISBN 978-0-8156-3248-1 (pbk. : alk. paper)
   1. Oklahoma City Federal Building Bombing, Oklahoma City, Okla., 1995.
   2. Political violence—Oklahoma—Oklahoma City.   3. Right-wing extremists—United States.   I. Title.
   HV6432.6.N63 2010
   976.6'38053—dc21   2010043510

This book is dedicated to my wife and very best friend, Kay;

to my wonderful, beautiful six children—

Tara, Stephen, Beth, Jirijah, Jared, and Davaar—

who bring me honor and joy, and who give me purpose in life;

and to my grandchildren, Shannon, Julia, Rachael, Mikaila,

Isaiah, and Robert, who have so much to live for.

Kerry Noble, a Christian minister since 1972, has been speaking publicly against racism and violence since 1995. Kerry is also the author of *Tabernacle of Hope: Bridging Your Darkened Past Toward a Brighter Future.*

Contents

Illustrations

So (the Lord) drove out the man;
and He placed at the east
of the garden of Eden
Cherubim, and a flaming sword,
which turned every way,
to keep the way of the tree of life.
                    —Genesis 3:24

Introduction

CRITICAL INCIDENTS

Twenty-five years after the FBI laid siege to a Christian white-supremacist colony on the banks of Bull Shoals Lake in the Ozark Mountains, the narrative of what happened there is shaped by streams of
memories from the participants. The colony named itself the Covenant, the Sword and the Arm of the Lord (CSA). It expected God to
destroy the world in an orgy of disasters chronicled in the New Testament's book of *Revelation*. The men converted guns to illegal automatic weapons, constructed a tank, and stored cyanide. They built a
mock "Silhouette City" in which they practiced killing enemy hordes
expected to descend on them from the decaying urban areas. The idea
of attacking the Murrah Federal Building in Oklahoma City originated at CSA (Noble 1998, 162, *new pages 158–59*). It was bombed on
April 19, 1995, by Timothy McVeigh exactly ten years after the FBI
siege began. After fugitives from the Order,[1] a white-supremacist cell,
fled to the colony in the spring of 1985, the FBI's elite Hostage Rescue Team (HRT) surrounded CSA and demanded its surrender. In a
break from the FBI's usual separation between their tactical team and
their negotiation team, Danny Coulson, the HRT's field commander,
was also designated as the lead negotiator. His mission improbable
was to persuade CSA's charismatic leader, James Ellison, to accept

1. The Order, or "Silent Brotherhood," began as a domestic terrorism cell of
nine men (later it grew to twenty-three members) who took an oath to defend the
white race and reclaim their land in imitation of a fictional group of the same name
in William Pierce (under the pseudonym Andrew MacDonald) 1996, 73. Coulson
and Shannon 1999, 193.

arrest and trial on weapons charges and to deliver the colony into the government's hands.

Danny Coulson remembers sitting with Ellison on the ground during their first meeting. Ellison picked poison ivy leaves and invited him to chew a few (Coulson and Shannon 1999, 299). Coulson sensibly declined, but Ellison stuffed the leaves in his mouth to demonstrate how extraordinary he was.

CSA's propaganda chief and Bible teacher, Kerry Noble, remembers how close the colony came to a gun battle with the Hostage Rescue Team. The FBI employed Ellison's own pastor, Robert Millar, as a "third party intermediary" in their negotiations and thought he was encouraging Ellison to submit. However, Noble, who was inside with Millar and Ellison, reveals that Millar intended to serve as a witness for the fugitives from the Order, who favored shooting it out on April 20, Hitler's birthday (Noble 1998, 166, *new page 198*).

An FBI psychologist noticed that James Ellison was impressed by all things military, including the display of two hundred armed agents around his property. Although Coulson treated Ellison with respect, he privately considered him a weak and vain adversary. He was astonished when Ellison delayed the surrender on April 22 in order to comb his hair.

Attempts to explain how self-styled prophets such as James Ellison, Jim Jones of Peoples Temple, or David Koresh of the Branch Davidians gain a following often rely upon a theory of "cult leaders" derived from studies of American prisoners of war during the Korean War that has been largely misapplied to new religious movements.[2] Cult theorists transfer their moral frame of good and evil from the American prisoner (good) and communist "brainwasher" (evil) and impose it upon the "cult" recruit (good, until brainwashed) and the cult leader (evil). Jim Jones and David Koresh are enshrined in our

---

2. Margaret Thaler Singer (with Janja Lalich), 1995. Cult theory is a product of the behavioral analysis of individual prisoners of enemy armies in wartime that has been analogized to the religious and social behavior of communities led by charismatic leaders in peacetime.

national narratives as evil men who brainwashed their passive followers, thereby reducing both men to a uniform moral category that does
not encourage us to pose specific, critical questions about how they
succeeded and failed, with traumatic outcomes for all parties to a conflict.[3] James Ellison may have had a great deal in common with Jones
and Koresh, but he escaped their fate. While the mass deaths at Jonestown (1978) and Waco (1993) have promoted a media fixation on
"doomsday cults," CSA fades from our collective memory—despite
the fact that Kerry Noble links it to the bombing of the Murrah Federal Building. It is this horrific event that rightly or wrongly drives
Noble's sense of guilt and sorrow and need to tell his story (Coulson
and Shannon 1999, 534–35).

During the tense, four-day standoff in the Ozarks, members of
Ellison's group beamed their own loudspeakers full of "praise" music
and propaganda at the about two hundred FBI agents who surrounded
their commune. Unlike the fiery denouement at Waco in 1993, the
CSA standoff eight years earlier ended peacefully because of Coulson's outreach to Noble, Noble's decision to work with Coulson, and
because God gave a message to Ellison's wife.

Ollie Ellison told her husband that "a feeling came over her" con-
veying that God intended the FBI to set her free, not to kill them. She
pointed out that a freak thunderstorm had detonated all the land mines
they had planted only a week before the FBI arrived. She convinced
Ellison this was a "sign from God" that the CSA "must lay down arms
and live to fight another day" (Coulson and Shannon 1999, 307–8).
Ollie's critical intervention proves that the actual exercise of power
in a religious community is complicated. Within an isolated group,
decision-making does not always originate in the leader. In the case
of CSA, the voice of God transmitted to a woman overcame the fierce

3. An FBI psychiatrist conveyed that some agents involved in the Branch
Davidian incident suffered from post-traumatic stress. What Robert J. Lifton terms
"survivor mission" appears to have affected survivors of both groups as well as some
of their relatives and government officials and some reporters who were at the sites.
See Lifton, 2003, 137–58.

demands of violent fugitives for a gun battle and resolved Ellison's nervous indecisiveness. It was also a revelation "from God" received by a woman in another confrontation twelve years later that helped resolve the longest FBI siege in American history during the Montana Freemen standoff.[4] Thus, discerning how spiritual authority actually is distributed among members of a male-dominated religious group may be helpful in defusing a hostile situation. God can act paradoxically, defying human logical expectations.

The FBI labels sieges of intractable armed groups "critical incidents." How the critical incident at Bull Shoals Lake arose and was resolved without loss of life is a major contribution to our understanding of these potentially explosive situations. Danny Coulson remembers his side of the story in *No Heroes: Inside the FBI's Secret Counter-Terror Force*. From 1991 to 1998 Kerry Noble wrote his account of CSA as he underwent a deep change of heart, a *metanoia*, that turned him into a warner of those who embrace eliminationist doctrines with utopian themes, such as Christian Identity, racial holy war, imminent apocalypse, and government conspiracies. *Tabernacle of Hate* may be the most instructive, forthright, unamended text we have that explains how a peaceable spiritual community can mutate into a terrorist group, and it clearly demonstrates how religion operates—for good and evil—as an overriding motive for human behavior.

Noble's account demonstrates how a disparate group of seekers achieves communal cohesion. Danny Coulson holds CSA up as a "lesson in peer pressure" and "mob mentality." He believes that James Ellison had to plan acts of violence against designated enemies in order to maintain his waning leadership. Coulson recognized that taking action against the "bad guys" operated to bind members of the FBI's elite Hostage Rescue Team together, as well.[5] The HRT's purpose is expressed in the motto *servare vitas*, "to save lives,"

4. Gloria Teneuvial Ward and her two children exited a farmhouse surrounded by the FBI after she got a message from her jailed pastor. She believed he received that message from God. See Rosenfeld 2000, 335.

5. Telephone conversation with Danny Coulson, August 2009.

whereas the CSA was committed to saving the white race and killing demonized others to achieve their purpose. Only a few missteps—interpreted as signs from God—prevented Ellison's men from assassinating government officials and gays before the FBI arrived at their threshold. It is not enough to eat poison ivy with impunity if the leader cannot protect his group from invasion by outsiders or compel God to save them from accidents and death. Ellison may have turned to a paranoid agenda in order to maintain his self-bestowed role as "King of the Ozarks."

SEEKERS AND THE SPIRITUAL ENTREPRENEUR

Initially, James Ellison gathered his flock together after the civil rights movement of the 1950s and 1960s overlapped the the "sex, drugs, and rock and roll" youth culture of the Vietnam years, which culminated in the feminist movement and *Roe v. Wade*'s legalization of abortion. Members withdrew into the Ozark Mountains to await God's judgment of a society that, in their eyes, rivaled Sodom and Gomorrah. In May 1977 Kerry and Kay Noble visited the Bull Shoals colony on the invitation of friends. Ironically, the friends left the community, but the Nobles stayed, driven by their search for God and a sanctified place to raise their children away from urban pollutants. They thought they had found a source of ultimate knowledge and spiritual power in the voice of James Ellison. But Ellison's separatist "praise" church became increasingly militant as it shared in the destiny of rural Americans who lost their properties during the farm crisis in the 1970s and turned to magical remedies offered by self-styled "freemen" and militia "patriots."[6] In 1983 Ellison's community fell behind on its mortgage, and the bank foreclosed on their lakeside property. After it was auctioned off on August 23, 1984, the judge ordered everyone to vacate the land. Noble's response was: "Our men are on full alert . . . armed to defend our property. We will not leave. We are believing in a miracle from God that will allow us to peacefully remain . . ." (Noble

---

6. See Dyer 1997, Aho 1990, Neiwert 1999.

1998, 150, *new page 178*).[7] That miracle, according to Ollie Ellison's message from God, came in the surprising form of the FBI, and it resulted instead in their final expulsion from CSA.

Above all, it is Ellison who dominates the pages of *Tabernacle of Hate* in his role as a spiritual entrepreneur who draws seekers of God to the mountains and a purer existence. Noble recounts how Ellison won the loyalty of his followers, how charismatic authority operates, and how the leader forfeits it. His book unveils the intensely personal relationship between follower and leader, leader and divine source of power, and it chronicles how that relationship becomes the lodestone of meaning in the lives of those afflicted by despair and millennial anxieties. As the character of the group changes, Noble begins to doubt himself and the group's mission. His disillusionment with the downward trajectory of the colony is softened by the avoidance of violence at the end of CSA and even more by his gradual recovery from despair, after his connection to Ellison is broken.

How do seekers of revelation from God become converts to holy war? How can a man of Noble's intrinsic intelligence accept conspiracy theories and notions of spiritual elitism as ultimate knowledge? It is easy to understand how Kerry, who remembers being sickly and weak as a child, would try to compensate by becoming a feller of trees and builder of a settlement in the wilderness. Perhaps more significantly, Noble appears to have arrived at Bull Shoals looking for a place he had never quite found in the churches of his youth. His aesthetic attachment to "the farm" at Bull Shoal's Lake, his tender feelings for his wife and children, and his intellectual drive to teach and write down everything of note in his daily experience all bear witness to an artistic and inquiring sensibility. Noble is a person readers easily identify with even when he takes up bombs or contemplates adultery. In the American "Bible belt," such personalities often turn to preaching—a type of dramatic performance—as an outlet for their talents. It is only

---

7. Wilson and Zimmerman 2009, frontispiece. See also *Silhouette City: God, Guns, Government,* a documentary film by Wilson and Zimmerman.

a small leap for the reader to recognize similar exceptionalities in Jim Ellison, prophet and magician, and to finally figure out what brought these two men together in such a dubious enterprise.

Ellison is a spiritual entrepreneur who must actualize his ideas. He is loathe to accept the teachings of others unless he can synthesize them in service to his own vision of God's special role for himself and his disciples. What attracts and mystifies others is his apparent immunity to disappointment and shame. Contributing to their sense of awe are his amazing powers not only to recover but to heal: he claims he was relatively unaffected by serious injuries in an accident; he readily forgives his first wife and a good friend for their mutual infidelity; and his son is cured after a near-death experience. Ellison meets Max Weber's criterion for charismatic leadership: he is a person seemingly set apart by a divine power from ordinary men.

Significantly, Ellison does not force his ideas on anyone else. His friends remain free to come to their own conclusions about his teachings. It is this quality, above all others, that entices Kerry Noble away from orthodox theology and practices. In a small, isolated community with intense daily "praise" meetings, Noble comes eventually to the conclusion that Ellison's obscure doctrines are intellectually compelling. His story of conversion to the hateful Christian Identity creed is both chilling and convincing, and as "boiling frogs"[8] readers collaborate in that experience, as it unfolds bit by bit.

CHARISMATIC LEADERSHIP

Charisma refers to the grace bestowed upon an individual who is "called" by a transcendent power. Proof of the power's favor and its in-breaking operation in ordinary time is provided by the remarkable deeds a person is able to perform. Recognition of power in operation through the leader by his or her followers is what attracts a community of adherents to the leader's "charismatic authority."

---

8. Noble employs the fable of the boiling frog several times to drive home the moral that exposure by small degrees to the lethal "heat" of hateful ideas will entice the "frog" to accept even the most contrary-to-fact ideologies.

Spiritual power is well-documented as a fundamental feature of religions throughout the world (Van der Leeuw 1963, 23–28, I.1-I.6). It is hard to imagine the rise of new religions or the maintenance of institutionalized religions without spiritual power. It is always channeled through some person or vessel that the community recognizes as a source of transcendent authority. Among Protestant congregations in America, the source of spiritual power is God's word, incorporated in the Biblical text and expounded by preachers or given voice by prophets. But Noble extracts from the book of *Revelation* a more sinister power:

> The word Nicolaitan means "power over the laity (or people)." It is that possessive, controlling attitude over people that leads them astray, that ministers deception, and causes followers to take extreme actions. I oppose it knowing that same element was once so strong in me (Noble 1998, 230, *new page 296*).

The word for "power" in the work of sociologist Max Weber is *Herrschaft,* which means "the power to compel people to obey" (Adair-Toteff 2005, 191). Weber's two concepts of traditional and of bureaucratic[9] *Herrschaft* may best be translated as "domination," but when he speaks of a third, charismatic *Herrschaft,* the word is better translated as "leadership," because of the three types of authority, only charismatic power is personal (Adair-Toteff 2005, 191–92). It inheres in the bond established between leader and follower. A priest, judge, or prime minister who exercises traditional or bureaucratic power claims a routine, this-worldly, ordinary authority, but politicians, prophets, and magicians who exercise charismatic leadership "derive their power simply from their personal gifts" (ibid., 195). Danny Coulson exercised the government's bureaucratic domination in a show of overwhelming paramilitary force to the members of CSA, but James Ellison demonstrated his charismatic leadership by swallowing poison

---

9. Bureaucratic power is also termed "rational-legal" or "legal" authority.

ivy without any ill effect. As Weber observed, charismatic leadership obtains devotion from followers by seeming to be able to perform miracles. According to Weber, the personal leader possesses magical charisma, is heroic, and specifically extraordinary.

The most interesting difference between ordinary social power and charismatic leadership is that charisma is temporary. Like any other personal bond, the devotion of a follower to a leader can break. Noble documents how Ellison won devotion from followers by *allowing them to think for themselves,* while impressing them with his extraordinary gifts. Over time, Noble came to doubt Ellison's leadership, a fact that supports Weber's theory of the impermanence of charismatic authority: "It seems as if the charismatic leader possesses the power and holds sway over his followers. However . . . the charismatic leader is dependent upon the followers for recognition" (ibid.). Noble exposes in detail how a charismatic prophet leads his willing followers toward a paranoid view of the world. He conspires with Ellison by becoming an "elder" and disseminating CSA's conspiracist beliefs in pamphlets that use scripture as "proof texts" for racist, anti-Semitic, and revolutionary doctrines. As James Ellison's CSA became increasingly militant, Kerry Noble incited his followers to "Prepare War!" Like the seeker in *Pilgrim's Progress* and the sinner in *Faust,* Noble is recognizable as a contemporary Everyman who, like any of us, can be enticed by Nicolaitan power.

According to Max Weber retention of this power by the leader depends upon the continuing affirmation of his disciples. When the miracles stop, the magic evaporates, a challenger overcomes the leader, the crisis ends, or the enemies win, his charisma wanes and the extraordinary person reverts to ordinary status. The lesson is that a "cult" is not dominated by its "cult leader" without the consent of each follower, and that consent comes with a time limit built in. Even Weber's archetype of the charismatic leader, Napoleon Bonaparte, could not work miracles forever.

Noble relates that James Ellison claimed to receive a divine "call" on April 29, 1970, at 9:45 a.m. when

God caused a building to collapse around me while I was working on it. I broke twenty-eight bones and my lung was punctured. But in fifteen days I was out of the hospital and back to work in two months. I learned to say what God has told me to say! (Noble 1998, 100, *new page 117*)

Ellison's charisma began to leave him in March 1981 on the day that a child died in a fall at the Bull Shoals settlement. It was the first death on their sacred property. The child was the daughter of Randall Rader, who challenged Ellison's leadership without success and left the settlement in 1982. Rader then joined the Order, was captured by the FBI, and became a source of information to the government about CSA (Coulson and Shannon 1999, 230). A second indication that the leader's charisma was waning occurred in late 1982 when the builders of CSA's fortress-church noticed that it was not square, but "more of a parallelogram" and "off" by twelve inches. Since twelve was a sacred number signifying God's government, the construction crew took this as a sign that the community's own foundation was off and were upset that Ellison refused to correct it (Noble 1998, 115–16, *new pages 135–37*). A third decline in Ellison's power occurred in late 1984 when God prevented him from carrying out his "ultimate goal" in Oklahoma City (Noble 1998, 134, *new page 158*). CSA planned to stage a rocket attack on the Murrah Federal Building, which Ellison and two followers[10] had reconnoitered in 1983, but a rocket blew up in a member's hands and, "It was interpreted as a sign from God that another plan was to be implemented" (Noble 1998, 135, *new page 158*). Over time other incidents were thwarted and Ellison's charisma waned, as Noble observed that "Ellison was losing control over the group" and "We, as CSA, were dying spiritually" by the time Coulson's agents surrounded them (Noble 1998, 162, *new page*

---

10. Noble 1998, 134. The two men were Steve Scott and Richard Wayne Snell, a messenger among radical right groups and a "Christian Patriot" who was executed for murder on the day of the Oklahoma City bombing, April 19, 1995.

193). Coulson told Noble that he was the stronger person, not Ellison, when the time came to negotiate a resolution.

CODED MEANING

Another lesson Noble teaches us from his CSA experience is that symbols and dates are of vital significance to radical right-wing movements. April 19 is a holy day in the ideology of Christian Identity, Christian Patriotism, the American militia movements of the 1990s, and of neo-Nazi imitators like Timothy McVeigh, Terry Nichols, and the "silent brotherhood" of the Order, because so many events that are significant to their ideology and experience occurred on that date.[11] The confrontation between the FBI and Ellison's militants provided "textbook lessons" to the government, particularly that negotiations with religious groups are "entirely different" from those conducted in "normal hostage situations." The difference is that God or a transcendent power is a party to the negotiations.[12] Nine years after CSA was disbanded, Kerry Noble tried to intervene in the FBI siege of the Branch Davidians, because he recognized that "[David Koresh] will not surrender unless he can see by revelation that it is God's will for him to do so." After the deaths at Waco, Noble asked, "What can law-enforcement do?" and answered, "First of all, they must understand the symbology and doctrines of the groups" (Noble 1998, 224, *new page 288*).

Coded language is party of a group's symbolic expression. CSA members believed that Ayn Rand's novel, *Atlas Shrugged,* encoded the "takeover plan" of the Illuminati, a secret international cabal of

11. Among them are the battles of Lexington and Concord, the Passover uprising in the Warsaw Ghetto, the siege of CSA, the burning of the Branch Davidian compound, the Oklahoma City bombing, the execution of Wayne Snell, and the date of birth entered on Tim McVeigh's false driver's license. April 19 was designated by the American antigovernment milieu as "Militia Day," according to Danny Coulson (1999, 455). It is also one day before the April 20 birthday of Adolph Hitler, venerated by neo-Nazis.

12. See Docherty 2001.

Jews and their co-conspirators who sought to eradicate Christianity (Noble 1998, 72, *new page 79*). In any religion, the act of naming is also regarded as an enactment of something, a deed. A name stands for the group's identification with its conception of ultimate reality. When Ellison gathered together his first community of post-sixties hippies and druggies, he called it Zarephath for the place where the prophet Elijah sought refuge from his enemies and protection from God. As he drew in young couples from the Bible belt like Kerry and Kay Noble, the group became Zarephath-Horeb, affixing the alternative name for Mt. Sinai, where God revealed his Law to the chosen people in the wilderness. After accepting Identity Christianity,[13] in 1981 the elders renamed the colony the Covenant, Sword and Arm of the Lord, a title that expressed their group's mission of physically defending white people during God's apocalypse. As the names changed, peaceable members left and were replaced by those who prepared for war. Ellison reconnoitered the Murrah Federal Building in 1983 and provided refuge for members of the Order in 1985.

THE CROSSOVER

Christian Identity infected Ellison's group around 1979–1980, when Noble and Ellison introduced conspiracy theories from outside the commune that were both oppositional and revolutionary. Ellison hosted a "convocation" of radical right-wing leaders and groups, and Noble wrote up and circulated CSA's new sacred texts about a presumed Illuminati takeover of the world and the identity of the "true Israelites," who were not Jewish, but white Christians. The new faith justified CSA's participation in resistance to the U.S. government

---

13. Identity Christianity, or "two-seedline" Christian Identity, teaches a racist, anti-Semitic interpretation of the Biblical myth of Creation. Identity Christians believe that the white race descended from the lost ten tribes of Israel and are God's chosen people, while Jews are descended from Cain, who is the offspring of Eve and the serpent, who is Satan. They believe all other races were separately created as "beasts" or "mud people" before God created Adam, the father of the white race, the "true Israelites."

along with Aryan Nations, the Christian Patriot Defense League, militia groups, and the Order, all of whom believed in defending America against its presumed internal and external enemies, variously defined as liberals, Jews, Zionist Occupation Government, the United Nations, minorities, and "race traitors."

The case of CSA illustrates what could happen in the United States if the neo-Nazi movement, which justifies genocidal violence but has very few followers, crossed with the Christian religion, which has millions of devotees. In fact, National Socialist activists had dreamed of this convergence for decades before Ellison turned to Identity (Kaplan and Weinberg 1998, 101–24). Identity Christianity arose alongside the neo-Nazi movement in America after World War II, and both groups fixed on race and nationality as sacred, ultimate concerns. Both expected a revolution/apocalypse to eliminate Jews, "minorities," and "race traitors." Both were chiliastic, expecting whites to rule in a future utopia. Both justified violence in defense of their ultimate concerns and as a means of attaining a racialist apotheosis. The possibility that a racist Christianity might couple with fascist organizers and produce a chimerical Christian fascism is the *bête noire* of those who monitor anti-Semitism and racism.[14]

In the mid-1980s David Lane, a member of the Order, was convicted of conspiracy to murder a Jewish talk show host with a gun that was illegally converted to an automatic weapon at CSA (Lane 1999, 17–22).[15] It was Lane who created the Fourteen Words, a motto that he hoped would unite the American radical right—from Christian Identity to the cosmotheism of William Pierce's National Alliance—as an expression of one sacred mission: "We must secure the existence of our people and a future for White children" (Lane 1999, passim). In keeping with the penchant of religious innovators to codify meaning in numbers, Lane's use of Fourteen Words

14. See Department of Homeland Security 2009; Southern Poverty Law Center 2009; Neiwert 2009.

15. The actual charges were conspiracy to violate the victim's civil rights. The gun was given by Randall Rader to Lane's co-defendant.

magically counters Woodrow Wilson's Fourteen Points in the Treaty of Versailles, which historian Walter Russell Mead observes still guide world politics today, including the United Nations.[16] Even though American fascists worship gods other than Yahweh and Christ, they also have dreamed of a united front with radical Christian leaders, such as Gerald L. K. Smith, Gerald Winrod, Richard Girnt Butler, and Robert Millar. Timothy McVeigh followed a script from a neo-Nazi revolutionary novel, *The Turner Diaries,* and executed a plan conceived by members of CSA. Thus, the Oklahoma City bombing symbolically enacted the dreaded crossover of fascism and Christianity, but contrary to McVeigh's hopes, it drove the militias and "Patriots" underground for a decade.

FASCISM

One cannot attribute the appearance of fascism as a twentieth-century *weltanschauung* either to liberal or conservative political philosophies.[17] It originated fulsomely in Italy after World War I as a vaunted "Third Way." Race and nationalism were potently combined in Nazi Germany to justify the appropriation of "living space" for Germans by military invasion. Charismatic leaders of fascist parties, Mussolini and Hitler, were never elected to office by majorities, but were granted the reins of national government by traditional parties in coalition arrangements

16. I am indebted to David C. Rapoport for bringing to my attention the backlash to the Fourteen Points during the rise of the Nazi Party in Germany. See Mead 2001, 2.

17. Polemicists of left and right have unfortunately appropriated the term "fascism" to score points in their endless discourse, but it is not really attributable either to socialist or conservative philosophies. Fascists invariably court and deceive conservatives by first attacking their traditional opponents on the political spectrum: communists, socialists, liberals. However, after achieving legitimate power to govern, fascists neutralize traditional institutions, such as state churches, and eliminate bureaucratic sources of authority by replacing conservative personnel with fascist ideologues or collaborators. The Quisling government in Norway and the Vichy French regime provide examples of fascist replacement of personnel in "rational-legal" institutions and state security agencies.

that acceded to their abilities to rally masses to their ultranationalist agendas. At the heart of these agendas is a soaring vision of a utopia based upon the virtues of "the people," as defined by the fascist party. The American imitators of Nazism seek to provoke a world revolution that will eliminate all ethnicities except the white race.

Kevin Passmore notes that fascist movements seek not only to eliminate communists and liberals but also to subvert traditional institutions and conservative political parties (Passmore 2002, *passim*). For a fascist movement to attain ruling status, it is necessary for the churches to stand aside, a dominant center or conservative majority to align with the fascists in order to unify the nation, and a charismatic figure to ascend by votes and/or political acquiescence to head of state. Because, so often, a parliamentary system relies on coalitions to govern, it can be exploited to enable fascist parties. Few instances of fascist rule have occurred in the modern era, but many proto-fascist organizations have arisen in democratic states. Each country breeds its own varietal of fascism, depending upon its culture, politics, history, ethnicities, and identity, among other sociological factors.

Scholars debate the definition of fascism, which presents problems for those who would confront and deal with it before it becomes the romantic motivation for a mass outpouring of ultranationalism. Unless it can be corralled, labeled, and watched, it can deceive the public as a beast with another name, such as patriotism, populism, traditionalism, or, in the case of the United States, "Americanism." Roger Griffin defines it as "palingenetic," meaning literally "born again," which specifically connotes a total regeneration of the nation by ordinary people who are fed up with all governing parties. When a critical mass of citizens—not necessarily a majority—coalesce around a polarizing charismatic leader with a message of national renewal that unifies the citizenry by defining their enemies and furnishing a program to overcome them, traditional political parties are tempted to capitulate to this popular enthusiasm. For dominant conservative parties, fascism promises to weaken the vote-getting power of their liberal opponents. For dominant liberal parties, fascism offers a popular alternative to tired agendas and revives their message.

Fascism is essentially charismatic; it replaces bureaucratic institutions with its own "parallel" entities and displaces traditional and bureaucratic authority with the new charismatic authority, removing power from ordinary loci and investing it in new organs of control and persuasion. It also introduces the crowd-pleasing elements of coercion by thuggery and vigilantism into the political system, giving power directly to "the people" in a Nicolaitan coup and representing the will of "the people" embodied in a charismatic leader.

The appeal of ultranationalism unified a new organization that rode the trend of urbanization in America in the early twentieth century. As the nation admitted Jewish refugees from pogroms in Russia and the Ukraine, *The Protocols of the Elders of Zion* was circulated (under the title "The International Jew") by Henry Ford's newspaper, and an enthusiastic Fundamentalist Christian movement took hold in the heartland. That organization was the nationwide Ku Klux Klan. It fed on a reawakened nativist response to the influx of immigrants, the de facto "sundown towns," and Jim Crow laws that excluded African-Americans from new suburbs and white establishments, the Christian anti-communist response to the atheist Bolshevik Revolution, and the loss of community cohesion through rapid urbanization (Bennett 2005; Neiwert 2009, 176–78).

A second fascist upwelling occurred in the 1930s as the national Klan movement was breaking up into local splinters, due to scandals and state legislation aimed at weakening it. The German American Bund and the Silver Shirts arose in support of Hitler on the West Coast. Although the advent of a second World War and investigations and trials of targeted fascists in the "Brown Scare" ended these ephemeral organizations, the fascist milieu persisted and threw off new conspiratorial movements, including the groups that James Ellison courted in 1983, when he attended a conference sponsored at Aryan Nations in Idaho. By converting to Christian Identity, the Bull Shoals seekers were "born again" as "true Israelites" to whom the promise of land and infinite descendents was covenanted by God with the white race exclusively. That land, according to the assorted fascists, Odinists, patriots, and militia members who "converged" in the

1980s at Aryan Nations and CSA, was the North American continent, specifically the United States. To reclaim their land and ensure the survival of the white race, it would be imperative to declare war on the Zionist Occupation Government. The Order and CSA both issued declarations of war on the government and took hostile action to advance their utopian agendas.

Not all groups that hope for divine judgment against their perceived tormentors take up arms against them. Most apocalyptic communities are passive and very few are aggressive,[18] but those few can cause disproportional mayhem. Ellison joined with racists, anti-Semites, and neo-Nazis to promote a revolution against the U.S. government. The eschatology of a white-supremacist racial holy war depicted in *The Turner Diaries* and the eschatology of the book of Revelation were syncretized at CSA in a microcosm of what could mushroom on a national scale if the radical right were able to fulfill David Lane's dream of harnessing a united white-supremacist movement to a race-based version of Christianity in the ultimate war of good against evil.

According to Noble, Identity Christians share a belief in the "potent combination" of race, religion, and nationality. In Europe and America fascism has combined a belief in the "white race"[19] with ultranationalism. The Oklahoma City bombing and the use of airplanes as missiles to destroy the World Trade Center, the Pentagon, and the Capitol are two expressions of the same international "wave" of religious terrorism, which originated in 1979—the year of

18. Included among aggressive groups are Aum Shinrikyo, the Order of the Solar Temple, the Movement for the Restoration of the Ten Commandments of God, and al-Qaida.

19. It should be mentioned that the concept of race is not biological or anthropological, but is socially and politically constructed. There is one human species, indivisible, on earth at this time. "White" is descriptive of skin color only and not indicative of the origin of the species, which physical anthropologists locate in Africa. Thus, use of the phrase "white race" reflects the label assigned to certain populations in certain countries by racialists and separatists, not any designation accepted by scientists or social scientists.

the Iranian revolution and James Ellison's general date for the Christian Apocalypse. Were it not for Noble's text, we would know much less about the current wave of religious terrorism that has manifested itself in Christianity, Judaism, Islam, and Hinduism since the late 1970s. Like ocean waves, these trends in world history build slowly, crescendo, and recede in, roughly, forty-year generations (Rapoport 2004, 9–37; Barkun 2003).

The final quarter of the twentieth century was marked by apocalypticism—a despairing response to deeply felt injustices combined with the paradoxical hope that divine power will soon intervene to punish the wicked and establish an ultimate utopia.

According to Kevin Passmore, there has been a resurgence of fascism in Western countries since the 1990s. David A. Neiwert pinpoints fascism's 1990s resurgence in the United States in "an economically disenfranchised rural America (Neiwert 2009, 237). He regards the phenomenon of talk radio as a "transmission" belt of conspiracist ideas throughout this widespread area, cautioning us to "have a clear view of what fascism is . . . as a real-life phenomenon. Fascism is not an extinct political force" (ibid., 105). He traces the American version of fascism through our "eliminationist" treatment of nonwhites throughout our history, from Indian tribes to African slaves to Chinese laborers and "illegal" Hispanic immigrants. Our varietal of fascism is racist, ultranationalist, and utopian. It is latent and awaits a "crisis of democracy" to become a viable charismatic threat to our constitutional regime (ibid., 236–37).

In a sense, the journey of Kerry Noble into the eliminationist paranoia of CSA and his gradual journey back to "values that all people can participate in" furnishes a *qal v'homer* blueprint for avoiding a descent into ultranationalism and nativism by the body politic (Noble 1998, 226, *new page 291*).[20] Part of the blueprint requires our collective recognition of "what we are up against—namely a form of

---

20. *Qal v'homer* is a mode of argument that maintains what is true in the lesser case is therefore true in the greater (analogous) case.

fascism" (Neiwert 2009, 239)—in the message of charismatic preachers, prophets, or talk show hosts who transmit the conspiracy theories of a Dan Gayman, David Lane, William Pierce, or Robert Millar. If we turn away from the word "fascism" itself or use it cavalierly against any designated political opponent, we relinquish the opportunity to exert that "eternal vigilance" that preservation of democracy requires.

Ultimately, human beings imitate the behavior of their gods. They express in symbolic terms—texts, rituals, architecture, calendars, inter alia—how, ideally, a social world should work and what its overarching purpose should be. Creating a "religious," that is, *meaningful,* context for daily life and routines is a recurrent endeavor in history. Charismatic leadership can save a people from death and destruction by a superior enemy, as it did in the Eastern European forests of Lithuania at ground zero during the Holocaust.[21] Conversely, it can threaten innocent members of society by naming them as an enemy to be eliminated in the name of God, as it did in the lakes and mountains of Arkansas and Idaho in the waning years of the second millennium AD. Christians can choose to follow their pacific Lamb of God or their militant Christ with a Sword. Whom they choose to imitate determines their impact not only on their souls but also on their worlds.

---

21. See Tec 2009, wherein the story of the Bielsky brothers' charismatic leadership saved Jews from genocide by creating a society de novo in the forest.

In Appreciation

To Ollie, whose mere presence illuminates a room and fills the soul with light. To Cheryl S., my spiritual twin sister, for always being there. To Gary and Billy, two friends who are closer than brothers. To Donna Jean, Cindy, Bill T., friends who have added immensely to my life.

Jack N., Eric, Henry, Gary, David, Tim, and Rudy: you should never have gotten in trouble; it was not your fault.

My sincere apologies to Larry and Donna, Greg and Nancy, Tom and Barbara, Dan, Alton, Barry, Hoyte and Charlotte, Rodney and Susie, Annie, Trent, Bruce and Phyllis, Richard and Connie, Kent, Jack and Sybil, the kind folks of Pontiac, Gainesville, and Mountain Home, and to anyone else I may have hurt in any way.

Special thanks to Dennis Graves, a news reporter with integrity and compassion, and all the other media that acted truthfully and without bias; attorney John VanWinkle; U.S. Assistant Attorney Steve Snyder; Gene Irby of the Arkansas State Police Criminal Investigation Division; Federal Agents Jack Knox, Danny Coulson, Bill Buford, Bill Hobbs, and all the other Federal Bureau of Investigation and Bureau of Alcohol, Tobacco and Firearms agents who rescued me and helped restore my confidence and respect in the United States government. Thanks to Agent Mark Dukeshier for his support. And to Carol, who treated me like a human being while I was in prison. To Bill Buford of the Bureau of Alcohol, Tobacco and Firearms and Thomas Garrett of the Baxter Bulletin for permission to use some of their photographs.

To Mike Farrell, of TV's *M.A.S.H.*, for his encouraging telephone call to me. To the Cult Awareness Network, the Anti-Defamation League, the Southern Poverty Law Center, other human rights organizations and various law-enforcement seminar officials: thank you for your encouragement.

To "Plus Two" Toastmasters for accepting me and for being a sounding-board, allowing me to work out inner emotions, without rejecting or judging me. Your encouragement has been a blessing.

Special thanks to friends Peter Pactor and Tana Grubb for pushing me concerning this book. To Bob Henry for listening and giving me insight into the production of this book. To Howard Goldenthal of the Canadian Broadcasting Company for believing in my story to recommend it; to Sean Fordyce, my original publisher; to Peggy Hubble and Jennifer Hill, my publicists, for taking a chance on me.

To the late George Hawtin, the late A. E. Knoch, and the late Ernest L. Martin, for their insights into the historical, scientific, spiritual, and doctrinal background of scripture.

To Kay, Brenda, Tommy, Red, Danny, Monica, Pam, Helen, Barry, Terry, Stanley, Steve, Bertha, Alton, Sam, Mike, Donna, Mike K., and Marcie—childhood friends who gave me such wonderful memories. To all my school teachers—especially Mrs. Sadler, Mr. Decker, Mr. McCoy, and Mr. Rock—who taught me a love and thirst for learning and to always ask questions.

To Mike, David, Susan, Diane, Gary and Larry: employers and bosses who gave me a chance after coming home from prison.

Finally, eternal thanks to my mom and dad, my grandmother (and grandfather, now deceased) and all my family, and to my wife's entire family, for being supportive of me even when I broke your hearts. I love you all. Especially to my sister, Karen: my battles have been nothing compared to yours. Your strength and courage have always been an inspiration to me.

Tabernacle of Hate

Prologue

O Lord, I know that the way of man is not in himself;
it is not in man that walks to direct his steps.
The steps of a man are ordered by the Lord.
                    —Jeremiah 10:23; Psalm 37:23

On April 19, 1995, at 9:02 in the morning, the heartbeat of America flatlined as the Murrah Federal Building in Oklahoma City exploded into rubble, killing 168 innocent men, women and children (and wounding over 500 more) in the largest terrorist act ever committed in the United States.

Twelve hours later, white-supremacist Richard Wayne Snell, already serving life in prison without parole for shooting and killing a black state trooper, would be executed in Arkansas for the previous murder of a pawn shop owner (an unsolved murder at the time of his first conviction). Snell spoke just two weeks before his execution about an upcoming event that would have to do with a bombing. While watching the news televising the Murrah building devastation, the bloody bodies being carried away and the rising death toll being announced, guard records reveal that Snell smiled and laughed. Then while being strapped down, awaiting the injection that would end his life, Richard Wayne Snell proudly proclaimed, "Hail his victory."

On April 19, 1993, the world watched in horror as over eighty men, women and children were sacrificed as a burnt offering to their messiah, David Koresh, rather than surrender to federal agents. For fifty-one days, America had been praying for a peaceful end to the standoff at Waco.

Are there interconnecting threads between these three fabrics of insanity? Is their common date, April 19th, significant?

On April 19, 1985, another religious community engaged a stand-off with many of the same agents that were later at the Branch Davidian compound. During that four-day standoff, I was the negotiator between that group and the United States government.

From May 1977 to May 1985 I was a member and one of the leaders of an organization in northern Arkansas that evolved from a quiet, rural community church into a violent, paramilitary, right-wing, white supremacist group. We were well-armed, formed paramilitary units, built bunkers and practiced military-style maneuvers. That organization, formerly known as Zarephath-Horeb Community Church, came to be known nationally and internationally as CSA: the Covenant, the Sword and the Arm of the Lord. From January 1981 to October 1982 we received constant attention from the news media. I was the group's spokesman.

In April 1985, we were invaded by over 200 law enforcement officers from the FBI, the Bureau of Alcohol, Tobacco and Firearms (ATF), and various state, county and local police agencies, for weapons violations and terrorist acts. It was the first time in FBI history that they raided a domestic terrorist group as militarily trained as ours. We became the case study for federal agents for several years.

How will history remember Kerry Wayne Noble? The Federal Bureau of Investigation lists me as the number two leader of the second most dangerous domestic terrorist organization of the United States of America in 1985. That's the negative side.

On the positive side, I am, to the best of my knowledge, and by the admission of the FBI, the only leader of a religious, paramilitary, extremist organization who has been involved in a siege/standoff situation with the federal government to have gone to prison, and to have turned around for the good — by the actions of the government I once condemned. This places me in a unique position, as an individual who has insight into both sides: the mindset of the ultra-right groups and the intentions of the government.

Today I speak to law-enforcement, civic organizations, and other groups about the dangers of the right-wing movement, its paranoid mentality and philosophy, its future and how law-enforcement should approach the various religious, nationalist and racist groups so that future Oklahoma City/Waco-type tragedies can be avoided.

I believe that not only should people understand what the right-wing movement is all about, but also how easy it is to get seduced by its philosophy. How and why did I get involved in the right-wing to begin with? What prompted my changing back — my awakening? How is my story like those of others? How is my story different? These are the reasons for this book.

I hope that this book will be a beam of light for those who, for an enormous variety of reasons, are afraid that the government of America is planning to take away, not merely their guns or constitutional rights, but also their cherished way of life. *Tabernacle of Hate* will examine dissident groups in a manner never previously undertaken. What are their true motives, their real beliefs, their potential dangers? I also hope to provide an understanding of the world of right-wing citizens, which to most is a broad, gray, menacing area. This book will examine the three ingredients, needed to create an extremist as well as the catalysts that will cause that person to cross the line to becoming lethally dangerous.

We all have concerns about our personal futures and the future of our country. This nation was built upon the premise of not trusting government. But America—with its government of the people, by the people, for the people—was also founded upon a belief in a Supreme Being which controls the destiny of men and nations.

Unlike during my years at CSA, it is now my personal belief that we are headed toward the best years in the history of our nation.

It has taken me years to write this book. My desire is not vindication, monetary gain, publicity, or blame. It has been therapeutic in its writing. I do not contend that all the dialogue quoted in this book represents the actual words spoken at the time, nor that all the events represented here are absolutely accurate, but are well within the parameters of my memory, of the documentation which I possess, and of the feedback of former CSA members. It is, however, best to remember that this book is from my perspective and no one else's.

The Biblical or spiritual discussions contained within are not designed to proselytize or to convince the reader of any doctrine or experience. The vast majority of these teachings I no longer adhere to. They are included only as background information in order for the reader to further understand the mindset of those involved. Obviously some offensive material rests in the following pages. I apologize for that but accuracy dictates its inclusion. As with the right-wing teachings that I once espoused, my former racial attitudes are no longer applicable.

My years in Arkansas were literally the best and the worst of times. I pray this book will help others not to take the path that I took, and that it be something of a healing balm to those who have taken the same path.

Part One | **The End Begins**

1

The Siege Begins

Yea, though I walk through the valley of the shadow of death,
I will fear no evil: for You are with me;
Your rod and Your staff they comfort me.
You prepare a table before me in the presence of my enemies;
You anoint my head with oil: my cup runs over . . .

—Psalms 23:4, 5

"Snipers!" came the scream of a frightened man. "Kerry!" the voice yelled, as the pounding on the door continued. "Wake up! Wake up!"

Go away! I thought.

It was April 20, 1985. I was hoping the last six days, especially the previous one, had been a dream. I looked at the clock. Six o'clock in the morning. Jesus!

My wife, Kay, let the armed, camouflage-clothed soldier in.

"Yeah?" I asked as the man entered our bedroom.

"Snipers. All around us. Must've come in during the night. Two of our men were walking their rounds near the perimeter right before dawn. They accidentally came upon one of the snipers, who then ordered our men to return to camp. Now we can see several of them from the bunkers and north guard tower. James wants you to go out there and speak to them."

"Okay. I'll be at James' house in a few minutes."

I dressed in civilian clothing instead of an American-camouflage uniform like the morning messenger had on. No need to spook whoever was out there.

"I'll have breakfast ready for you when you return," Kay offered, the concern on her face evident. She was doing well to not cry.

I left to go to James Ellison's house. I felt like I'd been fasting for a week; I was mentally and emotionally numb, and tired. I just wanted it all to end. It was Ellison who had brought us to this. The arrest warrant was for him. No one else. It was obvious who was out there and what they wanted. It wasn't like we hadn't been warned. Why wouldn't he just surrender?

To make things worse, five of our men had been unable to return from town the day before. They had been stopped by the roadblock and refused entrance.

It was Saturday morning. Our Sabbath.

As I walked to Ellison's house, armed men were scurrying to various bunker positions, trenches and foxholes. Panic was obvious in their voices. I mentally pictured where some of the other men might be—one in the communications building, maybe one on the tower, two or three in the munitions building, one or two trying to comfort the women and children, several with Ellison or simply walking guard. Then I tried to imagine where the enemy might be: snipers all around us, both roads cut off with vehicles, law-enforcement officers posted throughout the woods.

"It looks like they got their men positioned about every ten to fifteen yards, completely surrounding us," one of our scouts was telling James, as I entered Ellison's kitchen. Eight men, each armed with rifle and pistol and wearing the standard American camouflage uniforms, stood around James, waiting for orders. The table was covered with guns.

"What are we gonna do?" one of the young zealots questioned.

"Are we gonna kill us some feds today?" another demanded.

"I'm ready!" a third proudly interjected. "Been looking forward to this for a long time now. Let the war begin! It'll be a tribute to Hitler's birthday! We'll teach them not to mess with CSA." The other men laughed with heightened anticipation. I couldn't help but notice the contrast between the unstable men and the unemotional weapons.

Still another man, the anxiety showing in his voice, asked, "How many do you think are out there, James?"

Ellison quietly continued cleaning the guns, the gears turning in his head. He was always quick to listen and slow to speak. This time, however, he didn't even respond to the question. Ollie, James' wife, was trying to serve him breakfast. She was accustomed to several men being in her kitchen early in the mornings, though it still bothered her.

"Obviously," James finally said as he meticulously cleaned a rifle. "We knew this was coming. I guess this is it."

Ellison looked down the barrel of the rifle. "I suspect the snipers have night vision goggles, just like us. I want you to continue getting all the weapons out of the stashes today," he ordered the men, "and get them ready. Also the grenades and the LAW rocket. Everyone is to be on alert. Let the women and children do their normal activities outside. With women and kids outside, the feds won't shoot. Make sure the tank is ready if I need it . . . Kerry," he said, acknowledging my presence for the first time, "you know what to do. Talk to them. Tell them I'm not ready to surrender yet."

One of the men from the Order raised his rifle defiantly. "Surrender? We're not going to surrender, are we?"

"Of course not," Ellison stated calmly, "but I want them to think I might. That will give us time to prepare and to plan."

"Plan for what?" I asked. My stomach tightened. There were too many variables for me to stay calm.

"For a shoot-out, an escape, for whatever God wants."

"James, what escape? I thought they had us surrounded. And surely you're not thinking of shooting it out with the feds over a warrant that has a five-year maximum on it? Not with the women and children here!"

James lost his patience with me. He had for some time now. He knew my discomfort with the paramilitary, automatic weapons and handgrenades. It seemed all we had done for a long time was argue. He thought I was a coward and I was beginning to conclude he was crazy. "Understand this clearly, Kerry. I'm not going to surrender. And anyone who walks down that hill to surrender, I'll shoot them in the back myself! Do you understand me?" Ellison stood for the first time since my arrival that morning.

"I haven't come this far to surrender to the enemy now! It's not God's will. The feds started this war, not me. We could win without firing a shot, if that's what God wants. God can open the earth and swallow the feds if He wants. Or He can cause them to go blind. He can even have us die and then resurrect us in three days! Is anything too hard for the Lord? I don't care what He does or how He does it, but I know He doesn't want us to surrender!" Ellison looked intently at the men.

"Rumor has it," he continued, "that Klan, neo-Nazi and Patriot groups are already headed this way, ready to fight for us and with us. If this is where the Second American Revolution starts, in order to open the eyes of the American people, then so be it. And you know God can cause us to be victorious, don't you?"

"James," I argued, "He can do whatever He wants. But will He?"

"No, Kerry" he said, staring intently at me, "the question is, are you going to be afraid of the enemy and take the easy way out or are you going to have faith? That's the only question. Now, how long will you stand between two opinions? If Yahweh is God, follow Him; but if Baal is, then follow him. As for me and my family, I'll die before I surrender. Now get out there and do your job!"

I left James' house and the main settlement of our compound with my instructions. See what they want. Stall. Assess the situation. The air was crisp and cool on that April morning. I walked down our dirt driveway toward the iron-rod front gate scanning the area. I spotted a few of the snipers, some behind trees, some behind rocks and old, fallen tree trunks. I opened the gate, went through and locked it behind me. Then I crossed the rock-laden county road that went through our property.

I warily walked through the barbed-wire second gate and then slowed and located the sniper I chose to confront. He was about two hundred yards from James' house, in a prone position behind some rocks and dried brush, scoped rifle expertly held. I had spotted others, rifles targeted on me or the ten farmhouses I had just left behind. I extended my arms outward from my sides.

Would they shoot me down in cold blood—saying I provoked them? Would they arrest me on the spot? Hold me hostage? All possible scenarios ran through my mind. Was I afraid like James had said?

Was it wrong to feel fear? It felt like I was moving in slow motion. I advanced to within twenty feet of my target.

"Halt!" he commanded. "Do not come any closer!" He then spoke into the headphone mike of his communication radio. Crouched behind a fallen tree trunk, his face painted with camouflage, the federal agent looked menacing and serious.

"What are you doing here?" I demanded, as if in charge myself. "Are you trying to start a war?"

"Are you willing to talk to our commander?" he asked, completely ignoring my two questions.

"Yes."

He spoke again into the headset. "Very well. Leave and walk down the road toward the area you call 'the Valley.' You'll be met down there."

I did as I was told. It was a quarter mile to the Valley. The Valley of the Shadow of Death, I mused at myself. And behind me was Hell. The Valley was the settlement I had lived in for six years, before moving to the main settlement.

I walked cautiously. Having enemy guns aimed at me for the first time was disconcerting. I spotted federal "soldiers" throughout the woods, watching me. Will the feds be like the zealots inside, and simply want to shoot their enemy on sight? I wondered.

We were as isolated as one could get. Located near Bull Shoals Lake in northern Arkansas, we were surrounded by hills, trees and rough, rocky roads. The nearest town of any size was forty miles to the south—Mountain Home, Arkansas—population 4000. The winding, rocky road on the Arkansas side snaked from our property for nine miles before it met the paved state highway. Two miles to the north lay another rocky road that was drivable only as long as the lake wasn't up. It joined the highway to Pontiac, Missouri, an almost-hidden lakefront resort town with a population of about two hundred. For eight years I had lived between these two towns.

As I neared the valley, I was surprised to see two lines of vehicles parked on that county road, stretching past the next hill. At least thirty cars and vans rested where normally only one or two unfamiliar vehicles passed in any given month. I sighed deeply.

I purposely walked even slower. Let them wait on me. I thought about the events of the last few days.

Five days earlier, on Monday, April 15, 1985, the news blared across the radio and the compound's sole television set. Twenty-two-year-old David Tate had shot two Missouri state patrolmen, Jimmie Linegar and Allen Hines, near the Missouri-Arkansas line, between Harrison, Arkansas and Branson, Missouri, with a MAC-10 fully automatic machine-pistol. One officer, Linegar, was dead; the other in serious condition.

Two hundred police officers were immediately called in to help search for Tate, who had left his van and fled on foot into the area woods that covered hundreds of square miles. Tate had left behind a vehicle loaded with machine guns, ammunition, silencers and hand-grenades. He was a member of the neo-Nazi group Aryan Nations, located at Hayden Lake, Idaho. Law-enforcement officials believed he might be headed for our group, CSA: the Covenant, Sword and Arm of the Lord.

Later that same afternoon the news worsened. Fourteen members of another right-wing organization known as "the Order" became wanted fugitives when federal indictments were handed down that morning by the Grand Jury in Seattle, Washington. The indictments included charges of armored car heists in Washington state and California, counterfeiting, and for murdering a Jewish radio talk show host, Alan Berg, in Denver, Colorado.

Two of the fourteen were ex-CSA members. Two others were currently hiding on our property, now surrounded as we were, along with two more Order members not mentioned in the news reports.

In addition, Governor Bill Clinton had just signed into law a new anti-paramilitary statute designed by the Jewish Anti-Defamation League (ADL), which we believed would be used to make our group illegal.

That same day, Order member Frank Silva was arrested near Rogers, Arkansas. Named in the federal charges brought down from

Seattle, he now joined Order member Ardie McBrearty—arrested April 4th—in the county jail.

It had been a busy day.

On Tuesday, April 16, news media began arriving early. As the public-relations person and spokesman for our group, I met them at the front gate. No one was allowed in. All of our men were visibly seen dressed in camouflage and heavily armed.

"May we come in?" one newsman asked.

"No," I replied.

"Why not?"

"Due to circumstances, we feel it wise not to allow visitors at this time."

"Why are your men dressed like that?" another asked, pointing to the men.

"We're on alert. It's precautionary, that's all. It's not meant to be threatening."

"Did you know David Tate?" a third inquired.

"David Tate had been here once in 1982. He hasn't been here since."

"Was he headed for CSA?"

"Not that I am aware of. We've had no contact with him in almost three years, so I see no reason to assume he was headed here."

"Do you think he's headed here now?"

"According to the news," I responded, "Tate's on foot. The incident took place probably sixty miles from here as the crow flies. Again, I see no reason to assume he might be headed here."

"If he were and if he arrived here, would CSA hide David Tate?"

"I can't answer that."

"Kerry," the first reporter asked, "it's reported that CSA is harboring fugitives from the Order. Is that true?"

I laughed at the audacity of the question and knew I had to lie. "No, it's not true."

"You have no one from the Order here?"

"We do not."

"Then may we come in and look around?"

"No."

"Why not, if you have nothing to hide?" It was clear the reporters were getting frustrated.

"Our lives have been disrupted enough. We don't need any more disruption. Our people have a right to privacy."

"What about James Ellison? Can we talk to him? He's still in charge, isn't he?"

"Yes, he's still in charge here, but I do the speaking for CSA."

"Kerry," another reporter asked, "do you think the authorities will come to question you soon?"

"You'll have to ask them that question."

"It's been reported that law-enforcement officers have heard automatic gunfire coming from CSA. Do you have fully automatic weapons and handgrenades here?"

Again I had to lie. "No; now if you'll excuse me, I haven't had my breakfast yet."

The questions continued but I ignored them and headed back to my house. Technically, I thought, I didn't lie about that last question. I didn't personally have any illegal weapons here, even though I knew the group obviously did. I smiled at the semantics of the question and my answer.

More and more media personnel arrived Wednesday and Thursday. Almost all of my time was occupied speaking with them.

David Tate had not been captured by Thursday, April 18.

And then it got worse again.

On Thursday afternoon, a friend from the Arkansas State Police Criminal Investigation Division, Gene Irby, drove to our front gate. He asked me to get into the vehicle. I asked the media to leave us alone.

"How's it going?" Gene asked.

"Tiring."

To the point, Gene stated, "Kerry, I need to speak to James. Is he here?"

"I don't know, Gene." I knew I had to act ignorant. "What's up?"

"I've got a federal warrant for his arrest, Kerry. I want him to surrender peacefully and come with me to Mountain Home."

James Ellison was the leader and founder of our church, Zarephath-Horeb, and of our paramilitary unit, CSA.

"What's the warrant for?" I sighed, closing my eyes and hanging my head.

"Conspiracy to possess unregistered weapons. You know, fully automatic machine-guns. Kerry," he pleaded, "it carries a five-year maximum sentence. If James comes in voluntarily it'll look good on his behalf. He'd probably do less than two years." Gene's concern showed.

"Let me go talk to him. I'll be back in a few minutes."

I returned an hour later.

"Well?" Gene asked, after I got back into his car.

"He wants tonight to pray about it, Gene, and to talk it over with the elders."

"What's to pray about?"

"Gene," I implored, "give us till tomorrow morning. I'll let you know then. Please?"

"Okay. I'll be back at eight o'clock in the morning."

"Thanks, Gene." I got out of the car and walked over to the driver's side.

"Kerry, talk to him. This is serious."

Two months earlier I had secretly met with Irby at his office in Mountain Home, Arkansas. Absolutely no one from CSA—not even my wife—knew I had been there. James would have considered it an act of cowardice and betrayal, and I knew it. Gene and I had spoken often since first meeting in August 1984. He was a personable fellow, probably ten years older than me.

"Gene," I said at that clandestine meeting, "do me a favor. If a warrant ever comes down for James' arrest, come tell me first so I can make it easier for James to surrender. And come alone. If a bunch of vehicles drive up at one time, I can guarantee he would not surrender, for fear of the cops destroying the place after taking him away. And if a bunch of cops come in force, like they're ready to shoot it out, you'd have a war this country would never forget. I wouldn't be able to stop the bloodshed that would follow."

Then I looked as serious as possible at Irby and said, "And, Gene . . . there would be a lot of bloodshed."

He understood. "Very well. I know of no forthcoming warrant, but if a warrant is ever issued, I'll do what I can."

I hoped and prayed Gene would never have to do as I had asked.

In Fort Smith, Arkansas on Friday, April 19, 1985, the Order's "Declaration of War" was revealed at Silva's bond hearing.

Gene Irby arrived at eight o'clock sharp at our front gate.

So did the media.

I got into his car. I knew he wouldn't like what I had to say.

"Well, Kerry?" he asked.

"I'm sorry, Gene. He won't surrender."

"Damn. Kerry, you've got to make James understand. There's a lot at stake here."

"I really tried. I think he ought to surrender now, too. But he wants more time to pray about it." I hesitated. "Now what?"

"You know what. By five o'clock this afternoon roadblocks will be set up preventing anyone from entering or leaving. Kerry, talk to him. He has no idea what's going on here."

"I'll try, Gene, but you know how he is."

"Yeah, I know."

"And Gene . . ."

"Yeah?"

"Remember. Don't try to bulldoze your way in or try to sneak in. I wouldn't be able to prevent a shoot-out if the cops come charging in to hurt our people or our property."

"Don't worry. That won't happen."

But I was worried.

I relayed the conversation to James. Immediately he sent six of our men, including myself, to town, in three vehicles, for gasoline and supplies. We were told to be back by early afternoon.

Three roadblocks had been set up by noon Friday, April 19, 1985, five hours earlier than anticipated. All of our neighbors had been evacuated from their homes and housed in Mountain Home. The media were not allowed in, and were forced back about two miles away. The hills and woods kept them from observing the situation. Air traffic was forbidden over our property.

Those of us who had gone into town that morning had been stopped and detained upon returning to our property. Our men and supplies were prevented from returning to CSA. Lest all hell should break loose, I was allowed to return with one vehicle.

Ellison became upset when I reported to him. "They tricked us! They lied! Irby said it would be five o'clock before the roadblocks would be in place! We oughta go to war now, but we need more time. More time to see what God has planned."

I knew what Ellison was thinking. Five of our best military men had been taken out without a shot. Those five men made up about one-quarter of our military might.

But the feds had taken a chance; their action could have backfired and provoked the others into retaliating. Fortunately, however, the men waited to see what Ellison would do.

By the time I returned to the compound, the two outlying settlements had already been evacuated, their families now at the main settlement. Like settlers barricaded in an encircled wagon train, we waited for the attack. Friday night was a long night.

I continued down the dirt road to the Valley. Upon my arrival, several men dressed in Vietnam-style, American camouflage surrounded me. One of them patted me down to see if I had any weapons on me.

"Kerry Noble," an older, muscular, shorter man called to me, extending his right hand, "thanks for coming down here to meet with us. I'm Danny Coulson of the FBI's Washington, D.C. SWAT unit. I'm in charge here." Danny Coulson, I discovered later, wasn't just with some average SWAT team. He was the head of the FBI's Hostage Rescue Team, or HRT, a newly formed unit specifically designed to combat terrorist situations.

Coulson was like a lion lording over his territory. There was no doubt who was in charge. I looked around in amazement. Here were sixty, maybe seventy law-enforcement officers; each one dressed for war, decorated with camouflage facepaint, toting rifle and pistol.

These men here, plus the snipers surrounding the main settlement, plus no telling how many more I hadn't seen yet, represented a significant force. I said a silent prayer.

Although I had assumed that after all these years I would be prepared for this day, I wasn't. I felt completely alone.

"Listen carefully, Kerry," Coulson related, "I have over 200 officers here. FBI, BATF, Arkansas State Police, Marion County Sheriff's Department, Baxter County Sheriff's Department, Missouri State Police, Missouri Water Patrol, and even the National Guard if I need more.

"Over the hill," he continued, "sits a Huey helicopter with orders to level your place if one shot is fired. There's a 50-caliber machine gun sitting on top of the hill where you burn your trash. It's powerful enough to blow huge holes in any of your buildings. If that weren't enough, we also have an Armored Personnel Carrier around the bend, near the settlement you call 'the Plateau.' I have weaponry here, Kerry, the United States military doesn't have yet.

"The aircraft that has been circling your property the last few days carries heat-seeking devices on it and can spot anyone trying to leave. As you know snipers surround your main settlement. Each of them carries night-vision goggles. If any one attempts to escape through my men, he or she will be stopped immediately. We can watch your every move, day or night. Do you understand me?"

I arched my eyebrows and nodded my head. Again, there was no doubt Coulson sought to intimidate and overwhelm me. This is the enemy's camp, I thought. Were his words just more government rhetoric or were they reality? I prayed for the right words to say.

"Yes, Sir," I responded. "I sure do. But why so much?"

"Because your organization is considered by the government to be the best trained civilian paramilitary group in America. That's why we're here. We're only sent against the best." Coulson smiled for the first time. "Consider it a compliment and an honor." I smiled back.

"Are you thirsty?" Coulson asked me.

"Yes, Sir." My throat had dried up as soon as I had walked into the enemy's camp. I was extremely nervous, but I couldn't afford to let them know that. It was important to me that the negotiations went well. Everyone else at our compound might want a shoot-out, I thought. Groups like ours all across the country might want us to shoot it out. Again I felt alone.

"Please, call me Danny. No 'sir' stuff. Okay?"

Funny, I thought, I already like him. Something about him, an honesty, an integrity, a confidence, his spirit—something.

"Yes, Sir." I smiled at Danny Coulson and shrugged my shoulders. "Sorry. It's a lifelong habit." Coulson laughed. Coulson and I moved toward his encampment. I recognized several law-enforcement officials, including Bill Buford of the Bureau of Alcohol, Tobacco and Firearms, Gene Irby, and some local deputies. Coulson introduced me to other officers. After I drank the water, the conversation continued.

"Now what are we going to do, Kerry? It's Saturday morning. Let's hurry this up, can we? Is James ready to surrender?"

I looked Coulson in the eyes and held the gaze. "No, Danny, he's not."

"Why not? You know we're not leaving here until we have him."

"I know that. But James feels that the patriotic people of America have been pushed around by the government long enough. He believes that maybe it's time for a showdown."

"Listen to me," Coulson responded, alerted by my statement, "there will be no showdown. We are not going to shoot first. We have no desire to hurt anyone. You have women and children up there. I don't want to see them hurt. But make no mistake, Kerry, if your men shoot first, my chopper immediately flies in, the APC heads in, the 50-caliber will begin shooting, and it'll be over in less than thirty seconds. No one will survive and all your buildings will be leveled. Is that what you want?"

I knew Coulson was serious. "No, Sir," I answered, "but what I want is not important. It's what God wants that counts."

"Kerry, I can appreciate the Christian faith your people have. But I cannot believe God would have innocent men, women and children die over a warrant for James' arrest."

"It's more than that, Danny."

"Kerry, you know we can wait you out. You're cut off from supplies. We can have food and water brought in here at any time for us. You can't. At least let the women and children leave."

Who's he kidding? I thought. "We can't do that, Danny. They've chosen to stay."

I didn't think it wise to inform him that we also had an unlimited water supply, plus five years worth of food stored at the main settlement. In addition, everyone owned several kerosene lamps, with plenty of kerosene reserves; and with wood stoves to cook on, the government could cut the power and the effect would be minimal. We had been preparing for this for seven years.

"How many people do you have up there?" Coulson inquired.

"Over a hundred," I answered. We actually had less than sixty, but I wanted him to think we had more. I needed some advantage in this mental chess game.

"Kerry, someday you'll realize that many of our beliefs are similar to yours. I know you people feel we're the enemy. But that's not true. Let me prove it to you. Go up and talk to James again, Okay?"

"I'll try."

"Good," Coulson stated. "By the way, would you be willing to take a military fieldphone back with you, along with the wire, so we can communicate over the phone?"

"No problem," I agreed.

The wire and phone were made ready. I began to walk away, laying the phone wire in place.

"Call me, Kerry, and let me know what's going on. I'll expect good news." Coulson shook hands again and I left to return to the main settlement.

I knew, though, what James Ellison's response would be.

As I headed back my mind drifted back to when I first drove over these chug-holed roads of northern Arkansas. Eight years. That's all it took for a dream to turn into a nightmare.

2

I Have a Dream

Surely goodness and mercy
shall follow me all the days of my life,
and I will dwell in the house of the Lord forever.

—Psalm 23:6

"How ya' doing?" I asked my twenty-two-year-old pregnant wife as we drove around another bumpy curve in the road. I turned to check on our daughter, Tara, almost two years old, asleep in the back seat.

"I'm fine," Kay replied. "Just drive slower and I'll remain fine." She smiled, massaging her swollen belly of eight-and-a-half months. Her face radiated. She often said how she enjoyed being pregnant.

I glanced at the speedometer and realized I was driving over 45 miles an hour on this pothole-infested road. I decelerated, so not to injure Kay or our old Ford station wagon.

It seemed like we had been driving for years on that day of May 15, 1977, having started the five-hundred-mile trip from Dallas, Texas early that morning. I wasn't used to driving such distances in one day. I also hadn't realized dirt roads still existed in America, but they were here in the Ozark Mountains of northern Arkansas, stretching into eternity it seemed. Even the asphalt roads that we had just left snaked around the hills continuously, without the relative safety of guardrails or width. Surrounding us on both sides of the narrow, hilly road, cedar and oak trees stood so close together at times that only darkened shadows could move between them. Occasionally a deer or two ran across the road in front of us. I had never seen wild deer before.

I topped a hill and stopped the car. To the right we could see three parts of Bull Shoals Lake, the setting sun reflecting off its waters. The sight was beautiful and breathtaking. Neither of us had ever visited

21

Arkansas before. Our friend Barbara had written that the area was heavenly. She was right. Its scenic beauty and serenity captivated us with its sharp contrast to the Dallas-Fort Worth environment we lived and worked in.

Here on the shores of Bull Shoals Lake nestled a fledgling community, anticipating a Bible teacher that their charismatic leader, Jim Ellison, told them was coming. Unknown to me at the time, Ellison already had decided I was that teacher.

"Don't worry," Kay said, trying to encourage me. "I'm sure Tom and Barbara are all right."

"I hope so. Surely they haven't been taken in by yet another cult."

"I hope not. But we'll just have to wait and see."

Barbara's letters had worried me. Some of the doctrines she espoused sounded like the ones the Bible school we attended warned us about in our studies concerning cults. Surely, after all they had been through, Tom and Barbara would know better.

I followed the map Barbara had sent. It couldn't be much further, I thought. We rounded another dusty curve when suddenly we saw seven small white cabins situated in a circle like a wagon train prepared to fight a tribe of warring Indians.

This was Mountain Creek Resort, an old resort, closed for several years now, where deer hunters used to stay during hunting season. The owner allowed Tom and the others to live there in exchange for taking care of the property. Each of the six smaller cabins contained a bathroom, a small kitchen and a bedroom, much like an efficiency apartment. Tom and Barbara lived in the seventh cabin, the main house. It possessed a living room, kitchen, bathroom, utility room and two bedrooms. A single, circular, dirt driveway ran in front of all the cabins.

Tom and Barbara greeted and hugged us as soon as we drove up and got out of the car. Soon, some of the other women came to greet us.

"The men are working, but should be in soon," Tom told us.

"How was your trip?" Barbara asked.

"Long. Jesus, couldn't you have moved further into the sticks?"

Barbara laughed. "We tried, but this was the best we could do. Now, tell me," she almost demanded, lifting her hands to the surrounding scenery of rolling hills, trees of green and brown and the smooth lake, "how do you like it?"

I looked at the tip of the lake down the hill and then to the beautiful rolling hills and gigantic trees that surrounded and seemed to be welcoming and hugging us. What else could I say? "It's Okay," I shrugged nonchalantly, not wanting to commit myself. Barbara laughed.

"It's beautiful," Kay added, "and so quiet!"

"Yes," Barbara said, smiling, looking at me, "and it's the perfect place to raise a family."

Barbara knew me like no woman had ever known me, except my wife. She knew my thoughts, my desires, my dreams. Tall, thin, with flowing dark-red hair, Barbara was like an older sister to me. During the year that she and Tom, with their two daughters, and Kay and I, with our daughter, had lived together in the same house in Dallas, Texas, we had come to share many secrets and experiences. Tom, with dark brown hair and a beard and a few inches shorter than Barbara, was my best friend. Life with them had been my first taste of communal living and I loved it.

I had always wanted a large family, and to live in the country, far from the dangers and pace of city life. For as long as I could remember, I wanted to live and work with Christians and raise my family in a truly Christian environment. Not a churchy environment, full of hypocrisy and church politics, but where Christianity was a lifestyle, not a set of stuffy doctrines and traditions.

We had met Tom and Barbara in early 1975, who only a few months before had escaped a cult that sprang from the 1960s "Jesus freak" movement. The "Children of God" had been founded by David Berg, who later called himself Moses David.

Tom and I started working at a Dallas newspaper on that same January day and became friends instantly. In time, once they felt comfortable with Kay and me, Tom and Barbara shared their experiences about the Children of God, both good and bad, and the hunger grew in me for a lifestyle similar to the earlier good days of the Children of God.

A few months later, we decided it was the will of God for us to move in together, into a two-story house, where the women would share the kitchen and home responsibilities and Tom and I would work and pay the bills.

It had absolutely been the best year of my life—constant fellowship, Bible studies, learning how to worship the Lord in spirit, no disagreements over natural matters or doctrines. This was how the early church existed, I believed, and this was how I wanted to live.

An opportunity opened in 1976 for Tom and Barbara to move to a newly established fellowship, a community where a man named Jim Ellison was helping young people recover from drugs or from cults like the Children of God. Ellison, I discovered years later, knew that people who had used drugs or who had previously been in cults were basically discontent with society and the kind of people he wanted, who would be easier to mold than regular church people.

People often join groups like this because they are discontent with or alienated from society, and to find a community-sense of belonging. One of Ellison's favorite scriptures read: "David therefore departed and escaped to the cave Adullam. . . . And every one that was in distress, and every one that was in debt, and every one that was discontented, gathered themselves unto him; and he became a captain over them, and there were with him about four hundred men."

Although I didn't realize it at the time, here was the first ingredient necessary for creating an extremist: a philosophical or theological premise, based upon discontent, fear, unbelief, hate, despair, or some other negative emotion. In other words, a person's view of the present and future had to be dark and bleak.

A former leader of the Children of God, a friend of Tom and Barbara's, had met Ellison while on a trip through southern Missouri and came to Dallas to tell my friends about the group. Tom envisioned a ministry there for him and Barbara, so they moved to Ellison's group after a brief visit, shortly before the group relocated to northern Arkansas. Kay and I made plans to attend a pentecostal Bible school in Dallas called Christ for the Nations, where we could learn more about the Charismatic Movement, where people stress the gifts of the Spirit: speaking in unknown tongues, physical healings, miracles and God directing and speaking to people through prophecies, dreams and visions. They stressed worshipping God openly and freely, with emotional fervor. This was the opposite of how I was raised in the Southern Baptist church, where form was more important that substance.

When Kay became pregnant with our second child, we decided to deliver the baby by natural childbirth and not in a hospital again, because of complications when Tara was born. But the Bible school wouldn't let us birth the baby in the apartment we lived in on campus, so we had to make other arrangements. Barbara invited us to Arkansas to visit and have our newborn by natural childbirth there, which was the common way at their group. God had opened the doors for us to go, and go we did.

After Kay and I settled into the only vacant cabin, we went to visit Tom and Barbara. The four of us talked for the rest of the afternoon, catching up the last nine months since we had parted. Each of us could sense the concern of the other.

"Don't worry," said Barbara, trying to reassure me, "it's not like the Children of God. There's a freedom in the Spirit here that I've never experienced before. I know you've worried about us, but believe me, if you'd get to know the people here, you'd love this place." It did appear that Tom seemed content here. More than he did in Dallas. But I still sensed something was bothering him.

Later that evening the men arrived from work, covered in the cedar sap that was the trademark of their profession. "Christian Brothers Cedar"—the business name of the community—had contracted to clear over 3000 acres of cedar trees. The men worked six days a week from sunrise to sunset. Each man received one hundred dollars a week for his labor.

Thirty-six-year-old James Dennis Ellison rose from the back of the work truck, dirtier than everyone else. With his five-foot-ten frame and a big smile, he swaggered over to greet me.

"You must be Kerry," he said, extending his hand.

"Yes, Sir," I answered, "and you must be Jim."

"That's me," he grinned. "Glad you made it. Where's your wife?"

"Inside with Barbara."

"Well, tell her I'll meet her at the meeting tonight. I better get cleaned up and eat supper. See you later, Okay?"

"Yes, Sir."

He looked back over his shoulder, still smiling. "The name's Jim, not Sir, Okay?"

"Okay, Jim." In spite of my concerns about the place, I found myself immediately liking Ellison. Something about him, I thought. A humility, a confidence, his spirit, charisma, something.

Ellison lived in a travel trailer parked at Mountain Creek. Tom had already informed me that Ellison was trying to purchase some nearby property that had been given to Campus Crusade for Christ, a fundamental evangelistic organization in California, but it would take a few months for the paperwork to be finalized.

Barbara and Kay fixed supper while Tom and I fed the chickens. It felt like the old days. It was good seeing Tom again. Hard to believe it had been nine months since we had last seen each other.

After supper, we attended our first church service, or "praise meeting" as it was called. "Zarephath"—this Pentecostal-type fellowship—also emphasized prophecies, speaking in tongues, healings, visions, dreams, and miracles. They believed that Christian-community living, which they called "body-life," was the highest ideal God had for His people, that He dealt with individuals through a corporate fellowship.

Because of the way I felt God had moved in my life when He called me into the ministry, I also believed that He dealt with people on an individual basis in miraculous ways, even in small, trivial circumstances. While at Christ for the Nations, for example, I learned about the practice of "laying on of hands," for healing of the sick. I decided to take the practice a step further one day when our vehicle was acting up and I was short on money.

"In the name of Jesus," I scoffingly prayed, with Kay and I laying hands on the hood of the car, "be healed from any and all mechanical problems that you have." We then thanked the Lord and went on. The car never gave us another problem after that. I knew the car's repair wasn't due to any special power I had, but it was simply fixed by the grace of God because of our willingness to believe in His loving care, and to teach me a humbling lesson.

The music at Zarephath's praise meeting was similar to the music at Christ for the Nations, snappy and lively, with guitars and tambourines abundant. Sitting in folding chairs in a circle, people lifted their arms and hands upward to the Lord while singing or praying in tongues. Occasionally a prophecy, or word from God, would come forth for someone from a member of the group. When the music seemed to subside—almost two hours later—it appeared everyone was waiting for someone to speak.

I knew they had what was called an "open pulpit," meaning that whoever felt he had a word from the Lord could speak. As I expected, Jim Ellison stood.

This ought to be interesting, I thought.

"Open your Bibles, please," Ellison started, as he flipped through the pages of his Bible, "and turn to Revelation, chapter eighteen, verse four. 'Come out of her, my people, that you be not partakers of her sins, and that you receive not of her plagues.'" Ellison then laid his Bible on his chair.

"Tonight I want to talk to you of a vision, a vision for yourselves, a vision for this place, a vision from God! Tonight I want to stir your spirit with this vision; for without a vision, the people perish! We are commanded by God, especially in this hour, to come out of Babylon, Mystery Babylon, the Great Whore. Babylon, with its meaning of 'confusion,' accurately describes the world we live in. Men call that which is good, evil; and that which is evil, good. The thoughts and intents of people in America are only evil continually! Society is degenerate today, just as it was in Noah's day. Jesus said that when that type of day occurred again, He would judge the earth! Judge her for her sins!"

I watched, mesmerized by Ellison, preaching like I'd never heard before. He captivated his audience, confident in his mannerisms and stance. No microphone was needed, for his voice projected loudly and clearly. I watched the others as they listened intently to Ellison. Periodically someone would shout "Amen!" or "That's right!"

With encouragement from his congregation, Ellison continued. "The sins of America, the most godly nation to arise since Solomon's time, have reached heights beyond that of the Tower of Babel: Prostitution, pornography, violence, crime, drugs, adultery, government corruption, alcoholism, homosexuality, child abuse.

"Years ago the Lord showed me a vision of the filth and degradation of the cities, a symbol of our nation's moral decay and depravation. He showed me that as it was in Lot's day, so it is now. There aren't enough righteous men left for God to spare the cities any longer. Therefore, judgment has begun! That's the word and vision He gave me just a few years ago—a word I hesitated on until God got my attention.

"In 1970 God had to collapse a building around me and kill me so He could get my attention. Then He brought me back from death's grip. I'll tell you this, though—I didn't want to come back. Where I was, it was peaceful and quiet, the best place I'd ever been. But He brought me back for a purpose. His purpose!

"The only hope for America, God told me, is for Christians to leave the cities and organized churches and to build refuges in isolated sections of the country, so others will have a place to come when the Tribulation Period hits. When God does judge America for its sins, good people will need somewhere to go, and that's why we're here—to learn from God, first, and then to take care of others when the time comes.

"You here in this room have chosen to obey Jesus and come out of Babylon. And when God, through His five-fold ministry, raises His Body of people into Sonship, to walk in the realm where Jesus walked, then you will be a part of that Body!

"This is the vision I want us all to see. Of not only our purpose here when God judges the earth, but your purpose also in Him, when He shall raise you up in the spirit of Sonship as God's anointed, as God's Christ Body! Hallelujah."

"Amen!" someone returned. "Glory be to God!"

Part Two | **God, Guns and Glory**

3

Home

Behold, how good and how pleasant
it is for brethren to dwell together in unity!
—Psalm 133:1

Long before my arrival, ingredient number two—a charismatic leader—had been added to the first ingredient. Without my being aware of it, the extremist recipe now needed only one more ingredient.

After preaching for almost an hour, Ellison sat down and the room quieted to see if anyone else had a Word from God. No one did and in a few minutes we sang a final song and closed the meeting. Kay and I met everyone else, and after a brief time of fellowship, retreated to the cabin provided for us.

I didn't sleep well that night. Ellison's sermon had confirmed my fears about the group. Christ for the Nations had warned us about two new doctrines being taught throughout the country, called "Sonship" and the "Five-Fold Ministry." Barbara had alluded to them in some of her letters. And now Ellison lightly preached on them.

The "Sonship" teaching is a belief that God's Christ, or Anointed One, is not just Jesus, but that Jesus is only the Head of the Christ Body. The Body of Christ, according to the doctrine, is composed of several people—some say it's the 144,000 spoken of in the Book of Revelation. Whether that's a literal or symbolic number depends upon whom one listens to. In time, the doctrine teaches, these members that make up God's Christ-Body will ascend spiritually into the realm of perfection that Jesus walked in—called "Sonship," meaning "being placed as a mature son" (translated "adoption" in the King James Bible)—where, although in a mortal body, one would be incapable of sinning and would always walk in the Spirit.

Together, the teaching states, this Christ-Body, with the Christ-Head, make up the one Christ, moving as one man under the rulership of Jesus. Then, during the 1000-year reign of God's many-membered Christ (typified as Adam), the rest of the Church/Israel would be spiritually prepared to become the Bride of Christ (Eve). Following the Millennium, the period known as "the Dispensation of the Fullness of Times" would begin and all who had ever lived would be resurrected and would eventually realize their salvation and would come to know Jesus Christ as Savior, at which time Christ would hand the Kingdom back to the Father. Christ for the Nations taught that this sonship doctrine lessened the Headship, or authority, of Jesus and opened the teaching for the deification steps of man to become God. It seemed this was what Ellison taught.

The teaching called the "Five-Fold Ministry" said that there were still apostles and prophets in the church today, as well as pastors, teachers, and evangelists. According to the teaching, the five-fold ministry was needed in every local church, for the perfecting of the saints into sonship.

The Bible school believed this doctrine to be a false one, bringing believers into a system called "shepherding," in which the followers were taught to obey the "apostle," or leader, just as they would Jesus, because the leader or leaders supposedly received special revelations from God.

During the next three weeks, while waiting on Kay to have the baby, I spent my time getting to know this part of northern Arkansas and the people of Zarephath. The area was breathtakingly beautiful—clear lakes, fresh air, woods of green and brown, wild deer and turkey, quiet and remote. It was the most unbelievably serene place I had ever seen.

Friendly local folk waved at strangers and greeted people as they passed by. I felt a sense of community among the townsfolk that seemed so opposite to the Dallas-Fort Worth area. People here weren't afraid of their neighbors. I didn't see people lock their car doors then look around to see if anyone was watching them. It was almost as if crime was a foreign concept to them.

One day I asked if I could go along and work in the woods with Ellison and his men.

"Are you sure?" Jim asked. "It's difficult work. Why don't you stay here at the resort and just visit with Tom and Barbara?"

■   ■   ■

I had never done much hard, manual work before. When I was a teenager, my family lived on a small twenty-acre farm for almost four years. I fed our few animals, worked in the garden during the summer and grubbed the mesquite saplings. Having suffered from chronic bronchitis for ten years as a child, my endurance level had always been low. In the first grade, I even had to be in girls' PE because I couldn't keep up with the boys. I don't know if I ever got over the shame and humiliation of not being able to keep up with the other boys—or even with some of the girls.

"Remember," my mother would tell me over and over during that first year of grade school and for many years thereafter, "other boys may tease you because you're a little weaker than most children. But even if they try to pick a fight with you, don't ever fight back. Violence and fighting never solved anything. If I find out that you've been involved in a fight and hit someone, I'll spank you myself." I did get picked on, sometimes even hit. But I obeyed my mother—I never fought back.

Then one day, when I was thirteen years old, my brother-in-law and I were building a shed on our little farm. My endurance and enthusiasm were giving out, and he suddenly threw down his hammer and yelled at me, "If you can't keep up better than this, then just get the hell out of here!" His anger and bitterness continued. "You'll never amount to a damn, you know it? Hell, you ain't even worth a goddamn now. Now go on and get the hell out of here!"

I was crushed. It wasn't my fault I couldn't use a hammer very well; no one had ever taught me. I really tried to work hard. All my life I had been told not to exert myself, because of the bronchitis, but I especially wanted to help my brother-in-law that day. I wanted to be like him, like my step-father and like my older step-brother—rugged, hard-working men, with self-confidence. But I never was like them.

And now, at the age of twenty-four, I still wanted to be just like they were. I was still trying to prove myself to them and to myself. I still wanted to be worth a damn.

. . .

"Thanks, Jim," I replied, "but I really would like to work in the woods with y'all, if it's all right."

Ellison smiled as he waved me onto the back of the truck.

The men of Zarephath were known as "the Cedar Boys" by the local folk. The Cedar Boys had an excellent reputation in the area as hard workers, willing to help out neighbors for free, and keeping to themselves without getting into any trouble. They sold the cedar they cut to two of the local sawmills, which fashioned it into cedar closet lining or ground it into landscaping mulch.

I stood in amazement as I watched the men once we got to the timber woods. Working in unison, everyone knew exactly what to do. First, a road had to be cut through the woods for the four-wheel-drive, flatbed pickup to drive over. As two of the men were doing that, the others were sawing the trees down with their forty-six-inch-long, sixteen-pound Stihl chainsaws. Then the men sliced the limbs off the trees, cut the trees into blocks, and left them lying there for someone to haul them to the truck.

That someone today was me.

Blocks of cedar wood that were to be ground into mulch shavings had to be three to five-and-a-half inches in diameter on the small end and were cut thirty-two inches long, later to be loaded on a semi-truck. The larger blocks that were to be taken to the closet-lining saw-mill had to be at least six inches in diameter on the little end and cut fifty-two inches long. A "six-inch block" weighed about fifty pounds. The larger blocks, with diameters up to sixteen inches, could weigh as much as three hundred fifty pounds; blocks bigger than that usually required two men to carry them.

Jim told me my job for the day was to carry the blocks to the pickup and then stack them onto the flatbed. The truck was anywhere from ten to about one hundred feet from the blocks.

I tried to lift that first small block to my chest and carry it out. I couldn't do it. Even fifty pounds was too much for my six-foot, one-hundred-sixty-pound frame to carry. One of the men then showed me how to "flip-flop" the blocks, picking one end up, throwing it past the opposite end, and then repeating the action until I was at the truck. Flip-flopping was fine for the smaller blocks, but I couldn't even pick up one end of the larger blocks. Those I had to "roll" to the truck, getting on my knees and pushing them over cut stobs and rocks.

Once I arrived at the truck, though, I still couldn't pick up the blocks to put them on the flatbed, so I had to build a lower tier on which to flip-flop a block, and then once again flip-flop the block onto the truck. Then, by repeating the tier-strategy on the truck itself, I could finally stack the blocks on the truck.

The pickup, I had been told, should hold about fifty blocks once it was fully loaded. The men normally tried to take three or four loads a day into town. At the rate I was going, I figured it would take me all day to load the pickup just one time.

I looked at my watch after that first block; it was almost eight o'clock in the morning. Over twelve hours to go.

Unknown to me at the time, Jim had told the others for no one to help me that first day, except for instructions or tips on what to do. He wanted to see if I would last on my own. I was determined to last that first day, knowing I was only there for a visit, and not actually living there. It wasn't like I was going to be doing this for a living. Work a couple of days in the woods, maybe a week, and then I could go back to Dallas and tell my friends that I was a real lumberjack for a while.

As I expected, it took me all day to load that one truck. We didn't even have time to take it to the sawmill in town and unload it. When the men dropped me off in front of Tom's house, Kay came out to greet me.

"Are you all right?" she asked, concern in her voice.

"I think so," I replied. "Not sure, though; I hurt too much to tell."

I crawled up the stairs to the porch, too weak and sore to walk. I was covered with cedar sap from head to foot. I felt like I'd been beaten within an inch of my life. But, boy, did I feel proud! I had done it! I had worked hard all day long, and hadn't complained about it once. I actually enjoyed it, especially the camaraderie with the men.

Two men came to visit during our church service one evening. Called "Branhamites," they were disciples of William Branham, a 1950s Pentecostal preacher, who started preaching during the same time period as Oral Roberts and others. They spoke about how Branham was the Christ and how we should be following his teachings, even though Branham was now dead. They expected him, however, to resurrect at any time.

Ellison patiently listened to them and let them have their say. I threw a fit after they left.

"How can you sit there," I demanded of Ellison, "and let them say that garbage about William Branham being Christ?"

"Remember, Kerry," he tried to explain, "God's house has many types of vessels. He can use anyone he wants, to some degree or another. I know they were here to try and take some people with them, but a true shepherd can't lose any sheep. If anyone here wants to follow the Branhamites, they're free to do so. If they do go, they really weren't here anyway. True sheep cannot be driven away, just as a true shepherd doesn't lose his sheep. Otherwise, they really weren't his to begin with.

"As far as their teachings go, I believe that if you have a clear river, and a muddy stream runs into it, sure the river will get a little dirty for a while, but down the road apiece, given enough time, the river will, by its own nature, clean itself out again.

"That's how false teachings are when they come to anyone that really seeks the Lord. Never be afraid to listen to any teaching; it can't really hurt you if you're flowing in the Spirit. And you might actually learn something in the process."

I listened to his words in amazement. This man is too complicated for me, I thought.

One single woman, with two daughters, lived with the group. Margie had been with the Children of God at a time when they were taught that the women should be willing to do anything for the Lord or the group. "Hookers for Jesus" was the media name for the practice of women providing sex to bring men (and other women) into the Children of God. It was one of the reasons Tom and Barbara decided to leave that group.

Margie had been one of the hookers, and apparently brought the practice to Mountain Creek Resort, where she had seduced and bedded all of the single men at one time or another. No one really knew what to do about Margie, though her practice did concern some of the married women, for obvious reasons.

One day, after I found out what was going on with Margie, one of the single men, Bruce, told me to follow him to her house. When we went inside, Bruce asked Margie to play the Children of God version of "House of the Rising Sun."

Margie gladly accepted the invitation to perform. She picked up her guitar, and began to play and sing. She closed her eyes, her head pointed upward while singing the song. Bruce walked over to Margie and stood behind her.

"Watch this," he told me. Bruce then leaned over with his mouth near Margie's ear, and screamed as loud as he could, "MARRRRRG-GIIIEEEEEEEE!!!" She never missed a beat. I don't think she even heard him, she was so far gone to God-knows-where. We left her house, with Margie still playing and singing.

"Well? What'd you think?" Bruce asked me.

I didn't know what to think at first. I'd never seen anything like that. I just looked at Bruce, bewildered, wondering.

"Yeah, I've slept with her," Bruce confessed. "Ain't none too proud of it, either. All us single guys have had sex with her. Funny thing is, no one can stand her. But, what can a man do? She gets him to her house and flaunts her goods, and that's all it takes.

"Something's wrong with her and something ought to be done about her. But no one seems to know what to do. Kerry, she teaches her two young daughters to masturbate. I've seen her." Bruce looked desperate. "Anyway, I thought you ought to know what's going on around here."

Later that evening I talked to Tom about Margie.

"Obviously, it's some sort of demonic spirit," I told Tom, "and it's got to be dealt with." I knew about the abominations of the Children of God and I also knew a little about demonic activity, being taught about it at Christ for the Nations.

"What do you suggest?" Tom asked.

"Why not get together with her after the praise meeting tonight and cast the demonic spirit out of her? You and I can anoint her with oil or whatever we need to do, and take dominion over that devil." I knew I had no experience at this type of situation, but I arrogantly believed Tom and I had enough faith and knowledge of the Scriptures that we could cast any devils out of Margie.

That evening, after the meeting, we asked Margie over to my cabin. Kay went to Barbara's house to wait for us. We asked Margie to sit down; I sat in front of her, Tom stood behind her.

I began to talk to Margie about what she was doing and suddenly her face tightened, her eyes widened, and I was being choked. Not by Margie or anyone else in a physical sense. I was literally being choked until I couldn't breathe, by an invisible hand, by what I perceived to be the demon in Margie.

My first encounter with a demon and its lesson alerted me quickly as to its dangers. I couldn't speak and, therefore, couldn't tell Tom what was going on. So I simply thought to myself, "In the Name of Jesus, you foul spirit, let go of me and be gone!" Instantly, I could breathe again.

Margie's eyes were closed now, her face expressionless. Tom and I then laid our hands on her head and shoulders, a Charismatic practice, and began to pray in tongues and cast the spirit of darkness and lust out of Margie. We prayed that way for a long time, rebuking any spirit we could think of. Eventually we quit and then sat down to talk to Margie.

Margie didn't completely understand what was going on; she seemed in a daze. She asked us what she should do next. I asked her if she still had any of the writings from the Children of God with her. She admitted she did. I told her to get them, bring them to the trash barrels outside, and burn them. The writings, I informed her, were the link to her problems. She did as we told her and she burned the books.

Margie behaved for a while after that, but, unfortunately, it didn't last. I discovered she had only burned some of the many Children of God books she owned. About two months later, she left Mountain Creek.

Margie was my first experience with demon possession. Most importantly, to me, it was a sign from God of the power that I had only heard about at Bible school, but had never exercised. It scared me, yes, but it was exhilarating at the same time. I had just taken another step in the walk of faith that I desired with God.

Faith, to me, was simply believing and obeying God when He told you to do something or when He led you into a situation. Believing that He directs, it followed that He would also provide and protect at the same time. Whether the direction was in relocating, living communally, casting out demons, or having a baby by natural childbirth—faith was the key. It all centered around the idea or belief that God still directed and moved in the lives of individuals today, that He dealt with people as sons and daughters, while conforming them into the image of His Son, Jesus.

I worked a few days in the woods off and on after that, until it was time for Kay to have our baby. When we had Tara in a hospital, our tiny daughter developed yellow jaundice and had to stay two weeks under ultra-violet light with gauze on her eyes. In addition, Kay was very sore from the delivery for well over a week. Very dissatisfied with the service at the hospital, we decided later to have our second child naturally. We studied books and watched a television special on natural childbirth and were excited to try it. Our families were afraid for us, but we weren't. We knew God would watch over us.

Now the time had come and we were ready. The early morning light filtered in through the windows. Barbara and one of the women, Leslie, helped us with the delivery. Both women had previously given birth at home and had assisted others. My job, they said, was to catch the baby when it came out.

As the contractions got closer and closer, and Kay dilated more and more, the four of us sang songs of praise and worship, laughing and praising God for the miracle of life. The two women encouraged Kay at every step, ministering faith and hope to her. Kay breathed as Leslie and Barbara instructed her to, and she appeared to have it all under control. I was a nervous wreck.

Kay's labor was brief, especially compared to the time with Tara, and the moment arrived for our second child to enter the world. As the head began to crown, or come out, I thought it was its wrinkled face at first, frowning at me.

"He's looking at me!" I exclaimed.

"No, he's not," Leslie laughed, "that's the top of his head. Now get ready. He'll hesitate for a little bit at first, and then all of a sudden, there he'll slide out, right into your hands."

Just as she said, the baby plopped out and I was holding him.

"It's a boy!" Barbara shouted. Kay and I started to cry and laugh.

Leslie looked at the clock. "Hallelujah! It's seven o'clock exactly." Leslie wrote the time down on a piece of paper. "Now, Kerry," Leslie commanded, "gently lay the baby on Momma's belly and let her suckle him. We gotta wait for the cord to get cold before we cut it."

Kay and I held each other's hands, looking at one another and then the baby.

"I love you," she said.

"And I love you," I replied.

■ ■ ■

I had always loved Kay, from the moment I first saw her glowing on that October 1972 morning, as she sat in the choir of the rural Baptist church that I was visiting.

A friend had invited me to church, telling me she had the perfect girl for me. I didn't know it at the time, but the eighteen-year-old girl in the choir and the girl my friend had picked out were the same. As soon as I saw her, the Lord spoke to me and told me that this was the girl I would marry.

I guess it surprised me somehow that not everyone got as excited as I did about hearing God. I told Kay on our first date that we would someday get married, that it was God's will. It must have scared her, because she wouldn't talk to me or go out with me again for four more months.

Finally, after constantly calling her and bugging her, she agreed to a second date. The next month, we were engaged. Five months after that, on September 2, 1973, she became my wife.

"I told you I had someone for you," my friend said at the wedding, smiling. Yes, she did. And so had God.

. . .

Leslie cut the cord of our newborn son and weighed him. "Thank you, Jesus! Look at this! He weighs exactly seven pounds, seven ounces!"

I wasn't sure what Leslie was so excited about.

"Don't you see? Your son was born 6-7-77 at 7 a.m., weighing 7 pounds, 7 ounces!"

I had learned in Bible school of the significance of numbers in the Scriptures. I knew seven was considered a good number—the number for perfection—but six was not necessarily a good number, being the number for man.

"Don't you get it?" Leslie rambled. "All sevens except for one number. In fact six sevens. Six times seven is forty-two, which is the number for 'fullness of times.' In other words, time for something to be fulfilled. Six sevens is also almost 'perfect perfection!' All perfect except for one thing. The month. But 'month' is the same Hebrew word as 'the moon' in the Scriptures, and the moon is a symbol of the church, being only a reflection of the sun, or the Son." I must have looked puzzled.

"You still don't get it?" Leslie asked in disbelief, barely containing her excitement. She explained it to me again.

Then it hit me. Could our son's birth be a sign from God? That this place, this church, was as close to perfection as we could get? That this church was a reflection of all that we considered perfect, of how a church should be? And that our time had come for God to accomplish His purpose in us?

"I guess it's true," I acknowledged. "It must be a sign. We're home. We're finally home."

Numbers, I discovered later, are extremely significant in the Scriptures. Numerical meanings are a code, signifying why God unfolds circumstances as He does, so that we might spiritually understand His purpose. Five, for example, signifies grace; eight, new beginnings; fifty, the anointing; and one hundred, deliverance. The eighth day, as an example, marks a new week; Israelite males were circumcised on the eighth day; eight souls were saved from the flood in Noah's day.

In the original Scriptures, in their original languages, each letter and each number was significant. The Hebrew letters, for example, each have their own meanings. Vav, pronounced "vaw," is the sixth letter in the Hebrew alphabet. It represents the number six, but the letter itself also means "nail." Therefore, by breaking down the individual letters in a Hebrew word, one could understand more spiritual significance in what God was doing, by deciphering the numerical value of words and phrases and the meaning of each letter.

I also later learned that parts of the body reveal significant dealings from the Lord. For example, arthritis signified bitterness; the right hand represented the ministry; the left hand had to do with relationship with God; the knees corresponded with a person's prayer life; the back meant support; a stiff neck revealed stubbornness; and the arm represented strength.

Numbers and letter meanings and body symbolism, therefore, could reveal God's dealing with an individual through a code in the Scriptures—a proof of the perfection of its Divine author, a path to enlightened, esoteric understanding.

The difference between this birth and our first one was like night and day. By noon, Kay was doing laundry, not having any pain. She moved around easily. Even though our newborn son had a little jaundice-look himself, Kay simply laid him near a window for the sunlight to hit him, and he recovered quickly. We decided natural childbirth was the only way to go with all of our future children.

On the eighth day, as the Scriptures commanded, I circumcised our son. I believed that circumcising him myself would cause a bond between us that few fathers and sons would have. It was somewhat difficult to put the razor to him initially, but once the cut began, it went smoothly after that. The bleeding lasted only a short while and he quickly went back to sleep. We dedicated him that evening at the praise meeting.

"What is his name?" Jim asked, officiating the dedication. Kay and I looked at each other.

"Stephen Josiah Noble," I replied, proudly. We had originally decided to name him Philip Daniel, but when Kay first lifted him to her breast, she instinctively called him Stephen. She didn't know why; we had never discussed that name before.

He was our first child to have a Biblical name. Stephen Josiah, in the Scripture definition, meant "A crown founded by God." It seemed somehow that the name tied us to this place.

The owner of the property where the men were clearing timber asked Tom and Barbara to move to his ranch. Since he lived in Pittsburgh most of the time, he offered them free rent in exchange for them taking care of the home, plus he would pay Tom for working the ranch. That meant Tom and Barbara would be leaving Mountain Creek Resort.

Jim Ellison, upon Tom's decision to move, put his arm around my shoulders one night on the way to a praise meeting. He then asked me, "Why don't you and Kay move into the main house?"

"Jim," I replied, "that wouldn't make sense. In a few days, we'll be going back to Dallas, so Kay and I can finish school. Then next year we can move back here. Go ahead and let one of the other families live there."

"I was hoping," Jim implored, "that you might consider staying with us and not worry about school." He then arched his eyebrows, smiled, and softly stated, "We do need a Bible teacher, you know."

"I appreciate the offer, Jim, but I need to finish school."

"Well, just pray about it, would you?" he asked, mischievously grinning. Somehow, I knew I was in trouble. I really didn't want to pray about it. I wanted to go back to school.

Over the next few days, although I didn't pray about the situation per se, I did catch myself wondering what it would be like to live there. I knew Kay absolutely enjoyed the fellowship with the women. I also felt close to the people, even though most of the men thought that my Bible doctrines were traditional and churchy.

"What's bothering you?" Kay asked me a couple of days later.

"Well, it seems that I'm going to school, paying money to learn to be a preacher . . ."

"But," she interrupted me, "you're thinking about staying here."

"Well, yeah. I mean, why go to school and pay money, when I can learn by experience right here for free?" I looked for some reassurance. "Do you like it here as much as I do?"

"More, probably," she laughed. "Honey, if you think the Lord wants us to stay then let's stay."

I smiled and gazed into Kay's eyes. She was always willing to follow me wherever I believed the Lord wanted us to go. "I think I'm also supposed to stay so that I can help these people, to make sure they get a good Biblical foundation, and not get swayed so much by Jim's teachings. He seems a good man, but some of his teachings are just plain wrong."

"Then let's stay," she concluded.

I told Jim and the men we would be staying. Everyone was excited to have us. That night, Tom and I were anointed and set in place as the church's first ordained elders. I was now a part of the ministry of this place. I also became the bookkeeper for the church, with my name added to the church checking account.

Interestingly enough, I wasn't disappointed in not finishing Bible school like I thought I should be. So many other things in my life that I had wanted to finish, I had been unable to finish, usually because our family moved so often during my childhood. But this time was different; this time it was my decision, and not someone else's—that I could live with.

Later that week, Kay and I drove to Dallas to get our belongings. We said our good-byes to our families and excitedly headed back to Arkansas. Tom and Barbara had moved to the neighbor's ranch and we moved into the main house.

I started teaching Bible studies on a regular basis, arguing often with the men over my doctrines. Most of them had no church background, being new in the Christian faith. By the time I had moved to Arkansas, I had all my pet doctrines down solidly and was ready to defend them at any opportunity. I had all my Bible notes scribbled in my worn-out Bible, and by this time was past memorizing verses—I was memorizing entire chapters of the Bible. A good Christian, I taught, knew what he believed and could prove why he believed it.

During that first summer of 1977, Ellison and his family, with three of the single men, went to Minnesota to work and minister. Jim left Tom and me in charge, being the only two official elders of the church.

Tom helped out at Mountain Creek while working at his new home; I worked in the woods with two of the men. I didn't set the best work-example in the woods, I admit; I was more interested in talking about the Bible with the men than I was in working hard.

"Why did y'all move here?" I asked them one day.

"To get away from the big city," Hoyte answered, "away from the crime and the pollution, so I could raise my kids safely."

"Yeah," Billy continued, "and to learn more about God. Jim's a good leader and teacher. I knew some of the other men before moving here and I saw how living here had changed them. I wanted the same thing they had." They both agreed that even though they hadn't lived there very long, it was the best move they'd ever made.

I learned to work fairly hard that summer, with the help of these two men, and I felt good. I also did most of the preaching at the praise meetings and played guitar with Tom during the music portion. At summer's end, though, Jim and the men, two of them now married, returned to Mountain Creek Resort. The other single man, who also came from the Children of God, had stayed in Minnesota. The spotlight was back on Ellison now, so I settled back, trying to find my place in the group.

We had praise meetings almost every night, ranging anywhere from thirty minutes to five hours in length, depending upon the mood or spirit of the meeting. One night a week, for about an hour or so, I taught Bible studies, which everyone had to attend. Saturday was our Sabbath, so everyone rested; town trips were discouraged on that day.

I also did a couple of things that really bothered a lot of people in the beginning. When Kay and I were going to Bible school, even though I was working full time, we needed financial help, so we started getting food stamps. I continued that practice in Arkansas because the hundred dollars a week we were being paid still qualified us.

No one else at Mountain Creek received food stamps, because welfare was a "Mark of the Beast." I didn't know if food stamps were Satanic; I just knew they put extra food on the table. It was noticeable, though, that although everyone was against food stamps, no one was against eating the ice cream and sweets or drinking the colas at the only home that had them. In time everyone applied for and received food stamps.

The other thing I did that startled many was when Jim Ellison would preach a doctrine I disagreed with, I would get up and preach the opposite. I would warn the people to be careful of "false prophets" and "wolves in sheep's clothing." But Jim Ellison never said anything to me; he never defended himself or his doctrines after I got up; he never came against me. The others expected him to; I expected him to. But he never did. It would be several months before I would understand why.

And it would be for that reason that I would bond myself to him and commit myself to him for the next several years.

The second ingredient was about to get me.

4

The Revelation

And (the word of the Lord) said, 'Go forth,
and stand upon the mount before the Lord.'
And, behold, the Lord passed by,
and a great and strong wind rent the mountains,
and broke in pieces the rocks before the Lord;
but the Lord was not in the wind;
and after the wind an earthquake,
but the Lord was not in the earthquake;
and after the earthquake, a fire;
but the Lord was not in the fire;
and after the fire a still, small voice.

—1 Kings 19:11, 12

Tom's wife, Barbara, ran to Jim and me, screaming. "Oh, God, Jim, I didn't mean to do it!" she cried out, sobbing, barely able to catch her breath.

"Slow down," Jim tried to calm her and find out what was the matter. "Didn't mean to do what?" We were in the woods cutting timber. Everyone quit sawing and ran over to Jim, Barbara and me.

"I didn't mean to," Barbara continued to weep. "I'm so sorry. Please forgive me." She hung her head in her hands and sobbed.

"Barbara, it's all right." Jim was frustrated as well as concerned. "What's wrong? What did you do?"

She couldn't look up. "It's Joseph," she cried. "I ran over Joseph."

Jim looked like he had been shot in the stomach. Joseph was his eighteen-month-old son, his firstborn with Ollie. But after a moment he calmly put his arm around Barbara and tried to comfort her. "It's all right," he told her. "Let's go look at him."

The three of us got into the truck and headed back to the resort. "I didn't see him," Barbara pleaded. "I was backing out of the driveway and could tell I had driven over something. Then, for some reason, I pulled back up. I felt the back tire go over it again. I just figured it was a piece of firewood or something. I started to get out and move whatever was there, but the truck wasn't in gear. By the time I could stop the truck, it had rolled over him a third time. When I got out to see what was in the road . . ." Barbara's voice trailed off as she began sobbing uncontrollably.

"I just started screaming," she began again. "I picked Joseph up. He was just limp, not breathing at all. I'm so sorry, Jim. I'm so sorry."

Jim began praying and praising God. I looked at him in astonishment. How could he be so calm? His son may be dead and he's praising God!

We drove to Jim's trailer. Ollie came out, carrying Joseph in her arms. "He's breathing again," she said, "but his body is still hurt."

I could see abrasions and tire marks across Joseph's chest and face, and deep indentions from the gravel, forced into him by the pressure of the truck on top of him.

"After Barbara started screaming," Ollie continued, "I ran outside, saw what had happened, and took Joseph from her. Then I saw the angel of death trying to take Joseph, but I refused and took him back. His body was broken, Jim, but I prayed for him, that God would heal his internal organs. While Barbara had gone after you, Joseph was able to stand on his own."

"Let's go ahead and get him to the doctor, anyway." Jim told Ollie. "I'll call ahead on the CB and let them know we're coming."

Jim looked at Barbara. "It'll be all right. Quit worrying." Then he turned to me. "Stay here and keep everyone calm. We'll be back later. Have everybody pray for a miracle."

The three of them drove off, a cloud of dust revealing their route. I watched the dust rise, praying more for Barbara than for Joseph. Was this a warning from God? Maybe I wasn't supposed to be here after all.

It had only been a couple of weeks since Kay and I had moved here, and now a child had been run over. And why Barbara? She would never hurt anyone. God, I thought, why is this happening?

The doctor's clinic was a little over thirty miles away, yet in less than three hours, Jim and Ollie returned. Joseph was alert, laughing, ready to play. I couldn't believe it. Ollie was smiling as she walked up and hugged Barbara. Jim approached me and the other men. He lifted his hands toward the sky and proudly proclaimed, "The Lord be magnified! He alone is God!"

"What happened?" I asked, still shocked to see Joseph.

"We went to the clinic," Jim explained, "told them what had happened, and they took Joseph for X-rays. The doctor came out a little later and said he couldn't explain it. He couldn't find anything wrong with Joseph, even though he could see by the tire marks and abrasions that Joseph had been run over. He even called in another doctor and took more X-rays. All they could find was a small fracture on one arm, which wasn't bad enough to even put a cast on. So we thanked the doctor, took Joseph, and left. By the time we got back here, even the tire marks and abrasions were gone. God had answered our prayers! Jesus raised Joseph from the dead!"

"Hallelujah!" one of the men shouted.

Almost everyone seemed to take what happened with Joseph being raised from the dead like it was a normal everyday occurrence. They expected God to perform a miracle. I, however, was stunned.

I had heard of such occurrences but had never before seen someone raised from the dead. And that's the way it seemed to me. Teachers at Christ for the Nations had said that God directed His people with signs and wonders throughout the Bible, and that He does so now, in order to reveal Himself to His church.

Later that evening Jim Ellison confided in me his source of faith. "The Bible says that God has set apart him that is godly for Himself. I know that I am set apart for God; but more importantly, my family is set apart for God also. And this place, with those who have chosen to follow me. Learn to let God do that which is right in His own sight, Kerry, and you will learn to have peace and trust. I knew Joseph wouldn't die; no one will ever die here, as long as we trust Jesus and do what is right in His own sight."

It seemed God had now confirmed with signs and wonders that He was indeed active in these people's lives. I believed God was definitely moving in this place and now I was really convinced Kay and I were meant to be here.

Winter loomed; my first winter in Arkansas, my first winter anywhere other than in Texas. It had been an exciting six months. The birth of our son, the decision to stay, being anointed as an elder, learning to work hard, and the miracle with Joseph had all been important steps. But the next step in my adhesion to the group proved the most traumatic for me.

Everyone could tell as soon as we got to the meeting that night that something was different. We could sense the presence of God's Spirit and that something deep and intense was going to happen. We only sang a few songs when suddenly a prophecy came forth through one of the men, Trent.

"You have been a faithful people, says the Lord, a people that have chosen to bond together. Yet, there are some that are holding back from my dealings. Does not my word say that judgment must begin in the house of God? Do you not know that before I can judge the world, I must first of all cleanse my Body? A change is coming, says God. There are three of you that tonight must confess your sins and ask for deliverance. Do not ask, 'Who is it, Lord?' Do not look at the others and say, 'It is you.' For you know who you are. You are Rick; you are Eric; You are Tom. You have the sin of pride, pride which I hate, pride which holds you back. Confess that sin tonight which is covered up by your pride and I will deliver you, says the Lord, or else be purged from this people. For tonight a purging begins; tonight judgment must begin in the house of God."

This type of meeting was in sharp contrast to the churches I had been in, where openly mentioning a member's sins was taboo. To think that God still dealt with people in a real and vital sense exhilarated me. This was not an invasion of privacy, but a clear indication that God cared about His Body, that "when one suffers, we all suffer."

Prophecies like this one were accepted at face value as being from God. As long as the prophecy, or the one giving it, was not in direct

conflict or violation with the Scriptures or in how the group understood God's dealing with them, every prophecy was readily accepted.

A deathly silence lingered in the meeting room as heads bowed
in prayer. One by one everyone looked at the three men mentioned
by name. Rick—a big, burly twenty-four-year-old man with a long,
pre-maturely white beard—got up first and sat in the chair in the
middle of the room, used when one wanted prayer. He confessed his
pride and ask for deliverance from anger and self-righteousness. We
gathered around him, praying in tongues, laying hands upon him, and
asked for God to deliver Leslie's husband, Rick, of his pride.

A few minutes later, Eric—his long red hair and rope-woven san-
dals indicative of his hippie days—sat in the chair, confessing bitterness and pride. The deliverance process was repeated.

We waited for Tom to get up. He never did. He never said anything. After a long wait, the meeting was adjourned. I followed Tom
outside. "What happened in there?" I asked him.

"Nothing. I don't want to talk about it."

"Tom, you were named in the prophecy. Rick and Eric both got
up. I don't know what God is dealing with you about, other than
pride, but it's not that big of a deal to sit in the chair and ask for deliverance or prayer. Why didn't you follow Rick and Eric?"

Tom got irate. "Leave me alone! Can't you see I don't want to talk
about it? You don't need to sit in some chair to get deliverance from
something. The Lord is very capable of listening to me at home and
delivering me from some sin right there."

"I agree," I told him, "but that's not what He told you to do. He
said to ask for prayer at the meeting. What is so terrible that you cannot ask for prayer in front of the others? I know you too well, Tom.
What's eating at you?"

Tom sat on the ground and began to cry. I had never seen Tom
cry before. "Oh, Kerry, I'm so ashamed." He sobbed for a long time
before confessing his sin to me. "I picked it up while we were with
the Children of God. We were taught that it was healthy for us. I've
tried to stop, but I can't. I know it spiritually hurts me; I know emotionally hurts Barbara." Tom looked at me for the first time since he

started crying. "But I can't tell the others. And you can't, either. No one must know. Promise me."

"What about the prophecy?" I asked. "You don't have to mention this particular problem; just asked for deliverance from pride like God said."

"God will have to deliver me from this without my confessing it in front of everyone, and that's all there is to it."

That wasn't all there was to it. I still didn't understand completely about "the chair." I understood it was only a symbol in which to humble oneself in front of the group before asking for prayer, openly confessing what one needed. But I also believed that if God wanted Tom to get in the chair in order to be set free from this or any other affliction, Tom would have to obey God. But he wouldn't. Tom refused to get in the chair for the next several meetings. Then he began to avoid coming to the meetings altogether. Ellison knew this couldn't continue.

About three weeks after the initial prophecy of purging the camp, another prophecy came through one of the women, Donna. The prophecy said that we would have to be willing to sacrifice much for the good of the group, that only by our fusing together into one body could He accomplish His will in us. The word said that we would have to set the priorities of the group above our own individual priorities. And then it said that whoever would not follow this word would have to be cast from the group.

We believed that God wanted our individualities to die, that our rebellion would have to go. Within a week after that meeting, Jim determined that all the men would have to cut their hair short and shave off their beards. Those were symbols of our rebellious years in a rebellious society. Then within a month we were no longer being paid to work in the cedar woods. All of the money, it was agreed, would go to the group, to purchase the land we wanted, to build houses for each other, and to buy supplies. The people had a higher vision now.

We were united in our belief that "the Body" was more important than our own individual desires. "The Body" would take care of each other's needs. By now, however, everyone was on food stamps and other welfare programs, an act we considered to simply be "spoiling Egypt." Tom, however, said he wouldn't work for nothing, that it was too much like the Children of God.

Jim cornered Tom and told him that the pay was not the issue and Tom knew it. "You're running from God, Tom. You're an elder here, now act like it!"

"Then maybe I don't need to be an elder here," Tom argued. "I don't agree with what's going on." Tom looked at me. "Do you?"

I knew he wanted me to choose him over Jim Ellison. But to me it wasn't a choice between him or Ellison; it was a choice of whether to obey God or not. And Tom knew where I stood on that. "I admit I don't understand everything, Tom. But you're refusing to do what God wants you to do. Quit resisting before it's too late."

"It's already too late," Tom quietly said. "I no longer want to be an elder here. My family will no longer fellowship here. And if you know what's good for you, Kerry, you'll get out, too, before it's too late. Before this becomes another Children of God."

Tom had been my best friend for almost three years. I watched him drive away and leave the resort. I found it eerie and ironic. I originally came to save Tom and Barbara from this group and now he was trying to save me from it. I cried as he drove off. I knew I had lost my best friend.

That evening I shaved my head. It was my way of symbolizing that the old covering I had—Tom, the one I had previously sworn my allegiance to—would no longer be my covering. I would have a new covering now, a new allegiance. Ellison and the others understood the gesture. I was one step closer.

After Tom left our group, Jim anointed two of the other men, Trent and Randall, as elders. Trent, a couple of years younger than me, had been with Jim for about three years and was the main singer and guitar player during the services. He was one of the single men that had gone north that summer with Jim, and had returned married, to a woman named Annie. Often, Trent would preach at the meetings.

Randall, a year older than me, was a native of the Ozarks, a true mountain man. He was a little taller than me, with a muscular build.

He was also a guitar player in the meetings. Randall possessed the only gun in the group, a single-shot .22 caliber rifle. He and his wife would often come to the meetings in a horse-drawn covered wagon, the one they had driven in a wagon train during the nation's bicentennial in 1976. I don't think Randall liked me too much at first. He didn't like attending my Bible studies. When it came to the Bible, Randall actually got on my nerves.

"Why do you go to this much trouble about the Bible?" he would ask me. "You're making it too complicated."

"What do you mean?" I asked.

Randall knew only one Scripture by memory, and it was his trademark in his Christian walk. "There's only one truth I live by: 'Thou shalt love the Lord thy God with all thy heart, and with all thy soul, and with all thy mind, and with all thy strength. And thou shalt love thy neighbor as thyself.' If you can do this," Randall said, "you've accomplished all that's required in the law. That's what I live by. When you think about it, what does the Lord really require of us but to do justly, to love mercy and to walk humbly with our God?"

I didn't understand this simplicity, and told him there was more to our walk with God than that. He disagreed, shrugged his shoulders, and walked off.

Randall's philosophy was a little different from the group's. He didn't really see God moving in every situation of a person's life. He believed a person should do the very best that he or she was capable of doing, and if more was needed, then God would step in. This philosophy would pose a problem for Randall later on.

Knowing we would soon be moving to the new property Jim was buying, Randall built a small round house—with a dirt floor—at one end of the property.

Once Randall realized I was really going to stay, he tried to help me adjust to the hills. "Okay," he once said, "if'n you're gonna stay, you gotta learn to talk hillbilly and not Texican no more. So ya' gotta learn some lingo. Now tell me what 'rainch' means."

"Rainch?" I replied.

"Rainch." Randall repeated.

I thought about it for a moment. "That's a tool that you use to tighten a nut or bolt with."

"No," Randall said, "that would be a wrench."

"Okay, then it would be a lot of land with cattle on it," I figured.

"No, no, no," Randall laughed. "That would be a ranch. Don't they teach you'uns anything in Texas?"

"I give up." I couldn't figure out what "rainch" could mean.

Randall stepped closer and answered, "Rainch is what you do after you warsh your clothes. First you warsh them, then you rainch them out!" He kiddingly hit me on the arm and laughed.

Randall's humility and big heart was in direct proportion to his strength. It was here that I began to respect Randall Rader. In the woods, Randall was in charge of the crew loading the cedar blocks. He would always pick up the biggest blocks himself. "If'n you're gonna expect to be an example to the people here," he told me one day in the woods, "and lead 'em, you gotta be the first person to the blocks, and you gotta pick up the biggest ones. Like Jim always says: 'Whatever your hands find to do, do with all your might.' I've watched you pick up the smaller ones yourself and leave the bigger ones for others. I know you still ain't used to loadin' cedar, but you never will be unless you git the big ones first. Understand?"

Yes, I understood. Randall really cared about me, about people.

A few days later, Randall and I were building a barbed-wire fence for a neighbor.

"Randall," I said, "I don't understand the prophecy you got when you were anointed an elder. You know, about you having the strength of Samson."

Randall Rader proceeded to pick up the sixteen-pound postmaul he used to drive posts into the ground. Holding the long handle at one end and then extending his arm straight in front of him, Randall slowly bent his wrist (and not his elbow) and lowered the head of the postmaul to his nose—a feat of unquivering strength. He then raised the maul back up.

"I couldn't do that before the prophecy," he shrugged. "Everyday I feel stronger than the day before."

I looked at him in awe, hoping to one day be as strong as Randall Rader.

I then asked Randall to tell me how he met Jim and why he decided to move to the property after being non-committal to the group for the last few years. He told me about growing up in the Missouri hills; of going to California for a few years so he could play his music, do drugs, and have all the sex he wanted; then getting tired of that scene and returning to the hills, wanting to find some meaning for his life. Then he told me about Jim Ellison.

"I've never met a man like Jim," he told me. "He's got more compassion and mercy in him than anyone I've ever known, without being a wimp about it. He's a strong, hard-working man, in control of himself and his family.

"You never knew his first wife. She slept around on Jim for years. I didn't know that, of course, when I first met them at their farm in Elijah, Missouri. But she kept coming on to me and one day I gave in to her seductions. We were in bed getting it on, when Jim came in. He didn't scream, he didn't yell—nothing. Just turned around and left. I got up and ran away.

"I told him later I was sorry, that it had only happened that one time. And you know what he said to me? He said he forgave me. Said it was all right. Said it wasn't the first time he'd caught her with someone else. But he loved her and wanted their marriage to work. He was just hoping she would change."

Randall laughed a little bit, shaking his head. "But you know, she never changed. She left him and their kids a little while later and divorced him. I was glad she left. Ollie's a lot better for him.

"Why do I follow Jim Ellison? Because he forgave me when no other man would have. I still don't understand how he could do it; I couldn't've. But he did, so I owe him for that. As long as there's a breath in me, I'll follow him and I'll protect him."

I watched Randall as he turned to continue working. I had the feeling that he didn't share his thoughts with people much.

I still preached against some of the things Ellison taught, especially the "sonship" message. I asked some of the men to explain it to me, to show it to me in the Scriptures. No one could. None of them knew the Scriptures that well, and what they did know, they "spiritualized" to mean something other than the literal letter of what it said.

To spiritualize a scripture means to try to see a different or deeper meaning to it than the one commonly taught. The group believed that the Bible was not so much literal as it was symbolic, that the letter or literal meaning would kill the spirit of the scripture. I didn't believe that.

And, of course, I never asked Ellison to prove his teachings to me. Nor did he offer to. But one day he approached me with an idea.

"Your wife's family," Jim asked, "lives in Lubbock, Texas, right?"

"Yes, Sir. Why?"

"There's a man I know, an apostle, who has established churches all over the world. His name is Sam Fife. Every Christmas he has a large meeting in Lubbock with the church there. People come from all over for that meeting. Why don't you and your family go to Lubbock and visit Kay's family, and while you're there, go to Sam's meetings? I think you'd find them very interesting."

I agreed to go. We drove to Lubbock for the holidays. The prospect of seeing her family excited Kay. I wanted to see this Sam Fife character. Christ for the Nations had warned about him, claiming he was one of the main false teachers in the church.

Kay and I went to the meeting while her parents watched our two children. After an hour of praise music, which we really enjoyed, the meeting got quiet. A man walked to the microphone. "Good evening, brethren," he began, "I'm Buddy Tucker, one of the teachers for Sam Fife. I'm going to be brief tonight, and then Sam will preach to you. I'm here to speak about a message, a doctrine, that some of you are having trouble with. This teaching is called 'sonship' and many of you are in doubt of it. I can understand that. Probably up till now, no one has shown you this teaching in the Word of God. They may have spouted some rhetoric about it; they may have spiritualized some scriptures for you. But they couldn't show you concrete evidence of it in the Bible.

"Tonight, I'm going to show you fourteen Bible verses that speak about sonship. I'm not going to expound upon them nor explain them. I'll let the Holy Spirit do that. Thirteen of those Scriptures I want you to take literally for what they say. The last verse I will share with you, the fourteenth one, is the only one I want to spiritualize. You will understand its spiritual meaning by the time I get to it. Are you ready?"

I was beside myself. This was what I had been asking about for several months now. I couldn't believe what was happening. It was as if the speaker knew I was coming and was speaking directly to me.

"Now open your Bible," Buddy began, "to First Corinthians, chapter twelve, verses twelve to fourteen: 'For as the body is one, and has many members, and all the members of that one body, being many, are one body: so also is Christ. For by one Spirit are we all baptized into one body, whether we are Jews or Gentiles, whether we are bond or free; and have been all made to drink into one Spirit. For the body is not one member, but many.'"

I listened intently as Sam Fife's Bible teacher spoke, turning to every scripture he named, underlining that scripture, and reading the context around it. "Next, Romans chapter twelve, verses four and five: 'For as we have many members in one body, and all members have not the same office: so we, being many, are one body in Christ, and every one members one of another.'"

Buddy continued until he finished all fourteen verses. True to his word, he never expounded on them nor tried to explain those scriptures. He didn't have to. It was so simple, I couldn't believe I hadn't seen it before. There it was, in black and white, right before my eyes. Sonship.

I couldn't move, I was so awestruck by this meeting. I could see the hand of God in it, as if destiny determined for me to be there. Later Sam Fife preached and more songs were sung. I was in a fog the whole time, thinking only about what Buddy Tucker had said and how God had arranged circumstances.

After the meeting, I purchased all fifty booklets written by Sam Fife. I wanted to learn as much as I could of this teaching and any others that Fife taught. We drove back to Arkansas the next day. When we arrived Jim asked what I thought about Fife's meeting. I told him everything that had occurred. He just smiled.

The following day it snowed so much we couldn't go anywhere for three days. No work, no town trips, no distractions.

My only break from reading and studying Fife's material was when all the men took the four-wheel-drive truck to the pasture and "hood-skied." We turned an old car hood upside-down, chained it to the back of the truck, and skied behind it. It was wild. I loved the playful antics of the men while we took turns skiing. I loved the feeling of belonging. I loved this place.

I sat at my desk during those three days, reading and absorbing Sam Fife's books. I thought my brain would fry. The knowledge that man possessed of the Scriptures astounded me. Most of it was beyond my comprehension, but one thing was sure: I now began to understand the sonship message.

I no longer felt threatened by Ellison or his teachings, but craved to learn all he knew. I asked him to teach me all he could. "In time," he would say, "in time."

I never felt so alive with the Scriptures. It was amazing. Reading Fife was self-revealing. Now I not only recognized the erroneous teachings I had learned (and subsequently taught) from the Baptist church and the Charismatic Movement, I also began to understand the garbage of religious pride that still resided within me. I thought I had been delivered from it two years before, when I had confessed my pride to God while Tom and Barbara prayed for me.

It had been easy for me to tear down a person's doctrines if they were different from mine. Now, for the second time in my life (the first being with Tom), someone challenged my thinking. I was overwhelmed. Now the Bible by itself wasn't enough. I had to find more writings like Fife's that would challenge me, that would stimulate me, that would open the Word of God to me.

For three months I read and studied like I had never read and studied before. Then one day it happened.

Jim Ellison and I were in the back of the woods truck returning to the resort. I turned to him and told him, "You knew what I was teaching before. You knew I'd been teaching denominational garbage to the people here, yet you told them to go to my Bible studies anyway, even when they complained to you about me." Jim acknowledged what I said.

"Why?" I asked, "Why did you tell them to go? Why didn't you ever say anything to me about what I was teaching?"

He looked straight at me, humbled by my questions and his own forthcoming answer, and simply stated, "They that are led by the Spirit of God, Kerry, they are the sons of God. I did what I was told to do. I did what love would do. Always remember, Kerry, in any situation, always ask yourself, 'What would love do? What would Jesus do?' That should be the motive for all that you do."

Then he smiled slightly and looked away. "I knew you were coming to live with us, when you thought you were only coming to visit and try to save Tom and Barbara. I knew you were to be the Bible teacher I needed here. And I knew I had to wait until it was God's time to reveal certain truths to you before I could say anything. I knew I had to wait for Him and for you. And I know you understand what I mean."

I understood exactly what he meant. He did what God had told him to do. Jim had to wait until I was ready, wait until I questioned him about his teachings. This was the man of God I had sought for so many years. As the truck continued toward home, we remained silent. My thoughts carried me to another place, another time, to a decisive moment in my Christian growth.

■　■　■

"It seems you don't approve of my teaching methods or of some of my beliefs," I told the deacons and pastor. I had asked for a meeting with them after discovering they had been discussing me at church.

"That's right. In your teaching the young people's class on Sundays, you're using only the Bible and not the Baptist Quarterly teaching guide and that you had Communion with them at your house during Bible study one evening. Is that correct?"

"Yes, Sir, it is. We were discussing what angels really look like according to the Bible. I already told the pastor, before becoming a member here, how I teach. He said that was no problem." The pastor looked away. He had been my pastor six years earlier when I was in high school near Lubbock, Texas. He was the reason I had decided to join this Dallas church.

I was now feeling betrayed by my own pastor. Why won't he speak up in my defense? I wondered.

"Well we do, however, disapprove of what you're doing. Only the pastor is allowed to offer communion."

"Where does it say that in the Bible?" I asked.

"It's what we teach in the Baptist church. Besides," he added, "we heard you had wine at the communion so you could get the teenage girls drunk and have sex with them."

"What!" I screamed. "Who told you a thing like that? Each person had only one sip of wine. One sip! Are you telling me that I would expect an orgy after only one sip of wine?"

"It's what we were told. Besides, the main issue is your refusal to teach out of the Quarterly. Do you think you're smarter than the Baptist board that wrote the Quarterly?" the head deacon asked.

"Who is more intelligent has nothing to do with it," I stated. "I simply prefer the Bible itself."

"Why do you want to study this stuff about angels anyway?"

"Why?" I was shocked by the deacon's question. "Why not? If it's in the Bible, it's got to be important. Why would we not want to study everything the Bible talks about?"

"The only thing important," the deacon continued, "is whether a person is saved or not. That's what we need to study and discuss, not all this unimportant stuff."

Unimportant? I was starting to get mad, but was determined to stay calm.

"Okay, show me scripturally my error and I'll repent."

The head deacon offered no scripture. He simply said, "If you wish to teach here, you must teach Baptist doctrine, the Baptist way."

"And if the Bible contradicts Baptist doctrine?" I asked, horrified at his response. "Is the Bible not the final authority?"

"You must teach Baptist doctrine!" he repeated.

"Even though the Scriptures might disprove?"

Then the head deacon, in the presence of the pastor and other deacons, looked straight at me and stated matter-of-factly, "You must teach Baptist doctrine the Baptist way, or you cannot teach here at all. What you think the Bible teaches is of no importance."

I was stunned that a Baptist church would demand tradition and doctrinal adherence over the Bible itself, that I had been betrayed by a Baptist pastor, and that a Baptist deacon would be uninterested in all that the Bible taught. But all I said was, "I'm sorry. I can't do that." I walked out of the meeting, shaking the dust off my shoes in front of the pastor and deacons. I knew they would get the message. Tom had been right when he said I wouldn't last in the Baptist church.

I further realized the hypocrisy of the church when I counseled for Pat Robertson's *The 700 Club* in Dallas during the fall of 1975. As a telephone counselor for *The 700 Club,* I would pray for people's needs when they called in, then fill out a form so that we could keep track of the needs we had prayed for. At the end of the program each evening, all of the counselors would gather the forms into one pile, lay hands upon them, and claim victory for those prayer requests. Therefore, if one hundred people had asked prayer for a physical healing that day, we proudly proclaimed that one hundred people got healed.

I was new to the Charismatic movement, and ignorantly asked those in charge of the local *700 Club,* "Why don't we call these people back periodically to see how they're doing, or maybe even go by and visit them?"

"We're not allowed to do that," I was told. "That would be a lack of faith on our part." Right—just like questioning our church's doctrines would be a lack of faith. I left *The 700 Club* shortly after leaving the Baptist Church.

■   ■   ■

I had gotten in trouble at the Baptist church for doing something my pastor said I could do, for something I considered a minor incident. If I had done there what I had done in Arkansas, I'd have been disfellowshipped in a heartbeat. Yet, here was Jim Ellison, knowing what I was overtly doing and saying and teaching, waiting patiently for God to deal with me. I had never witnessed a man so secure in his position before, so sure of his relationship to God, that he didn't feel intimidated or threatened by anyone. Ellison loved God enough to love me in spite of myself. Here was the man I yearned to follow, that I wanted to learn from, that I wanted to be like.

"Why don't you and Kay come over for supper tonight?" Jim asked, as I gathered my thoughts. "We could talk some more."

"Sounds good," I replied. "I'd enjoy that."

After the meal, Jim and I walked outside. I was a little apprehensive, but excited. For the first time in the nine months since moving to Arkansas, I would find out some important background and insights into Jim Ellison.

"I believe beyond any doubt, Kerry, that we're in the last days. I believe there are still apostles and prophets in the church today. This is known as the five-fold ministry, which I've begun to teach you about. And I believe that God will do nothing without telling His prophets first. As you know I came from the Disciples of Christ Church, which does not believe in the five-fold ministry, the gifts of the Spirit, nor in the move of the Spirit in people's lives today.

"I went to college in Illinois, until a friend and I got expelled for questioning the doctrines of the church during our senior year. We did this because we had both recently received the baptism of the Spirit. I woke up one night to find a swirling ball of fire hovering above my feet. The colors were unbelievably beautiful, almost alive. I felt such peace while I watched it. I had never experienced anything supernatural or spiritual before, but even though it was new to me, I knew it was a visitation from the Lord."

The fact that God had visited Ellison perked my attention.

"In 1962," he continued, "I heard about a Spirit-filled church in San Antonio, Texas, called the School of the Ministry and decided to check it out. When I arrived, the elders of the church received me and said they had been expecting me. One of the prophets said that he had seen me in a dream wearing a certain suit. I was informed that the Lord had given them instructions to give me money and tell me to return to my home and bring my wife and children to San Antonio, to receive special training. I knew the Lord was directing them in truth.

"When I did return to Illinois, my first wife thought I was crazy to even consider such a thing as moving to Texas, but I told her we were going, so we did. She hadn't received the baptism of the Spirit yet, and knew nothing of the witness of the Spirit or of the blessings of God. When we arrived in San Antonio, the ministries of the church said that even though I was willing to work that I was not to look for a job, but that I was to give my complete attention to studying and seeking the Father. The church provided us with a nearly-new four bedroom house, rent free, with utilities turned on and with groceries and other necessities.

"At this time, the School of the Ministry was alive with the Spirit. The ministries and the people were completely involved in prayer and fasting, with seeking Jesus' will and in study, with meetings six days and nights every week. They were warning the people of San Antonio, and the United States, about avoiding the judgments of God. They rented full-sized billboard signs along the highway in the city and purchased radio time.

"I spent six months in this intense training, on faith, repentance, judgment, the ministry of prophets, seeking the will of God, and other truths found in the Bible. All these things were done with an air of urgency as the judgment of the church and the nation, with the appearance of Jesus, were felt to be imminent. The tone or nature of my own ministry, giving it an end-time and prophetic flavor, was set."

The School of the Ministry sounded a lot like Christ for the Nations to me.

"For about three years I traveled and ministered where our Father directed me across the nation. Periodically I would return to the School of the Ministry. One time when I later returned to San Antonio, something had changed. At first I couldn't understand it. Most of the people and ministries were the same, but something was wrong.

"I learned the reason soon enough. When the judgment and destruction of the nation and the establishment of the kingdom didn't come as quickly as some had felt they would, many grew cold. You see, the people had grown tired of waiting, and the word of God took second place to the people's homes, businesses, families, and other possessions. Some members even felt relieved that the church no longer preached about the coming judgments; but that word began to come strongly to me. I didn't understand at first why the church wasn't preaching about the judgments as much.

"But I continued to preach and prophesy about the coming destruction. The older ministries later took me aside and said to leave it alone. Wanting to be in submission, I foolishly said I would do so. I felt like Peter denying Jesus. Then on April 29, 1970, God reached out His hand and put me straight. While working on a building as an iron worker—that was my trade in those days—the building began to collapse, with me hanging upside down on a steel beam. I couldn't escape. The beam followed me and broke twenty-eight of my bones, with various other injuries.

"My back was broken, both legs were broken in several places, all my ribs were broken, and my left ankle was crushed. When the beam trapped me, I died. It had doubled me over, and would've decapitated me had one end of the girder not landed on another steel beam. I left this world and went to a quiet place, peaceful and blue. It was the most joyous feeling I've ever known. But I eventually returned to my body."

While Ellison was speaking, I realized for the first time how he had been able to remain so calm when Barbara had told him she had run over Joseph. If God could bring Jim back from the dead, why not Joseph?

"The doctors didn't expect me to live, so for the first three days I was in the hospital they didn't even give me any medicine or pain killers, or even set my bones. But I knew I wouldn't die. I knew I would preach again. And I knew I had to speak God's word regardless of the feelings or wishes of men. This I did about seventeen days later, standing in the church shortly after walking out of the hospital.

"Many were obviously surprised by how soon I had come to church following such extreme injuries. I wasn't afraid to speak the truth this time. I walked to the front of the sanctuary and picked up the plastic bottle that contained the anointing oil that we used to pray for the sick. I held it up and prophesied that the Spirit of God was leaving this church. Then I let go of the bottle and it dropped to the thick carpet that covered our floor, where it shattered in pieces, like glass hitting concrete. The people gasped as they understood the symbolism involved. The anointing was gone from the ministries at the school.

"I spoke forth the judgments of God for the next nine months, demanding obedience to God, until seven families and my family finally left San Antonio for the Ozark Mountains, to establish a place of refuge. The Lord had told me to take a map of the United States and draw circles representing a one-hundred-mile radius around every major city of one hundred thousand people or more. When I did that, there were only about six areas in the entire country that were not within the circles. I chose the Ozark Mountains area to move to.

"When some of the brethren and I came to the Ozarks, I was led to the farm at Elijah, Missouri, which we later called 'Cherith Brook.' Over the next few years, the families from San Antonio grew disillusioned that God hadn't judged America, and they left. My first wife left also, and then divorced me, leaving our children with me. Some time later I met Ollie, the wife you know, and we married. She's been the half of me that my first wife never was.

"I've known two women in my whole life, Kerry, and both of them I've married. I've never smoked a cigarette and have never been drunk. The ways of the world just never appealed to me. My dad died in a car wreck when I was fourteen. I had to grow up fast and help my mother with my brother and sister. I couldn't even afford the luxury of feeling the pain of his death, so I learned to ignore pain. I've never really been close to my sister and brother.

"Then last year, right before you arrived, my mother died. That severed all my family ties, leaving me free to obey God without being hindered by what my family might think. Anyway, at Cherith Brook I met many of the people who are living here now. Then came the contact with those that left the Children of God, and through them you came to know of us. And now you've come to Mountain Creek."

I sat there next to Jim Ellison, overwhelmed at the similarities between him and me. He put his arm around me and continued. "As

I've told you before, I knew you were coming here to be the teacher I needed. You have much to learn, and much more to teach. Kerry, you have no idea yet how much potential you have as a teacher of God. Already you're asking questions of me that took me years to ask. Your growth in God astounds me. Someday . . . someday you will ask questions whose answers won't even concern me." Then Ellison smiled.

"I've wanted to personally share some of the directions of God in my life with you for some time now, but I wanted to wait until the right time. I don't know how much Tom might have told you, but I never shared much with him."

I felt the bond between Jim and me strengthen.

"I had the best childhood possible," I began revealing to Jim, "growing up in an absolutely safe and idyllic environment. My mom was a Sunday School teacher at a Baptist church. She always taught my sister and me about the Lord. I can honestly say that I've never known a time when I didn't love the Lord. I wasn't a strong Christian, I guess, but I tried to do my best. When I was with other Christians, I was fine. When I wasn't with other Christians, I sometimes wasn't so fine.

"After graduating from high school, I worked at a newspaper in Dallas. In time, through my friends there, I discovered marijuana and other drugs. My life had no direction, no meaning, at that time. It seemed that every goal I had set in life had de-materialized. In March of 1972, I was living alone, and one night, after smoking a joint, I went to bed. During the night I found myself all of a sudden standing before God, even though all I could see was His arm and hand. Then He spoke. His voice seemed to echo throughout the entire place. Then I saw a book on a table and the Lord was turning the pages. As He did so, He would tell me things about my life and why He had done as He did in those events. It totally changed my understanding about my life. God began to tell me what He had planned for me and what He wanted me to do. He said He had given me the gifts of teaching and pastoring.

"The place I was in was so peaceful and so full of light, yet somehow dark at the same time. Anyway, I woke up and felt a power in my life I had never felt before. I went to a Christian bookstore and bought a pocket-size Bible to carry to work. Then I went to see a Baptist preacher at a church down the street and told him about my experience. He simply said I had been called to the ministry. It wasn't until three years later that I realized I had experienced the baptism of the Spirit as well.

"When I got to work, I told everyone what had happened. They said it was just the marijuana. But I ignored them and began to read the Bible every day, every chance I got. I read it through, underlining verses and memorizing scriptures, and then I would read it again, cover to cover, over and over. I couldn't get enough of it.

"Later, I left Dallas and moved to Lubbock. There I married Kay. Two years later we moved back to Dallas, and that's when I met Tom and Barbara. It was through their laying hands on me, on the night of my twenty-third birthday, at the house that we lived in with them, that I tasted my second supernatural experience. While I was praying for the Lord to cleanse me from religious pride, I left my body and watched the entire scene while hovering above. It was so powerful, Jim, that I can still picture it today. Living with Tom and Barbara was the best year of my life." I stopped suddenly and felt the pain in my chest.

"And now Tom's gone. But I gotta go on and do what God wants. All I've ever wanted to do was to know Jesus better and to love Him more and more. I hunger for Him and for the knowledge of Him. Do you know what I mean?"

"Of course, I do," Jim assured me. "That's why you're here."

In the spring of 1978 we moved about two miles from Mountain Creek Resort to the 224-acre property we bought from Campus Crusade for Christ. Jim had been living in an old farmhouse there for a few months by the time we began to build him a two-story house. Soon we were building other smaller houses and moving in some trailer houses. For a while we had our church services in the living room of Jim's new house.

"Brethren," Jim began one night in a meeting, "we've come a long way together these few years. Tonight we take another step forward.

Those of you who lived with us near Elijah, Missouri know that we named our farm 'Cherith Brook.'

"It was at Cherith Brook in the Bible that the prophet Elijah sojourned and was fed by the ravens. When the brook dried up, Elijah went to Zarephath, where a widow woman shared her last bit of food with the prophet. Her act of faith secured a miracle from God, so that she and her son never did without food, though they never had abundance either.

"Later Elijah challenged the prophets of Baal so that Israel would choose to follow God. From there Elijah fled to Horeb, the mount of God, also known as Sinai, where he was divinely sustained for forty days and forty nights, and where Elijah—amidst the winds, earthquakes, and fire—learned the still, small voice of God. This is the same place where Moses saw the burning bush and learned the name and nature of God.

"At our own Cherith Brook, God fed us, but that place dried up. Then we came to Mountain Creek, which some of us called 'Zarephath.' Zarephath, in the Hebrew, means 'a purging place.' That is the spiritual realm the Lord has taken us to, a place for purging, or refining. Our Father's purpose here is to refine us, to purge from us those worldly and carnal things which hinder our relationship to Him, so that, even in the midst of trials and tribulations, we might learn His still, small voice.

"We are in a transition period," Ellison continued. "We are no longer just Zarephath; we are now moving to Horeb. Therefore, the Lord has impressed upon me that we shall call ourselves by a new name, by a name that signifies His dealing with us. From now on we will be known as 'Zarephath-Horeb Community Church.' May He guide us and teach us to walk in Him, and to know Him as He knows us!"

We praised God for this new name, this new message. An electrifying excitement reverberated between us all. I had caught the revelation—"enlightened"—that here at Zarephath-Horeb and throughout the world, God was conforming a people into His image, a people who would truly know His voice.

Months before, after finishing the books by Sam Fife, I began to drill Jim Ellison with question after question about the Bible. Areas of thought opened up to me that I had never considered before. When he felt I was ready for it, Jim loaned me some booklets entitled, *The Page*, written by George Hawtin, a man from Canada. I ate, breathed, wore, and dreamed about the teachings within those "Pages"—more revelations, more invigorating power.

George Hawtin was a former Assemblies of God preacher and, at one time, the superintendent of the largest Assembly of God school in Canada. Hawtin was later rejected by the Assemblies, once he began to question his denomination's doctrines. He began writing *The Page* in 1960. His primary emphases in writing were commonly on sonship, coming out of Babylon's church system, and the eventual salvation of all creation.

I began to correspond with Hawtin and gained tremendous respect for him and his writings. Hawtin, however, believed that every group, church, fellowship, or whatever name they chose to call themselves, no matter how good and sincere they were when they started out, would eventually become part and parcel to spiritual Babylon, and would become corrupted. Hawtin warned me to separate myself from our church group. No matter how much we may try not to be like the Babylonian church system, Hawtin taught, by nature it was inevitable for us to become another harlot daughter. I believed he was premature in his judgment and would change his mind if he ever visited us. Only years later did I finally begin to understand the truth of his statement.

We lived by a simple standard, although a high one, at Zarephath-Horeb. Besides requiring a love for Jesus and a high desire to follow and obey Him, we allowed no smoking, no drinking beer (wine was allowed in moderation, since we used wine for the Lord's Supper), no cussing, no drugs. Everyone had to attend the praise meetings and Bible studies. Members of our church had to live on our property and were required to work with us instead of in town on their own. If a person was not willing to follow this standard, Zarephath-Horeb was not the place to live.

A typical day at Zarephath-Horeb would find most of the men cutting timber in the cedar woods. Other men would probably be building the homes or repairing a vehicle in the garage. Several women—under the direction of Ollie Ellison—might be preparing a town trip together in a van or other vehicle for groceries. The women who didn't go to town that particular day might be canning, working in the garden, sorting clothes that neighbors donated to us, or baby-sitting. The days were full and productive with each member preparing themselves spiritually for the praise meeting or Bible study that would take place almost every night.

Beginning in the spring of 1978, I taught a six-month Bible study about the Old Testament tabernacle that God instructed Moses to build and the truths that the tabernacle were symbolic of. I built a four-by-eight foot replica of the Tabernacle as a visual aid for the classes. Through teaching about the tabernacle, I found the Bible to indeed be a book of tremendous symbology, with spiritualized meanings, as well as literal interpretations. This made Christianity an esoteric philosophy to me and not an exoteric religion. This was important, since our group believed that it should be normal for God to speak to His people, to deal personally with them.

I also learned that "the shewbread in the tabernacle was changed every Sabbath," which meant that revelation was progressive, that as long as we continue in the Lord, the old doctrines and understandings were continuously superseded by new truths. We were to constantly learn about the purpose and nature of God, as God unveiled Himself to us.

Studying the tabernacle also introduced me to the truth concerning fasting. Traditional churches never taught fasting as a way of understanding God, but I found it to be the quickest, surest way of discovering God, as well as myself. Over the next two years I fasted several times, from one day fasts to a twenty-one-day fast, my longest. Three to seven-day fasts were the most typical.

Trent, Annie and Randall wrote most of the songs that we sang at our praise meetings. In 1978 I wrote my first song for our community, entitled "River Jordan." It symbolized where I was at that time in the Lord and thought it might apply to the other members as well. It became one of the favorites at our farm.

We continued to grow collectively at Zarephath-Horeb, until a distraction occurred in the group.

Until our priorities changed.

5

Now We Have Guns

And I saw heaven opened, and behold a white horse,
and he that sat upon him was called Faithful and True,
and in righteousness he does judge and make war.
His eyes were as a flame of fire,
and on his head were many crowns;
and he had a name written,
that no man knew, but he himself.
And he was clothed with a vesture dipped in blood:
and his name is called The Word of God.
— Revelation 19:11-13

We believed God had established Zarephath-Horeb not just for our own refinement and spiritual growth, but so that when the time came for God to judge the world—and especially America—Christians would have a place to go and dwell safely away from the government of the Antichrist. We did not believe in a "rapture," whereby Christians would be taken away from the earth before the tribulation period. We believed that Christians were to go through the tribulation, that period of time when God would judge the sins of nations. During this time, we believed we were to house, feed, and clothe those who would come to us.

In the summer of 1978 we received some material by David Ebaugh, a preacher from the northeastern part of the United States. He predicted that the judgments of God would begin on the Jewish day of the ninth of Ab, which corresponded to our 12th of August that year. He predicted natural catastrophes beyond measure, including flooding on all coasts of the United States in a band two hundred miles wide.

This preacher gave some historical significance to the ninth-of-Ab teaching, as well as some scriptures. The prophet Jeremiah commanded the Jews to read the Book of Lamentations on the ninth of Ab, the fifth month of the Ecclesiastical Calendar. It commemorated the day on which the Temple was destroyed by fire by the King of Babylon and was the exact same day that the Temple went up in flames in the Roman/Jewish War in 70 AD. The ninth of Ab became a day of fasting that figured prominently throughout Jewish history as a day of infamy. We were hoping that the time had come for Jesus to establish His kingdom.

In preparation for this possible day of destruction, we sold everything we could of value—watches, silver coins, wedding rings, high school rings, any metals we could, in order to buy food and materials for our families. We also had a bonfire and burned everything we considered "Babylonian," that is, associated with the ways of the world. The saying of the day became "Redeem the time." I burned high school annuals, a lot of photographs and old keepsakes. We trashed televisions, radios and all other tokens or reminders of the "outside world's propaganda."

I have often regretted our actions during this time, especially burning photographs and school annuals and the selling of wedding rings. Separation from the past is a common ploy of cults. Ingredient number three—isolation—was beginning. The third ingredient to the creation of an extremist is itself composed of three parts: the limitation of information not coming from the group itself, a Savior mentality, and a perceived enemy or limited options. By getting rid of our televisions, radios, newspapers and magazines, information coming into the group was now limited, filtered primarily through either Jim Ellison or myself.

I decided to visit my parents in Fort Worth before the ninth of Ab, a sort of last good-bye. While there I visited several former work or Bible-school friends in Dallas to warn them of the coming destruction. My old co-workers rejected me, shrugging me off as a cult member. But some Bible school friends, who had once visited us in Arkansas, gave me an audio tape by a man that had recently been preaching in Dallas. His name was John Todd and, in time, he would accelerate the direction of our group.

I kept Todd's tape to myself for a while, without listening to it, since the day of judgment was now quickly approaching. However, the ninth of Ab came and went, with nothing unusual occurring. We were disappointed that God's judgment didn't come, but still anticipated its arrival as being near. A few days later I listened to Todd's tape and then enthusiastically shared it with the elders of the church.

John Todd identified himself as a former member of an organization called "The Grand-Druid Council of 13," the witchcraft innermost circle of the organizers for a one-world government. He introduced us to terms like the Illuminati, the Bilderbergers, the Council on Foreign Relations, the Trilateral Commission, the Federal Reserve System and the International Bankers. He mentioned the Masonic Lodge, Satanists, and others he claimed were involved in a worldwide conspiracy to rule the world for the devil.

John Todd brought the Illuminati and the Council of 13 into modern-day perspective. He was the first person we had ever heard mention the conspirators by name. He mentioned not only political leaders, but religious leaders, movie stars, media personalities, and corporate leaders. Going from church to church preaching about the Illuminati's purposes, he caused quite a stir.

According to the Bible, Noah's great-grandson, Nimrod (through Ham, then Cush), built Babel (Babylon) and other cities. He later opposed God and proclaimed himself to be the Messiah.

John Todd said that Nimrod's Tower of Babel—discussed in Genesis, chapter eleven—was an ancient "United Nations," seeking to bring about a one-world, one-religion government. God later confused the people of Babel with various languages and scattered them.

According to Todd, Babylon, with its "New World Order," went underground and became the pagan "Mysteries." He said that their hidden temples (called "groves" in the Scriptures) eventually became the modern Masons, Elks, Shriners, and Moose Lodges of today.

John Todd taught that the mystery religion of Babylon, with its Trinitarian worship of Isis, Horus and Seb, and its incestuous mother-son worship, remained underground, until Constantine made it the state religion, a so-called Christianity, in the fourth century.

Then, according to Todd, in the mid-1700s, Adam Weishaupt, a professor of Canon Law at the University of Ingalstadt, Bavaria, came on the scene. Weishaupt was born a Jew and later converted to Catholicism. He became a Jesuit priest, but later broke from the Order and spent the next five years in meditation.

Weishaupt had friends in the French royal court who practiced black magic, baby sacrificing, and other occult rites. Weishaupt desired copies of *The Kabbalah, The Major Keys of Solomon,* and *The Lesser Keys of Solomon,* books that showed how demons could be controlled by occult practices. The House of Rothschild, a European banking family, supposedly had these books and heard that Weishaupt was interested in them.

With the financial and occult backing of the Rothschilds—according to Todd—Adam Weishaupt then took these books, along with *The Book of Shadows* and *The Necronomicon,* two occult books that taught how to control demonic forces, and conceived a plan for the building of an organization called the Illuminati, or "Enlightened Ones." Their goal was the rebuilding of Nimrod's "One World" Babylon. Weishaupt's aims for world domination were simple. They included the abolition of all governments, of all private property, of all inheritance, of patriotism, of family life, marriage and communal education of children, and of all religion. This read like the Communist Manifesto. Weishaupt and the Rothschilds then started their private witchcraft coven, called the "Golden Dawn." Todd, additionally, said that the American Illuminati was formed on May 1, 1776.

Then in 1785, a courier for the Illuminati was struck by lightning and killed. This courier was carrying secret Illuminati papers, which the Bavarian government got hold of and then raided the Illuminati headquarters. The Illuminati had to go underground, just as Nimrod did. In 1829, so the story goes, the Illuminati created a philosophy called "communism" and the plan was again in progress.

On August 1, 1972, according to John Todd, Philippe Rothschild sent some papers to a meeting of the Council of 13, a Luciferian Priesthood of the top witches in the world, of which John Todd was supposedly a member. Besides the usual pay-off notes and progress reports, the papers included a projected takeover plan.

The plan included removing the President and vice-president (Nixon and Ford) and replacing them with a Democrat (Jimmy Carter), who would enact federal gun laws, remove tax exemptions from churches, institute martial law in the country after some planned catastrophe such as an oil crisis and begin World War III, the last planned war that was to bring about a one-world order.

Under the open organizations of the Trilateral Commission and the Council on Foreign Relations, the Illuminati was aided by top-ranking government officials, news media, scientists, movie and television personalities, recording artists and religious leaders, all of whom were supposedly deeply involved with witchcraft. Todd rebuked the idea of a Jewish-controlled conspiracy, saying the primary evildoers were Gentiles, not Jews.

The political-social warfare in reality, Todd said, was a spiritual warfare, a warfare between the forces of darkness and the forces of light, between Lucifer and Jesus and would be waged in both spiritual and physical arenas.

John Todd was supposedly backed by Dr. Tom Berry, a pastor of one of the largest Baptist churches in the country. Chick Publications, a Christian organization in California, also published a series of comic books based upon Todd's messages. With these two credentials, Todd's story seemed to have some credibility.

Only later, as I examined Todd's audio tapes that I had kept, did I realize the deception of his conspiratorial theories. We wanted to believe Todd. With that first John Todd tape I was given, our group embraced everything Todd preached. He seemed to confirm all that we felt was wrong in this country, as well as what we believed would happen in the future. He explained the source of our problems. Todd's explanation especially hit home with me and with Randall Rader. John Todd challenged me, just like Sam Fife had done, just like George Hawtin had done.

John Todd named many religious leaders as infiltrators for the Illuminati, including the founder of Christ for the Nations Bible

School. Todd said that the Charismatic Movement was started by the Illuminati as a way of getting witchcraft into the church, through rock music and divination (false prophecy). While attending Christ for the Nations, I had studied the writings of most of the other ministries Todd mentioned. Even then I had questioned some of their tactics or motives.

The only preacher of the 1950s that John Todd stood up for was William Branham, whose followers I had encountered earlier at Mountain Creek. Todd said Branham knew that the other ministries were fake and called them devils one night at a revival. Supposedly, Branham was later murdered by the Illuminati.

Randall Rader had spent three years in California as a rock musician. He confirmed many of Todd's statements about the occult influence in the music industry and about the witchcraft practices themselves.

According to John Todd, *Dunwich Horror,* a 1969 movie with Dean Stockwell and Sandra Dee was the most accurate movie on the occult ever made. *Three Days of the Condor,* with Robert Redford, was supposedly about a code book, *Atlas Shrugged,* discovered by a CIA agent. The recently-released *Star Wars* sequel, *The Empire Strikes Back,* was supposedly about the battle for world dominion between Black Witchcraft (Satanism) and White Witchcraft (which the Illuminati practiced and believed was "true" Christianity).

With the way the economy was, under President Carter, it seemed America was primed for an economic collapse. Todd said Carter had already betrayed us militarily as a nation, so a communist take-over was potentially nearer than most people suspected. Adding the fact that the Supreme Court had kicked God out of schools and legalized abortion in recent years, and with the Gun Control Act of 1968, America's time for judgment, we felt, was surely at hand.

True to my nature, in no time at all I purchased all of John Todd's tapes and his book. I also bought several other books about the Illuminati and the international banking system. But the eye-opener for me came with a novel that Todd mentioned. Ayn Rand wrote *Atlas*

Shrugged in the 1950s. I read its 1100-plus pages in less than two days. The book absolutely overwhelmed me.

Atlas Shrugged, according to Todd, was the code book about the takeover plan of the Illuminati. Todd revealed the code, which laid out how the government would cause the collapse of the United States and then other countries.

According to John Todd, the secret to *Atlas Shrugged* was in knowing the code. John Galt was supposed to be Philippe Rothschild, head of the Illuminati at that time. Dagny Taggard was Ayn Rand herself, Rothschild's mistress. Dagny's brother was the combined railroad systems. John Wyatt was David Rockefeller, head of the American arm of the Illuminati. Hank Reardon was the steel industry; Francisco D'Antonio, the copper industry; and the Pirate, piracy itself that was occurring at the time. Galt, D'Antonio, and the Pirate formed the Rothschild Tribunal.

The tribunal in the book went around convincing certain major corporation presidents of the Illuminati philosophy and plan, getting the corporate heads to bankrupt their own businesses. The owners of these companies would then vanish and leave with either Galt or D'Antonio to a retreat area in the Colorado mountain regions, the code name for the Bermuda Triangle, the place where the key figures of the Illuminati would be when the world system crashed.

As these corporations were bankrupting themselves, the tribunal began setting off riots, plane and train wrecks, grain bin explosions, inflation, a stock market crash by means of the gold price, and other ways of causing more panic and more governmental controls. We viewed these events as current in America.

Most important to us, however, were the philosophies of the enemy that were spelled out in *Atlas Shrugged*. The powers-that-be declared: "The only power any government has is the power to crack down on criminals. Well, when there aren't enough criminals, one makes them. One declares so many things to be a crime that it becomes impossible for men to live without breaking laws. . . . Freedom has been given a chance and has failed. Therefore, more stringent controls are necessary. Since men are unable and unwilling to solve their problems voluntarily, they must be forced to do it. . . . Fear is the only practical means to deal with people. . . . There is no way to disarm any man except through guilt. Through that which he himself has accepted as guilt. If a man has ever stolen a dime, you can impose on him the punishment intended for a bank robber and he will take it. He'll bear any form of misery, he'll feel that he deserves no better. If there's not enough guilt in the world, we must create it. If we teach a man that it's evil to look at spring flowers and he believes us and then does it—we'll be able to do whatever we please with him. He won't defend himself. He won't feel he is worth it. He won't fight. But save us from the man who lives up to his own standards. Save us from the man of clean conscience. He's the man who will beat us."

That was the key! That was where we came in! In the writings of the enemy they foretold who would beat them and how!

We believed that the satanic enemy had prophesied about us, and people like us, people like those at Zarephath-Horeb. Our purpose became more focused, more fine-tuned. Fear and guilt would not take hold of us! We would be men of clean conscience!

So, even more, we rose to the standard of God at our church, to His purpose in refining us, and we took our first major step to our own self-destruction. The ingredients were nearing completion. We took on a "Savior Mentality." We became Christian Survivalists!

The message that John Todd preached that Randall Rader especially got excited about was Todd's demands that Christians prepare militarily for the coming chaos in America. John Todd said it wasn't enough to have rural housing, food storage, and clothing for the coming days of chaos, but that Christians would need to protect themselves defensively with weapons against the riotous criminals and gangs in society. John Todd said we needed guns!

Randall had long advocated that members of our church needed guns when the collapse of America occurred. Todd reinforced that belief in Rader. And now Jim Ellison caught the revelation. It only seemed logical that if we were going to house, clothe, and feed droves of people from the cities during the Tribulation period, that we also would have to protect them as well, now that Todd spoke about the coming riots planned for America.

It all made sense to us. Now we had a perceived enemy: the government, the Illuminati, the One-Worlders. The ingredients became spicier. The mixture was complete!

So from August 1978 to December 1979, we spent $52,000 on weapons, ammunition, and military equipment, and we began to train militarily. We primarily bought 9mm, .38 and .45 caliber pistols; Ruger-10 .22-caliber rifles; Mini-14 .223-caliber assault rifles; HK-91 .308-caliber rifles; and Remington-870 12-gauge shotguns.

We practiced military maneuvers and learned weaponry. Every man was issued a pistol and rifle, with full military gear. Although Jim was the "General," Randall was in charge of the paramilitary training. Rader had no formal military training, but he owned several military fieldcraft books, studied tactics and was more familiar with weapons than anyone else at the farm.

We built our homes with defense in mind, strategically placing them against an attack from the outside. Many of the houses had bunkers built underneath. Those that didn't usually had a foxhole bunker built nearby. We aggressively began to store ammunition, food and clothing. We wholeheartedly embraced the survivalist mentality.

Another step in our being survivalists was to wear our pistols, openly holstered to our sides, into two local towns on the Missouri side. In a small way, we were proclaiming ourselves as a standard, as "the man of clean conscience." We had discovered that, by law, as long as the pistols were strapped down, whether loaded or unloaded, we could carry them legally almost anywhere in town, including banks. The townspeople watched us nervously, but the authorities said we were within our rights.

Survivalists are those people who not only believe in the imminent collapse of our nation, perpetrated by our own leaders, but also believe in preparing for it and living it. As Christian survivalists, we believed the downfall of civilization was imminent, and that we were required to help people during that time. Economic and social collapse, racial wars in cities, a failed government taken over by communists, pestilence and even nuclear war awaited the country, soon afterward to spread worldwide.

Based upon our interpretation of some isolated scriptures, we estimated ninety percent of the earth's population would die within a very short time period—possibly within the first hour—leaving an elect people to rebuild society and help usher in the millennial rule of Christ. This false premise of an evil apocalypse, I discovered years too late, would be the basis for our misguidance.

With Todd's warnings in mind, we built our homes in three locations on our property. The first, called "the main settlement" (also known as "the compound")—containing the home for Ellison and his family, the trailer houses, the barn, the church building, the workshop/garage, the communications building, the munitions basement, the office and some other houses—was the only settlement that had electricity and running water. It was this central settlement where we would have our meetings and carry on with the business of the group.

The main compound was also the settlement where everyone would retreat if we came under attack. The trees in the main settlement were cut and landscaped so that we could see out a lot easier than someone could see in. Trees surrounded and hid the compound in a one-hundred-yard diameter; all trees past that perimeter, for another two hundred yards, were cut down, so an enemy seeking to do us harm would have no protection or hiding place. Past that area, the remaining trees and debris were significantly thinned.

The other two settlements were "the plateau" and "the valley." Randall oversaw the former, which contained five homes and was located on the Missouri side of the property. I oversaw the latter—located on the Arkansas side—with its five homes. These two settlements were the "preparation" settlements, where many of us would learn to live without electricity or running water, to prepare us for the day when there would be no such luxuries.

In the fall of 1978, we built my house—much like we did most of the houses—out of rough oak lumber. Mine was built on locust tree piers on the side of a hill. It was a 24-foot by 24-foot frame house—which cost the church $1000 to build—with a high-pitched tin roof, so that the center upstairs formed two twelve-foot-by-twelve-foot bedrooms. Downstairs had the master bedroom, living room and kitchen. The entire house had no insulation, no running water, no electricity. I loved it!

In October 1978, just when the winter winds were beginning to blow, a pregnant Kay, I and our two children, moved into our new home that still had no doors or windows. We warmed ourselves with a wood stove, cooked on a wood cook stove, and used kerosene lamps or a Coleman lantern as lighting. We stacked firewood underneath the six-foot tall porch in front of our house, and built "the only on-porch outhouse in America" at one end of that porch. Kay and I got our water from a creek in front of the house, when it flowed, or in plastic jugs filled at the main settlement. The next year we drilled wells in the middle of our settlement and at the Plateau, so we could use a rope and bucket to get water. We kept refrigerated items in an ice chest, with frozen water jugs to keep the food cool. We bathed in a medium-sized, oval galvanized tub located on the small porch in back of the house.

Kay often did laundry by hand, with a scrub board (even though the main settlement had one washer and dryer for everyone to use) and hung the clothes to dry on our clothesline. It was a constant irritation for Ollie that Jim had money for more guns, but not for more washers and dryers, or for toilets and showers for the other houses in the main settlement. As far as I was concerned, let the main settlement have their "luxuries;" I loved the survivalist lifestyle in our home.

The overhangs on each side of the upstairs bedrooms of our house were designed for food storage. At one point I had over 3000 pounds of food stored there. The weight once caused the roof to begin sagging and I had to redistribute some of the food to an underground food bunker.

Much to everyone's chagrin, I flew the Texas flag from a tree near my front porch.

"Why do you fly that flag in front of your house?" Bruce once asked me. "This is Arkansas, not 'Texico.'" Bruce, a native of Arkansas, liked to harass me about my love for Texas.

"I'm proud of my home state," I replied. "That's how Texans are raised, to be proud of Texas. We were the only state to have been an independent nation first. We have the Alamo and the Texas Rangers law-enforcement agency. It's the biggest continental state and the most colorful state historically. Yeah, I'm proud to be a Texan." I figured everyone should be proud of their own state.

"I'll bet you can even tell me when Texas became a state, can't you?" he joked.

"Of course. It was 1836."

"What about the state flower?" Bruce asked. He thought he had me. "What's the state flower?"

"The bluebonnet," I stated, and quickly added, "and the state bird is the mockingbird. The state tree is the pecan and the state song is 'Texas, our Texas.'"

"That's sick!" Bruce exclaimed.

"All right," I asked, "what's the state flower of Arkansas?"

"Who cares?" he shrugged.

"That's the difference," I responded, "between Texans and people from other states. We do care because we're proud of our state. Heritage means a lot to Texans."

Bruce, and most of the other men, never understood why I felt as I did about Texas. I never understood their not understanding.

I was notorious for eating any kind of wild meat. I ate not only rabbit, deer and squirrel, but also coyote, possum, raccoon and even cat. I believed the survivalist message, lived the survivalist lifestyle, and loved the survivalist way of life. It was heaven-on-earth to me. Except for the winters.

I never got used to the winters in Arkansas—too cold; too much snow. I had to get used to wearing thermal underwear ("longjohns") all winter long. It took me a while, also, to learn to work our wood stove properly. A layer of smoke usually settled near the ceiling in our home. Many a morning, we would find the kitchen water in the five-gallon buckets frozen solid. It was so cold in our home during those Arkansas winters that it was not unusual for us to stand beside our heat stove, the sides of it red from the intense heat, and still be able to see our breath in the air.

The hot part of summer was also a test for endurance. With no insulation in our home, small windows that allowed little circulation and a tin roof that captured the heat, the temperature inside our home was unusually high in the summer. We often had to rinse off several times during the night in our galvanized tub on the back porch just to get comfortable.

Our third child, a daughter, was the first to be born in our new home. She was also the first and only child that Kay and I delivered by ourselves. Kay panted and pushed, and I prepared to catch the baby. With my head about a foot from the birth canal, Kay's water broke and sprayed all over my face and head. Kay laughed so hard, the baby had no choice but to come out.

Born in December, we named her Beth Shalom—"House of Peace"—because that's what this house meant to us. We loved that house and the peacefulness of it. This daughter would be symbolic of that peace, we believed, with a name prophetic to her own life and nature—a prophetic word we envisioned that would also symbolize this place we called Zarephath-Horeb.

My parents came to visit us shortly after we moved in our new home. I wasn't sure what they would think of our new lifestyle. But I think my dad really appreciated what Jim Ellison had done for me. My dad saw me working harder than he had ever seen me work, willing to do whatever I needed to do. I had muscles where my Dad (and me) never thought I would have muscles. My forearms had shape, my chest had a "V" to it, my body was bulking. I had a confidence I never experienced while growing up. I hoped, and wanted to believe, that my dad was proud of me there in Arkansas.

My mom saw me dressed in camouflage and wearing guns one day while they were visiting. I figured she would say something about it, since she had reared me to be anti-gun and anti-violence. She didn't. Before they left I asked her why she hadn't.

"I raised you to do what's right and what you believed the Lord wanted you to do. If you're doing that, even if I don't understand it, then who am I to question what you might be doing?" I loved her for that faith in me.

"Besides," she added, smiling only slightly, "what I don't know won't hurt me."

Zarephath-Horeb practiced a patriarchal system, where the men were in charge. Women were not allowed to be elders of the church, though we did have prophetesses and deaconesses, as well as some women in the paramilitary. The basic function of the woman was to keep the home and to bear children. The men happily kept their women pregnant, believing in the scripture that said, "Lo, children are a heritage of the Lord; and the fruit of the womb is his reward. As arrows are in the hand of a mighty man, so are children of the youth. Happy is the man that has his quiver full of them."

Within a few years, many of the women were having so many children so quickly that they were developing serious physical problems to the point of endangering their lives.

In the fall of 1978 we began a practice based upon a scripture which mentioned that Abraham's wife, Sarah, called him "Lord." Therefore, for quite a few months, the women were encouraged, as a sign of respect, to call their husbands "Lord" when speaking to them or when the husband asked the wife to do something. Religious men usually like to quote the scripture that says, "Wives, be in submission to your husbands," but often forget what follows: "Husbands, love your wives as Christ loved the church."

On the only television set in our group, at Ellison's house, we watched the news reports in November 1978 as the pictures showed the mass suicide of over nine hundred men, women, and children at Jim Jones' Jonestown. How could people be so stupid as to follow a man to their deaths?

By the end of 1978, Zarephath-Horeb had about twelve families, comprising about fifty individuals. Many of the children were attending the local school, and many more were nearing school age. Since we believed the message of coming out of Babylon, we decided to teach our children in our own school.

We started our children's education at the age of four, with the basic requirements of the four R's—reading, 'riting, 'rithmetic and religion—and used a Christian-based correspondence curriculum. Jim wasn't too concerned about the children's education, since he believed the country would collapse at any moment and education would be useless. Many of us, however, did desire for our children to be intelligent, especially if they were to be the future leaders of the newly-established kingdom after the coming war and Jesus' return. Three of the women—Ollie, Cheryl (also our main midwife) and Cindy—became our teachers; a few years later, when the children entered their high school years, I also taught.

Although we didn't realize it at the time, all the ingredients necessary to create an extremist were now mixed into our church. First of all, we were built, not upon faith and love like we thought we were, but upon a false premise based in fear and despair, a premise that declared the future to be a bleak one, full of judgments and destruction. Then, we had a charismatic leader to manipulate us and direct us to where he believed God would have us go. Lastly, our physical and mental isolation led us to a "Savior Mentality"—with a perceived enemy and with limited options—brought upon us by extremely limited, unbalanced information. All that was needed to make us cross the line into dangerous extremism were the catalysts of "heat" and "time." With those catalysts, the ingredients would rise into a cake of destruction.

Part Three | The Origin and Rise of CSA

6

Identity

Awake, awake, put on strength,
O arm of the Lord;
awake, as in the ancient days,
in the generations of old.
—Isaiah 51:9

John Todd foretold a major truckers' strike which was to occur in the spring of 1979 and would cripple the economy of the United States sending the country into collapse, with riots and chaos. The strike did occur, but not with the results Todd predicted. But the exactness of his predictions were close enough to warrant listening to him about other "planned" events.

We intensely continued to train militarily. Classes were held on Wednesday nights. We learned about weapons and studied tactics. Sunday became "military day." We practiced maneuvers in every scenario imaginable and camped in the heat, snow or rain. We had wake-up drills in the middle of the night, to see how fast we could assemble in an alert situation. At the shooting range Rader designed, we became proficient and confident in our abilities. With continuing target practice, each man was able to hit various sizes of targets—head shots, heart shots, body shots—at various distances.

The men made a pact one night during a weekly military meeting to serve each other, to serve our military commanders, to serve God's army and that any traitors or deserters during battle would be shot in the back. Each man passed through an archway made by the raised weapons of the other men. "Lord," Randall prayed in closing, "teach our hands to war and our fingers to fight. Teach us to love and teach us to hate. In Jesus' name. Amen."

The hope of Ellison and Rader in performing this pact was to instill loyalty in the men; the result, instead, was fear of the "officers."

Ollie Ellison later recounted to me that Jim somehow changed right before this meeting. After getting his first military-style haircut, he gazed at himself in the mirror for a long time, preparing to inspect the men. She noticed a change in Jim's countenance, a different look in his eyes.

Although I was uncomfortable with the military aspect itself, I actually did enjoy learning to shoot weapons, which surprised me since my mother had reared me to be anti-gun and anti-violence. But the feeling that I could, in some way, protect myself made me feel better about myself.

I had never learned to protect myself. My mother reared me to never fight, even in self-defense. This made me a perfect target for bullies while I was growing up. Moving so many times as a child didn't help either. Though I had been beaten up often, one memory was burned in my mind more than any other. . . .

■ ■ ■

"What did you do that for?" I demanded.

"He was beating you up!"

"I don't care! It's better to get beat up than to have your little sister come along and pounce the guy." I cried from shame. "You don't know what you've done!" I hung my head as I sobbed. I was in the sixth grade, at a new school. Eleven years old and my little sister could fight better than me.

"He kept hitting you," she insisted, "and you did nothing to fight back. Why didn't you fight back instead of just layin' there?" That remark tightened my stomach. I couldn't fight back; I didn't know how.

■ ■ ■

In addition to the weapons and military training, we also began guard duty. Military training was bad enough. I told Jim that I always felt like a fish-out-of-water when I was dressed in military camouflage, like some kind of wanna-be. I hated camping out, marching, drills and maneuvers. But everyone had to be in the paramilitary.

"If you aren't in the military," Jim once told me, "then others might not want to be. Then we don't have cohesion. You'll probably never be in any offensive duty once the war begins, but you know as well as I do that we gotta have a defensive unit to protect our women, children and property once most of the men are away. That's where you'll come in, and others like you that don't quite fit into the military. That's why you gotta really try in the military. You're in charge of Home Guard; be an example."

Home Guard? I laughed to myself. Home Guard? What a joke! I'm in charge of a unit that has a man fifteen years older than me that has an artificial leg; I got an epileptic, retarded man; two half-blind, fat, young men; and two men who could care less about the military than I do. That's a squad that's supposed to protect Zarephath-Horeb? But I quit arguing.

Guard duty—that was the worst. The guard had to stay awake all night, by himself. He was responsible for the safety of the group, in case anyone tried to come in without permission. Although we were secluded in the middle of nowhere—with a reputation by now of having several weapons—we actually imagined someone still might try to walk in at night. We primarily practiced guard duty, however, for later on, for after the government collapsed.

I hated guard duty because it brought all my fears to the surface. Every horror movie I had ever seen as a kid flashed back into my memory. Every sound I heard was a monster coming to devour me or an enemy coming to kill me. I would hide in the dark shadows, afraid I might accidentally shoot one of our horses or someone taking a midnight stroll who didn't say the password quickly enough, wondering what I would do if someone actually did show up unexpectedly. Would I shoot? Would I fight? Or would I run scared, crying like some sixth-grader? I honestly didn't know. All I knew was that I was scared—and I hated being scared.

In the early summer of 1979 we came across a group in Flora, Illinois—the Christian-Patriots Defense League—founded in 1959, and headed by John "Johnny Bob" Harrell and retired U.S. Army Colonel

Jack Mohr. It was here that we learned of the patriotic movement, with its tax protesters, federal government protesters, second amendment activists and states' rights advocates.

Here were men and women who seemed to dearly love this country, who were concerned about its future, who were disconcerted about what the federal government was doing, who saw no hope that the government would change for the better.

According to John Todd, the government had purposely devalued the American dollar and the American economy, in order to bring about a new currency, a world currency. Here at the Christian-Patriots Defense League, the tax protesters preached that the Federal Reserve and the income tax were unconstitutional. The second-amendment activists warned of gun control and government tyranny. Others warned of the coming Antichrist's mark, the 666 that the Bible spoke of.

"Pull out a dollar bill," one of the speakers ordered his listeners. "In the upper left corner it reads, 'This Note is Legal Tender for All Debts, Public and Private.' All currency is now like that. But contrast the current bills with a 1934 bill that stated, 'This Note is Legal Tender for All Debts Public and Private and is Redeemable in Lawful Money at the United States Treasury or at any Federal Reserve Bank.' Thus, paper currency in 1934 clearly stated that it was not lawful money, but a ticket that could be exchanged for such. This is no longer the case. Now the fake money cannot be redeemed for gold and silver; it's only a note, an IOU. Today's money causes inflation and feeds the illegal Federal Reserve System, an unlawful and unconstitutional system that cannot be audited, a private corporation that is above the government itself!"

"Executive Order 11490," another speaker stated, "signed by Richard Nixon, established a dictatorship in this country! A Regionalism government that abolishes Congress, the Constitution, the Supreme Court, and states' rights, under a 'Martial Law National Emergency.' Nixon signed into law Executive Order 11647 on February 12, 1972, dividing the United States into ten Federal Regions, to be run by 'Federal Regional Councils.'

"Furthermore," the speaker added, "in 1971, the Office of Management and Budget formed a planned disbursement of the remaining Americans after the planned internal revolution against the people. No city or town will have less than 50,000 people in population. Wyoming and the Upper Peninsula of Michigan will be barren with no people allowed to live there. Under Presidential Directive 41, anyone thirty years of age or older who does not cooperate with the system will be liquidated or confined in a Federal Enemy Camp. These detention facilities are located in places like Allenwood, Pennsylvania; Greenville, South Carolina; Montgomery, Alabama; El Reno, Oklahoma; Florence, Arizona; Elmendorf, Alaska; Wickenberg, Arizona; and Nevada, Missouri.

"Prepare, people," the speaker concluded, "because they're coming for you!"

Still a third speaker warned everyone about the 666 in the Bible. "The World Bank Number is 666," he said. "A laser tattoo gun is being used for registering fish. It places a tattoo number on them in one thirty-billionth of a second. It's effective and painless. IBM reportedly has developed laser tattoo guns for people and the scanners with which to read the invisible marks. How soon before they want to tattoo you? Before they want to tattoo your children?

"The bar codes on the products you buy," the excited speaker proclaimed, "is a 666 product of the Beast government. This Universal Product Code has the same symbol in the front of the first five numbers, in the middle, and at the end of the last five numbers. This dividing symbol is the UPC symbol for the number six, thus giving us 666 on everything we buy! And these bar codes can be scanned from aircraft, just like they're scanned at the grocery store, so that the government can find out how much food you have stored in your home!"

I listened intently to the speakers. Whole worlds of knowledge, of some major conspiracy, opened before me. Were the men and women in attendance at this meeting perhaps fellow soldiers who would help destroy the evil Antichrist beast in the coming judgment? I wondered. Or were they raving lunatics?

I listened to the speakers, examining the messages, but open to accepting them. Their credibility seemed heightened by two books in particular that were offered: *The International Jew* by Henry Ford, and *Protocols of the Learned Elders of Zion*. Both books described a so-called Jewish plan for world dominion.

We also met a number of people who were involved with the Ku Klux Klan and the neo-Nazis, but we weren't interested in their message, or in their propaganda. Books with titles like *Martin Lucifer Koon* (about King's communist affiliations and womanizing) and *Great Accomplishments of the Negro Race* (which was full of blank pages only) were sold to those attending the meeting. Pamphlets admonished readers to use the term "jew" instead of "Jew," since capital letters were reserved for proper nouns and not common nouns, and "there is nothing proper about a common jew."

Also obnoxious were the "Yahweh" people, those who said that the name "Jesus" was a pagan name and that only "Yahweh" or "Yahveh" was the correct name for God. With a cigarette in one hand and a beer in the other, the foul-mouth, cussing preacher Colonel William Gale—a co-founder of the Posse Comitatus—made me want to vomit. He had heard me speak and use the name "Lord." Self-righteously he approached me and informed me that using the term "Lord" was the same as calling God "Baal." He ordered me to repent. I shook my head in disgust and walked away.

Due to the involvement of these three types of people at the Christian-Patriots Defense League, we didn't attend the meetings the next year, though we did return the following year.

Most of the speakers made for interesting thought, though. So again I bought as many books as possible—books like *Gun Control Means People Control*; *When Your Money Fails*; *Secrets of the Federal Reserve*; and *Fourth Reich of the Rich*—and absorbed their messages, teachings that basically confirmed what John Todd had said. Again I was taken in by the messages. I learned the teachings and began to teach the patriotic message. Ellison, however, did not understand or like my appetite for so many books.

"Why must you always buy so many books?" he asked.

"Because I want to learn," I responded. "To me, knowledge is a key. How can I teach if I don't completely understand the subject?"

"Yes, but you go overboard," Ellison warned. "You absorb yourself in books to the point of not reading your Bible as much."

"Nonsense," I retorted. "I read my Bible as much as I do these books."

That wasn't quite true. Later, I received a prophecy from a woman who didn't know of the conversation between Ellison and me. The prophecy stated, "Yea, I say unto you, that you must put away these things from me. They are flesh, they are idols to you. You must put away the things that are not of my word. You must keep me and me only. Kerry, you must cleanse your mind from all this trash and stuff that you've read, the books you've read. You must put them away from you now. For if you don't put them away from you, then I, the Lord, say unto you this night that you'll lose the path you follow; you'll lose sight of the Lord; you'll lose the way that I have put before you. You need to get back on that path that is set before you."

Then later in a church meeting Ellison prophesied to me, "Yea, for thus says the Lord unto you my son: From the time that you were young and small in your own sight, the desire of your heart has been to know and understand. I will give you understanding. I shall open your understanding, and your knowledge shall increase and your understanding shall come clear. Yea, it shall not be by strife, but shall be by peace, says the Lord your God. By peace and by my spirit you shall have revelation and you shall know the truth. You shall surely discern between truth and error, between tradition and life. I will encourage you this night, seek me early and seek me late. Wait for me by your spirit. Offer your spirit unto me, and by my spirit I shall cleanse the spirit you offer up and renew a right spirit within you."

But I never quit reading the books. I couldn't. Knowledge was everything to me. Knowledge was my power. The only power I had ever possessed.

To make some extra money for the group, while the rest of us cut timber, Jim worked in Missouri building missile silos for the military in late summer 1979. We needed more money for more guns and more housing. Ellison believed the downfall of the government and the country was imminent.

While away, he left Randall in charge. Jim expected to be gone for about three or four months, but planned to come home for one weekend after the first two months. While Ellison was gone, something happened to Randall. Something snapped.

Within a month after Jim first left, Randall began to tell me privately that Ellison had heart trouble and would die soon, leaving Rader in charge permanently. He said that was the real reason Jim was gone, so no one would see him die. Randall said the Lord had shown him that he was to take the group into the promised land, like Joshua did, when Moses wasn't allowed to.

This was news to me! I knew nothing of Jim having any heart trouble. But Randall said to keep the news to myself, so I did. Randall turned into a dictator, wanting to rule by fear and intimidation. Almost overnight, he wasn't the same Randall that I had come to admire and love. Suddenly he was wearing a Nazi-like uniform, often carrying a small whip and even wearing a monocle.

I grew concerned, as did others. Later, I went to speak to one of the prophetesses about it. While I was at her house, Randall showed up.

"What are you doing here?" he demanded. "Why aren't you outside working?"

"Randall," I replied, "please sit down; we gotta talk."

He wouldn't sit down, but, instead, stood directly over me while I was seated. "Randall, people are getting scared of you. They're afraid."

With that, Randall reached down with his right hand and grabbed me around the throat, choking me until I couldn't breathe. I panicked. When he finally let go, he said, "Now that's fear! That's what you need to be afraid of. Now get up and go to work!" He was right, that was fear and I was indeed afraid of Randall Rader.

That night, at our praise meeting, Randall rose, took a long sword that he had made, and violently struck an upright post that stood in the middle of our meeting house. He declared that in the Old Testament times, dissenters would have been killed and rebellion would not have been tolerated. He said he was tired of the rebellion in the group, that it was the same as witchcraft according to the Scriptures. "Obedience," he screamed, "is better than sacrifice!"

Then Randall Rader also decreed, "I'm tired of waiting. If God doesn't start the riots soon and the collapse of our government, then I will!"

Many of us were numb with shock. Those who sided with Rader began to convert the legal semi-automatic weapons into illegal fully-automatic machine guns, as well as manufacturing silencers and hand-grenades. The rest of us were ready for Ellison to hurry home so we could inform him of Rader's actions.

In two weeks Jim returned and we hit him hard and fast with the news. He immediately took the reins back from Rader, scolding him for converting the weapons. Rader explained that when the hordes of rioters come from the cities to the country, once the government had collapsed, we would need machine guns and handgrenades to protect ourselves. Ellison saw the logic of Rader's reasoning, and regardless of the arguments from the rest of us, conceded to keeping the weapons. Now we were an illegal group, and many of us didn't like it.

Rader saw a power struggle between himself and Ellison. He secretly spoke to the elders individually to get them to side with him. Those who were pro-paramilitary sided with Rader; those who were anti-paramilitary sided with Ellison. But Jim had to go back to Missouri for another month, to clear up the work there, before returning home.

When Jim did return, he brought with him something that would again hone the direction of our group. He called the elders together to his house, pulled out a cassette, and played it for us.

Some kind of church service was on the tape, but instead of singing the typical church songs, they sang patriotic songs like *America, the Beautiful* and *My Country 'Tis of Thee*. Then a man got up and preached about who the Anglo-Saxon people were—the "true Israel" as he put it. He went into detail about something called "Identity," of how we had forgotten who we were racially. He spoke of God's election on America, how the Declaration of Independence and the Constitution were inspired documents of God, about the Christian inheritance the founding fathers had left us, and how this nation was founded upon Christian principles. He spoke of high ideals of patriotism, love of country, and of the heraldry and symbolism of the United States. He then quoted Scriptures that he believed prophesied about the United States. And he said the troubles that have come to our nation were the result of our having forsaken the Old Testament laws of God and of allowing God's enemies to rule over us.

The preacher's name was Dan Gayman, pastor of the Church of Israel, in Schell City, Missouri. Jim had met him while working in the area, and Gayman had been teaching Jim about the "new Israel."

Most of the elders rebelled. "You mean our parents were right?" they asked. "God, country, and mom's apple pie? That sort of thing? We came out of the 1960s rebellion against our government, not out of the pro-America 1950s like you, Jim." I, however, loved the patriotic flavor. It reminded me of a time in my youth. . . .

■   ■   ■

"How's it coming?" my mother asked, looking at my eighth-grade science project.

"Good. I finally got the model put together yesterday, and I'm working on the papers today."

"Have you heard from the Air Force yet?"

"No, not yet," I sighed. "I just hope they send me some information and photos about the space program soon. I don't expect them to really bother much with some kid's science project, but I'd sure be happy just to get some pictures of the rockets and Cape Canaveral."

Early the following Saturday, a knock shook the door.

"Kerry Noble?" one of the two officers asked after I opened the door.

"Yes, Sir?"

"I'm Sergeant Brower from Dyess Air Force Base; this is Sergeant Littner. We received your letter about your Cape Canaveral science project and thought we would personally deliver the information you requested and spend a little time with you today, if that's okay."

I was ecstatic. The officers spent the next three hours with me, in which they explained NASA's space program, showed me the photographs they brought me, and pointed out different areas on the launch platform model I had assembled. I couldn't believe that they cared enough about some kid they didn't even know. If this is what our government was about, I thought, I want to be in the government!

I later watched the two officers drive away. They really cared, I thought. The government really cares about its citizens. I couldn't get over it. The government really cared about me.

▪   ▪   ▪

"The Declaration of Independence," Jim began to preach, "says that whenever any form of government becomes destructive of our rights to life, liberty and the pursuit of happiness, that it is the right of the people to alter or to abolish it and to institute new government that to them shall seem most likely to effect their safety and happiness. It goes on to say that all experience has shown that mankind are more disposed to suffer, while evils are sufferable, than to right themselves by abolishing the forms to which they are accustomed. I'm here to tell you, brethren, that Americans have gotten accustomed to several evils. And we have suffered them long enough! But, after a while," Jim continued, "after those abuses of government reduce the people under absolute despotism, it is the right of the people, nay it is their duty, to throw off such government!

"Men of Israel, we have a clear mission before us. It is the destiny of the patriotic people of today, like our forefathers of two centuries ago, to throw off our government and to provide for the future of our children. We have tried two hundred years of voting and petitioning, only to find that our government officials have sold us down the river, betrayed us, enslaved us. A multitude of new offices have been erected and sent to harass our people, and to eat out their substance. OSHA, the IRS, the FBI, the Bureau of Alcohol, Tobacco, and Firearms, the EPA, and others are destroying the rights of the people. This Antichrist government has imposed new taxes on us without our consent. It has deprived us, in many cases, of the benefits of trial by jury. It has taken away our charters, abolished our most valuable laws and has fundamentally altered the forms of our government. This nation of ours is supposed to be a republic, not a democracy!"

Holding up a copy of the Declaration of Independence and the Constitution of the United States in one hand, and his Bible in the other, Ellison continued paraphrasing. "This government—not my government, not your government—this Jewish-controlled government, is transporting large armies of foreign mercenaries to complete the works of death, desolation, and tyranny. It has incited domestic insurrections amongst us, and has endeavored to bring on the inhabitants of a white America, the merciless nigger savages, trained to kill in the government-created ghettos and in prison! The Jews have declared war on our race, promoting race-mixing and thereby polluting the pure seed of God. This government is killing our white babies through abortion! It is destroying white minds with its humanistic teachings of evolution! I tell you this—niggers may be descended from apes, but my ancestors never swung on trees by their tails! In order to preserve our Christian heritage and race, it is our right, our patriotic duty, to overthrow this Antichrist government. Standing by and doing nothing against the tyranny of this government is open rebellion to God! Prepare war, O Israel! Wake up the mighty men! Let all the men of war come near. Beat your plowshares into swords and your pruning-hooks into spears. Let the weak say, 'I am strong!'"

And the men, clothed in camouflage, armed with rifle and pistol, rose and saluted an almost Nazi-like salute, while shouting, "I am strong!"

"Saviors," Ellison loudly concluded, "shall come up on Mount Zion to judge the mount of Esau; and the Kingdom shall be the Lord's. Just as Jesus scourged the Jewish moneychangers out of the temple of God, so shall we destroy the Jewish international bankers! The inhabitants of the world will learn righteousness!"

The patriotic message energized me and the others. It stirred within me the roots of my childhood, the hopes for the future, and the love for our country and government. Again, I felt challenged in my thinking. Gayman reinforced what John Todd had said, but took it a step further. Everything was always a step further. Unfortunately, without realizing it at the time, it was always a step in the wrong direction. The enemy's face now began to take shape.

I loved what Dan Gayman had taught us. Except for one part, about the other races and that the Jews were not God's true Israel. I didn't understand that. Although, as a child, my teachers in church never had an answer when I asked them why there were various races of people if we all came from Adam, I had always been taught that the Jews were God's chosen people. And as a young preacher in Dallas, I often ministered to blacks and had several black friends. Now I was confused about what their place in God might be.

Gayman wrote a book—*The Two Seeds of Genesis 3:15*—and as usual, I bought that book and every book I could find on the subject of the Jews not being God's people. This was a difficult concept to grasp, but a few months later, I did grasp it, and I taught it to the others.

A second step had been taken. Now we were no longer just Christian Survivalists, we were white supremacists!

The Identity teaching is that the Jews are not God's chosen people, but that the Anglo-Saxon race (meaning the white race) is the true Israel. This extremist philosophy teaches that the Jews are the literal children of Satan. Blacks, Orientals and Polynesians—according to Identity—are not descended from Adam and Eve, but are separate, pre-Adamic, inferior creations.

A neo-Hebrew doctrine, Identity teaches the observance of the Mosaic dietary and holy-day laws, as well as America's destiny in Biblical prophecy and the heritage belonging to it. True Israel, according to the teaching, scattered through the Caucasus Mountains after the Assyrian captivity (hence the word "Caucasians") and settled Europe, each tribe of Israel forming a separate European nation.

Identity had its roots in a doctrine called "British-Israelism," which began in the 1790s by Richard Brothers. It gained prominence in the United States with Howard Rand, founder of the Anglo-Saxon Federation, in the late 1920s. Later carriers of the torch included Gerald L. K. Smith, Conrad Gaard, Bertrand Comparet, William Potter Gale and Wesley Swift in the 1940s and 1950s. It was during this period that British-Israelism—which taught the Jews as the House of Judah and the Anglo-Saxon nations as the House of Israel (or Ten

Lost Tribes)—evolved into Identity. In the 1960s and 1970s, the message was preached primarily by Dan Gayman, Richard Butler, James Warner and Raymond Capt. It would be thirteen years before I could fully discern Identity's seductiveness and see it for the evil it is.

It is interesting to note that before we were introduced to the Identity teaching, Ellison was proud of the fact that he had American Indian blood in him. His grandmother, he often told us, was Cherokee. Yet, after we accepted the Identity teaching, Ellison never mentioned his Indian ancestry again.

As white supremacists, we now believed that other races and those who would betray the white cause in America were destined to be destroyed in the future chaos. We were now not only the elect spiritually, but racially as well. As the propaganda teacher, I learned the divisive Identity message only too well.

"Adam," I taught my students, "was the first white man, created in the image of God. The Hebrew Concordance shows that Adam means, 'ruddy, able to show blood in the face, to flush or blush.' Now, I ask you, which race is the only race that can blush and show blood in the face? Can the black man?"

"No!" someone would respond.

"Can the yellow man?"

"No!"

"The brown man?"

"No," the answer came, "only the white man can blush!"

"That's right! Only the white man can. Therefore, Adam had to be white. And since Eve came from Adam, Eve had to be a white woman. This is further shown in the twins Jacob and Esau, sons of Isaac. Esau was red and hairy. Only one race is born with red hair—the white race. Then later on, the Philistine Goliath sees that David is ruddy and of a fair countenance. Ruddy means 'to be red or reddish,' and a 'fair countenance' means to be 'light-complected.' Only a member of the white race can have a reddish, light complexion by nature!

"This means that the race that has kept itself pure, from Adam to Jacob to David, and on to Jesus—that race that is called by God—is the white, Anglo-Saxon race. That is what the Scriptures teach! That's why the book of Genesis says that the Bible is only for the white race, the sons of Adam, because only the white race is created in the image of God.

"But what about the black, yellow and brown races? Who are they? Where are they to be found in Scripture? The Bible, as all of you know by now, is a coded book, a book, we are now discovering, whose secrets are open only to the white race, the true Israel of God. Therefore, the Scriptures use symbols when speaking about the other races, about those races that were created before Adam. These races can know God as their Creator, but they cannot know Him as their father, because only Adam is called the Son of God in the Bible—except, of course, for Christ Jesus Himself.

"In the creation story, the pre-Adamic races are called by symbolic names. The blacks are the 'beasts of the field.' The yellow races are the 'fowls of heaven.' And the brown races are the 'creeping things of the earth.' An example of this can be seen in Jonah, chapter three, verses seven and eight. Here we find the king has issued a proclamation: 'Let neither man nor beast, herd nor flock, taste any thing; let them not feed, nor drink water. But let man and beast be covered with sack-cloth, and cry mightily unto God: yea, let them turn every one from his evil way, and from the violence that is in their hands.'

"We know that the beasts here are not animals, because animals cannot fast, cannot pray unto God and cannot repent of the evil they have done. Animals also don't have hands, as mentioned here! Obviously, the beasts must refer to someone else other than man. 'Man,' of course, is the same word as 'Adam.' Therefore, the beasts are those who lived in the land at that time who were not Adamic, or white. Those people, historically, were black!

"We also read in Ezekiel twenty-nine, verse eleven: 'No foot of man shall pass through it (Egypt), nor foot of beast shall pass through it, neither shall it be inhabited forty years.' Do animals have feet? No, but those who resemble white man do. Again, the blacks.

"The Bible says in Genesis and in the book of Acts that God separated the races. We are not to mix geographically; we are not to mix socially; and we are never to mix sexually! Kind is to produce after kind. A white man and a white woman could live to be a thousand years old, and though they have a child a year, they would never give birth to a black child, or a brown child, or a yellow child! It is genetically impossible. God has decreed the separation of the races! This is why the Holy Spirit would not allow the Apostle Paul to go into Asia and preach; instead he ministered in Rome and then Europe—all white nations!

"And what about the Jews? Aren't they God's chosen people?" I asked the congregation. "Did you know that there is no scripture that specifically says that the Jews are God's chosen people? Not one. It's a lie perpetrated by the counterfeit race. The Jews aren't even mentioned in the Bible until the book of Kings! Moses wasn't Jewish; Abraham, Isaac and Jacob weren't Jewish; Sarah and Rebekah weren't Jews. And Jesus was not a Jew! 'Jew' is simply a derivative of 'Judah,' one of Jacob's sons, a derivative arrived at after the Babylonian captivity, when the Judahites mixed with the Babylonians. Judaism, therefore, is really a Babylonian religion. Judeo-Christianity is an oxymoron, a contradiction of terms.

"When Jesus was speaking to the Jews, He told them they were of their father, the devil. He told them their father was a murderer from the beginning and a liar. Jesus is telling us that the Jews are liars, just as their father, the devil, is a liar! They are murderers, just as their father, the devil, is a murderer!

"How did the devil become their father? The seducer, the devil, whose name was Nachash, seduced Eve. That's right. Seduced her sexually! Eve had sex with Satan. This is confirmed when God curses Nachash and says that He will put enmity between his seed and the seed of the woman!

"You see, after Eve had sex with Nachash, the devil, she then had sex with Adam, and conceived with both seeds! Thus, Cain and Abel, the offspring of Satan and Adam, were born at the same time! Same mother, but different fathers! Cain, whom John says 'is of that wicked one,' hated Abel and killed him, just as evil always seeks to destroy good, just as the Jews historically have always tried to destroy the godly white Christian race! And who was Nachash? From the Hebrew word Nachash comes the Arabic word Chanas, 'to seduce.'

"From this is derived the Arabic words Akhnas, Khanasa and Khanoos, all of which mean 'ape.' Further derived is the Arabic word Khanas, 'devil.' Jesus, in the books of John and Revelation, tell us that the serpent was the devil himself. But further study reveals that Nachash, the devil-serpent, was also a black man, the father of the ape-race!

"Further proof is seen when we see that Cain, the devil's offspring through Eve, is from the Hebrew word Cayin, which is derived from the root word Koon, 'to chant.' Thus, Cain, a half-breed, reveals the origin of our modern-day 'Cajuns' and 'coons.'"

The people at our church became excited by this revelation. As with others in the right-wing movement, we blamed the Jews for the problems of the world, for the pornography, the lack of morality, for the economic situation in America, for minority rights over white rights, and for kicking God out of the schools. Even though most of us had never personally known a Jew, we became convinced they were the enemies of God, the tares that were choking out the wheat in God's field. Tares, we believed, that would one day need to taken and destroyed.

Identity. It's seductive; it's twisting of the Scriptures; it's a poison. It's extremely difficult to purge from your system once you've partaken of it.

Even though I accepted Identity in time, I still had unanswered questions concerning its teaching. If Eve's sin was sexually partaking of the fruit of the Tree of the Knowledge of Good and Evil (a man-like creature, the devil) then wouldn't that logically mean that Adam's sin would be likewise? That he had to commit a homosexual act with the devil? That interpretation was unacceptable to me. And if "Adam" by definition meant the white race, then why wasn't it accepted in Identity that Simeon—a teacher and prophet in the Christian church, mentioned in Acts, chapter thirteen, verse one—was a black man, since "Niger" means "black?" And what about the traditionally-known examples of other blacks in the Bible: Moses' wife, Zipporah, described as a Cushite woman; the Queen of Sheba; and Noah's son,

Ham? Were they not black? And if the "beasts of the field" could repent, then why were we supposed to destroy them in the coming judgments?

These and other questions haunted me, yet I could find no one who could satisfactorily answer my questions. But instead of continuing to question, I simply accepted Identity because "it seemed as if that's where the Lord was leading us to."

The race question was the most difficult for me to answer in later years. It was also the last hurdle in my turning around completely. I finally realized that the name "Adam" which we were taught to mean "able to show blood in the face" was a metaphor. Adam was separated from the other creatures in that he could blush or be flushed, that is, he could be embarrassed. Adam (all humankind, not just the white race) had a conscience.

With the infiltration of the hate-filled Identity teaching—and our zeal at its peak—and with all the machine guns, silencers, and handgrenades built by Rader and the others, we were only a step away in our transition from a defensive to an offensive stance, and only a year away from getting the FBI and BATF's full attention.

Ellison continued to deal with Randall in the meetings about Rader's rebellion. Randall would go through the motions, but he only got worse. In Randall's eyes he was "trying" to do right—"if God wanted to change him, He could." Randall had become, in a sense, like Tom—unwilling to rest in the grace of God and unwilling to open himself to the group's forgiveness. Thus, the chasm between Ellison and Rader—between the spiritual faction and the military faction—continued to widen.

We sincerely believed that we were Christians first, and Survivalists or Identity second. But we always took what we believed to extreme.

In the spring of 1980, after fully accepting the Identity message, and after selling all of the hogs we owned (which were considered unclean under the law of Moses), we celebrated our first Passover. But we wanted Passover to be more than just "the Lord's Supper." We wanted to experience Passover, experience it the way Moses and the children of Israel had done. Gathered together in Jim Ellison's yard, one of the men held a male lamb while Randall cut its throat, and we all watched the yearling lamb die. The lamb stood quietly still until he bled to death, never uttering a sound. The teaching of Jesus being the Lamb of God was never more real to us. We sprinkled the lamb's blood on the door posts of Jim's house, cooked the Passover meal (complete with unleavened bread and bitter herbs), and we all stayed in Jim's house that night.

The men dressed in their military uniforms, armed with weaponry, ready for battle. All of us prayed that the angel of death would come and would kill the firstborn of all the "Egyptians" that still lived in America. We were disappointed when we awoke the next morning not to find a plague having struck the nation.

We celebrated the three Israelite feast days of Passover, Weeks, and Tabernacles in a way that no other Identity group would do. We believed that of the three Biblical feast days that we celebrated, Passover, especially, was a tremendous time of God dealing with all of us. We looked forward to the feast days, to see what God would do next in our lives.

The Identity teaching also introduced us to the health field, including herbs and natural foods. We quit using pesticides in the garden, started buying natural foods without preservatives, drank herbal teas, and learned about reflexology, acupressure, iridology, and chiropractic holistic healing.

The Identity teaching also made our heritage real to us. I began to study about Ireland and England, since my family is Irish-English. Soon I discovered the meaning to the name God had given our first child: Tara Tralee. 'Tara' was the ancient capital of Ireland and 'Tralee' is the county seat of County Kerry. Thus, I perceived, my older daughter's name was a personal prophecy to me that our racial heritage was important. "First that which is natural," the Scriptures teach, "then that which is spiritual." Thus, for me, our firstborn seemed to confirm this new revelation called Identity.

In April of 1980, Ellison's sister came to ask him a favor. She and her husband needed a lot of money and asked Jim if he could arrange for their trailer house to burn down so they could collect on the insurance money. He agreed to arrange it. On the night on the eighteenth, after his sister had removed what she wanted saved, Jim Ellison and Randall Rader crossed state lines and set fire to the trailer house. His sister did indeed collect the insurance money: eleven thousand dollars. Our first outside crime had now been committed. First, food stamp fraud. Then, illegal weapons. Now, arson and insurance fraud. But it was all justified because we were "making war against the Beast." By the summer of 1980, although I hadn't realized it yet, we had become a destructive cult. The group believed itself to be above the law—even the law of God.

By now, Ellison would often preach, "Follow me as I follow Christ." He believed that he could no longer sin. God had a purpose for Ellison, he stated, and would see to it that nothing prevented that purpose, not even sin. Sinless, therefore perfect.

It is not uncommon for the leadership of groups to enter into the "Christ-Mentality" where the leader believes himself to be perfect or sinless. Once "anointed" or "chosen," it only becomes a matter of time before the anointing becomes so "strong," that the leader separates himself completely from the rest of the group. The leader must keep the spiritual gap between him and the people as large as possible, or he will lose control of the group.

Cults are totalitarian. Members have to ask permission to do anything and are dependent upon the group for everything: food, clothing, shelter, transportation, and health care. Medical care is often negligible. Education is inferior. The world is generally taught to be a hostile, evil place.

At our place, members had to ask permission to do almost anything. We controlled basically what people ate and wore, their daily routines, how their homes would be built, and when they could go to town. Ellison couldn't care less about the children's education, while I stressed the need for it. Doctors were tolerated only in an emergency, so many had to deal with illnesses on their own, although one of our members was a former military medic.

It's actually a minor miracle that we didn't have community eating facilities, believing instead that the family ought to eat together in its own home. Yet, to further enslave the members of our group, we lowered ourselves to the point of often bringing home thrown-away McDonald's hamburgers or donuts from the trash bins in town for everyone to eat. This was also how the men sustained themselves while on trips away from the farm.

All individualism is discouraged in a cult. Cult members are taught to suppress any negative feelings they have about the group. A cult member is taught that loyalty and devotion are the most highly respected emotions. Never doubt; never criticize. Character tests are given to see if the member will lie, steal or cheat for the group.

Another component of cults is the control of information. Their truth is the only truth. Block out any information not essential to the group. Disbelieve any criticism. Since the doctrine is perfect and the leader is perfect, any problem is assumed to be the fault of the individual member. Guilt is the emotional control. Ellison and I controlled the information coming into our group. We did ninety-five percent of the preaching and teaching. In my pride I could not understand why anyone would not want to be taught by us.

A person's mind is controlled once his identity, beliefs, behavior, thinking and emotions are replaced with a new identity. This new identity is the one which the original would strongly object to, if it knew in advance what was in store. For the core members of the group, if Zarephath had been in 1977 like it was by 1980, none of us would have moved there. This became evident for me when a childhood friend of mine finally moved his family to our farm in late 1979. I had been trying for over a year to get them to live with us. They lasted less than two days, quickly deciding to leave after attending the military meeting where the men practiced throwing dummy handgrenades. My friend almost left without saying good-bye. I never heard from him again. A friendship of fifteen years was over within two days.

A common technique of cults is the "hot seat" or "chair." Here the individual sits before the group and confesses his shortcomings, problems, and failures to the group and asks for help. These discussions are often very intimate. The group, therefore, becomes the mediator between God and man. I never realized this mediation factor in the beginning, when we had utilized the chair in the praise meetings. Only years later did I understand the idolatry and mind-control that the chair really represented.

Entwined with control and deception were the teachings of the "virtues" of death-to-self, self-sacrifice, submission to authority, putting Body-life above individual desires, and so-called faith. The true purpose of these teachings is not freedom of spirit, but guilt and bondage to the flesh.

Cult thinking is black versus white, good versus evil, us versus them. Under this mindset, Ellison was always more concerned with immediate results than with the future, disregarding all legal and accounting advice. The leader and, therefore, the group become "chosen" and "anointed" to fulfill God's purpose. To leave the group is to leave God. And leaving the group was almost financially impossible for the one wanting to leave. Leaving our group was almost unthinkable, for who knew how God would punish the one who left? And when anyone would leave, the "love" formerly directed to him or her would turn into anger, hatred and ridicule.

The first step toward our deceiving ourselves actually began with the traditional church backgrounds Ellison and I came from. Two major points are made in most churches, regardless of the denomination or the subject matter. One: society and people are corrupt and evil, with sin rampant and out of control, and both are going to hell. Two: if you don't want to go to hell with the rest of the world, then (although you do not deserve it) get saved by whichever method that denomination dictates.

From childhood we were taught that sin was getting worse and worse, setting the stage for the Antichrist who would destroy Christians until the Rapture occurs, after which time God would fiercely judge the world. So our basic spiritual outlook was negative, perceiving the future as a bleak, evil, foreboding time in which all hell would break loose, with God barely winning over the Devil.

The second force that had an effect upon us was the perceived change in society while we were growing up. The "American Dream" 1950s confused its citizens with the "Red Scare" of Communism, air raid sirens and bomb shelters, while we tried to identify with *Father Knows Best* on television. This gave way to the upheavals of the 1960s, with its assassinations, drug culture and Vietnam War. Then finally came the despondent and difficult 1970s, with inflation and American apathy.

America itself in twenty short years had drastically changed. We wanted to know why. All over the world, people were "coming out" of society and joining various groups—hippie communes to religious communities. Safety and sanity, it seemed, were only to be found if one was separated from society.

And that is where the third and most important step towards our self-deception occurred: Isolation!

We were not content to be merely separated from society; we put ourselves in a position to be totally isolated and insulated from it. We rarely kept up with the news of the world. The only input we were eventually receiving was from publications by various neo-Nazi and KKK groups, other Christian survivalists groups, or individuals like John Todd—constantly feeding us fear, hate, and paranoia. "Garbage in, garbage out."

As a society and as individuals, we typically fear what we do not understand. That's all right as long as we face that fear and get understanding. But when we don't face it, fear becomes paranoia and we become obsessed.

We at Zarephath-Horeb became obsessed with setting dates for the destruction of America—first it was in August of 1978; then in the spring of 1979; then again the summer of 1979. Our apocalyptic timetables got so ridiculous that when nothing would occur one season, Ellison said it could not possibly last another season, and so we would prepare for the economic and social collapse of society for the next season. Meanwhile, the mental and emotional pressure began to wear many of us down.

Hate is the result of an individual's or of society's refusal to accept responsibility for its own actions and to face its fears. The right-wing extremists (and many others in society and in history) are famous for this. Rather than admit that we failed to act responsibly and were indeed able to change our conditions positively, we chose instead to blame others for our conditions.

The Jews, we said, controlled the money and the politicians; the Blacks were destroying the cities with their ghettos and welfare status; the Asians were taking away American jobs. So we covered ourselves in the cloak of constitutional rights—the income tax was unconstitutional, so we would not pay taxes (which was just an excuse for greed); guns were constitutional, so we didn't need to legally register our machine guns (an excuse for rebellion or violence); and why should the Blacks get all the benefits, so we stayed on food stamps and welfare (an excuse so we could keep our own people from being productive and financially responsible).

No one, however, really sets out wanting to hate. The problem is, most people don't want to examine their fears or belief system in a positive, enlightened, introspective manner. Hate, anger and paranoia are simply easier.

Oh, we stood in our righteous robes all right, but that was the result of the final factor—pride. We had to be right: we were God's holy instruments. "Identity" as a belief system was founded on fear, hate and pride. Now we were not just some Gentiles who came into the covenants by grace, we were Israel by race and had a right to the covenants!

And God have mercy on whoever stood in our way to that right.

By 1980, we had grown to about sixty members, including children. Kay gave birth to our fourth child that summer, on July 2. We named her "Jirijah Jubilee," which means, "to bring forth joy and the fear of the Lord." That was how I was feeling at the time. We needed joy in our group again—still suffering from the tribulation-rule of "Heir Rader"—and we needed to be reacquainted with the reverence and awe of God.

George Hawtin mailed his final publication of *The Page* in December 1980, declaring that God had shown him that he had finished the task God had given him; that the messages he proclaimed had been sent out as God saw fit; and that the end of his ministry had arrived. He saw no sense in trying to continue something that God was saying was over. He had been faithful and it was time to quit.

I had so much respect for Hawtin that I asked Ellison if it were possible that Hawtin's "retirement" might be a sign from God that it was time for all groups built upon the same revelations as Hawtin's to also retire. He said it wasn't, that it was just time for the older ministries to step down, to give way to the new ministries, the armies of God. I accepted that to some degree, but Hawtin's attitude, of being willing to end his ministry because God said so, remained with me.

The timber-cutting business had slowed down, and we began to do construction work to earn money for the community. More guns—this time Uzis, MAC-10s and MAC-11s—had been purchased and converted. Our paramilitary unit had grown into squads by now. We built a large obstacle course like one in a Marine bootcamp. And we built "Silhouette City," a four-block mock town in which to practice urban warfare.

As if all that were not enough, December 1980 brought another shift into the group.

7

The Birth of CSA

Prepare War!
Wake up the Mighty Men!
Beat your plowshares into swords
and your pruninghooks into spears.
—Joel 3:9, 10

I stood in the midst of the meeting, once the music had ended and prophesied that God was going to set us as a beacon in the night, that as He had spread our name across the local area, so would He spread our name across the country, to draw others to Himself and to His purpose in this hour. Within three weeks of the prophecy, during our January 1981 visit to John Harrell's Christian Patriots' Defense League in Illinois, Jim Ellison was briefly interviewed on *ABC World News Tonight*. The occasion? We were among the hate-mongers, and we had made our presence known.

Jim Ellison stood behind the pulpit at John Harrell's. He was dressed in American camouflage with a military-style haircut. Clearly angry, he began to preach to the group of dissidents.

"I'm here today," Ellison began, "to bring you a word from God, a word to Israel. In the Bible there are rules of warfare—how to pick good soldiers, how to invade a city. We've been preparing for war for a long time. John told you a little about our place in Arkansas. We only want committed Israelites there, committed soldiers. Don't come if you're not committed. Don't come. This is a nation guilty before God. America calls good, evil and evil, good. America has been lied to and deceived by its schools and its preachers. But God will have a remnant to rule with Him, a people for Him. I'm here today to get you stirred up. Get ready! For judgment is coming to America! For if

God does not judge America for her sins, then He owes Sodom and Gomorrah an apology. Do you hear me?"

Amens echoed from the audience.

"We live rough in Arkansas. Because we have to! Because we're serious with God! And guess what? You're going to have to get serious with God, if you're not already. You'll have to learn to live like we do. I've committed my family, my fortune and my life to Him. He owns them anyway! Yes, I know my family is in danger from the government. But if I have to sacrifice my children for what God's doing, then I'll have to do it! I tried before not to do what God required of me and it cost me. On April 29, 1970, at 9:45 a.m., God caused a building to collapse around me while I was working on it. I broke twenty-eight bones and my lung was punctured. But in fifteen days I was out of the hospital and back to work in two months. I learned to say what God has told me to say! People won't leave the cities until the blood is ankle deep. But I'm telling you now that it's later than you think! War is coming!"

Jim stood tall before the clapping audience as John Harrell nervously thanked Ellison for his message.

Upon returning to Arkansas, the elders of the church were convened by Ellison. "Our name is spreading," he began, "even as the prophecy said it would. Do we want that name to be Zarephath-Horeb?"

It was determined that our church name was too complicated for the public and too special to us. We needed a public name, a name that would symbolize our paramilitary function. That name, Ellison decided, would be CSA—the Covenant, Sword and Arm of the Lord.

"The Covenant," he explained, "speaks of all the covenants of God from Adam to Christ and especially of the covenants He has made with us in this last hour. It also speaks of the covenant that He has made with each of you individually and that you have made with Him and with each other and with this Body.

"The Sword speaks of all the judgments of God from the time of the Garden, but especially of the coming judgment upon America. The Arm is those people whom God will use to administer the final end-time judgment. And we are part of that people.

"Our symbol shall be a military patch that shows a flaming sword with a rainbow above it. The flaming sword speaks to us of Eden and the way back to paradise, through purging and tribulation. The rainbow speaks of Noah's day and the peacefulness that comes after God's judgment of the world. The colors remind us of the tabernacle coverings which are the anointing that we, the tabernacle of God, have upon us."

The name and the symbol were readily accepted by the elders.

Zarephath-Horeb Community Church, a small, peaceful community-minded group of Christians, whose vision was to know Christ better, now gave birth to CSA, a soon-to-be-aggressive, outspoken, hate-filled group of zealots, whose vision was the collapse of "Babylon" and, therefore, our absolute rule over the Ozarks. Step three was about to be completed. Soon we would be right-wing extremists!

In March of 1981, Randall Rader's thirteen-month-old daughter, Julie, stepped out of the house one day without her mother's knowledge and fell face-down into an unfinished basement being built for a small house. It had been raining, and the little girl's coat soaked up the water, weighing her down. By the time anyone found her, she was dead. The men and women performed CPR on her for two hours, trying to revive her, but to no avail.

Hers was the first death on our property. As a body of believers, we never got over that death, for we had always believed that none of our people would ever die on our property which was supposed to be sacred and protected by God. That baby's death, though no one dared voice it, meant we were not as protected as we once believed. And if a baby could die, then what of the other members?

According to state law, if we buried Randall's daughter within twenty-four hours after dying and after being examined by the coroner, she would not have to be embalmed. So the carpenters built her a small casket and we buried her the next day.

Randall blamed Jim for his daughter's death. He never got over Julie's death.

In the spring of 1981, Kay also suffered a miscarriage. I suppressed the feeling that, like the births of my three previous children, this was a symbol of how I saw God moving in our church. Was our "body" sick, needing to reject something that might be harmful to it? Had the spirit of death now invaded our paradise? I wouldn't allow myself to dwell upon it, but the miscarriage and Julie's death bothered me for a long time.

In 1981 we began to publish our own *CSA Journal,* a monthly newsletter, in booklet form, circulated to a 2000-name mailing list. I was in charge of the writing and production of the Journal, which included articles on Survivalism, Identity and Bible teachings, military fieldcraft and right-wing rhetoric. I wrote in one CSA Journal that the coming war was a step toward God's government.

I began to write booklets for the group, as propaganda to send to other groups or to sell to individuals in order to obtain money for our group. From 1981-1983, I wrote: *Witchcraft and the Illuminati* (an 88-page booklet about witchcraft in the international plan for world dominion, the organizations and individuals involved, and the demonic jewelry created by the Illuminati); *Prepare War!* (a 32-page booklet showing the Scriptural basis for Christian militantism and our justification for violence); *Betrayal: 100 Facts* (a 60-page booklet revealing how the United States government had betrayed its own citizens in order to bring about a one-world government); *The Jews: 100 Facts* (a 44-page booklet "proving" our justification for hate and why the Jews were the enemy of white, Christian people); *CSA Survival Manual* (this 174-page book, co-written with others from CSA, became the training manual for the right-wing, giving instructions in firearms, weapons, knives and gear; personal home defense; how to store food; natural survival; and first-aid and nuclear survival); *Freedom: The Strength of America* (a 44-page treatise on the Godly heritage of the Declaration of Independence and the Constitution, and our justification for overthrowing the government); and *The Most Dangerous and Violent Group in America: A Study of the Anti-Defamation League of B'Nai B'Rith* (in our viewpoint at that time, the number one enemy in America).

From January 1981 to October 1982 we were the focus of various media. I was selected to be the group's spokesman. Among others, we were covered by the *LA Times; PM Magazine;* the British Broadcasting Corporation; WCCO television in Minneapolis; *Eagle Magazine;* the *Arkansas Democrat;* the *Huntsville Times;* the *Tennessean;* the *Kansas City Times; Springfield News-Leader;* the *Arizona Republic;* the *Dallas Morning News;* and television stations from Springfield, Missouri; St. Louis, Missouri; Detroit, Michigan; and Illinois.

So good was I at debating the Jewish or Black "enemy," that, according to one television reporter, the word had spread for no one to debate me on live television. On one live talk show, I had embarrassed the black Urban League leader, who had confused us with another group, so that he shut up quickly; I made the liberal preacher admit he did not believe the Bible to be the inspired Word of God; and I tricked the Jewish Rabbi into admitting on live television that he would not kiss the flag of the United States of America. I, on the other hand, arrogantly kissed the flag and confessed faith in the Scriptures.

In the WCCO television report, Jim Ellison could be seen raising his rifle and declaring that the rod of iron that Jesus spoke about in the book of Revelation was a gun. I was seen saying, in that same report, "I'm not looking forward at this particular point to have to kill somebody. I've never had to kill anybody before. I can do it, but it's not something I look forward to. I look more forward to the righteousness that comes afterwards. Yet, I know because of certain people on this earth, that they're the ones who are causing the filth and the degradation on this earth, that it would be better if they were not here."

By this time, I was accepting what we believed even though I was internally questioning some aspects of Identity.

Our name had indeed spread—from Mountain Home, Arkansas all the way to Europe. The newspaper headlines in those days included "God's Guns . . . and Gentle People," "Holocaust Homecoming: Dead Serious About Survival," "With Prayer and Firepower," "Fundamentalist Firepower Alarms Ozarks," "The Doomsday Watch: Survivalists Prepare for the Apocalypse," "Christian Soldiers March as to War—in the Ozarks," and "Survivalists Worry Police."

I must admit, however, that with all the right-wing talk of the "biased, leftist liberal press," at least eighty percent of the media coverage on us in 1981-82 was accurate and fair, even positive and favorable to a degree. They wrote often that although our doctrine was extreme, we were considered hard workers by the neighbors, that we didn't cause problems, that we cared for our children, and that our praise music was enjoyable.

Why was the coverage not slanted more in opposition to us? I think a number of reporters actually liked and respected us, and even envied us to some degree. We were a hard-working and friendly people who did what few did—we got along well together. We had our own private school, with the children unaffected by drugs, violence, abusive parents, child molesters, or kidnappers. We had a high standard of righteousness that was adhered to. Anyone could speak in the church meetings, not just Ellison or myself. We treated visitors like family, with most reporters eating meals at my home.

Outwardly CSA looked like the ideal Christian example of love and hospitality, in spite of our "hate" doctrines. Obviously, though, we were not totally honest with the media.

Illegal fully automatic machine guns, silencers and handgrenades were not all that we possessed. While teaching at a survivalist seminar in Detroit during the summer of 1981, we also obtained a thirty-gallon barrel of cyanide from Robert Miles, a Klan leader of "the Mountain Kirk" in Michigan. The purpose for the cyanide was so that in the future, when the judgment time had arrived, we could dump the cyanide into the water supply systems of major cities, condemning hundreds of thousands of people to death for their sins. Until that time occurred, however, the cyanide served only one purpose—one of our munitions men placed some of the cyanide in sealed tips of hollow-point bullets, so that even a graze shot would kill a man. The rest of the cyanide was safely stored away from the children.

Randall Rader, meanwhile, also prepared plans for blowing up area dams and for taking control of our three-county area. He also toyed with the idea of running for County Constable—the only person who had the power to arrest the Sheriff.

The other right-wing extremists were taking notice of us. We attended gun shows across the country and sold goods for money for the group, while prostelyzing for membership. Many good contacts were made at gun shows, the most common place for dissenters to meet.

Silhouette City, with its year-round survivalist training school, had become the training ground for those who wanted more than talk. We threw handgrenades into old cars to see the effects when they blew up. With burning tires and junk vehicles on fire, with smoke and tear gas exploding in the buildings (which we entered, sometimes wearing protective masks and sometimes not), and with practices that included shooting at each other so we would know what it felt like and sounded like, our training was intense as we practiced urban warfare.

Throughout Silhouette City bullet-riddled cardboard cutouts of state troopers, Jews, and blacks stood as practice targets for elimination. In the survival school we taught urban and rural warfare, basic rifle and pistol use, a weapons proficiency course, general military fieldcraft, natural wilderness survival, personal home defense, Christian martial arts, and Christian military truths. *Eagle Magazine,* a survivalist magazine, called us "the number one civilian SWAT team in America."

The local authorities were obviously getting concerned about us. We were especially having trouble with two officers on the Missouri side. These two law-enforcement agents continually harassed our people whenever we went into Gainesville, Missouri. One of them, a Missouri state trooper, even tried to provoke a fight with me after illegally handcuffing me over a trumped-up traffic citation and taking me to jail. There he tweaked my nose and dared me to do something about it. He informed me that he didn't like our group and would do everything possible to drive us away from the area.

After that incident, our paramilitary snipers would often stalk these two officers in town or at their homes, in what we called "dry shooting." They would aim their unloaded weapons at the officers, get them in the rifles' sights and pull the triggers.

One time, after watching the home of the officer that threatened me and observing him sleeping on the couch with a magazine draped across his chest, the snipers called him on the phone and said, "Instead of lying on the couch after reading a magazine, you ought to go see *First Blood* (the recent movie with Sylvester Stallone, in which a trained ex-Green Beret takes vengeance upon a town and its sheriff). And learn the lesson well!"

First Blood and *Red Dawn* (about a failed Russian military invasion and takeover of the United States) were two favorite movies at CSA.

After that incident, the trooper's boss paid me a visit and asked what he could do to calm down the situation. I told him what the trooper had done to me and said, "All the trooper needs to do is leave us alone. But if he continues to harass us for no reason, then we've got a major problem." The trooper's boss kept him away from the area for almost a year after that.

In the spring of 1982, John Harrell of the Christian-Patriots Defense League asked us to provide security for his annual Freedom Festival. We were instructed not to let any Jews, Blacks, or other minorities in. It was discovered during the Festival, however, that a suspected Jew was attending the meetings and Ellison told him to leave. The man insisted he had a right to stay, that he was a concerned patriot and citizen. John Harrell said he had invited the man to the meetings, that he would let anyone in he wanted to, especially if they were patriots. Ellison and other leaders got upset with Harrell and we left the meeting, never again to return to the Christian-Patriots Defense League. Ellison later accused Harrell of being a federal informer and that the Freedom Festivals were set-ups to find out who was in the movement.

This solidified the split between John Harrell and James Ellison. Later, when I went to Harrell, to try to soothe things between him and Ellison, he told me, "Kerry, Ellison is trouble for the movement. He's trouble for you and all of your members at your farm. And he'll get all of you in trouble with him. He's only concerned with himself. Get away from him while you can."

In 1982, in the *CSA Journal #7*, we published our *Declaration of Non-Surrender,* written by one of our members. It read . . .

We, the undersigned, knowing that we stand in the presence of God Almighty and His Son, Jesus Christ, do commit our signature and our willing approval to this document.

In the event of the collapse of this Great Republic or the consideration of surrender of our sovereignty by our duly elected government officials to an internal or external power, we the undersigned, acting in the spirit of our Forefathers and these great documents—the Declaration of Independence and the Constitution of these United States—refuse any and all such treaty, pact or declaration of surrender.

We acknowledge that there can exist no compromise between the principle of Freedom under God and the establishment of a world order based on humanism, materialism, socialism, and communism. We accept the principle that it is better to stand, and if need be fall for the cause of Christ and Country than to submit to the coming attempt of satanic and socialistic world order.

Let it be affirmed in the name of Jesus Christ and in the spirit of our Forefathers.

The people of Zarephath-Horeb and C.S.A.

This declaration followed a reprinted article in our *CSA Journal* that was being widely circulated at the time, *When Will It Happen?* We envisioned this scenario as the most likely to occur. I repeat the imagined radio announcement so that the reader may understand the mindset at CSA at the time . . .

Announcer: "And now, direct from the Oval Office of the White House, the President of the United States of America."

President: "Good evening, ladies and gentlemen. There is no cause for public panic or alarm; however, I must reveal the events of the last day. Yesterday afternoon, representatives of the Union of Soviet Socialist Republics presented your President with an ultimatum: If the United States were not to lay down all arms and transfer its national sovereignty to the World Socialist Democratic Alliance within 24 hours, an immediate, full-scale nuclear attack would be launched against our nation by the Alliance. I immediately summoned the Joint Chiefs of Staff, the National Security Council, and all presidential advisers to the White House. Since that time we have been in continual conference and debate. Every option and alternative has been considered. Our decision was finally dictated by the following factors:

"The USSR has far outpaced us in nuclear and military capability. While we supplied the technology, money, material and food for peace, the socialist nations diverted these resources to preparations for war.

"Our allies are unable to come to our assistance. The secretary general of the UN informs me that his organization is both unwilling and unable to change or thwart the designs of the Alliance.

"The USSR possesses far superior civil defense. In full-scale nuclear warfare, only 5 to 10% of the Russian people would be endangered, while fully 60% of the U.S. population is vulnerable to nuclear attack.

"Based upon these realities, we had no alternative. We have unconditionally accepted the terms of the Alliance. Therefore, effective immediately, all governmental authority is hereby transferred to the new interim government appointed by the Democratic Alliance. Alliance troops will begin to arrive shortly at all major U.S. air and sea ports.

"I repeat, there is no cause for panic. Throughout our negotiations, the Alliance displayed a spirit of charity, understanding, and sympathy, but I am compelled to announce the following:

"To ensure the public safety, a dawn to dusk curfew will be rigidly enforced. No one will travel more than one-half mile from his present location, and will return to his present location by dusk. Use of all vehicles and telephones by the general public is strictly prohibited. All banks will be temporarily closed, and no withdrawals or transfers will be permitted until the new currency is implemented. All physicians are hereby ordered to be on 24-hour emergency call. All food, fuel and medical supplies will be impounded for the good of the people. As soon as possible, all men 16 years of age and over will register at their nearest police station.

All firearms will be delivered to the authorities as soon as receiving centers are operable.

"All fundamental, independent, Bible-centered congregations will cease operation at once. All publications and distribution of conservative Christian, patriotic and nationalist oriented literature will cease immediately. Public use and conveyance of the Bible is especially forbidden. These measures do not comprise persecution of any form; they have been initiated to ensure public order and safety.

"This is my last appearance as your President. Neither apologies nor excuses will ease the pain of this moment. History is not amendable to alteration. What has occurred today is the inevitable consequence of a long chain of unwise decisions and priorities which cannot be undone or prayed away.

"Thank you for your support. Good night. And may God Almighty have mercy upon us."

Announcer: "You have just heard an address by the former President of the United States of America. Stay tuned to this station for further directives."

8

CSA National Convocation

Go through, go through the gates;
prepare ye the way of the people;
lift up a standard for the people,
and you shall be called,
Sought out, A city not forsaken.
—Isaiah 62:10-12

In August 1982, I approached Ellison and the elders with an idea.

"We've seen a lot of people in various groups," I said, "that are no longer satisfied with just rhetoric and talk. They want action. But they need a leader, someone to bond them together."

"What are you suggesting?" James asked. We had started calling Ellison "James" instead of "Jim," since it sounded more dignified.

"I propose a meeting this fall. We're basically centrally located in the United States. I suggest that we invite Aryan Nations, the Klan, the patriotic groups, the Christian-Patriots Defense League, the Posse Comitatus, any who want more than John Harrell offers. We can invite the various leaders to speak; we can hold classes like we do in the survival courses; then we can talk to the people and the leaders about forming a coalition. We're stronger together than we are apart. Our goal is simple. We want to unify the splintered, autonomous extremists into one national organization, with James Ellison of CSA as its leader! No more talking—'action' will be the word of the day."

Everyone loved the idea. I was to get the information out to the various groups and invite the speakers. We invited Richard Butler of Aryan Nations, Robert Miles of the Mountain Church, and Colonel Jack Mohr of the Christian-Patriots Defense League to be the main speakers. Also invited were Thom Robb of the Klan, Richard Scutari (a martial arts expert), and several others to teach classes at the meeting.

James wanted to do the meeting right. He knew we couldn't fit everyone into our small meeting house, so it was decided we should build a new meeting house, a sanctuary built especially for the occasion.

In less than three weeks, we broke the ground, poured the concrete, and erected a forty-foot by fifty-foot, two-story concrete block building with thick, elaborate rock work on the outside. On each side of the double-door entrance, the flaming sword of our emblem stood immortalized in rock. The downstairs was our new meeting place, while the upstairs would serve as a library and school. The downstairs windows were built like narrow gun ports, with scriptural references of war or Identity written above them, and with the tabernacle colors of blue, purple, white and red as the curtains.

In the center of our new Sanctuary stood a large, stone fireplace. On each side of it we hung a shield and weapon, corresponding to each of the four divisions of the tribes of Israel.

On the second floor we built a winding, narrow passageway that led to a defensive port, from which to see the enemy at great distances and to defend ourselves against attack. The sanctuary was designed to be our Alamo in case the feds or enemy armies came against us in large numbers and broke the outer perimeter.

At the opposite end of the main settlement we had built our communications building, complete with ham radios, police scanners and a landmine-detonation panel that controlled the perimeter explosives. Atop that building was a sixty-foot tower, with a sandbagged platform on top of it. This was our lookout tower, enabling us to see anyone coming up to three miles away. By this time CSA had one hundred fifty members, made up of some thirty-two families and several single people.

"Why do you want to move here?" I asked one perspective member.

"The guns, man. You guys are the best paramilitary group in the country. Hell, everybody talks about CSA; you guys are like gods. Everybody expects you guys to start the war." I sighed. Nothing about God, Jesus or the Bible. Nothing about love of the brethren. Guns and war. That's all he wanted. That's all anybody wanted who moved to CSA now.

"The Bible," Ellison tried to instruct me, "says that man looks on the outward appearance; but God looks on the heart. I see men who need a shepherd; you see men who don't quite measure up to your expectations."

"No," I countered, "you see men to add to your army; I see men whose hearts have never been touched by God."

The meeting, now called the CSA National Convocation, was scheduled for October 1982, and was well received by the various groups. Of course they didn't know about our plan to appoint James Ellison as the new leader of a united extreme right.

Attendance was higher than expected, with well over three hundred people from all over the country. Men, women and even children freely walked around with weapons, enjoyed the classes, partook of the food we prepared for them and welcomed the chance to meet the infamous CSA and James Ellison. Leaders spoke out against the Jewish-controlled media, banking systems and federal government. Hate, fear and paranoia were in the air infecting everyone.

In one meeting, Ellison (copying a tactic Louis Beam had previously used when he visited CSA) threw out a piece of raw meat for "the federal dogs" that were controlled by ZOG, the Zionist Occupied Government, and challenged any of the BATFAGS present to identify themselves. "Batfags" was right-wing slang for agents of the BATF—the Bureau of Alcohol, Tobacco, and Firearms.

At the Convocation Ellison also received a prophecy from an outside ministry we had never met before. During one of the meetings, the middle-aged, gray-haired man, though short in stature, stood proudly and confidently in the center-right of our sanctuary, forefinger pointed to Ellison, while all eyes were fixed upon him. This prophecy would become the pivotal point for Ellison, one that would become his guiding trademark.

The visitor proclaimed, "You my son have desired to bring unity. You have tried to lay down your life for those who have gathered around you. I say unto you, surely you shall also be betrayed. Though you have been seen at times as a prophet, certain things have been hid that you might be deceived. But I say unto you, surely my son you shall succeed. I will cause you to prosper. Be true unto Me and in that day be not discouraged when those that are near you turn from you. Be true to the vision; walk in the word that sings within your own heart. And in due season, after I have purified in the midst, you shall surely stand and be expanded. Be glad and full of rejoicing, for that which I have begun in this place shall come to pass."

The man who had so captivated Ellison's attention was Canadian-born Robert Millar—known to his followers as "Grandpa"—founder of a spiritual community near Muldrow, Oklahoma, called "Elohim City." The group had lived on their several hundred acres since the early 1970s. Its name could mean either "The City of the Gods" or "The City of God."

Elohim City built round dome-shaped houses, believing that rectangular or squared buildings somehow hindered the electrical flow that was contained in each of us. A pacifistic community, their eyes were opened, upon attending the Convocation, to a more military stance. After meeting us, Millar's group began to purchase weapons and train militarily.

We received two influences from Millar and Elohim City. The first was to incorporate dances into our praise songs. Elohim City believed in expressing its praise and worship of God in dance as well as song. We found the experience to be enlightening and that it added excitement to the meetings.

The second was a revelation—a new name for God: Yahuah. I had shared with Millar that I was never comfortable with the name "Yahveh" because it was too "hard" in its pronunciation. "I was taught once at a Baptist college," I mentioned to Millar, "that God's name, as revealed to Moses at the burning bush, should sound like a musical breeze blowing gently through the trees—since "spirit," "wind" and "breath" have similar roots in the Hebrew—but that it should also sound like a strong wind or hurricane, that His name should be heard distinctly in both instances. 'Yahweh' comes closer, but somehow still seems off, to me."

"That's interesting," Millar responded, "because we recently had a prophecy given by one of our women that used another name for God—a new name we had never used before. It's 'Yahuah.'"

"I love that!" I enthusiastically said. "Yahuah. That makes sense, since Jesus' name in the original scriptures is Yashuah."

I could hear its magical music singing in the wind. "Yahuah" became the name of God we most often used at CSA, although at various times we still retained "Yahweh" and even "Yahveh" because of its familiarity with Identity.

Millar's prophecy consumed Ellison. James analyzed it, and interpreted it in every way he could think of, bringing it up for discussion at every opportunity. It became *the* word of God for him. He awaited the time that he would be betrayed. By this time James Ellison was solidly convinced that not only did he have the anointing of King David of the Old Testament upon him, but that he was indeed King David reincarnated genetically and spiritually.

As far as Ellison was concerned he was David. His word was God's word; his law, God's law. No harm could come to him, nor could any stand before him. No one else, nothing else, meant anything to him, but the purpose of God that he perceived for his life. The land was his to rule, and rule it he would. God was with him, in him, for him. What else mattered?

Ellison believed that Millar would be his "Nathan," his servant-prophet, a counselor for him for times of guidance. Even though Millar had more learning, more wisdom and more years of experience that Ellison did, Ellison was convinced of his superiority and standing with God over Millar.

The 1982 Convocation was a failure in bringing a unified cause; each group exalted only its own leader. After the five-day affair was over, each group wrote glorified articles in their own newsletters about the drawing together of the various groups, and that an army was truly being raised by God. The names of CSA and of James Ellison were being proclaimed, however, and we continued to believe that in time, unification under our banner would occur. So plans began for the 1983 Convocation.

Part Four | **The Fall of CSA**

9

The Foundation Not Square

Except the Lord build the house,
they labor in vain that build it;
except the Lord keep the city,
the watchman wakes but in vain.

—Psalm 127:1

The last days previous to the October 1982 Convocation were darkened for two reasons. After the construction of the new sanctuary building began, one of the younger elders came to me.

"I need to talk to you," Billy told me one evening. I could see he was troubled. Billy was also the Bible teacher for the younger members.

"What is it?" I asked.

"The sanctuary isn't square."

"What do you mean, not square?"

"I mean it's off. Corner to corner through one diagonal is twelve inches longer than the other corner-to-corner measurement. Twelve inches! That means the building is more of a parallelogram than it is a rectangle. The corner angles are not ninety degrees like they're supposed to be."

"How can that be?" I asked. "The men are putting the roof on it now. Have you told James?"

"Yeah, I've told him. I didn't notice it while we were putting the joists in, because you line up the joists with the walls. But once I started nailing the plywood down for the upstairs floor, I caught the mistake, and told James. He then checked the measurements and said there was nothing we could do about it, that he'd have to correct it with the roof."

"I guess he can do that, then? So what's the problem?"

"Don't you see? There's no way anyone could have measured that wall wrong when we first began to build it." Billy emphasized. "Not by twelve inches! Yet there it is. Exactly twelve inches! I've helped build every building here, and I've never been out of square by more than maybe half an inch."

I looked at him, puzzled. Carpentry wasn't my calling, although I did understand numbers. "Yeah, twelve inches. I know that's a lot, but if James is correcting it with the roof, then why worry about it?"

"You don't get it. You're not listening to me. We missed something we should never have missed. Something major. Twelve is the number of God's government, right?"

"Right," I replied.

"There's something major wrong," Billy continued, "in the government here, in the eldership here, in its foundation. But instead of finding out what it is, instead of going back and correcting it, James wants to simply cover it up so that no one can tell. He says it's too costly to go back and correct it, that it's too late now.

"Kerry, James physically laid the foundation to the sanctuary himself and he laid out the lower layers of the concrete block walls. Spiritually, he laid the foundation and built the walls of Zarephath-Horeb and then CSA. But now he wants to finagle the roof, our spiritual covering if you will, so the problem won't show. Don't you see it, now?"

I understood. "Yeah," I acknowledged, "I see what you're saying. You believe that God caused the measurement of the sanctuary's foundation to be off by exactly twelve inches, as a sign that we're missing it somewhere, and that we aren't trying to recognize and solve the problem, that we're just trying to cover it up, to lie about it. And that the problem is with our own basic foundation. Right?"

"Right. And that bothers me," Billy responded. "I don't care about the building itself—we can fix that. But the building is a symbol about us as a people. We have a problem and James doesn't care about the solution. That really bothers me."

It bothered me also.

But it really bothered Billy. He never got over it. To him, God was saying that James knew there was a problem; that he may even have known what the problem was, or may have even caused the problem.

And, further, that James didn't care, because it was too costly to fix; it would mean having to start over. Billy had never seen this side of Ellison before.

But what part of the foundation was off? Was it our involvement with the right-wing and Identity? Was it the paramilitary? Was it "body-life" itself? Or did it go back even further? I wasn't completely sure. But I had questions. And I wanted answers.

Then, only a few days before the 1982 Convocation was to begin, one of the elders, Trent, called for an elders' meeting. I had no idea what it was about. In the meeting, Trent declared he was leaving our group. Most of us were shocked. No core member had ever left our farm before.

"Why would you leave?" someone asked.

"I must confess a sin and ask your forgiveness. But, first, let me say that this sin is too much for me to bear and to stay here among you. Once you know of this sin, you'll recognize that my ministry here is finished. I can't stay." Trent looked over at James and then hung his head low. "I've committed adultery against Annie." A deathly quiet hung over the room. No one moved, no one spoke.

"It had been a long time coming," Trent continued, "and it's been going on for some time now." When someone asked him who it was with, Trent couldn't answer.

James spoke up. "It's with my older daughter." A shock settled in everyone present. James' daughter? But she's only fourteen!

Trent then went into details about the affair, about his decision to leave, and about leaving his wife, Annie, with their children, in James' care. James and one other elder, Bruce, had known what Trent had been doing. The rest of us were taken by surprise.

Trent left the farm shortly after his announcement.

In early November James called another elders' meeting.

"All of you know about Trent and why he left. The Lord has shown me that Trent is spiritually dead now. He and Annie are no longer married. God has also told me that I am to take Annie as my second wife."

Randall stood up and hollered, "What? What are you talking about? It was decided years ago that the polygamy issue would not be brought up again! You can't do this! What's Ollie say about this?"

Ellison waited for Randall to calm down. "Ollie and I have discussed this. I must do this. I have no choice. It's what God wants. I want you all to pray about this and we'll speak of it later. But be assured, I won't do this without the blessing of the elders."

The elders left James' house, most of them confused and hurt.

This wasn't the first time polygamy had been mentioned at the farm. I spoke of it first in 1978, when I asked Ellison one day in the woods, "Jim, if God is going to restore everything the way that it used to be, then I have a question. In Isaiah, the Bible says, 'And in that day seven women shall take hold of one man, saying, We will eat our own bread, and wear our own apparel: only let us be called by your name, to take away our reproach.' The early patriarchs and most of the kings of Israel had more than one wife. Does that mean that God will restore polygamy in the earth in the last days and that men will have more than one wife?"

"I think so," Jim answered, "but not until after the judgments begin." After the men had talked all day at work about multiple wives, we discussed it with our own wives when we got home, with anticipated reactions. All of the men were in favor of it; none of the women were. The women got mad at me. The subject was dropped.

Two years later, in 1980, the subject of polygamy came up again. This time, one of the elders discussed it with one of the single women. The elder, of course, was married. Ellison and I were in Texas working, with some of the other men, while this was going on. Randall was again in charge. But Randall forbid the discussion of it any further. When we returned from Texas, Jim agreed with Randall's decision and said to never discuss polygamy again. As far as Ellison was concerned, during the tribulation period a lot of men would die, leaving more women than men, and then those women would need to be taken care of. But not until then.

After the Convocation, Billy's revelation, Trent's confession, and then James' bulletin, I began to more seriously question the direction of CSA. But I still kept my concerns to myself. It seemed that no new revelations or understandings were coming forth, no "changing of the shewbread in the tabernacle." If new understandings—new shewbread—weren't coming forth, then our old understandings, our old bread, would become stale and of no use. That meant that we would not be growing spiritually in the Lord.

I discovered a scripture in Isaiah that foretold of God giving us the treasures of darkness that had been hidden in secret. So I began to study things like astrology, the chi, yoga, auras, meditation, chakras, color therapy, aromatherapy, palmistry, numerology, horoscopes, pyramidology, the Kabala and other topics we normally associated with witchcraft or the new age. These studies caused me to view Christianity as mystical, deepening my previous belief in the esoteric philosophy of Christianity.

Rader threw a fit over my new studies. Ellison questioned the validity of these subjects. "Why dig through a quagmire of manure for a few coins at the bottom?" he asked. "Yes, you may discover a little bit of value, but is it really worth getting dirty over?"

"Maybe not for a few coins," I replied. "But, what if there's a fortune buried under all that dung, then would you dig for it?"

"Possibly. I don't know," he shrugged as he walked away. "I guess it doesn't matter, though, you're already polluted and corrupted anyway."

That response really bothered me at first, but as I thought about it, I knew Ellison was right. He could tell I was no longer one hundred percent committed to our purpose, our vision. I couldn't help it. I had too many unanswered questions. I had always questioned things. I was willing to get dirty if it meant finding the truth. And I believed deeper truth had to be found.

While a student at Texas Tech University in the early 1970s, I delved into Transcendental Meditation and made application to learn the practice. Because I was in the Christian ministry, I was personally invited by the Maharishi Mahesh Yogi to be taught by him in Hawaii and then to have my own school. I declined the offer, however, and decided not to take the TM courses. I had often regretted that decision. Now I regretted it again.

On November 20, 1982, I prophesied in a meeting, "For thus says the Lord unto you, 'You have many pillars of strength. But these pillars shall crumble before your eyes. For you have forgotten my admonition, that judgment must begin in the house of God. Yea, I have told you before that this house is the latter house. For who can defy the Lord God? Who can stand before me?' says God."

I knew as soon as I prophesied it that the prophecy was speaking about Randall and the paramilitary leaders. The arm of the flesh had become our strength. Another purging was due.

1982 was the first year that we didn't celebrate Thanksgiving, the only holiday besides July Fourth or the Israelite Feast Days that we did observe. We meagerly attempted to celebrate Thanksgiving that year but it was a failure because not everyone participated.

"What's there to be thankful for?" Randall asked James. "You're wanting to take a second wife; Kerry's teaching witchcraft; and we ain't going to war anytime soon."

In another elders' meeting, James asked who would stand with him in God wanting him to take Annie as his second wife. Elder after elder said, "No." I was the only one in favor of it, the only one to side with James. One of the other elders, Bill, said he would reluctantly submit to it. No one else agreed with it. I recognized the opportunity, though, as not just a show of loyalty to James, but with an ulterior motive.

If it were time for James to have a second wife, I reasoned, then since God had first given me the revelation of it, wouldn't it make sense that I would be next in line, especially since the other elders had no desire for a second wife? Also, since my siding with James showed my allegiance to him, wouldn't that help to elevate my position in our group, from just the lowly teacher?

Randall stood in the elders' meeting and demanded an answer from James. "You said you would not marry Annie unless all the elders gave their consent. Do you still say that?"

"When I said that," James answered, "I figured you would all agree with me soon. You know me, you know how I have withstood the polygamy question for years. But now God is telling me it's time. And if it's time, then who is the obvious choice to go first? Wouldn't it have to be the apostle? Wouldn't it have to be me? I have been found faithful with Ollie, and God has seen fit to increase my stewardship."

"But why Annie?" Randall asked. I knew that Randall had never liked Annie. He thought she was too Yankee, too prim and proper.

"I don't know why," James replied, "but I know she's the one. Maybe it's because Trent left her in my care when he left. All that matters to me is that she is the one God has chosen."

"But none of us," Randall continued, "except maybe Kerry, agrees with this. Are you going to choose a woman over the military? 'Cause that's what you're gonna do if you choose her. 'Cause me and the others ain't staying if you marry her."

James stood his ground. "I have no choice. I have to marry her."

With that Randall Rader and the other elders left James' house. Only I stayed.

"I want you to do something for me," James told me. "I want you to give me and Ollie and Annie the VSA test. I want to know what it will reveal."

"All right," I said. "I'll get it ready."

The Voice Stress Analyzer test, using a series of red and green lights, was a wireless machine (unlike a lie detector) that measured the stress in a person's voice, indicating whether the person was lying or telling the truth when asked a series of yes-no questions. The machine was given to us by a friend, Ardie McBrearty. I had been entrusted with its care and was trained to use it. We had tested it on all of our men to judge their dedication to the group. In addition, after 1981, any one who desired to join CSA had to take the VSA test, as well as fill out an allegiance oath and an application for a background check (which we never checked).

During the Convocation, I showed the Voice Stress Analyzer to Richard Butler from Aryan Nations. He wanted me to test it on his men. One of them, David Tate, a young red-haired man, was excited about the test. He wanted to prove his loyalty to Butler and to the white race. Butler considered Tate one of his best and most devoted men, since Tate's parents had long been with Butler and Aryan Nations. After some basic questions concerning his name, address, age, and hair color, I asked Tate some important questions.

"Do you believe in the white race?"

"Yes." All green lights revealed he told the truth.

"Do you admire Richard Butler?"

"Yes." Again, the truth.

"Would you ever betray Aryan Nations?"

"No." Two of the analyzer's four red lights showed that Tate lied to some degree. Richard Butler's eyebrows raised.

"Have you ever betrayed Aryan Nations?"

"No," Tate emphasized. He lied.

"I would trust David with my life," Butler whispered to me.

I accepted this statement and knew where to go with the questions. "David, do you read material from any group other than Aryan Nations?"

"Yes." He told the truth.

"Do you feel any guilt about reading the other material?"

"Yes," he answered, reluctantly. Again, the truth.

"David, other than reading any material from any other group other than Aryan Nations, have you ever betrayed Aryan Nations?"

"No." All green lights. David Tate told the truth. Richard Butler was ecstatic.

"David feels guilty about reading other material," I explained, "as if it's an act of betrayal to read anything else other than what you write, Richard. He's not sure if you or the other men would approve."

David looked down at the floor. Butler laughed and rested his hand on Tate's shoulder. He told him not to feel guilty, that he didn't consider it an act of betrayal. But the incident affirmed Butler's confidence in the machine and in me.

I prepared to administer the test to James, Ollie, and Annie. Everyone was a little apprehensive. I decided to test them individually with no one else present.

"James, do you believe that it is God's will for you to marry Annie?"

"Yes." Green lights. The truth.

"Do you have any ulterior motives in marrying her?"

"No."

"Are you tired or bored being married to Ollie?"

"No."

"Are you willing to marry Annie in spite of any objections of the elders?"

"Yes." One red light.

"Do you love Ollie?"

"Yes."

"Do you love Annie?"

"Yes."

The green lights came on every time.

After some more questions, I proceeded to Ollie.

"Ollie, do you believe James is supposed to marry Annie?"

"Yes." She wasn't convinced.

"Do you have anything against Annie?"

"No." She did.

"Are you willing for James to marry Annie if that's what God wants?"

"Yes." The truth.

Again, after some more questions, I proceeded to Annie.

"Annie, do you believe you are to become James' second wife?"

"Yes." All green lights.

"Do you have any ulterior motives in becoming James' second wife?"

"No." She lied.

"Do you love Ollie?"

"Yes." Some truth.

"Will you give her the respect due her as James' first wife?"

"Yes." Again, she lied.

"Are you willing to do anything for James?"

"Yes." The truth.

After questioning all three, we gathered together in James' living room.

"Well?" James asked.

"According to the questions asked and the answers all of you gave, these are my conclusions. James, you're obviously convinced that God wants you to marry Annie, but you're a little apprehensive. Ollie, you're willing for James to marry Annie, but you don't want him to. You have nothing against Annie per se, but you're not ready to share James. That's understandable. Annie, you say that you have no ulterior motives in marrying James, but you do. You're bitter against Ollie because you don't think she's the wife she ought to be for James. In fact, your tests reveal that you want to replace Ollie, that you want to be wife number one. James, Annie's not ready, Ollie's not ready, you're basically the only one ready, but I'm not sure you know what you're getting into. My advice, based upon the Voice Stress Analyzer, is for you to wait.

"All right," James said, "we'll wait." James, I discovered later, lied.

Even though James said he would wait, Randall Rader and many of our military men left our group beginning in December of 1982. We lost two-thirds of our members within the next three months, down from one hundred fifty men, women, and children, to fifty. It was like going through a divorce. We were without direction, numb, as if family members had died. The pain was excruciating.

The purging of the camp had continued. Not only had we lost a large percentage of the core of the group, those who had been with us for a long time, but almost all of the people who were there for just Identity or guns also left. Ellison felt the betrayal begin and it grieved him.

We were so hurt and exhausted by the departure of some of our most solid members, that we decided to do no more media interviews. We also decided to cool it with the right-wing movement. There was no more military practice. Most of us who remained were hoping that we could just go back to being Zarephath-Horeb and let CSA die.

The tenth issue of *The CSA Journal* was our first to be printed after the 1982 Convocation and the split in CSA. It was also the last Journal that we ever published. It revealed a distinct difference from the previous nine. All of the articles in this last issue were spiritual or religious in nature; not war, not racial, not hate. We were trying to find our way back.

In the very first article of issue ten, entitled "Update on Zarephath-Horeb and CSA," I wrote:

> A visit with us now would shock any who visited us before October '82. No more do men walk around in fatigues or camouflage.

No more does CSA look like an army camp. Now we dress like everyone else; now there are only a few here; now we are returned to our first love, Zarephath-Horeb! By the grace of God He has spared us from ourselves. By His grace, we shall go on to perfection. God declared to us in December '80 that He was going to make us a Beacon to His people. He is still doing that. The people of God however do not need weapons training; they do not need racial get-togethers; they do not need refuges; they do not need another Identity or survival publication. They do need Jesus! In prophecy, our Heavenly Father told us that our pillars of strength would crumble before our very eyes. They did! Now we are more encouraged than ever before. What is happening with CSA? We are still here. But behold, now shall come forth its parent—Zarephath-Horeb Church!

Our fifth child, a son, was born on March 9, 1983. Kay and I named him Jared Kane, "descent of grace." I believed that God had shed His grace upon Zarephath-Horeb, providing a way for the paramilitary to die and the right-wing with it. I felt invigorated again and hopeful about the future.

Although I had not realized it at the time, our split at CSA was not over Ellison's taking a second wife and Rader's disagreement with it. The split was over a much more serious issue.

Our church government was based upon a plural ministry, the belief that the one-man ministry so common in traditional churches was dangerous and unscriptural. We believed in the checks-and-balances of more than one elder.

Even though Ellison was in charge, in times past if the other elders overruled him on an issue, he would submit to us. Now, for the first time, the votes of the elders meant nothing to Ellison. For the first time in our church, Ellison's "revelation" was more important than the counsel of the elders—more important than the basis of our ministry. Now, we had reverted to the "one-man ministry."

By the early months of 1983, I began to question the basic premise of our purpose. We had always believed that the end-time days were full of misery, gloom and doom, under the evil auspices of some dark, sinister Antichrist that would make war on all Christians. I began to study some scriptures that indicated the opposite. Although I didn't understand them completely, it seemed that perhaps the future would not be gloomy and full of chaos, but would be one of peace and prosperity, where hope was to be found in abundance, almost an Utopia.

I based this premise primarily upon Jesus' statement in Matthew, chapter twenty-four that said, " . . . if it were possible, they shall deceive even the very elect." The common teaching is that "they" refers to false prophets. I began, however, to see it referring to the latter days themselves, referred to a few verses earlier. If that were true, then how could the elect be deceived by the opposite of the kingdom of God? I thought. Deception comes primarily as a counterfeit to the real thing.

Then other scriptures began to fall into place. Ellison often quoted the scripture that said, "Peace, peace, when there is no peace," supposedly referring to the latter days. Yet we always interpreted that by today's values, that society said there was peace now. But there wasn't world peace yet and I knew it. However, now I understood that that scripture had to mean that one day people could honestly say there was peace in the world because there would be world peace! But that world peace would be deceptive because it would still fall short of God's glory! It would only be the best that man could do himself, but short of what God would ultimately do.

But what of Babylon? Weren't we supposed to come out of the confusion and chaos of society in order to become true children of God? Then I began to study about Babylon and realized that the ancient society was not an evil society, but a glorious one. It epitomized in its day the best that man could do on his own.

I concluded that the latter days had to look just like the kingdom of God in order to almost deceive the very elect. The latter-days could not be the opposite of the kingdom. This meant, instead of "doom and gloom," the latter days would actually be "prosperity and peace." As I studied this concept, I was able to bring other scriptures into harmony with this, scriptures that sometimes had puzzled me in the past.

I approached Ellison with another concept. "I don't believe some collapse of the government is coming any time soon, if ever. I now see a bright future for America and the world, a time of tremendous prosperity and peace. In fact, I question whether Jesus will actually return soon, that possibly it may be even twenty to thirty years from now. Maybe even not until after the Millennium."

James didn't like that. I shared with him my reasoning on this. "What are you suggesting, then?" he asked.

"I am of the opinion that we should be a testimony to the world about how Christianity ought to be. I call it 'Positive Christianity.' Let's abandon the military survival school and concentrate instead on having the best private school in the area. Let's build a Bible school where people can come to learn the ways of God. We have a tremendous amount of talent here with our people.

"We not only have mechanics and carpenters, we've got a talented painter and artist. We lay some of the best outside rock-work on houses in the area. One of our women was a children's photographer before moving here. Even though she's gone now, we've still got a lot of talent here. We could build a manufacturing plant on our property, or have a chicken ranch like a lot of people do in Arkansas. Or we could start a pet cemetery in the area. We could even build a self-storage complex in town, producing residual income.

"There's no limit to what we could do! Let's build businesses in town that can support our group, that can bless the area people, and that can enable all of us to get off welfare and food stamps, so that everyone can learn to be financially responsible for his own family. Let's plan for the future in a positive manner, instead of living season to season, hoping for some governmental collapse."

I thought Ellison was going to hurt himself with the way he carried on. He couldn't see my position at all and totally disagreed with my views. However, to pacify me, he did allow me to establish a business in Mountain Home, a health food store.

In April of 1983 we opened "Ozark Shepherds Natural Foods" with a storefront in the Wal-Mart Shopping Center. It was the third health food store in Mountain Home, but we did a fair business, although only enough to remain open for just one year. But Ellison's motive wasn't pure. The store was allowed because we could then launder food stamps through it, exchanging them for cash.

During that time, I met a man one day at our store. He owned an out-of-state business selling satellite dishes, and was looking for someone to franchise his up-and-coming business in the Ozarks. After talking for a while, he asked if I'd be interested in opening the only satellite dish business in the area, if he were to back me.

"Yes, Sir, I'd be interested. But I gotta talk to my partner first."

"Bring him in tomorrow," the visitor said, "and let me meet him. If I like him as much as I do you, we'll work up a deal." The next day he met Ellison. James was acting cocky, almost as if he purposefully wanted to insult the man. I remembered, years earlier, when a man had bought and placed a sawmill on our property under a business arrangement with Jim. Ellison never paid him for the lumber we had cut and sold. Eventually, disgusted, the man came and repossessed his sawmill and other equipment.

After James left the health food store, the satellite-dish man spoke honestly to me. "I'd do business with you in a heartbeat," he said, "but not with your partner."

"Sorry," I replied, "I can't do business without him."

The older gentleman looked seriously at me, leaning close. "Son, you're making a big mistake. Separate yourself from that man. He's no good for you."

The man left. I never saw him again. Someone else later opened a satellite dish business in town. It was extremely successful.

During a praise meeting in June 1983, Eric, now one of the elders, prophesied to James, "This night I anoint you as a King before my people. And I shall bless and enlarge your family. I say unto you this night take also your other wife; you shall not be turned away by your other wife. You shall be a glorious king. You shall stand before me and shall fight as a warrior in the days that I shall call forth. Thus says the Lord your God."

The remaining elders, Ollie and Annie were also prayed and prophesied over that God would bless them to stand with James in faith.

Then on June 12, the next night, Ollie washed Annie's feet during the praise service, and prophesied to her, "Lift up your voice in praise and honor him in all things. I have said before, says the Lord, that your voice would echo through the hills in praise of me. Your voice shall be heard among the nations, praising me, and glorifying me. You are a clean, honorable vessel in my house and worthy of this honor. Be humble before the congregation."

Then Ollie said to James, "Now in the sight of this congregation, as seven months ago I did, I give the release to my husband to take the woman for his wife. Let it be a pleasing thing to the congregation and in the sight of the Lord. I choose to honor my lord, my husband, my king. I will continue to serve the Lord as this man's wife. To love him, and to support him in all things and in this thing. I will be glad in this and I will rejoice."

As James, Ollie, Annie, and the other elders stood before the congregation, I said, "Fear not little flock, it is your Father's good pleasure to give you the kingdom. Because of your dedication to the Lord, to our Body, and to each other, by the authority given to me by our Heavenly Father, I do hereby solemnize this union to be a new beginning for our Body, and an ushering in of the coming age."

Then after James and I each prayed, Annie offered the commitment, "Thank you for my lord and thank you for my mistress, Jesus. And I ask that you make me worthy to dwell in their house. And that you'd make me a joy and strength to my lord, my king. And a reward and an honor to Ollie. For your name sake."

With that the meeting was dismissed and James Ellison officially had two wives. I was the only one who knew that he had already bedded Annie some time before while on a trip to western Arkansas. He had boasted of it to me, and I was grieved that he hadn't waited until the ceremony. Why sneak around if he was openly proud of the relationship? I thought.

What I didn't know, until years later (even though Ollie had alluded to it in her prayer the evening of the meeting), was that Ellison had first bedded Annie on November 13, 1982, the night that Ollie gave birth to one of James' sons, about the time that Ellison first talked to the elders about taking Annie as his second wife. That night, while Ollie was having difficulty in childbirth, Ellison was with Annie instead of his childbearing wife.

Ellison said he would wait for the approval of the elders before marrying Annie. But he didn't; he never had any intentions of waiting. During the eighth month of Ollie's fifth pregnancy, Ellison told her that he was now perfect and that God had made him king. And being king, God wanted Ellison to take a second wife. Though she tried to argue against Ellison's polygamous stand, Ollie's efforts were in vain. Ellison told Ollie that she wouldn't go into labor unless she gave him permission to go unto Annie. Fearful of the fate of her unborn child, Ollie relented and gave Ellison permission. While Ollie laid recovering from childbirth, Ellison laid in another bed down the hall with another woman.

Annie lived in the same house with Jim and Ollie for several chaotic months before moving into her own dwelling. The entire time I had to watch Ollie being torn apart, humiliated and nearing a nervous breakdown. But I felt helpless to rescue her. At times she would cry to me for help, yet I was powerless to do anything but encourage her to be patient, that in time all would be better.

James took his two wives with him wherever he went, to every other group we knew. It was a sign of who he believed he was in God. A king in Israel. It is interesting to note that Ellison had never taken Ollie to these type of places before; only until he had two wives to show off did he ever care to have a wife along.

Could it be, I thought after the "wedding" ceremony, that we are on our way back to being a spiritually minded church, and not a right-wing paramilitary organization any longer? God, are You finally separating us from the right-wing?

10

The Battle Cry

And when he had opened the fifth seal,
I saw under the altar
the souls of them that were slain
for the word of God,
and for the testimony which they held.
And they cried with a loud voice, saying,
How long, O Lord holy and true,
do you not judge and avenge our blood
on them that dwell on the earth?
—Revelation 5:9, 10

All of the ingredients had been gathered and mixed. The formation of an extremist group was complete: First, a false philosophical or theological foundation based upon some negative emotion such as fear, lack of faith, hate or despair; then a charismatic leader that could manipulate and direct the people; lastly, physical and mental isolation with limited information, producing a savior-mentality with a perceived enemy and limited options. A quiet, rural Christian church had been transformed into Christian survivalists and then white supremacists. All that was needed to take this extremist group into terrorism was a catalyst that combined "heat" and "time."

In February of 1983, a man we had never heard of before was making news in North Dakota. His name was Gordon Kahl. He became our catalyst.

Sixty-three-year-old Gordon Kahl was a major leader in the state's Posse Comitatus, a tax-protesting organization. The five-foot-seven-inch Kahl had been a World War Two turret gunner, flying more than fifty combat missions and had received the Purple Heart. Kahl had accepted the Identity teaching during the latter 1960s. When the foreclosures began rising in the mid-west, Kahl discovered the Posse in 1974.

The Posse Comitatus (Latin for "power of the county") believed that the only legal law-enforcement officer in the United States and the supreme authority of the land was the county sheriff.

The sheriff was accountable and responsible only to the citizens of his county. If the sheriff failed to satisfactorily perform his duties, then the Posse Comitatus believed they had the lawful right under natural law to act in the name of the sheriff. The Posse believed the federal government had no right to interfere in local affairs.

Kahl spent eight months in prison in 1977 for failure to pay income taxes since 1967. After his release from prison he still refused to pay taxes. With his belief in Identity, Gordon Kahl hated "the Jewish-controlled" banking and tax systems in the United States. With the farm crises of the early 1980s, Kahl believed it to be time to stand against the Beast.

In February 1983, four U.S. Marshals and a deputy sheriff went to arrest Gordon Kahl. In the shoot-out that followed, Kahl's son, Yorie, was shot, and Kahl killed two white U.S. Marshals, Kenneth Muir and Robert Cheshire, the latter of whom Kahl wounded first and then fired two bullets point blank into his head. A nationwide manhunt for Kahl followed.

In a sixteen-page manifesto, Kahl declared his desire to "put our nation back under Christian common law." He denounced Jews and spoke of efforts to amend the Constitution to prohibit them from living in the United States. "We are a conquered and occupied nation . . . by the Jews . . . (out) to destroy Christianity and the white race." Kahl spoke of a coming struggle "between the people of the Kingdom of God and the Kingdom of Satan."

Kahl implored, "Let each of you who says that the Lord Jesus Christ is your personal savior sell his garment and buy a sword" to use against the "Synagogue of Satan."

Gordon Kahl's activities in North Dakota were of no interest to us. In fact, we hadn't even heard about what had happened until sometime in late March. Then, by fate or destiny, Kahl showed up in Arkansas.

Some friends of ours were hiding Gordon Kahl, we had discovered, but still we had no dealings in the matter until June 3, when it was reported in the news that Kahl and a Sheriff Gene Matthews had killed each other after a federal raid on the home Kahl was hiding in—less than two hours from CSA, near Smithville, in northeastern Arkansas.

Gordon Kahl's death sucked us right back into the right-wing limelight. Again, it seemed to us, this was a sign from God, a direction from Him, leading us back to the right-wing.

Had I been wrong in my new revelation about the future? Was the government the evil Antichrist after all? I was more unsure of myself than ever. I really thought I had been on the right track.

Right-wing reports came in immediately that Kahl had killed the North Dakota Marshals only in self-defense. Some reports said that Kahl had been set up, that he didn't really kill the sheriff, but that the FBI had. Supposedly the Arkansas Sheriff was going to blow the whistle on government corruption in his county and he had tried to keep the feds from killing Kahl.

We went to the burned-out house where Kahl was supposed to have been murdered. What were we going to do about this unlawful action of the federal government, the right-wing wanted to know. Although we had never met Gordon Kahl, the new martyr of the patriotic movement was killed in our own backyard, so we were forced to act or lose credibility.

After his death, right-wing publications proclaimed, "At Last! We Have a Hero! Gordon Kahl, the First American Hero of the Second American Revolution!" An *Ode to Gordon Kahl* was published in several neo-Nazi and other right-wing newspapers, calling his death an heroic struggle. A ballad was even recorded about him and distributed to radio stations throughout the Farm Belt.

Some men from the patriotic movement who were involved with Kahl came to visit us and asked James and me exactly what we intended to do. Friends of ours had been indicted and arrested for harboring Kahl. We decided we would devise a plan of action and would let them know of our decision as soon as possible.

Aryan Nations always held their Annual Congress in July of each year. I advised James that if we were going to save face with the right-wing, he should go to Aryan Nations in Idaho, especially since Kahl had been killed in Arkansas. He agreed and took Ollie with him.

While there, a number of the leaders from various factions across the country gathered together to hear Ellison's report about Kahl, what actions should be taken, and about the future direction of the right-wing, since the federal government had obviously declared war on the patriots. James Ellison returned from Idaho with more energy and excitement than I had seen in him in a long, long time. He called for an elders' meeting, to give us a rundown of the events in Idaho.

"Thirteen men from various right-wing organizations met in Idaho," James began. "We discussed Gordon Kahl and I told the leaders that I was sorry I wasn't with Gordon Kahl when the feds found him in Arkansas. I said I wished I'd been there, that the sword is now out of the sheath, and it's ready to strike. I proclaimed that for every one of our people they kill, we ought to kill one hundred of theirs! Plans were discussed about financing the right-wing movement by illegal activities. If the left-wing could do it in the '60s, then the right-wing can do it in the '80s.

"Ideas were discussed such as counterfeiting, robbing armored cars or banks, stealing from stores, or whatever it takes. We also made a 'hit list' of people who need to be eliminated. We discussed targets like David Rockefeller and Morris Dees of Klanwatch. An Aryan 'points list' was designed to give points to those who commit illegal actions, where stealing would be worth a point, killing a nigger might be worth five points, killing a federal agent might be twenty points, killing a Jew might be worth fifty points, and so on. The point system would elevate our aggressive soldiers to positions of power.

"There was also talk about 'Silent Warriors,' those individuals who would go out alone and commit crimes and not tell anyone what they had done. The silent warrior, working alone, would simply bring back any spoils of war, like money, for the cause. He would be anonymous, not wanting personal glory. This would eliminate any chances of a leak if no one knew what the warrior had done. We also spoke about forming cells of warriors, with two to five men, who were to never combine with other cells. These would also bring back spoils of war, but their accomplishments would be recognized.

"At the close of the meeting, I passed a sheet of paper for everyone to sign, which they did. Then I told them that they had just committed conspiracy and treason against the United States of America, that the revolution had begun!"

"What type of actions are we considering?" someone asked Ellison.

"Dumping cyanide into the reservoirs of major cities, killing federal agents, blowing up an ADL building or overpasses in major cities; maybe even blowing up a federal building.

"The code name previously given me by Louis Beam is Warlord. I plan to live up to that name."

It was clear from Ellison's report that the mood of the right-wing had taken a major turn. He wanted this; he needed this. Action, not just talk, was now on the agenda. To aid us in that direction we had an individual more than happy to help us out. Richard Wayne Snell, a fifty-three-year-old messenger between the more radical groups, was ready for action and ready to help us overthrow the United States government.

We had met Snell at the Christian-Patriots Defense League in 1982, when Ellison had his disagreement with John Harrell. Ellison, and later Robert Millar, really liked Snell, seeing him as a God-fearing patriot. I, however, never trusted him. To me he wasn't a spiritual man and his seeking the Lord in our praise meetings was for show only and not sincere. But Snell was available for Ellison's use and use him Ellison did.

Ellison confessed to me during this time that it was his destiny to become famous, to go down in the history books in a major way. He informed me that he didn't care what it took, he would have his place in history. He saw himself as one of the major founding fathers of the Second American Revolution. We were now about to become an aggressive group of right-wing ultra-extremists. Phase three of our five-year transition had begun.

I prepared a four-page declaration of war declaring "War in '84," in which we at CSA stated that for every aggression the government did against the patriotic people of the United States, equal and opposite, if not greater, reaction would occur against the government. The proportional response, it was decided, would be double to seven times. If the government wanted war, war they would get. The document said that "it is inevitable that war is coming to the United States of America . . . It is predestined!" And that we had to meet force with force: "Terror will succeed only until it is met with equal terror!"

The declaration of war was entitled, *ATTACK—Aryan Tactical Treaty for the Advancement of Christ's Kingdom*. We envisioned that 1984 would be the year of the Second American Revolution. "The time has come," I wrote, "for the Spirit of Slumber to be lifted off our people! Arise, O Israel, and Shine, for thy light is come, and the glory of our Father is risen upon thee! We shall Attack and Advance into enemy territory within the next two years. Be prepared!" We then signed the document and circulated copies among the other groups as an example for them to do likewise.

Once the ingredients are mixed and the catalyst is introduced, all logic is forsaken, all emotion detached. The required catalyst must contain heat and time. That is, an emergency and a deadline. With this, the extremist group or individual will cross the line into terrorism. In this catalyst, Gordon Kahl became an emergency, a martyr, a battle cry. It was believed the government had decided to make war against the saints, the "enlightened" Christian-Patriots; therefore a deadline became imminent.

On August 9, 1983, James Ellison and one of our elders, Bill Thomas, poured gasoline through the front door mail slot of a Metropolitan Community Church. It was Springfield, Missouri's only homosexual church. The arson attempt was a dismal failure. No major damage was done other than charring the door.

On August 15, Bill Thomas and three other CSA members bombed the Jewish Community Center in Bloomington, Indiana and caused some damage. Ellison had wanted them to rob a bank, but Thomas and the other men couldn't bring themselves to do so.

During the months of these "road trips," as they were called, others of us shoplifted in various stores wherever we traveled, and would then return the merchandise for cash. It was one way of supporting the group financially. On one of these trips, in Fort Smith, Arkansas, Ellison got caught shoplifting in a grocery store. The management kicked us all out of the store, without calling the police. Ellison laughed about the incident; I was ashamed. I began to realize that it was all a head-trip to Ellison. He simply didn't care what anyone thought anymore.

On November 2, Bill Thomas went with Wayne Snell and Steve Scott, another non-CSA member, and taped a large amount of dynamite to a natural gas pipeline over the Red River, near Fulton, Arkansas, that ran from the Gulf of Mexico to Chicago. It was hoped that by blowing up the gas line, Chicago would be without heat and riots would break out. The dynamite, however, failed to break open the pipeline, only denting it.

Then the next day, the same three men drove to Texarkana. As Thomas sat behind the wheel of their vehicle, Snell and Scott went inside a pawnshop, and bound and gagged the owner. Wayne Snell shot the owner, Bill Stumpp, in the back of the head three times with a .22 caliber pistol which was once registered to Ellison—the silencer was built at CSA. Snell and Scott then robbed the store.

Upon returning to the car, both men bragged to Thomas about what they had done. Thomas, unaware that the men were going to kill someone and believing that only a robbery had been agreed upon, was shaken up. Returning to CSA, Snell handed the stolen merchandise to Ellison: jewelry, guns, and money. Ellison gave me two thousand dollars from the robbery, to pay bills with, and dispersed jewelry to some of the other elders and their wives.

That evening, Bill Thomas came to me, confessing what had occurred, and wept. He wanted out of the nightmare.

Wayne Snell justified the murder by saying that the pawnshop owner was Jewish and deserved it. Ellison, who had authorized the robbery, accepted that. Even murder was easily rationalized now.

Another pawnshop robbery was planned for Springfield, Missouri, but it never occurred. A jewelry heist was planned for Las Vegas, but it, also, never materialized.

But all these "baby" steps were taken until an ultimate goal came to mind. That goal became the bombing of the federal building in Oklahoma City. About mid-November—shortly after our CSA Second National Convocation—Wayne Snell and Steve Scott went to case out the Murrah Federal Building. They discovered that it housed several federal agencies and had minimal security. Snell and Scott asked Ellison to go with them and look at it for himself. Ellison went to Oklahoma City to gauge what it would take to damage or destroy the federal building. Upon his return, he ordered our new munitions man, Kent Yates, to devise a system of rockets that could be launched toward the federal building and would totally destroy it.

"We need something with a large body count to make the government sit up and take notice," Ellison proclaimed. "I want to be able to launch these rockets from a trailer some distance away. And I want the government to know that the right-wing has spoken, that the Second American Revolution has begun."

Kent Yates had only recently moved to CSA from a religious community in Indiana. Like Ellison, Yates also had two wives. Yates, unlike Ellison, had been a Green Beret in Vietnam and had been trained as a weapons, explosives, martial arts and assassination expert. Yates excelled at what he did.

"Are there people in the federal building working there besides feds?" someone asked Ellison.

"Doesn't much matter," Ellison replied. "There are no innocents in war. Those people have chosen to work in a federal building."

"What about children?" someone else asked. "Will there be any children there?"

"The sins of the fathers," Ellison quoted, "are visited upon the children." It was estimated that about five hundred people would probably die in that building—men, women . . . and children.

By the grace of God, in late November or early December, while preparing and testing the rockets to be used to crumble the Murrah Federal Building in Oklahoma City, a rocket exploded in Yates' hands and damaged them. It was interpreted as a sign from God that another plan was to be implemented. Had God not intervened, I believe CSA would have begun its war against the government with an attack on the federal building at that time.

On November 10, during our Second National Convocation (which was publicized as a spiritual and not a racial meeting), Robert Millar and some of the members of his Elohim City group came to visit us.

One of the recognized prophetesses of our church prophesied to James Ellison, "Yea, thus says the Lord unto you, when you were young you girded yourself and did what you willed. But now that you have gained wisdom, I the Lord gird you, and cause you to do what I will. I anoint you a King in Israel," she continued, while girding Ellison with a belt about the waist, "and all the seed that does come forth from you is blessed for me among my people. And the revelation and wisdom that I have given you is true, says the Lord."

The young prophetess then poured an entire bottle of anointing oil over James' head, signifying that, like King David, his cup had run over, that God's Spirit was upon Ellison without measure.

Then one of the women from Elohim City rubbed her hands in the oil that had spilled onto the floor from James' head and proceeded to rub the oil all over my head. It appeared that Ellison was now being recognized as a king in God's future kingdom and that I was his prince, to govern a territory as "King James" would.

Robert Millar then stood by Ellison and prophesied, "You have not feared the face of man. Neither have you feared physical pain in your mortal body. But you have feared greatly, fearing lest you should miss the Word of the Lord your God. And you do well, my son, you do very well. You will not fail, neither suffer defeat. I am directing your footsteps aright. You shall walk as you have not walked. You shall go where you have not gone. You shall perform what you have not performed. You shall be what you have not been. But fear not, for I am with you."

It seemed to us that God was saying that we had been going in the right direction, but that now it was time for events to occur even more quickly, perhaps that James would now be recognized amongst the leaders of the movement, many of whom were also at the meeting that night.

Then the young prophetess that initially prayed over James approached Kent Yates. The prophesy to Yates said, "If you heed this word this night, says the Lord, to follow James Ellison, I shall give you an anointing that others have turned down, that have left here." Now Ellison officially had a replacement for Randall Rader, a new military commander for his army.

"The Lord does also bring a further word unto this people," Millar then prophesied, "that dwells in this place at this time. For I have determined that I shall change your circumstances. You have suffered; you have done well; you have been willing to do without. I declare unto you, I am He that Provides. You shall see that a load has been lifted from him that I have placed over you. I will supply for each of you abundantly. You shall have abundance every one of you to give to him that lacks. This day shall you mark it upon your wall that your Father has spoken." If this word were true, I reasoned, then a lot of money should come our way, because we had surely suffered in the past, and had sacrificed a lot. The idea of more money coming in sounded good to me. A kingdom, in order to flourish, must have money.

Then Kent bowed before James, and the other men did likewise. The women bowed to Ollie. Millar then told Ellison to stand up and for his men to kiss James' right hand, which everyone did. The men put their right hands into the oil that had spilled over Ellison onto the floor. This signified a bonding to Ellison and to the anointing God had given him. We believed we would partake of his spirit and of his anointing.

Robert Millar addressed the people of CSA, "As Robert of Oklahoma, I speak before the heavens and before men, that I shall not hinder, neither shall I prevent, nor betray this one that is appointed; but I shall walk in friendship and in support, before God and before the men of this place."

Then Millar motioned Ellison to stand and to turn to the people. He then announced, "Ladies and gentlemen, I present him perfect before God through Jesus Christ."

With that the whole congregation shouted, "Amen!"

And James Ellison stood proudly as the newly anointed "King James of the Ozarks."

King James of the Ozarks. No one boasted of that more than Ellison himself. True anointing is supposed to be a humbling experience. True prophecy is supposed to glorify God. Now Millar and Ellison were either religious zealots caught up in vain self-deception or they were knowingly collaborating together for the furtherance of their own kingdoms regardless of all other considerations. I, however, continued to push my doubts and questions to the back of my mind. To what extent this was due to my own pride and hunger for recognition I cannot say.

The kerosene lamps barely lit the darkened room as I sat around the table with Ellison, Thomas, Snell and two of our men, Miller and McGuire. Even the atmosphere we created seemed to accentuate the significance of what we were doing.

"So it's agreed, then?" Ellison asked. "Tomorrow, December 26, the war begins. Let's go over the plan one more time. Kerry, Bill and I will be in Sulphur Springs, meeting with Robert Millar and making ourselves plainly visible, in order to establish alibis. Meanwhile, Wayne, you and the others will go on to Fort Smith, where the three of you will go to the homes of Judge Waters, Asa Hutchinson, and Jack Knox and assassinate them, as retribution for Gordon Kahl and for our friends in Cotter that have been arrested."

Waters was the federal judge in western Arkansas; Hutchinson, the federal prosecutor; Knox, the FBI agent in charge of arresting our friends. We had obtained their addresses months before by going through court records. Over time our men had sometimes followed them and had eventually stalked their houses, making plans for the day of judgment.

"David," Ellison continued, "will stand guard, watching for unwanted traffic, while Wayne and Lambert go to the front door of each house. There, you'll ring the doorbell. If the target-to-be-assassinated answers the door, you'll shoot him with the silenced weapons that you'll carry and then leave. If, however, someone else answers the door, then you'll kill that individual, go into the house and assassinate everyone in the home—every man, woman, and child."

It had been decided that God wanted us to pick a target that was more personal than the federal building in Oklahoma City. The assassination of a federal judge, prosecutor and law-enforcement agent would, in our opinion, send a clear message across the nation and directly to the federal authorities.

The day after Christmas was picked as an additional shock factor. I had called two leaders of the right-wing movement—Richard Butler of the Aryan Nations in Idaho and Robert Miles of the Mountain Kirk in Michigan—to let them know of our plan. They gave us their blessings and support for our willingness to lead the fight against ZOG.

"Let's load up the van and the second car tonight with the weapons," Ellison finished, "so we can leave bright and early in the morning."

We loaded the vehicles with rifles, pistols, explosives, handgrenades, ammunition and other military supplies. I gazed upon the stars. It was a clear, cold December night, nervous anticipation hovering in the air.

I felt drained, almost as if hypnotized. I dreaded what we were doing, but if it were what God wanted, how could I argue against it? My inner confidence was disintegrating. I was scared, but couldn't let James or the others know it. God, I thought, what are we doing?

The next morning we arose to find snow on the ground—a lot of snow. There had been no mention of snow in the forecast.

Ellison, Thomas, and I now felt uneasy about the plot. Why the snow? Was God trying to tell us something? But the other three wanted to go on, so we did. Ellison, Thomas and I went in the van, with Miller driving. Snell and McGuire went in the car behind us. Once we arrived at our alibi location, Miller would then go on with the other vehicle, while we stayed in town. That evening we would regather at CSA.

Before we left the farm, Ellison prayed for direction and protection from God. He asked that if this were indeed God's will, that God would cause everything to go as planned and no one would get caught. And if it was not what God wanted, then to reveal it to us before arriving at our destination.

Ellison and I sat behind Miller and Thomas as Miller drove through the snow on the winding Arkansas highways. Miller, I knew, was an experienced driver, and was being cautious in the snow, but I sensed that he was anxious to get to our destination, and it seemed like he was driving just a little too fast. I said something to Ellison about this when we were about halfway there. Ellison spoke to Miller about the driving conditions, suggesting that he slow down, but Miller said he had it all under control.

Within a few minutes, we were turning right around a curve, when suddenly an oncoming pickup appeared partly in our lane, and we hit them almost head-on. The collision totaled the front of our van, steam bellowing from the radiator.

Ellison and I looked at each other in acknowledgment: God obviously does not want us to complete this mission.

I went to check on the elderly couple that had run into us. Snell drove to the other side of the van, out of sight of the couple, while the men loaded the weaponry into the small Mazda car.

Later, as someone drove past us, we stopped them and asked them to call the highway patrol and report the accident. While Miller and I stayed with the wrecked van, the others went to town so as to not be connected with the scene. To make matters worse, our van was a stolen van, and we were afraid the officers might run the vehicle identification number through the computer. We weren't sure how we'd address that situation.

The two officers arrived, took reports from the four of us, called a wrecker for each of us, and left. They never even looked at the VIN. Later, the four other men returned and picked Miller and me up at the wrecker driver's garage.

"Are we going on to do the job now?" Miller asked.

"No," Ellison replied. "It would seem God doesn't want us to do this. Thomas and I wholeheartedly agreed. Snell and Miller tried to talk Ellison into going on with the mission. Ellison wouldn't listen to them. The two men were angry and disappointed. I was relieved.

In March of 1984, Kay called me from town one morning. She had been grocery shopping and had our son, Jared, with her. She was scared. "He's turning blue," she said, "and having trouble breathing. That infection in his throat has swollen. What do I do?"

"Take him to the hospital in Mountain Home," I told her, "and call me as soon as you know something."

Kay called a short time later to tell me that the local hospital couldn't do anything and they were on their way to the hospital in Harrison. I took one of the vehicles and went to meet her.

Before I left, Ollie hugged me and said, "Don't end up like Randall," a reference to Rader's turning bitter after his daughter died.

I smiled and returned the hug. "Don't worry; I won't. Whatever God does, He does."

When I got to the hospital, Jared was on the respirator. With tubes in his throat, he was crying out, but no sounds came. My heart ached for him because I knew he didn't understand what was happening, and couldn't say anything. I identified with that feeling.

Jared couldn't breathe on his own. The infection in his throat, caused by a lingering cold, had spread and was hindering the air flow through his windpipe. The doctor told Kay that if she had been thirty minutes later, Jared would have been dead.

The hospital at Harrison was also unable to do anything more for Jared and prepared to take him to the Children's Hospital in Little Rock. We followed the ambulance there.

The doctors at the Children's Hospital operated on Jared and told us it was the largest pus-pocket they had ever seen in a child. He survived, leaving only a three-inch scar on his throat.

While Jared was in the hospital, two events struck me. While there, Kay and I needed a place to stay and we could not depend on much money from the farm. The hospital recommended the Ronald McDonald House, where we could get a room for five dollars a day. The compassion at the House was overwhelming and made me realize again that there were good people and good organizations in the world. Secondly, Jared turned one year old in the hospital. For his first birthday, the floor nurses threw him a little party and gave him some gifts. Their compassion and kindness moved me and caused me to not be so critical of doctors, nurses and hospitals.

Although Jared could have died, I never believed he would. When we dedicated him when he was eight days old, I received a prophecy that stated, "The Lord says unto you, surely this child shall be a blessing unto you. I shall bless him and anoint him and he shall be a blessing unto me. See that you teach him my truth, that your hand might be upon him for correction for good. Surely, if you will cause him to fear my name, I shall bless you and bless him, says the Lord."

This was the first and only time one of my children had been mentioned in a prophecy. If the word were true, then I had to believe that nothing serious would happen to Jared. If he died, the prophecy would be of no effect. That was not a possibility to me.

Meanwhile, the "road-trips" continued, but, once again, we gave a cold shoulder to the right-wing, and they gave one to us, once they discovered we hadn't completed the assassination plot.

Bill Thomas felt continued pressure from James Ellison. Ellison had told Bill for several months, "God has shown me in a vision that you are to carry the sword of war for our group. You are to be the leader of these road trips."

Bill didn't necessarily agree with that vision; he just wanted to work the farmland that we had. He felt torn and divided over his allegiance to Ellison and the dreams in his own heart. Bill Thomas was a good-natured, kind man, like a big teddy bear. I could see the battle within him; I knew how he felt.

Early on the morning of April 1, 1984, I received a phone call over the military fieldphone that was now in my house.

"Bill's been arrested."

"Yeah, yeah, I know," I laughed, "April Fool's Day."

"No, seriously, he called this morning. He got arrested in Missouri with Eric and Henry."

"For what?" I asked.

"For stealing a flatbed trailer."

I groaned. "What were they stealing a trailer for?"

"Wait, it gets worse. The cops discovered a machine gun and silencer in the pickup when they searched it."

"I'll be right up there. Meet me at James'."

Bill called back that Monday afternoon. He told me as much as he could over the phone. The three of them had gone the day before to Missouri, to a business where trailers were sold and rented. Bill needed one for the farm. Ellison had advised them not to go, but Bill went anyway. It turned out that the owner of the trailer later saw our men pulling his trailer down the highway. He checked his lot, then called the cops.

I told Bill I would come up and see what I could do. Being the group's paralegal—or "barrister," as it was called—I immediately checked the Missouri Statute books that we owned, to verify the charges. We had bought the Missouri books, as well as a set of Arkansas Statute books, two years before, once it appeared we needed to understand more about the laws of the states we lived and operated in. I then checked the Federal Rules of Criminal Procedure, which we also owned.

I drove to Missouri and visited Bill and the others. They were considered flight risks and were denied bail. The charges were serious, and the local authorities were scared that CSA might cause trouble. Upon returning to Arkansas, I conferred with Ellison.

"It's serious. They caught them red-handed with the trailer, a trailer that had a rental sticker on it. They've got the automatic machine pistol and the silencer."

"Why did Bill have those on him?" James asked.

What a stupid question, I thought. "James, you've taught everyone to be prepared. You take illegal weapons with you all the time. So that's what they did."

"Well, I told him not to go on that trip anyway."

"That doesn't matter now. Now we have to decide how best to help the guys out."

"They should've shot it out with the troopers that pulled them over," James replied. "Maybe then the war would've started."

"Over a trailer? Yeah, right." I answered sarcastically. "James, Bill's scared. And Eric and Henry are looking to Bill for answers. What do you want them to do?"

"When Bill calls, tell him that they're to keep their boots on."

"What? What does that mean?"

"It means we'll break them out of jail. Bill will know what it means."

"You're crazy!" I exclaimed. "You can't break them out of jail. They got extra guards up there because they're scared of us. They got cops with scoped rifles, walking the jail roof. You can't break them out!"

"I won't leave my men to rot in jail! Now tell Bill what I told you!" Ellison ordered.

I did as I was told, but I knew nothing would happen. Bill and the other two men did as they were told. They kept their boots on all the time, waiting for us to break them out of jail. Every time I spoke to Bill, or saw him in person, he asked when we were coming. I had no answer for him.

Bill called one day to tell us that the federal government had offered him a plea bargain. If he would plead guilty to all three charges, then he'd be given a five-year sentence, to run concurrent, and would probably be out in twenty months. I advised Ellison for Bill to take the plea bargain; Ellison told him not to take it.

"James, he's got to take it!" I implored.

"No! He's going to go to trial and he'll be found not guilty. I've told Bill to make up a story about the trailer, that he bought it from some black man. And that he didn't know the machine gun and silencer were under the seat in the truck, because it wasn't his truck."

"No one will buy those stories," I argued. "He's got no receipt showing he bought the trailer, and his fingerprints are probably on the weapon. James, Bill's facing five years of state time and up to twenty years federal time. Even if they run the two federal charges concurrent with the state time, Bill could be forced to do the state time first and then start doing the federal time. He could do up to twelve years in prison that way!"

"Quit trying to take the easy way out!" Ellison screamed. "Stand up to the federal government! You're as smart as any lawyer. Go in there and defend our men!"

"James, I'm no attorney! The courts won't let me defend them."

"File a motion that it's Bill's constitutional right to have whoever he wants to defend him. The courts have to let you do it."

I pleaded with Bill to take the plea bargain; the other men would probably get probation if he told the court it was all his idea. But Bill obeyed Ellison.

The court would only allow me to sit at Bill's table during the trial with his court-appointed attorney. I could offer advice to Bill or his attorney, but I wasn't allowed to question anyone or to speak up and object to anything. Only the attorney could do that. I had Bill fire his first attorney and the court appointed him another one.

The judge told Bill that he was being ill-advised from outside sources. I knew the judge meant me. I, of course, agreed with the judge—Bill was being ill-advised. Not by me, but by James Ellison, "King of the Ozarks," who would rather see his men do more time than to compromise his personal beliefs.

As I expected, the jury found the three men guilty. The judge reluctantly sentenced them. He gave Eric a two-year prison sentence, to be served in state prison. Henry received five years' probation, on the condition that he leave CSA and move back to Indiana to his parents' home.

The judge told Bill that he should have taken the plea bargain. He said that the trailer was nothing to go to trial over, and gave Bill three years for that. He said he could even dismiss the machine gun as nothing, because he himself liked guns and could see no harm in a fully automatic one. But the silencer, as far as the judge was concerned, was for one thing: killing someone quietly. And for that the judge sentenced Bill to ten years in prison, to be served concurrently with the other sentences. Chances were Bill Thomas would spend six years in prison instead of twenty months.

It made me sick and angry. I knew Ellison would not bust Bill and the two men out of jail. I knew Bill should have accepted the plea bargain. The experience broke him. Bill Thomas was one of my best friends. We had grown in the Lord together, travailed together, traveled to gun shows together, appeared on live television together. I knew his heart, his desires. I knew it killed him to obey Ellison, to trust in him to rescue the men out of prison. I understood the doubts, the confusion, and the disappointment.

I felt like I had betrayed Bill somehow, that I had let him down. Maybe I could have argued with James more. But my loyalty was still to Ellison, so I kept my mouth shut as much as possible. I was still trying to earn a place in the kingdom. With Bill gone, I felt I had to do something. But life was complicated for me at that time.

In February of 1984, I had approached one of our young, single women to see if she felt any inclination to being my second wife. She said that she would be open to the situation. That evening I told my wife that I believed God might want me to take this woman as my second wife. It would have been much more merciful to have driven a knife through my wife's heart.

Kay had been dreading this possibility for a long time. Through her tears, however, she said, "If that's what God wants, then I'll support you." Then with the stoic humility that had always spoken well of her, she looked at me, and said, "Even if you sleep with her six nights a week after you marry, and with me only one night a week, I'd rather have you for one night than not at all." God knew and I knew that I didn't deserve Kay. But I went on anyway.

I informed James and Ollie of my desire. James said I had no idea what I was getting into. I agreed, but said I really believed it was what God wanted. Ollie's heart went out to Kay. I continued to court the young woman and we made plans to marry in May. Meanwhile, we closed the health food store. James was tired of it and really never supported the idea anyway.

I deeply loved Kay but had never really felt like we communicated spiritually. The other woman, on the other hand, knew the Scriptures and could talk about spiritual matters. But two days before we were to wed, the woman called off the wedding. It tore me up inside, devastating me. I did everything possible to talk her into marrying me.

James said he believed God didn't want me to have a second wife and to let it go.

I decided to leave the farm for a while. I told Kay I didn't know when I would be back. I left and spent the night in an abandoned house near the farm. While there, crying to the Lord, I begged God to justify me as His son, as one of His anointed ones, and to make the woman marry me.

An inner voice spoke to me clearly, sternly, saying, "You are not doing what you are supposed to be doing. I have taught you since you were a child," the Lord continued, "to be a certain way, to act a certain way, yet now you are trying to be what you are not, doing what you are not to do. Quit this vanity and be what I have created you to be. Do what you know you are supposed to do."

With that, the presence of the Lord left me and I sobbed, the pain causing me to have trouble breathing. I left the house, sneaked back to the farm, asked Ollie to shave my head for me, and then went to the praise meeting that was already in progress. I openly repented of my actions for the last several weeks and asked forgiveness.

Upon my repenting, a prophecy was given me that said, "My son, think not to yourself that you have failed me, but consider that the renting of the flesh is a painful thing. You shall go on, to fulfill that which I have set for you. Wait in patience. I have called you where I have set you, and I humble you. Walk in humility and strive not, neither struggle nor fret, and I will grant unto you the desires of your heart, because surely you have desired in your heart to serve me, says the Lord."

I knew I had been striving and struggling, trying to be what I thought Ellison wanted me to be, trying to establish myself a place in the kingdom of God. But I foolishly interpreted the prophecy to say that if I just rested in God, then He would cause the other woman to marry me.

Before the young woman had called off the wedding, Kay had given me permission to go unto her if I needed to, to have sex with her. I slept with the young woman one time. After she had called off the wedding, I deeply regretted having slept with her. It had been the only time in my life I had laid with any woman other than Kay.

My "second wife experience" brought the most shame into my life that I had ever experienced. It left me feeling worthless. For the first time in my life, I sincerely doubted my relationship with God. Where once I could be proud that I had only been with one woman—Kay—I knew I had betrayed that relationship. And where I once stood proudly as James Ellison's staunch supporter and defender, I had broken that relationship also. I had betrayed my wife, I had betrayed myself, I had betrayed James Ellison, and I had betrayed God. I had never felt so dirty, so alone, so confused, and so exhausted as I did by the summer of 1984.

To a religious man, nothing is worse than betrayal. Ironically, the shame brought upon me by these betrayals far outweighed any shames my criminal activity should have brought upon me. Bombing and assassination plots, knowledge of murder, statewide shoplifting, racism, stealing, fraud, and hate crimes were nothing to me compared to feeling that I had let people down.

In the latter part of June, trying desperately to win back James' favor, I approached Ellison with an idea.

"Do you really want the war to begin?" I asked Ellison.

"You know I do," he answered.

"Then let me ask you a question. How does God feel about it when a black man dies?"

"About like He does," James responded, "when a dog dies."

"All right, then have Kent make me a briefcase with C-4 explosives and dynamite in it, that I can detonate from outside the case. I'll take the bomb to Kansas City and will blow up an adult bookstore. I'll also take the .22 pistol with the silencer on it and will go to the queer park in Kansas City, and will kill some queers and niggers during the night." My desperation to earn a place in Ellison's kingdom now outweighed any value for human life.

Ellison loved the idea. He told Yates to do as I had requested. Yates was a genius at his work. I once saw him shoot a .45 caliber MAC pistol, attached with a silencer that he had made. The weapon made absolutely no noise when he shot it, except for the bolt opening and closing to expel the spent cartridge. I looked at him in awe.

"I'm working on fixing that, too," he responded, almost apologetic, "so the bolt will be silent also."

I laughed.

A federal government ATF agent, during Kent's trial the following year, testified that Kent Yates made better silencers than the government did.

Yates gave me the briefcase bomb. "Once you set the timer," he instructed me, "you got about three minutes before it goes off. Get away as quickly as possible, 'cause it'll level the entire building."

I drove to Kansas City with one of our other men on a Saturday afternoon, arriving there after dark. We circled the park known for being a hang-out for homosexuals. I had the pistol in hand, but couldn't find anyone walking in the park.

We then made our way to an adult bookstore, complete with video arcades of X-rated films, and I went inside with the briefcase. I had decided on an adult bookstore after remembering watching Ellison urinate once on some adult magazines while in a store. I figured I would take the briefcase to one of the back arcade booths, arm it, and leave. The operator of the bookstore, however, said I couldn't take the briefcase in, that I would have to leave it with him. I knew it would look suspicious leaving the case with him, even if I could manage to set the timer first without him seeing that, then trying to leave without it, so I left the bookstore with the bomb in hand.

The next morning, Sunday morning, the two of us discovered a Metropolitan Community Church in Kansas City—a gay church— and went in with the briefcase. The usher welcomed us in and we sat in one of the pews. I watched men hugging and kissing men, and women hugging and kissing women. I watched as the pastor of the church talked about his lover, the music director. And I prepared to set the timer.

It would have been, up till then, the largest domestic terrorist act in the history of our country, an act that would have ended the lives of over fifty to sixty people. I hesitated long enough to think and made "mistakes" that are to never be made in time of war.

I began to put a human face on the enemy. All I could envision was torn bodies, limbs ripped from torsos. I thought of bodies that might become unidentifiable, of people who had never personally done anything to me or to the people at CSA. I thought of these peoples' relatives and friends who would grieve for them, of the homes nearby that would be damaged and of those unknowing, innocent individuals living inside those homes who might be killed also.

Next, I tried to imagine how this one lone incident would start a revolution—and knew that it could not. The only thing it would accomplish was a large body count, some satisfaction for James Ellison, and my possibly spending the rest of my life in prison, being on death row, or dying in a shoot-out—none of which appealed to me. The consequences for my actions would be too costly.

The final step, though—my slap-in-the-face for the reality I was in—was when the congregation began to sing. I realized quickly that these were the same songs I grew up with and I watched these gays and lesbians reaching out to God as we did at the farm, as I did myself, trying to find their place in God. *How were they any different from me?* I began to realize. The Scripture that came to mind was, "Draw near to God and He will draw near to you." No exceptions; no qualifications. I knew at that moment that if I were to kill these men and women, I would be killing Christians. I could not justify that in my mind.

I thought about these things and much more as I turned to my partner in crime and said, "Let's go. We're through here," as I rose with briefcase in hand.

We arrived back at the farm that afternoon. Ellison was sitting in front of the television, waiting for the news about an explosion in Kansas City. He saw me walk in.

"What happened?" he asked.

I told him everything.

"What do you mean you couldn't do it?"

He was clearly disappointed in me.

By now, I desperately wanted to leave the farm. Ellison had begun letting people move to CSA that we wouldn't have let in years earlier.

Where cigarette smoking had once never been allowed, butts littered the grounds. Where beer drinking had previously not been tolerated, bottles cluttered the trash cans. Where years before a single cuss word was never uttered, foul language flowed steadily. Where once praise meetings were frequent and all were anxious to attend, we seldom had meetings and I wasn't teaching Bible studies any longer. Ellison was no longer looking for spiritual leaders. Now, he just wanted to build an army.

The core men who had been there for years rebelled against Ellison by growing our beards again. If he were going to lower the standard, then we would manifest our dissatisfaction to him also.

Every time I asked the Lord if I could leave—and I pleaded often— He would answer, "No, not yet. You have to stay a little longer." No explanation as to why I had to stay.

Since I had to continue living there and since I didn't care what the right-wing or even Ellison thought of me anymore, I was determined to get things back to what they used to be. I wanted CSA to die and for Zarephath-Horeb to be reborn.

One day I asked Ellison if I could build a playground for the children. I considered it a simple request. He didn't.

"Why do you want this?" he asked.

"I think the children would appreciate it," I answered.

"That's not the real reason and you know it." Ellison's voice was getting louder. "You're wanting to be 'normal.' When are you going to realize that there's no such thing as normal for us. That which is highly esteemed among men is abomination to the Lord. Quit trying to be like the world!"

"I'm not trying to be like the world!" I screamed. "Yeah, I want a little normalcy. Is that a sin? I want our children, I want all of us, to enjoy life. Is that so bad?"

"This ain't life," Ellison replied. "This world ain't life. Life is what we're trying to bring to the world. Let go of these fruitless desires of yours. Just let them go."

He didn't understand what I wanted. He didn't see what I was seeing. I built the playground, though, in spite of Ellison's objections. I needed something to give me hope for the future.

On June 30, 1984, Richard Wayne Snell was driving home to southeastern Oklahoma with a van full of illegal weapons and hand-grenades. Ellison told Snell it was foolish carrying so much weaponry, that it would be bad if he was pulled over for some traffic violation. Snell wouldn't listen.

Near DeQueen, Arkansas, Wayne Snell saw the red lights of an Arkansas State trooper behind him, wanting Snell to pull over. When the black officer Louis Bryant routinely approached the driver's door, in full daylight and with traffic passing them, Snell rolled out and shot the officer twice with a .45 caliber pistol that he stole from the pawnshop robbery. As the officer slumped to the pavement, Snell casually drove away. Louis Bryant lay dead in his own blood. Bryant's wife, on her way with their children to have lunch with him, discovered his dead body just a few minutes later.

A trucker witnessed the incident and radioed in a report. A roadblock was set up almost immediately near Broken Bow, Oklahoma, waiting for Snell.

When Wayne Snell saw the roadblock, he stopped his van, stepped out, and pulled his weapon on the dozens of police officers waiting for him. He then began shooting at them. The officers returned fire and Snell was shot seven times.

He should have died, but didn't. The police rushed Snell to the hospital, where Snell's heart stopped twice, but was revived each time. Snell later confessed at his trial to shooting the trooper, but claimed it was in self-defense, that the trooper had threatened him several times in the past. Snell was found guilty of murder and sentenced to life in prison without parole.

Some of the weapons in Snell's van were tied to CSA and James Ellison. The pressure was again mounting.

In July of 1984, Robert Miles visited us and informed Ellison that we were soon to receive a large amount of counterfeit money. We never received it.

Later that month, Kent Yates was arrested on the way to Mountain Home on a warrant out of New Mexico for a federal weapons violation from a time before he had moved to our farm. Ellison was with Yates at the time, but the agents let Ellison go. Years later, when I met one of the arresting officers, I was enlightened about that day.

"Yates had cold eyes," the agent told me. "He's the type of guy that could be eating breakfast with you, and then, without blinking, pull his knife, reach over and slit your throat, and then resume eating. But when we told Ellison to lie down on the ground, he was shaking so bad I thought he was going to pee in his pants. I never knew what you guys saw in him."

I had to agree.

Randall Rader, Bill Thomas, Wayne Snell, Kent Yates. All the king's mighty men were gone.

By now my family had lived at Ellison's castle longer than anyone other than the king's family. The military was vanity to me; I no longer saw any judgments of God as imminent. I no longer cared. I was too exhausted to care. George Orwell was right. 1984 was turning out to be one hell of a year.

That year, Governor Bill Clinton of Arkansas wanted to make available to all law-enforcement officials a list of suspected or known members of any paramilitary or white supremacist organizations in Arkansas. Arkansas was also considering passage of an ADL-formulated anti-paramilitary law. We considered both these actions in violation of our civil rights as Americans and I wrote Clinton asking for a meeting with him to discuss this.

An aide to Governor Clinton contacted me. We agreed to meet on July 25, my thirty-second birthday, at the State Police Headquarters in Harrison, Arkansas to discuss the matter. The meeting went as expected, with me sharing my concerns and the aide politely listening. He suggested I write my concerns in a letter to Governor Clinton, which I did. I never received a response.

The anti-paramilitary provision was signed into law by Governor Bill Clinton on April 15, 1985, four days before the federal government was to begin its siege on CSA.

The only bright spot in 1984 was the August birth of our sixth and last child, Honor Davaar, a daughter. I had been expecting a son during Kay's final pregnancy. With three daughters and only two sons, I wanted a balance. When our new daughter was born, I was temporarily disappointed. I really believed a son would be born to us.

While searching for a name, I felt that the Lord disapproved of my attitude toward this newest member of our family. My family crest is the falcon, so I looked up Hebrew words associated with the falcon. "D'va'ar" was the closest I could come to, and it meant "Falconer." So I transliterated it to Davaar. I felt the Lord seemed to say that my little daughter would be an honor to me if I simply accepted her as such—that honor was not just for men. So I called her Honor Davaar, the Honorable Falconer.

Davaar seemed a tie-in somehow to Tara, names of natural meanings, rather than spiritual, and I wondered if Davaar would be the last child we would have. The circle seemed complete; my quiver was full.

Could this mean my time at CSA was nearing completion also?

Because of financial losses from the timber market shutting down and our not finding enough work in which to make money, we had been unable to make bank payments on our property since the middle of 1983, shortly before our illegal right-wing activities began. Ellison didn't care about the payments.

"The land is mine," he said, "and no one is going to take it from us."

On December 20, 1983, the bank foreclosed. The property was auctioned off for $51,000 to Campus Crusade for Christ. An eviction hearing was held on August 23, 1984, and we were ordered by the judge to be off the property within ten days.

Ten days! That was unheard of. Even the statute books stated that we were to have ninety days. But the judge ordered the sheriff to remove us if we were not gone in ten days. He was obviously tired of hearing about CSA and wanted us out. Only if we came up with $75,000 within ten days could we stay.

We refused to move. The media gathered again and wanted to know what we were going to do.

"We've put years of our lives into this property," I told the media at a news conference I had called in Mountain Home. "We bought this property in 1978 for $70,000. At that time it had one house, an old barn, and some torn-down fences. The land hadn't been worked in over twenty years. During the next four-and-a-half years, we built all the fences that are now there. We built three stock tanks, put in three new wells, built seventeen houses and brought in four mobile homes. We've built a new church building with a school house above it, an office building, and a communications building. We've spent thousands of dollars in material and have increased the value of the property to about a quarter of a million dollars.

"By state law, the judge had to order an appraisal of the property value before it could be sold off, and the property had to sell for at least seventy percent of that. Then anything left over, after paying off the bank, would be ours. The judge didn't order the appraisal. Therefore, in our opinion, he broke the law, which invalidates the court order.

"In addition to the work and material we've put into those 224 acres, we've had over two hundred people living with us over the years. We've helped people get off of drugs; we've kept broken marriages together; we've cared for people that no one else wanted. We also worked for free for a lot of the area people, trying to give something back to this community. But the judge wants us to leave town. Now, we get along real well with the county sheriff, but I'm telling you this, we will not be forced off our property by any one. We do not want a confrontation with law-enforcement officials, let me make that clear right now. But we will not be illegally thrown off our property, either.

"Our men are on full alert, dressed in military camouflage and armed to defend our property. We will not leave. We are believing in a miracle from God that will allow us to peacefully remain on our property. In addition to staying, we have decided to form an organization called COPS—Citizens Opposed to a Police State. We believe the law-enforcement officials of this state and of this nation have gotten out of control. As many of you know I recently had a meeting with an aide from Governor Clinton's office about the Jewish Anti-Defamation League's anti-paramilitary law the state is trying to pass. The meeting was uneventful as I suspected it would be. The patriotic people of this great nation of ours are tired of being expected to obey laws they didn't create, when the government won't live up to its own standards. We have been swallowed up with regulations, forms and laws, all spewed upon us by an ever-pregnant bureaucracy. The police expect the citizens to know every law on the books but if you want to see their manual that tells how they are to treat the public, you're not allowed to see it.

"No longer! Our new organization, COPS, will monitor police harassment reports, study police procedures toward citizens, mediate police-citizen disputes, as well as monitor and lobby pending legislation. In a word, ladies and gentlemen, we put the police and judicial arms of the law on notice that, as soon as this land -dispute gets finalized, COPS will be watching them!"

I left the press conference angry.

The news media across Arkansas and Missouri proclaimed our message. The sheriff was not having a good day.

What I didn't mention at the press conference was that I was also making plans to sue the state of Arkansas in federal court over the issue of Separation of Church and State. The State Police and several county sheriffs' departments used the six-pointed star (the Jewish Star of David) as a symbol on their vehicles. If local governments weren't allowed to set up Nativity scenes or Christian crosses at courthouses during certain holidays, I saw no reason for a symbol that represented a foreign country, the Jewish religion, and the witchcraft religion to be continually used on government vehicles. I was hoping to bring the American Civil Liberties Union as an ally in this, pitting (what we considered) one leftist organization against another leftist organization, the Jewish Anti-Defamation League.

During this time period, we met Jim Wickstrom of the Posse Comitatus, who told us how to file motions in our county seat to stop the foreclosure proceedings. These motions were based upon Common Law, as the Founding Fathers had, and not on Equity Law, as the court systems currently had.

Wickstrom said we needed to rescind our driver's licenses, marriage licenses, hunting licenses—any licenses that the state had issued any of our people—and even birth certificates. We were also to write the IRS, rescinding our social security numbers. Doing this, he said, would be declaring ourselves as "sovereign citizens" and we could proclaim the property as ours under Common Law, rendering the judicial courts without jurisdiction in our case.

"If any clerk refuses to file your motions," Wickstrom advised, "add them to the law suit against the bank and the court. They cannot prevent you from being a sovereign citizen. If they continue to refuse you, have the Posse arrest them if the Sheriff won't."

We tried to file the Common Law motions as Wickstrom suggested; the courts threw out our motions after only one hearing. We never took further steps to being "sovereign citizens."

We were to be forcibly taken off the property on September 2, 1984, the eleventh anniversary of my marriage to Kay. In the last twelve hours before the sheriff was to arrive, a man we had met in 1980 telephoned us.

"Have you got the money, yet?" he asked Ellison.

"No."

"How much do you gotta have?"

"Seventy-five thousand dollars by tomorrow."

"All right, tell the authorities you'll have the money tomorrow. I'll loan you the money, interest free, if you sign the property over to me as collateral. Okay?"

"What's the catch?" James asked.

"No catch. You can continue living there, doing as you're doing. When you pay me back, I'll sign the deed back to you. Deal?"

"Deal."

The man on the phone, Jack Fredericks, had been in the Identity movement for a long time. I had been to his home a few times in the past and liked him. He had been instrumental in my earlier interest in herbs and health food. The money—his wife's family inheritance—was a nest egg for him and his wife, Sybil. Jack really liked us and didn't want to see anyone die over a piece of property.

A miracle had occurred. Everyone was astounded. The sheriff was elated. War had been averted.

We agreed to meet in Yellville, Arkansas the next day to sign the papers. Jack asked Ellison, "You will repay me, right? You can make monthly payments to me?"

Ellison looked at me. "We can probably afford to pay you five hundred dollars a month for now, and should be able to increase that later on. Don't you think so, Kerry?"

"Yes, Sir, I'd say so," I responded. I knew that look in Ellison's eyes. He had no intention of ever repaying Fredericks.

Suddenly, while at the attorney's office, one of our men ran in, shouting, "Cops! Everywhere! Get out of here, James!"

Ellison ran around the building after spotting several agents with what appeared to be fully automatic assault weapons.

"Halt!" one of them yelled. "Federal Marshals! We have a warrant for your arrest!"

Ellison dove into the nearby woods before anyone could catch him. Several agents tried to follow but lost him in the woods. They were ordered back for safety reasons. Ellison was armed.

"What's going on here?" I demanded.

"Who are you?" one of them asked.

He was interrupted by a man I had met at the press conference, Gene Irby. "Kerry, it's a misdemeanor bench warrant for contempt of court, because James didn't answer the subpoena to appear before the Grand Jury in Muskogee, Oklahoma."

"I wrote the prosecutor in Oklahoma," I explained, "asking for a delay in James' appearance. I informed him what was going on with our property and that James couldn't come yet. I asked him to give us a few days. When I didn't hear from him, James and I assumed we had been given the time. Are you trying to tell me," I demanded, "that federal Marshals are here to arrest James on a misdemeanor charge, with automatic weapons, like he's killed someone? Are they crazy? They're going to cause somebody to get hurt or killed if they're not careful."

Bill Buford, an agent with the Bureau of Alcohol, Tobacco, and Firearms, joined Irby and me. Buford was a big man, serious about his job. A former member of the 5th Special Forces in Vietnam, Buford still looked like a trained soldier, one that no sensible person would want to mess with.

Bill Buford had come to our compound a few days earlier with Irby and ATF agent Doyne Branch, in order to serve the Grand Jury subpoena to Ellison. Ellison wouldn't let Buford in unless he left his gun at the gate with Irby and allowed me to frisk him. Buford reluctantly did so. I was uncomfortable patting Buford down.

As Buford walked to Ellison's house with me, a number of the men, all armed, surrounded us. The scene was almost humorous: the only one without a gun was a federal agent, who later told me that it was one of the most intense situations he had ever been in. But it was also a pivotal first step in which Buford proved himself to me. I came to trust him and the ATF he represented.

"Kerry, can you talk James out of the woods so we can settle this?" Buford asked, while the federal Marshals nervously patrolled the edge of the woods Ellison was hiding in.

"Maybe. If I have some guarantees from y'all that we can complete our business here and I can take him back to the farm. Then we'll go to Oklahoma and he can appear before the Grand Jury, if you'll see to it that the bench warrant is dropped."

"I think all of that can be arranged," Buford replied.

Buford and Irby sequestered a news-media helicopter and had Ellison's wife, Ollie, and me flown above the woods.

We both spoke through a loudspeaker microphone asking James to surrender. He never came out.

"He probably couldn't hear you," Buford told us after we landed. "The wind muffled your voices. I could barely understand what you were saying. Our only choice is to go in there after him."

"I'll go after him," I offered.

"Do you think you can find him?" Buford and Irby asked in unison.

"I've been training with him for six years as you both know. I'll find him."

Actually, I had no idea how I would find him. If James Ellison wanted to hide, he could hide. I knew that. But I pretended I knew what I was doing so I could go in after him.

"James," I called out as I walked through the woods, "can you hear me? It's all right; everything's under control! It's safe!"

About ten minutes after going in, I heard a noise behind me. It was Ellison, covered with leaves and dirt, laughing, but clearly concerned as he looked around to see if anyone had followed me.

"What's going on here?" he wanted to know.

I explained everything to him. He agreed to come out. The U.S. Marshals had been told to leave; no one but our own people greeted us when we emerged from the woods.

We completed our legal business. The papers were signed. The property crisis was over. We would continue living on the farm.

James was a hero to the people of CSA. He outran and outsmarted the feds. He gloried in the attention.

A few days later, Ellison and I went to the courthouse in Oklahoma. While Ellison stood before the judge, a federal agent guarded me in the back of the courtroom. The judge was angry with Ellison, but agreed to the terms arranged between Buford and myself. Ellison appeared before the Grand Jury concerning issues about Wayne Snell, but pleaded ignorant of any answers for them. The charges were dropped against James.

With the property safe again and Ellison triumphant over the feds, I was now hoping that life could go on with some measure of sanity. However, by now I was not only seriously doubting the premise of our beliefs and ideology, but also the motives of Ellison and the right-wing.

11

The Order and the Siege on CSA

> For the time must come
> that judgment must begin
> at the house of God.
> —1 Peter 4:17

Ten months before our property crisis, in October of 1983, former members of Aryan Nations and the National Alliance (and later former members of CSA) were weary of waiting for judgment day and decided to act. They formed an organization based upon a book that was published in 1978 by neo-Nazi William Pierce, under the pseudonym Andrew MacDonald.

The Turner Diaries is a fictional memoir of a member of a racist underground network which, through a series of increasingly violent acts from 1991-99, gain power in the United States and eventually the entire world. In the book, FBI buildings are bombed, the Capitol attacked, public utilities and phone systems crippled and "the enemy" is targeted and assassinated. The book served as the blueprint for the number one domestic terrorist organization of the 1980s, the Order.

The Order, also known as Bruders Schweigen, was founded by thirty-one-year-old Robert Mathews. This group laid out six steps in which to accomplish their goal of financing a war against the United States. First of all, they had to establish their organization. Second, a war chest was to be set up. Third, they would acquire more money through armed robberies. Fourth, they would recruit new members. Fifth, they would assassinate enemies. Finally, they would carry out an armed guerrilla operation. Their oath, as later shown at one of their criminal trials, left little doubt concerning the determination of the organization:

I, as a free Aryan man, hereby swear an unrelenting oath upon the green graves of our sires, upon the children in the wombs of our wives, upon the throne of God Almighty, sacred be His Name, to join together in holy union with those brothers in this circle and to declare forthright that, from this moment on, I have no fear of death, no fear of foe, that I have a sacred duty to do whatever is necessary to deliver our people from the Jew and bring total victory to the Aryan race.

I, as an Aryan warrior, swear myself to complete secrecy to the Order and total loyalty to my comrades. Let me bear witness to you, my brothers, that should one of you fall in battle, that I will see to the welfare and well-being of your family.

Let me bear witness to you, my brothers, that should one of you be taken prisoner, I will do whatever is necessary to regain your freedom. Let me bear witness to you, my brothers, that should an enemy agent hurt you, I will chase him to the ends of the earth and remove his head from his body.

And furthermore, let me witness to you, my brothers, that if I break this oath, let me forever be cursed upon the lips of our people as a coward and an oath breaker.

My brothers, let us be His battle ax and weapons of war. Let us go forth by ones and twos, by scores and by legions, and as true Aryan men with pure hearts and strong minds face the enemies of our faith and our race with courage and determination.

We hereby invoke the blood covenant, and declare that we are in a full state of war and will not lay down our weapons until we have driven the enemy into the sea and reclaimed the land which was promised to our fathers of old, and through his will and our blood, becomes the land of our children to be.

In November 1983, shortly after the Aryan Nations' Congress that Ellison had attended and after we had distributed our *ATTACK—The Declaration of War in '84,* the Order began counterfeiting $50 bills.

The next month they robbed their first bank, bringing in $25,000. The following month, they robbed their second bank, this time netting only $3600.

Then in March of 1984, the Order committed the first of three successful armored car heists. The first netted $40,000. The second, one month later, brought in $500,000. The third armored car robbery, in July, gave the Order a whopping $3.6 million. Quite a war chest, indeed!

The money from the armored car heists was supposed to be dispersed among various right-wing groups to help finance their organizations. Rumor had it that CSA would receive $100,000. Randall Rader, however, prevented us getting any of the money, once he told the Order about Ellison's second wife and his being "King James of the Ozarks." The Order believed Ellison to be flaky.

In April, the Order bombed the largest Jewish synagogue in Idaho. The following month, they murdered their first suspected traitor, Walter West, by beating him in the head with a hammer and then shooting him. Only later was it discovered that West had never betrayed anyone.

In June of 1984, the Order furthered its assassination plans by brutally murdering outspoken Denver radio talk show host, Alan Berg, a Jew. Two members of the Order shot Berg over thirty times with a .45 caliber fully automatic assault pistol while he was getting out of his car.

After the July armored-car heist, the Order recruited ex-CSA paramilitary leader, Randall Rader, to train their army. Now they had money; they had accomplished a number of their goals; and they had a respected paramilitary leader. They were ready.

With CSA and the Order, two groups were prepared and ready to make war against the United States government.

On November 25, 1984, thirteen men of the Order's forty-one members signed a "Declaration of War," in which they stated:

> It is now a dark and dismal time in the history of our race. All about us lie the green graves of our sires, yet, in a land once ours, we have become a people dispossessed.
>
> By the millions, those not of our blood violate our borders and mock our claim to sovereignty. Yet our people react only with lethargy.

A great sickness has overcome us. Why do our people do nothing? What madness is this? Has the cancer of racial masochism consumed our very will to exist?

While we allow Mexicans by the legions to invade our soil, we murder our babies in equal numbers. Were the men of the Alamo only a myth? Whether by force of arms or force of the groin, the result of this invasion is the same. Yet our people do not resist. Our heroes and our culture have been insulted and degraded. The mongrel hordes clamor to sever us from our inheritance. Yet our people do not care.

Throughout this land our children are being coerced into accepting non-whites for their idols, their companions, and worst of all their mates. A course which is taking us straight into oblivion. Yet our people do not see.

Not by accident but by design these terrible things have come to pass. It is self-evident to all who have eyes to see that an evil shadow has fallen across our once fair land. Evidence abounds that a certain vile, alien people have taken control over our country.

How is it that a parasite has gained dominion over its host? Instead of being vigilant, our fathers have slept. What are we to do? How bleak these aliens have made our children's future.

All about us the land is dying. Our cities swarm with dusky hordes. The water is rancid and the air is rank. Our farms are being seized by usurious leeches and our people are being forced off the land. The capitalists and the communists pick gleefully at our bones while the vile hook-nosed masters of usury orchestrate our destruction. What is to become of our children in a land such as this? Yet still our people sleep!

Everyday the rich tighten the chains that lay heavy upon our people. How pitiful the white working class has become. Where is the brave Aryan yeoman so quick to smite the tyrant's hand?

They close the factories, the mills, the mines, and ship our jobs overseas. Yet our people do not awaken.

They send an army of agents into our midst to steal from our pockets and enforce their rule. Our forefathers under King George knew freedom more than we. Yet still, still our people sleep!

To those who awaken, the reality is grim. John Singer awoke. Concerned over the rampant drugs, homosexuality, and miscegenation in public schools, he tried to teach his children at home. He was a stout Aryan yeoman who loved his family dearly. Government agents shot him in the back.

Gordon Kahl awoke. After four decades of submission to the tyranny of the IRS he tried to resist. He was a stout Aryan yeoman who loved his family dearly. Government agents shot him in the back.

Arthur L. Kirk awoke. For three generations his family farmed the land the usurious banker was trying to steal. Kinsman Kirk tried to resist. He was a stout Aryan yeoman who loved his family dearly. Government agents shot him in the back.

To these three kinsmen we say: Rise, rise from your graves white brothers! Rise and join us! We go to avenge your deaths. The Aryan yeomanry is awakening. A long forgotten wind is starting to blow. Do you hear the approaching thunder? It is that of the awakened Saxon. War is upon the land. The tyrant's blood will flow.

By ones and by twos, by scores and by legions we will drive the enemy into the sea. Through our blood and God's will, the land promised to our fathers of old will become the land of our children to be.

We will resign ourselves no more to be ruled by a government based on mobacracy. We, from this day forward, declare that we no longer consider the regime in Washington to be a valid and lawful representative of all Aryans who refuse to submit to the coercion and subtle tyranny placed upon us by Tel Aviv and their lackeys in Washington. We recognize that the mass of our people have been put into a lobotomized, lethargic state of blind obedience and we will not take part anymore in collective racial suicide!

We hereby declare ourselves to be a free and sovereign people. We claim a territorial imperative which will consist of the entire North American continent north of Mexico.

As soldiers of the Aryan Resistance Movement (ARM) we will conduct ourselves in accordance with the Geneva Convention.

We now close this Declaration with an open letter to Congress and our signatures confirming our intent to do battle. Let friend and foe alike be made aware. This is war!

We, the following, being of sound mind and under no duress, do hereby sign this document of our own free will, stating forthrightly and without fear that we declare ourselves to be in a full and unrelenting state of war with those forces seeking and consciously promoting the destruction of our faith and our race.

Therefore, for blood, soil and honor, for the future of our children, and for our King, Jesus Christ, we commit ourselves to battle. Amen.

The Order made copies of the Declaration and distributed them to the editors of the one hundred fifty largest newspapers in the country, as well as to every member of the United States Congress.

In addition they enclosed an "Open Letter to the U.S. Congress":

All of you together are not solely responsible for what has happened to America, but each of you, without exception, is partly responsible. And the day will come when each of you will be called to account for that responsibility.

The day will come when your complicity in the betrayal of the 55,000 Americans who were sacrificed in Vietnam will be called to account. Whether you were a "hawk" or a "dove" will not carry much weight then. All that will matter is that you played politics while they were dying. All we will ask you is why you failed in your responsibility to them and to America, why you failed to use the full power of your office to expose the treason of your colleagues.

The day will come when your subservience to the anti-American "Israel lobby" will be called to account. Your votes to strip American arsenals so that Zionists can hold onto stolen land; your acquiescence in a policy which has turned all our Arab friends into enemies, seriously jeopardized our oil lifeline, and bankrupted our national economy—those things are inexcusable, and no plea that you "had to do it," that the Jewish pressure on you was too great to resist, will acquit you.

The day will come—if America survives—when you will pay dearly for having weakened America and strengthened our communist enemies all over the world. And don't try to tell us that Henry Kissinger is the one to blame for that! You confirmed Kissinger's appointment knowing full well what his policies were. You went along with Kissinger. You could have stopped him any time you wanted to.

And it was you who allowed the Soviet Union to overtake America on the seas, to whittle down our lead in missiles, to build its military might while ours dwindled. It was you who bought votes by taking money from our defense budget and spending it on "welfare" and "pork barrel" projects. It was you who caved in to the demand of the media liberals that we scrap military superiority and settle for "parity" with the Reds. That treason will cost us millions of lives one day, and so do not think that we will spare yours.

The day will come when, above all else, you will pay for betraying your race. Most of you will say that you are against the forced racial busing of school children, that you are against the black terror which stalks the streets of our cities, that you are against the "reverse discrimination" which takes jobs away from whites and gives them to blacks, that you are against the flooding of America with illegal immigrants, because you know all these things are unpopular.

But you brought every one of these plagues down on our heads. You passed the "civil rights" laws which gave us busing in the first place, and then you refused repeatedly to specifically outlaw this monstrous crime against our children. It was your scramble for black votes and your cowardice in the face of the controlled news media which allowed our cities to become crime-infested jungles. You set up the requirements that employers had to meet racial quotas. And you passed the immigration laws which started the flood of non-white immigrants into America—a flood which is now out of control.

We hold you responsible for all these things: for every white child terrorized in a racially mixed school, for every white person murdered in one of our urban jungles, for every white woman raped by one of the arrogant "equals" roaming our streets, for every white family hungry and desperate because a white worker's job was given to a black. Each day the list grows longer, but the day will come when the whole score will be settled and you will pay every one of these debts in full.

Don't try to explain to us that you voted right some of the time, that government is a game of give and take, and that you had to vote for bad laws in order to get others to vote for good laws. All we care about is that you have collectively ruined America and put our whole race in jeopardy.

We know what America used to be and what it could be today, and we can see what it has become instead—and you presided over that transformation. We placed our trust in you, we gave you the responsibility for our future, and you betrayed us.

You know how to lie smoothly and convincingly, how to talk out of both sides of your mouth at the same time, how to switch sides without blinking an eye. But when the American people finally rise up in righteous wrath and demand justice, none of your trickery and deceit will save you.

You may wave the flag then, but we will remember that when 55,000 young Americans were being butchered in Vietnam because the American government imposed suicidal "Rules of Engagement" on them which gave the enemy all the advantages, you did little or nothing.

You knew what was happening, and you did not shout it from the rooftops. You knew that our fighting men were being betrayed, and you did not attack the betrayers for all you were worth. You did not disrupt the councils of treason. You chose not to make a nuisance of yourself, to shout down the traitors on the floor of the House or the Senate, to give them no quarter. You remained a party to the treason, because you chose not to fight it so uncompromisingly that the chief traitors would have had either to back down or to expel you from the Congress.

Whether you were an instigator of the treason or whether you just went along for the ride will make little difference to us. We will not listen to your explanation that you were really on our side all the time.

We will only remember that when a man who once was an official of the Communist Party's Lawyers' Front and who was still an official of the Zionists' Secret Police Agency, the notorious ADL, was nominated to be Attorney General of the United States, not one of you voted against him—not one! We will only remember that you could have stopped what has happened to America, and, for whatever reason, you did not.

No, when the day comes, we will not ask whether you swung to the right or whether you swung to the left; we will simply swing you by the neck.

The lunacy of this action was obvious, but the Order, like CSA, had crossed the line, a line beyond which logic has no place.

On December 8, 1984, at Whidbey Island, Washington, Robert Mathews—following a thirty-six-hour standoff with two hundred law-enforcement officers—died in a fiery blaze at his retreat.

The right-wing now had its second significant martyr.

The other Order members were apprehended during 1985 and 1986. Thirteen of twenty-three indicted Order members negotiated plea bargains and cooperated with the government.

It is extremely important to note that the Order was established during a time of decline in the strength and influence of the far-right, when President Reagan's optimism was spreading throughout the land. It is during times like this that true extremists realize they must do something to awaken the members of their own movement, as well as society.

By January 1985, I was extremely tired. Tired of CSA, of the right-wing movement, of the hypocrisy, of struggling. Ellison and I were arguing constantly. I wanted to go back to just being Zarephath-Horeb, to let CSA die completely, to destroy everything illegal while we could. Ellison said we could never go back, that "the bull was out of the chute and there was no graceful way to get off."

Ellison toyed with the idea of a "Patriot Memorial," a large rock monument to be located near the front of CSA in which the names of patriotic martyrs and political prisoners would be written in stone as a witness to the movement and to the world. The idea never saw fruition.

The downfall of CSA was inevitable. Ellison was losing control over the group. Until now, I had always looked up to Ellison as a son to his father. Now, I no longer saw him as a spiritual father, but only as a brother, at best. That same gap had narrowed between most of the core members and Ellison. Without that element of control, a cult-like group cannot continue.

We, as CSA, were dying spiritually and I knew it. We had been for years now. No one even cared if we had church services anymore; I still wasn't teaching any Bible classes.

By now I fully realized what I personally had done to corrupt the group. It was *I* who had introduced food stamps and welfare. It was *I* who introduced the teaching of polygamy to the group. It was *I* who introduced the teaching of plundering the Egyptians, giving an excuse to steal. It was *I* who prophesied that God would set us as a beacon to the world, opening the door for the creation of CSA and the death of Zarephath-Horeb. It was *I* who taught the false doctrines of fear and hate, proclaiming its filthy message in books that may have contaminated literally thousands of minds. It was *I* who had supported Ellison marrying Annie, though I knew it to be a mistake. It was *I* who had deeply wounded my own wife, in my lust for another. It was *I* who talked Ellison into the 1982 Convocation and into going to Idaho in 1983, giving birth to the idea of a Declaration of War. It was *I* who almost committed the greatest domestic terrorist act in history. And it was *I* who was the only one who could have possibly stopped Ellison at any time, and didn't. Therefore, I believed, it was *I* who had taken us where we were.

That left me with two options. I could move away from the farm and leave everyone else in Ellison's hands. Or I could stay and try to make amends by changing the group's direction. I believed and feared that if I left, all would die in a shoot-out. So I decided I had to stay. At least for a while longer.

But, tiring of even God telling me I needed to stay, I finally decided that if things did not change by May 15, 1985—the eight-year anniversary of my arrival—I would take my family and leave. I believed that the Lord had kept telling me I had to stay a while longer; now I was at the point of not caring if God wanted me to stay or not. Everyone that I had cared about had already left by now—except for one family and Ellison's wife.

Either change things for the better by May 15, I argued to God, or I'm out of here. I should have packed earlier.

By February, rumors were circulating that we were going to get hit by the feds. Unknown to anyone at CSA, I secretly contacted Gene Irby later that month, with my plea not to come in force should a warrant be issued against Ellison.

In March, four members of the Order—including Randy Evans, one of the signers of the Order's Declaration of War—moved to CSA, much to my dismay. Several of the Order's members had already been arrested, including Randall Rader, who had now turned state's evidence against the Order and CSA. Bill Thomas, in jail for a year now, had contacted federal and state authorities about the pawnshop killing and other illegal activities at CSA. Both Rader and Thomas told the government about the illegal weapon stashes.

In March, also, Ellison began to build a thick, steel-plated armored personnel carrier (a tank) on the chassis of a four-wheel drive truck, to be mounted with our anti-aircraft Lewis machine gun. He declared that if the feds wanted a fight, a fight they would have.

"What are you doing?" I demanded.

"What's it look like I'm doing?" Ellison responded. "I'm preparing for war. I didn't start this war, they did! But I intend to finish it."

"The only reason the feds can come in here is because of the illegal weapons. We should have legally registered them years ago under a Class 3 Dealer's License, like Bruce wanted to! Since we didn't, then let's just get rid of them! Let's give the feds no reason to come in here, so we can continue in peace!"

"There is no peace!" Ellison screamed. "Don't you get it, yet? There is no peace! And there never will be! I won't register weapons to a beast government that our Constitution says we can own and I won't pay the huge taxes on them. And I damn sure won't toss them into the lake somewhere! Whether you like it or not, war is coming and judgment from God is coming!"

"I disagree, Sir!" I yelled back. "It's not time for war! It's not time for judgment!"

Ellison grew tired of my arguing with him and threw down the wrench he held in his hand. "Do you dare question me?" he demanded. "Do you dare to keep arguing with me? Then let's see who God honors more, you or me." By now, several men and women, upon hearing shouts, had gathered around us.

"We will both plead our cases before God, right here, right now, and believe that He will answer before all these witnesses who He honors amongst us. Decide this day, Kerry, who you will serve!"

I knew Ellison was challenging me to an "Elijah the prophet versus the prophets of Baal" contest. I knew he had to hold his position before the new Order members and our own members. And I knew I was the only one challenging him, questioning him. The only one who potentially could.

But I withdrew and said, "No, there's no need for this challenge. You win. You always win." I retreated, leaving Ellison to continue working on his war machine. Even in times like this, I could hear my mother in the background—telling me to never argue with my elders.

On March 12, 1985, a prophecy came through Ollie, that said, "Behold the day of the Lord is at hand. I would that you would gird up your loins and be prepared for battle, says the Lord. I would that there be a cleansing in this camp. Remember the standard that I have put before you to follow. I would that you guard your tongue; that you not give your pearls before the swine. Confess nothing to the enemy. Bridle your tongue, lest you fall into the pit that the enemy would build for you, says the Lord."

I heard two things in the prophecy: another cleansing of the camp and confess nothing to the enemy. I knew what the two previous cleansings had done. And I knew I had already talked to the enemy. Confusion increased in me. Was I going against God by resisting James or were my actions and desires for peace justified?

In early April we began to notice a number of "fed-like" vehicles at area motels, staying longer than usual. Ellison sent people into town every day to watch for strangers, especially men in suits. Our men spotted them everywhere.

We knew the feds were here; we weren't absolutely sure if it had to do with us, but what else could it mean? We were also able to monitor the authorities on the police scanners and radios we had in the communications building. We had obtained a manual years before that showed the various law-enforcement frequencies. It had come in handy a number of times.

In the second week in April, we were all awakened by an extremely loud explosion during the night. We were having a violent rainstorm, with lightning hitting nearby. The explosion we heard, though, was not lightning; it was landmines.

We had recently constructed about fifteen landmines near the perimeter of the fence, all tied into a detonation box. The lightning must have caused a surge in the current, which detonated the dynamite. A major part of our defense had been compromised. Fortunately, the explosions occurred at night and not during the daytime, when someone might have been near the landmines and been killed.

Then, on April 15, David Tate shot two Missouri state troopers, killing one of them. He fled on foot, leaving behind a van loaded with machine guns and handgrenades. The media began to converge on us and high-flying aircraft began circling our property. The FBI knew Tate was in the area and was planning to go to CSA with the weapons.

That same week U.S. Attorney General Edwin Meese visited Arkansas twice and was briefed about CSA. All actions involving domestic terrorism had to have authorization through the Attorney General. Former AG William French Smith had previously authorized investigation into CSA activities.

Earlier that week, authorities found a woman under a bridge in Oklahoma. She had been stabbed to death. Her name was Sue West, former wife of slain Order member Walter West. She had arrived with the Order members at CSA, but left a short time later.

On April 18—five years to the day after Ellison's first arson crime—Gene Irby initially came to CSA to deliver the news about the arrest warrant for Ellison.

The next day, April 19, upon being told Ellison would not surrender, the road blocks had been set up. The siege had begun. Several of our key men had been detained; our army was decidedly smaller, armed now with inexperienced and undisciplined men.

On Saturday, April 20, 1985, negotiations began between me and the FBI's Hostage Rescue Team commander, Danny Coulson.

Coulson was not the first man chosen as commander of the CSA operation. He was the third. The first choice had been an agent by the name of Jim Blasingame, who had been in charge of the Gordon Kahl incident in Arkansas, thus making him an enemy. The second choice was a black negotiator. But FBI psychological profile tests concerning Ellison revealed that he would probably only deal with someone he considered an equal. Eventually, it was decided that Danny Coulson was that equal.

The FBI was correct, and was extremely fortunate in its decision. Had Blasingame or the black agent been the negotiator, war would have broken out between us and the government. There would have been no negotiations.

"You know I could have you arrested right now," Coulson informed me during my first contact with him.

"You could," I responded, "but that would be the biggest mistake you could make. If I don't go back, there will be no negotiations, and you'll have a war you won't forget. We might not win, you might kill everyone up there at CSA, but the world will hear about it. The message will have gone forth."

Coulson looked at me. "You've got balls," he said.

"No, Sir," I answered, "Ellison's got balls. Big ones."

Coulson laughed. "Maybe so, but as far as we're concerned, you're the stabilizing factor in the group. You have been for a long time. We need you for the negotiations, so go back and let's end this thing peacefully." I took the fieldphone Coulson gave me and headed back to the main compound.

Ellison, who had now bleached his black hair almost white, as a disguise, unsuccessfully tried to come up with an adequate escape plan, so instead said God would deliver us miraculously. "Be still," Ellison quoted concerning God, "and know that I am God. Yahweh will vindicate us this day!" Ellison proclaimed.

Two of the Order members, including Randy Evans, emphatically wanted to shoot it out that day, since it was Hitler's birthday.

By mid-afternoon, I was going house to house telling everyone good-bye. "We're going to die," I cried to Cheryl, the wife of one of the other elders, and one of my dearest friends at the farm. We sat on her front porch and I cried from the fear and the helplessness. "We're going to die and I can't stop it," I said. "I don't want to die, Cheryl. I don't want anyone here to die. I just want to see my children grow up. I want to grow old with Kay. But I don't know if I can stop the war from happening. I tried, but I've failed." I didn't see any way that we could go into the night without a shoot-out.

Aerial view of CSA.

Entrance to CSA.

Kerry Noble in CSA
uniform, 1982.

James Ellison,
leader of CSA.

Kerry Noble's house at CSA.

James Ellison's house at CSA.

The CSA sanctuary.

Praise dancing.

CSA arm patch: rainbow and flaming sword.

Booklets published by CSA.

CSA defenses: bunker and "hedgehogs."

Silhouette City, CSA targets and CSA's training ground.

FOR ACTIVE CHRISTIAN-PATRIOTS ONLY!!

C.S.A. NATIONAL CONVOCATION

★ Christian ★ Identity ★ Patriotic ★ Survival

OCT. 8, 9, 10, 1982 — FREE Admission — Secluded

To Be Held on the Secluded 224-Acre CSA Property in Pontiac, Missouri

Primitive Camping Facilities available on property
or you can stay at one of the nearby resorts in Pontiac.

Guest Speakers: Col. Jack Mohr (Ret. US Army)
Bob Miles (Mountain Church)
Richard Butler (Aryan Nations)

Plus CSA's own instructors and other outside teachers! There will also be an open forum time for people to speak. PLUS the establishment of a National CSA Confederacy.

Informational and Participational Classes include:

Weapons	Income Tax	Health	Betrayal of America
Wilderness Survival	Shooting Weapons	Racial Truths	The Jews
Christian Army	Food Storage	Natural Childbirth at Home	
First Aid	Personal Home Defense	Self-Defense	Rappelling
Nuclear Survival	AND MUCH, MUCH MORE! ! !		

Facilities include classroom areas, shooting range, and our own "Silhouette City" for Military Training.

PRE-REGISTRATION is Required!! Only White, Patriotic, Serious CHRISTIANS need apply.

For Attendance Registration Form or for information, please write or call

The Covenant
The Sword
The Arm of the Lord

C.S.A. ENTERPRISES
RT. 1, BOX 128
PONTIAC, MO. 65729
501-431-8882

Plan To Attend!

CSA 1982 Convocation advertising poster.

Communications building.

CSA radio tower.

CSA's communication room.

CSA's LAW rocket

The armored personnel carrier constructed at CSA.

Canister used to bury weapons and ammunition to escape detection.

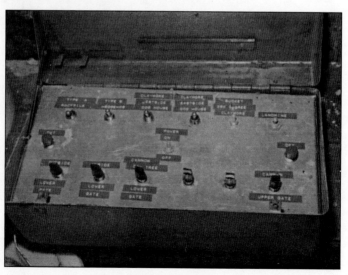

Detonation box for CSA minefield.

Some of the guns seized by authorities at CSA.

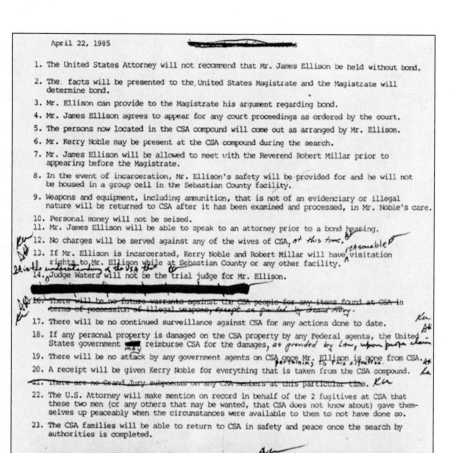

April 22, 1985

1. The United States Attorney will not recommend that Mr. James Ellison be held without bond.

2. The facts will be presented to the United States Magistrate and the Magistrate will determine bond.

3. Mr. Ellison can provide to the Magistrate his argument regarding bond.

4. Mr. James Ellison agrees to appear for any court proceedings as ordered by the court.

5. The persons now located in the CSA compound will come out as arranged by Mr. Ellison.

6. Mr. Kerry Noble may be present at the CSA compound during the search.

7. Mr. James Ellison will be allowed to meet with the Reverend Robert Millar prior to appearing before the Magistrate.

8. In the event of incarceration, Mr. Ellison's safety will be provided for and he will not be housed in a group cell in the Sebastian County facility.

9. Weapons and equipment, including ammunition, that is not of an evidenciary or illegal nature will be returned to CSA after it has been examined and processed, in Mr. Noble's care.

10. Personal money will not be seized.

11. Mr. James Ellison will be able to speak to an attorney prior to a bond hearing.

12. No charges will be served against any of the wives of CSA, *at this time.*

13. If Mr. Ellison is incarcerated, Kerry Noble and Robert Millar will have *reasonable* visitation rights to Mr. Ellison while at Sebastian County or any other facility.

14. *this is the understanding of the USA that* Judge Waters will not be the trial judge for Mr. Ellison.

16. ~~There will be no future warrants against the CSA people for any items found at CSA in terms of possession of illegal weapons, except as provided by Grand Atty.~~

17. There will be no continued surveillance against CSA for any actions done to date. *Ku At*

18. If any personal property is damaged on the CSA property by any Federal agents, the United States government ~~will~~ *may* reimburse CSA for the damages, *as provided by law, upon proper claim*

19. There will be no attack by any government agents on CSA once Mr. Ellison is gone from CSA. *pertaining to this situation*

20. A receipt will be given Kerry Noble for everything that is taken from the CSA compound. *La*

21. ~~There are no Grand Jury subpoenas on any CSA members at this particular time.~~ *Ku*

22. The U.S. Attorney will make mention on record in behalf of the 2 fugitives at CSA that these two men (or any others that may be wanted, that CSA does not know about) gave themselves up peaceably when the circumstances were available to them to not have done so.

23. The CSA families will be able to return to CSA in safety and peace once the search by authorities is completed.

| Asa Hutchinson | Danny Coulson | James Ellison | Kerry Noble |

The Murrah Federal Building destroyed April 19, 1995, Oklahoma City.

Metropolitan Community Church in Kansas City, targeted gay church.

Plaque "In the Arms of the Law" © 1989 Brodin Studios All
Rights Reserved, inspired by a scene after the peaceful end to the
siege at CSA. This plaque was produced by Brodin studios and is
available for sale to the public by Brodin Studios, Minneapolis,
MN. Tel. (612) 588-5194.

12

The Surrender

When a man's ways please the Lord,
He makes even his enemies
to be at peace with him.
                    —Proverbs 16:7

To Ollie and the others during the siege, there were only two options: miraculous deliverance by the hand of God or martyrdom. I chose a third: surrender—since I no longer believed in the former and had no desire for the latter. Yet a question haunted me: Would our lives in the hands of the federal government be worse than death—or better?

I still wasn't totally convinced that our premise concerning the end-time was wrong or that I could trust the government. For four days, though, I had to pretend that I was doing what Ellison wanted—stalling until he knew what God wanted him to do—while negotiating for the safety of our people. It was a juggling act.

Saturday evening Ellison allowed a number of the women and children to leave the compound. Maybe this was a good sign, maybe not. It could mean a possible surrender; it could mean a final showdown once some members had left. I didn't know which.

Mounted atop our lookout tower, we had loudspeakers. Through them we played praise music, war songs, and preached, encouraging federal agents to switch sides and join God's army instead of the devil's army. It had no effect.

Sunday morning arrived. Miraculously, we were still alive. Ellison had managed to keep the Order members calm. I traveled back and forth all day from Ellison's house to the FBI command post in the valley, trying to negotiate a peaceful surrender from James and guarantees from the government. Meanwhile, Ellison had instructed some of the men to destroy as much of the illegal weapons as possible "in case God wants me to surrender."

The so-called help that was supposed to be coming from the neo-Nazis and the Klan hadn't materialized. Ellison finally decided that if he were to surrender, "it would be nice if the feds found nothing illegal; then their siege and arrest warrant would backfire."

By Sunday, U.S. Attorney Asa Hutchinson, one of the three men we were going to assassinate in 1983, was brought in for the negotiations. Robert Millar from Elohim City had also been brought in as Ellison's spiritual advisor. The government thought Millar's role was as a negotiator for peace; we knew it to be as a witness in case the government attacked first. Meanwhile, I was preparing a surrender treaty in which CSA demands needed to be approved by Coulson and Hutchinson.

That afternoon Ellison sent word through me to Coulson that he wanted to talk to Coulson face to face and then return to CSA, to determine if Coulson were a man of his word, in case Ellison decided to surrender.

"I can't do that," Coulson responded. "I've got an arrest warrant for him. I've never had a man within arm's reach of me that I was to arrest and then let him go. We're not trained that way."

"Danny," I implored, "please, what can happen? Where can Ellison go once he leaves you? Only back to the compound. Show him that he can trust you, if you want a peaceful surrender."

Coulson reluctantly agreed to let Ellison come down the hill and meet him, then return. Ellison, his hair now dyed black again, did so. Not once, but two separate times that day. The first time was to meet Coulson personally. The second time, Ellison brought his wife, Ollie, to meet Coulson, to see how she felt about him. One thing was for sure—we were all impressed with Coulson's keeping his word and allowing Ellison to return to the main compound.

Then, the next day, Monday, April 22, Ellison met with Coulson a third time, to talk surrender. After that third visit, right before noon, Ellison told Coulson he needed to go back to CSA before he surrendered, so he could comb his hair! Coulson had no idea why

Ellison was so concerned about his hair. But again Coulson kept his word and let Ellison return to CSA. I was overwhelmingly impressed. Coulson had the opportunity three times to place Ellison under arrest, but didn't.

That morning, Ellison's wife, Ollie, prophesied to James that God wanted him to surrender. I had been encouraging him for five days to surrender. To both Ollie and me it was evident God wanted this thing to end peacefully.

I reiterated to Ellison the events of the last few years: how our foundation was off; that God had continuously taken his "men of war" out of the picture; how often we had sought to separate ourselves from the right-wing; that the plot on the federal building in Oklahoma City had been foiled; that the assassination plot had been foiled; that God had caused the landmines to prematurely detonate; that major Order members and more guns had been prevented from coming to CSA; that our own main men were not here with us during the siege itself; and that the right-wing was not coming to our aid and rescue, though they said they would.

"James," I told him, "the evidence is clear. It's time to end this. God wants a surrender. Do the time, get it over with, then come back and we can start all over again. You'll be out in a couple of years and Zarephath-Horeb can go on then."

It had been agreed by all for me to type up the terms of our surrender, our demands from the government. I presented them to Coulson and Hutchinson. We asked for the following:

1. The United States will not recommend that Mr. James Ellison be held without bond.

2. The facts will be presented to the United States Magistrate and the Magistrate will determine bond.

3. Mr. Ellison can provide to the Magistrate his argument regarding bond.

4. Mr. James Ellison agrees to appear for any court proceedings as ordered by the court.

5. The persons now located in the CSA compound will come out as arranged by Mr. Ellison.

6. Mr. Kerry Noble may be present at the CSA compound during the search.

7. Mr. James Ellison will be allowed to meet with the Reverend Robert Millar prior to appearing before the Magistrate.

8. In the event of incarceration, Mr. Ellison's safety will be provided for and he will not be housed in a group cell in the Sebastian County facility.

9. Weapons and equipment, including ammunition, that is not of an evidentiary or illegal nature, will be returned to CSA after it has been examined and processed, in Mr. Noble's care.

10. Personal money will not be seized.

11. Mr. James Ellison will be able to speak to an attorney prior to a bond hearing.

12. No charges will be served against any of the wives of CSA.

13. If Mr. Ellison is incarcerated, Kerry Noble and Robert Millar will have visitation rights to Mr. Ellison while at Sebastian County or any other facility.

14. Judge Waters will not be the trial judge for Mr. Ellison.

15. Mr. Ellison will be tried in Harrison, Arkansas.

16. There will be no future warrants against the CSA people for any items found at CSA in terms of possession of illegal weapons.

17. There will be no continued surveillance against CSA for any actions done to date.

18. If any personal property is damaged on the CSA property by any Federal agents, the United States government will reimburse CSA for the damages.

19. There will be no attack by any government agents on CSA once Mr. Ellison is gone from CSA.

20. A receipt will be given Kerry Noble for everything that is taken from the CSA compound.

21. There are no Grand Jury subpoenas on any CSA members at this particular time.

22. The U.S. Attorney will make mention on record on behalf of the two fugitives at CSA that these two men (or any others that may be wanted, that CSA does not know about) gave themselves up peaceably when the circumstances were available to them to not have done so.

23. The CSA families will be able to return to CSA in safety and peace once the search by authorities is completed.

It is understood that CSA has cooperated with the U.S. government during this time of the siege and that the Government has acted honorably; and that both sides understand that if the Government fulfills all concessions and agreements, that CSA considers this a time for a line of communication to be opened nationwide for the government and the right-wing people of America; and that the breaking of promises made will be considered an act of closing the door for any future trust between the free citizens of America and the U.S. Government.

I presented the agreement to Asa Hutchinson and Danny Coulson. Items fifteen, sixteen, and twenty-one, as well as the final paragraph were finally agreed to be smitten from the agreement and were marked out with a magic marker. Item twelve was amended to read, "at this time." Item thirteen was amended to read "reasonable" visitation rights. Item fourteen was amended to read, "It is the understanding of the U.S.A. that . . ." Item eighteen was amended to read "may" reimburse, instead of "will" reimburse, and "as provided by law, upon proper claim."

The agreement was then signed by Asa Hutchinson, Danny Coulson, James Ellison, and Kerry Noble. Ellison prepared his people to surrender.

Shortly after high noon, on Monday, April 22, 1985, after a four-day standoff, James Ellison and CSA surrendered.

The men left first, marching downhill in a two-line formation with James leading and me taking the rear position. The men sang praise songs the entire time while marching down the hill; I cried my heart out instead. Crying because a nightmare had not occurred and we were still alive; crying because a dream was now dead, a dream that had once brought me to this place of safety and serenity.

When the men arrived at the FBI encampment, Danny Coulson informed James Ellison that he had a warrant for his arrest. He then told Ellison, "Normally, when I arrest someone, I handcuff him. However, I am not going to handcuff you at this time, in front of your

men, because I would not want to be handcuffed in front of my men."
That statement and action again impressed Ellison and me both.

True to his word, Coulson did not handcuff Ellison until they
had driven away in the federal vehicle. The four men from the Order
were arrested and handcuffed, then all of the men, except for myself,
were driven into town, housed in motel rooms provided by the federal
government until the search of CSA was completed.

Then I went back to the main compound and got the remaining
women and children and brought them down to the FBI, where we
were all driven to town. Agents treated Ollie and the others will great
respect.

The next day's newspaper printed a photograph of the backside
of an ATF agent with a small blond-haired girl—Annie's daughter,
Hannah—laying her head on his shoulder. That photograph was carried nationwide. It later became a symbol on plaques that the ATF
awarded agents for various reasons.

The plaque by Brodin Studios—entitled *In the Arms of the Law*—
symbolized why the ATF did their job: to rescue those who needed
saving. Two copies of the plaques were given to the Houston and New
Orleans offices of the ATF, in memory of the four agents killed on
February 28, 1993, at the Branch Davidian compound in Waco. A
copy also hangs at ATF headquarters in Washington, D.C. and two
are donated each year to the "Untouchables Golf Tournament" sponsored by the ATF, the proceeds of which support the National Law
Enforcement Officers Memorial fund.

At the Baxter county jail in Mountain Home, I was interrogated
by Special Agent Bill Hobbs of the ATF, Arkansas State Police Sergeant Gene Irby, and FBI Special Agent Doug Berry. I told the three
officers how I came to live at CSA, about Rader's dissension with
Ellison, how the illegal weapons began, and about Kent Yates. The
interrogation continued till evening.

The next morning, I was brought in again for questioning, while
the search of CSA began. I became outraged and said that the government promised I would be at CSA during the search. The agents
called Hutchinson and Irby took me to CSA.

On Tuesday, April 23, I watched as dozens of federal officers searched the CSA compound for illegal weapons. Weapons were found and loaded into vehicles.

A large round tank filled with water was brought in so that the unstable explosives the feds discovered could be detonated in the water, with no one accidentally getting hurt. Those explosions lasted three days.

Four Minneapolis, Minnesota squad cars with explosive-sniffing police dogs had been brought in to help find the explosives that first day of the search. I showed the ATF where Ellison hid our LAW-rocket: in the guttering of his house. The ATF had been unable to locate it during their search.

During the search I noticed something unexpected. We had always been told that whenever the feds searched a property, they trashed the place, ripping furniture open, tearing out walls, destroying everything. Although the agents searching the property dug up waterlines, pulled back paneling from walls, cut holes in floors, went through every drawer, cupboard and closet in a massive effort to locate guns, ammunition, stolen money and jewels, and any other evidence in support of their case, it seemed to me and Ollie that they made a special effort not to destroy anything and to actually pick up after themselves. Again, I was impressed. The second day of the search was the same.

That evening, I gathered the elders together, with Ollie, to ask their permission for something. "When James decided he was going to surrender, he gave me a list of all the weapon stashes and told me to hide it. He ordered me to tell no one of its existence, so that when he was released from jail, he would have some guns with which to start over. I hid the list as he told me to. I'm telling y'all this so that you will know what I plan to do. I cannot live at CSA with illegal guns there. I refuse to go through this all over again. But I can't leave CSA. I can't walk away and leave everyone in danger. So this afternoon, after having watched how the feds took care of our property, I had Jack Knox call Asa Hutchinson.

"I told Hutchinson I would give the list to the government on three conditions. One, no more charges would be brought against

James. Two, no weapons charges would be brought against me, and I would plead guilty to Misprision of Felony, which means that I knew crimes were being committed, but did not report them. Three, no one else from CSA—not the elders and especially not the women—would be charged with any crimes. But Hutchinson said he could not agree to my conditions. The government has informed us that warrants will come down on the rest of the elders within a month. I've decided to give the list to the government anyway, even though Hutchinson isn't cooperating with me."

The elders got upset with me. "Don't give them the list," they said. "We'll take our chances. Do as James said."

"I can't do that." I answered. "I would like your permission and blessing to give the list to the feds, but I'm going to give it to them anyway, even without your approval. I will not go through another siege again!" The elders would not give their approval, but said they would reluctantly cooperate with me. The next morning, I contacted Agent Hobbs about the list. I retrieved it from its hiding place, then I, and the four remaining elders and deacons spent the third day of the federal search showing the agents what they had missed. They were astonished, not only that we were helping them, but also by how much they had missed.

Altogether the federal agents confiscated over 157 loaded and 16 unloaded magazines (clips) for various weapons; over 183 large ammo boxes full of ammunition for various weapons; 16 shotguns, 38 handguns, 74 assault weapons, and many other various types of rifles; over 30 machine guns, 50 handgrenades, and six silencers; the 30-gallon drum of cyanide; one anti-aircraft World War II .303-caliber Lewis machine gun; one M-72 LAW rocket (a light anti-tank weapon); and 86 packs of binary explosives, three 1/2-pound blocks of military C-4 plastic explosives, 2000 feet of detonation cord, and over 270 blasting caps. Not found, to the pleasant surprise of the federal authorities, were drugs. That was the one thing we never allowed in.

The one item that all the agents found fascinating was the unfinished tank. "Were you planning to use this against us?" one of the agents asked me.

"Yeah."

"Cool."

"Except that no one wanted to be in the tank," I informed him. "We were afraid that if a bullet came in through one of the portholes, that it would ricochet inside and hurt someone."

The agent laughed. "You're probably right."

By the time the search was completed, the authorities had picked up all of their trash and had cleaned the place up. In fact, CSA looked much better to me after the search than it had for the last few years. The officers had even fed the animals and livestock while our people were kept in town. But many of our members felt violated by the whole experience.

During the next few days I still had to answer questions from the media. I explained about the cleansing prophecy and said that CSA was dead. I apologized to the public and said everything would be better in the future.

My grandparents contacted me and said they would move me and my family to Texas if I would just leave CSA. I told them I couldn't do that; I had to stay and make sure everything was taken care of.

For four days the federal authorities questioned the men and women. Then we were finally allowed to come home, only to await our own arrests. So for the next thirty days we tried to figure out what to do. Meanwhile, as often as possible, I visited James in jail.

Ellison found out that I had turned over the weapons list and he wasn't pleased. I didn't care.

Besides the initial conspiracy-to-possess-unlawful-weapons warrant, additional charges had now been placed on Ellison for RICO (racketeering), which carried a maximum penalty of twenty years, plus various weapons violations, each carrying a maximum sentence of ten years in prison. He was now facing over 200 years worth of charges.

I was soon informed that the FBI would return on Friday, May 31, for my arrest. So the night before, Kay and I went out one last time together. Early the next morning, FBI Agent Jack Knox arrested me.

"If you promise not to try to escape, I won't handcuff you," Knox told me.

I laughed. "Jack, I've been here over a month waiting for you to arrest me and I haven't gone anywhere yet. I won't try to escape now. You have my word on it."

Knox drove me to Fort Smith, Arkansas, stopping along the way for us to eat at a restaurant for breakfast. He informed me the other elders, working at a job in Missouri, would also be arrested that day. I figured I would be released on my own recognizance at my hearing, set for Monday, and would be back at our farm then. After all—I reasoned—I had cooperated, I hadn't left the area, and it was my first offense.

I couldn't help but recognize the irony of the situation: Here I was with FBI agent Jack Knox, who knew that we had planned to assassinate him only 17 months previously, and he was buying me breakfast, taking me uncuffed to jail. Surely God can cause us to have peace with our "enemies," I thought.

Jack Knox later retired from the FBI because of the emotional impact CSA had made on him. Jack became very close to some of us, and helped many of our people over the following few years. The man who had originally sought to have our women arrested also (as a bargaining chip over the men), ended up becoming one of our staunchest allies.

I was fingerprinted at the jail, given my orange jumpsuit, and placed in the guarded, isolated cell with Ellison.

At Monday's bond hearing, I was informed of the charges against me. They included conspiracy to possess unlawful weapons, nineteen counts of actual possession of unlawful weapons and explosives, and one count of receiving stolen merchandise. I was facing 205 possible years. I was also questioned about the assassination plot on Waters, Hutchinson and Knox. I acted ignorant of it. Bail was denied and I was ordered to remain in jail.

What the court and the law-enforcement didn't know was what Ellison had been doing during our first three days in jail together.

Part Five | **Scattered Dreams**

13

A Frog in Boiling Water

Hope deferred makes the heart sick:
but when the desire comes,
it is a tree of life.

—Proverbs 13:12

There's an old saying that if you drop a frog in boiling water he'll immediately jump out. But if you drop him in cool water and then slowly heat it, the frog will stay in the water until he actually boils to death, because he has slowly gotten used to the water changes.

Deception is that way. Dropped into the boiling water of Jonestown in 1978, or CSA in 1985, or the Branch Davidians in 1993, most would immediately jump out. Yet, if that same person were to have been refreshed by the cool water of Jim Jones in the early 1970s, or of James Ellison in 1977, or of Vernon Howell (before he was David Koresh) in 1981, that individual might not have seen the immediate dangers until too late, until he was eventually boiled to death.

The irony of deception is that, by definition, if you are deceived, you do not know you are deceived.

How could Jonestown's mass suicide have occurred? How could people think Koresh was Christ and voluntarily die in a fiery blaze? How could people in the peaceful Ozark Mountains become so hate-filled and paranoid while still professing to be loving Christians?

I was a frog and didn't even know it, a frog boiling to death—until someone reached down and pulled me to safety. That someone, by the grace of God, was the federal government. Through the honest actions of the federal government, through the integrity of Danny Coulson, and through the compassion of the other agents involved, especially those involved in the search of CSA, my confidence in our government began to return.

In those few days of the siege and the search, I saw the government act more honorably and keep its word better than I had seen any group of right-wing individuals ever do. Yet, it still took nearly seven years after my arrest before the cobwebs of confusion were completely swept away.

I explained, earlier, how we had become a destructive cult and the steps that took us there. I had come to worship James Ellison as a god, had come to believe he was perfect and could not sin. Not until 1983 did I seriously question that belief and the premise of CSA.

When I was arrested and placed in a cell with James Ellison, I got to see the man as he really was and this was a revelation to me.

Ellison had been in jail for forty days when I got there. At first I was excited to see him, but almost immediately he just wanted to get down to business. He showed me a list of every person he could think of that had been associated with the right-wing, when he had met them, and any discussions with them that might prove they were guilty of something.

The purpose of this list? To trade information with the FBI in exchange for his freedom. To snitch out the brethren after less than six weeks? To betray "the cause" so quickly? This from a man who swore vengeance on any who would betray him? Who swore to shoot you in the back should you run during the fight? I simply could not believe it.

His list was full of exaggerations and lies, but that didn't matter to him.

"I've spoken to the FBI and the U.S. Marshals several times about this," he informed me, trying to justify his actions. "I believe something will be worked out. I can't go to prison, Kerry. CSA needs me; God needs me; the government needs me. I am more valuable to them outside of prison than I am in prison. I can be an infiltrator into other groups for the government. I've even talked to them about working for the CIA in clandestine operations!"

Ellison rambled on about how evil the right-wing was, how God had shown him that I had been right about the hypocrisy of the movement, that he now knew God wanted him to be the one to bring cleansing to America by getting rid of the right-wing! "But I need your help," he pleaded. "I can't remember it all. You were always better at remembering details than I was. Will you help me?"

Again, in blind devotion, I helped Ellison. I supplied names, dates and events that I was aware of. Only later did I stop to realize that not once had Ellison mentioned that he was doing this so that he could help all the men at CSA. Ellison was only interested in helping himself. Not only was he working to betray everyone in the extremist movement, he had in his heart already betrayed those who had been faithful to him and had followed him for years.

Many at CSA were convinced that Ellison was untouchable and that God would miraculously release Jim and me from jail, with all charges dropped, or that we would go to trial and be found not guilty. Either way, the group told itself, Ellison would somehow return and tell everyone what to do again, so CSA could go on. In my heart, however, I knew CSA was dead.

In the one hundred days during our time together in jail, I endured James Ellison's lofty ideas of being a "Rambo" for the government; of his going to trial for RICO and being found guilty of the charges; of his crying uncontrollably at times, saying he had failed us, while I had to comfort him with pitiful examples of him "only attempting to do good for us."

While preparing for my own weapons-violation trial, I also had to reject Ellison's contemplating our escape from a small understaffed county jail that we were temporarily housed in. And finally I had to carry the guilt trips he heaped upon me for not ministering to him enough and for my "betraying" him. All these had been small steps in opening my eyes concerning Ellison, reminders of why I'd better try to pull myself out of the boiling water.

In 1984, I had learned a valuable lesson concerning the judicial system, when Bill Thomas and the other two men from CSA were arrested in Missouri. I, therefore, had no intentions of going to trial. I knew the cards were stacked against me—and although I knew I personally never actually conspired to possess nor actually possessed any illegal weapons, I knew I would likely be found guilty on all counts and would no doubt be given a ten-year concurrent sentence. I also knew I had neither the strength nor the heart to "fight the good fight" any longer.

The government offered me a plea-bargain that would guarantee a maximum five-year sentence, even though I would not cooperate about the assassination conspiracy. I told the prosecutor I would also not testify against Ellison—that even for the trouble I was in, I owed him too much for what he had done for me in the years before.

I informed Ellison that he and the other elders could do as they pleased, but I instructed my court-appointed attorney to accept the plea bargain. I figured I had a good chance at getting probation with what jail time I had already served. Ellison considered this action a betrayal on my part, although he and the others later agreed to plea bargains also.

While in county jail, awaiting the time that we would all enter guilty pleas in exchange for our plea bargains, James Ellison asked me to tell the federal authorities that everything CSA had ever done was my idea, that I was the true power behind the throne, that I had been blackmailing Ellison for years (for something we would come up with later)—so that I could sacrifice myself and go to prison and he could be released to "save CSA."

"Are you kidding?" I asked, still shocked at his suggestion. "The feds would never believe that!"

"They'd believe it if you told them," he implored. "We've got to be willing to save CSA!"

"I don't give a damn about CSA!" I yelled, almost in tears. "I cared about Zarephath-Horeb and you let it die. All you care about is yourself!"

"But what about the prophecy," Ellison responded, "that Millar gave me? You know I've got to succeed!"

"I don't know anything anymore." I looked out the narrow window that gave the only light into the small exercise room we were alone in. "I don't know anything," I sighed, hanging my head.

Then Ellison looked at me, staring, and coldly stated, "So, you're going to betray me also."

I couldn't answer him. I was too numb. Betray you? I wanted to scream, but merely thought to myself, the government has guaranteed my release if I testify against you. They've guaranteed me absolutely no prison time. I'm the main person that could send you to prison for a long, long time and I'm not doing it. I'm risking going to prison rather than testify against you. And you dare to say that I'm betraying you?

The reality of the situation pierced my soul. It wasn't me that was betraying James Ellison. It was James Ellison betraying me, betraying the men and families who had followed him.

Instead of doing whatever he could to get his men off easier (as I had earlier attempted to do), James Ellison was only concerned with what would keep him out of prison. Never again would I see him as anything but a false shepherd, as just another con-artist who had ruined the lives of so many good people. All I wanted was to get away from him because of how dirty I felt near him.

When I was arrested and jailed, my entire family and my wife's family remained supportive. As the time neared for my sentencing, my mother wrote the judge, asking for leniency. In her letter she said, ". . . Your Honor, I know my son is accused of many things. His main fault in life has always been that he always saw just the good in people; he was never able to see the bad. . . ."

After pleading guilty, but before being sentenced, Ellison, Bill Thomas and I were temporarily moved to another county jail after rumors surfaced that someone might try to break us out. Bill and I asked the guards to put us together in the same cell. The guards were astonished that we made such a request, since they knew Thomas had testified against Ellison and me. But we both reassured the guards that it was all right.

I told the guards I held no animosity toward Bill or Randall Rader, as far as that was concerned. I understood the conflict in Bill; I knew it hurt him to testify against us. But the guilt he was carrying around was hurting him even more. I assured Bill that I forgave him and Rader and only wanted God's best for them.

Bill Thomas was my friend, one of my closest friends. I knew the motives of his heart and knew he never wanted to hurt anyone. Because I loved him as a friend, I could forgive him.

I confided in Bill that Ellison had wanted me to take the rap for everything the farm had done. Bill was not surprised.

The fellowship Bill Thomas and I shared those last couple of days together in jail made a world of difference for both of us. As we said good-bye, I realized even more the effects on anyone who exalts another upon the pedestal of divinity as we had all done with Ellison.

We were sentenced in federal court on September 4, 1985. Though he testified against Ellison, and against Snell for killing the pawn shop owner, Bill Thomas was given a twelve-year sentence for his actions at CSA, adding another three years in essence to the time already given him, since he had already served one year. Altogether, Bill served about six years in prison.

I had already pleaded guilty to one count of conspiracy to possess unregistered weapons. The other charges against me were dropped. My investigating probation officer recommended probation, stating I had a good background and a supportive family, and had learned my lesson. He was right, I had. Even the prosecuting attorney agreed not to argue against probation if I agreed to leave the area. I figured it was a cinch. But as soon as I walked before the judge I knew I was not going home that day. I could feel it in the air.

The federal judge asked me several questions, but one question he asked over and over again.

"Who was the number two man at CSA?" he wanted to know.

"I was, Your Honor," I responded. Not because I ever officially was, I thought, but who else could have been? I had lived there longer than anyone other than Ellison and his wife; I was the first elder ever ordained by our church; I had always been the main Bible teacher and the financial bookkeeper; I had done all the publicity and the negotiating. Who else could it have been, especially since all the others before me were gone? I thought I had simply inherited the title by default.

The judge asked me, "Was the man arrested in 1984, the former Green Beret, the number two man at CSA?"

"Kent Yates?" I exclaimed in shock. Him? Are you kidding? "No, Sir," I answered, looking rather puzzled.

"Are you sure?" he asked.

"Yes, Sir," I answered, not understanding his persistence in this matter. "I was the number two man at CSA."

"Okay, then," the judge responded. He then proceeded to give me the maximum sentence under the plea bargain agreement—five years in prison.

I was crushed and angry. What I didn't yet know was that Yates had previously stated in court and told the judge that he was the number two man at CSA and that I had nothing to do with actual possession of any illegal weapons and was openly opposed to them. Kent Yates, a man who owed me nothing, had done what Ellison should have done, but didn't.

I was taken back to where Ellison was being held. I told him of the judge's questions. And then Ellison hit me with a sledgehammer again. "Of course Kent was the number two man! You never were. I considered Yates second in command because the paramilitary never mattered to you, only the spiritual aspect of the farm did. In a war situation, I would have depended on Yates, not you."

He had said it as calmly as could be, as if I should easily accept his answer. Thanks for telling me, James; thanks for your honesty and devotion; thanks for giving the judge the justification he needed, so he could send me to prison. Thanks for nothing.

"Besides, you wanted to think you were the number two man, so I let you."

"But I just caused the judge to give me a five-year sentence for no reason at all."

Ellison looked at me and shrugged. "It'll do you good."

Do me good? I thought. *What do you mean it'll do me good? Well, if five years will do me good, imagine how good you're going to feel!* James Ellison received a 20-year sentence that day. That helped, I suppose, but not enough.

Now I realized that I was going to prison—not because of what I had done, but because of who the court thought I was.

Five years in prison seemed a lifetime to me, and why was I given five years?

Because I was the number two man at CSA? No.

Because I was a frog and didn't even know it.

14

Freedom

Bring my soul out of prison,
that I may praise your name.
—Psalm 142:7

Freedom. We take it for granted in this country. Like the air we breathe, we assume it's always going to be there, until the time comes when it's no longer available.

Fort Smith, Arkansas was a five-hour drive from CSA. Yet, every week, Kay faithfully made the drive for the allowed fifteen-minute, once-a-week visitation. Though no one else might stand behind me, I knew Kay would always be there. Visitation was through a small window, using telephones to communicate with. No physical contact; only a little privacy. But those fifteen minutes meant everything to me. Occasionally, one of the guards that liked me would allow Kay and me to kiss and hug briefly before she had to leave. I will never forget the guard's kind act of humanity.

For the first time in our marriage of twelve years, I began to no longer take Kay for granted. A deeper love developed for her, an appreciation I had never experienced before. I could never have made it through prison without her. I knew then that I owed her more than I could ever repay her.

When my parents came to see me in the county jail for the first time, I thought I was going into the room to see my attorney and my wife. I saw my folks and immediately broke down crying. I cried until I was weak. All I could say was, "I'm so sorry."

I had betrayed them—all the years they had spent teaching me, guiding me, protecting me, providing for me, instilling in me a sense of right and wrong, and here I was, showing my appreciation by landing in jail. Though they never yelled at me, condemned me or even questioned me, I knew their hearts had to be broken, their minds had to be crying out, Why? But they just asked how I was holding up, reassuring me everything would be all right: I would pay the consequences, my life would go on.

Jail was a foreign concept to me. I grew up respecting the law, never one to get into trouble. As a ninth-grader, I wanted to be an attorney. When I was a senior in high school, my counselor recommended me for the police academy. After high school, I volunteered for the military (although I was denied acceptance because of a history of illness).

The average prison cell is eight feet by five feet, housing two men for the steel bunk beds with paper-thin mattresses and pillows, a small locker (sometimes) and a dirty sink and toilet. The average jail cell, by comparison, is ten feet by ten feet, housing up to fifteen men with six steel bunk beds (the others sleep on the floor) and a dirty sink and toilet.

The Fort Smith, Arkansas, jail was crowded, dirty, and infested with cockroaches. Breakfast was a warm, watered-down cup of powdered milk or Tang, and two jelly rolls. Lunch and dinner consisted of a cup of warm Tang and a TV dinner. Recreation included watching inmates make a prison brew by distilling the alcohol from various hygiene products. It was a nasty introduction to the punishments of crime.

I cried the first day I was in jail. Although I didn't, it seemed like I wept everyday thereafter for twenty-six months. The humiliation of strip searches, being handcuffed, being fingerprinted, the fears, the feelings of frustration, the unsanitary conditions, the separation from family, and the sounds of jail cell doors locking behind me: a person never fully gets over prison. It robs your spirit and makes you feel impotent.

I guess I always took freedom for granted. In America we come and go as we please. We have no police state to tyrannize us. We as a people have never known anything but freedom, and when it is taken away, you soon realize it is the most precious commodity we have.

In going to prison, in one swift action, you go from "the sky's the limit" to your entire world being reduced to forty square feet. No longer is opportunity in life a heritage given you; now you must learn to survive in order to live. The game rule is no longer to do unto others as you would have them do unto you; it is now to trust no one, for everyone is out to get you.

The Federal Bureau of Prisons (BOP) is a system divided into basically three categories—maximum, medium and minimum security—and is scattered throughout the United States. A number of conditions—the person's crime, background, family ties, education, et cetera—determine which level he is assigned to and therefore which prison he might go to.

If, for example, an inmate is classified as a Level 2 minimum-security risk, he would never be assigned to a Level 5 maximum-security prison. As time passes on a prisoner's sentence, his security level can lower, as long as he has caused no problems while in prison. This means that, in time, he might be transferred to another, hopefully nicer, prison.

The BOP can move a prisoner anywhere, anytime, at its own discretion. When a prisoner is transferred, it is usually on a chain bus, a degrading part of the prison system. Here an inmate is handcuffed, which is then cuffed to a chain going around the waist, which is in turn chained to ankle cuffs, which are connected to the floor in front of the seated inmate. On the road the inmate is fed a peanut butter and jelly sandwich and an apple, usually with nothing to drink. The prisoner is not allowed to take any personal items.

After my sentencing—having been in county jail for three and a half months—I was transferred to a Level 4 federal prison in Memphis, Tennessee for holdover for about two weeks. I was a Level-2 medium-security prisoner, so I couldn't remain at Memphis for long. Still in transit, I was moved then to Texarkana, Arkansas for one month. Then to Level 2-3 Seagoville, Texas—where I was designated, or assigned—and where I spent about eight months.

Then I was sent to Big Spring, Texas (a minimum security camp, since my security level had been lowered to a Level 1-2), for six months. Then, as I will explain later, to Terminal Island, California, a Level 4 medium-security prison, for three months of solitary confinement. Then, finally, to Safford, Arizona—a Level 3 medium-security prison—for my last four months of prison life. This placed me in four county jails and six federal prisons during my twenty-six-month incarceration, an average of about two and a half months at each location.

Memphis and Texarkana, although they were only temporary holdover spots, were a great sense of freedom compared to county jail. After four months of county jail, prison food was like food prepared by a master chef, and here I could go outside to feel the warmth of the sun on my skin or go to the library. Texarkana even had an 18-hole miniature golf course and cable TV (more recreation is required in higher security prisons to keep the prisoners active and thus less likely to riot).

Seagoville, Texas, was fantastic. My wife and children, now living in the Dallas-Fort Worth area, were able to visit me every weekend. I had a great cellmate, so I didn't have to fear about my personal belongings being stolen. And I had an excellent job (the best one there, as far as I was concerned) in one of the business offices. I had my own office to work at and usually finished all my work in two or three hours.

My boss—although she wasn't supposed to—allowed me to bring books to work and study, and I could use the prison computer to type my Bible newsletter, which I would mail to Kay, for her to copy and mail to those on my mailing list. During these times, I could read and study my Bible, trying to sort out the right-wing propaganda that was still in my head. I will also never forget the kindness of my female supervisor.

In federal prison, every inmate had to work and was paid anywhere from 11¢ an hour to $1.10 an hour. I was making the maximum pay and sent half my money home every month to my wife, using the remainder for commissary privileges.

By the time I got to Seagoville, I was so discouraged and weak that when I got around to working out in the weight room (almost everyone worked out), I could barely bench-press just the bar with no weights added. All around me were men who worked out constantly and had the intimidating bodies and attitudes to prove it. Though it was a struggle, I hung in there and continued to work out. By doing so, the others gained respect for me. Respect in prison is essential.

As I mentioned before, a five-year sentence seemed like a lifetime when the judge pronounced it. A lifetime, that is, until I actually arrived at Seagoville and found men who had received twenty, thirty, even forty year sentences. Then my sentence, called "a nickel," seemed like nothing compared to the "dimes, quarters and odd change" that other inmates had to live with.

I realized early how fortunate I was. If any one of our major plans had gone through—the federal assassinations, the gay church bombing or the federal building bombing—I would have been in prison the rest of my life or on death row or already dead.

While at Seagoville, I discovered the sentences of the Order members I had known. Ex-CSA members involved with the Order were: Andy Barnhill, who received a forty-year sentence; Jack Norton, five years probation; and Randall Rader, six years probation.

Order members arrested at CSA were: Thomas Bentley, who received seven and a half years; Dwayne Butler, two years; Randy Evans, forty years; and Jim Wallington, who jumped bail and is still a federal fugitive today, although he would have received the same sentence as Butler.

Other Order members convicted of the armored-car robberies: Ardie McBrearty, who had taught me to use the Voice Stress Analyzer, received forty years; Bruce Carroll Pierce, for also killing Alan Berg, 252 years; David Lane, the driver in the Berg killing, 190 years; Richard Scutari, who had taught classes at the CSA Convocation, forty years; and Frank Silva, forty years.

In the fall of 1985, Robert Millar from Elohim City visited me at Seagoville prison. I had always liked Millar, respected him. But this day, I lost respect for him. "James shouldn't have surrendered, Kerry," Millar confessed to me. "CSA should have shot it out with the feds."

I couldn't believe what I just heard. "That's easy for you to say, Robert, you weren't on the inside of the compound with the guns aimed at you, with your family's lives on the line."

"CSA would have won," Robert argued. "God would have seen to that. It would have been a testimony to everyone in America, a testimony to God."

"I'm sorry you feel that way, Robert, because I don't believe it for a second. We would have lost; everyone would've died. And for what? For nothing!" I wanted to tell him that if he wanted to see God in action, then he could have his own standoff with the government, but I didn't.

Robert left shortly after that. It was clear he was disappointed in me. That was only fair—I was disappointed in him.

In 1986—while I was at Seagoville Prison—Asa Hutchinson, the U.S. Attorney that prosecuted us, resigned and ran for state senator. His platform was that he was the man who broke up CSA. He lost the election, but later ran as a U.S. Representative and won.

Also in 1986, I went to my first parole board hearing to find out how much of my five-year sentence I would have to serve in prison. A prison counselor went to speak on my behalf saying I should only have to do my minimum twenty months, which would allow for release in January of 1987.

The Parole Commission recognized that the most significant factor in my favor was my "acting as negotiator between law enforcement and Mr. Ellison." The panel acknowledged from file material that I "was somewhat of a stabilizer in the negotiations that took place with the government, and that it appears that he (I) was the one who convinced the leader of the organization to negotiate and eventually surrender to federal authorities." Nevertheless, the board told me to do the maximum forty months, not to be released until September 1988. I was deeply disappointed but I knew I could do the forty months if I had to.

Big Spring, Texas was even nicer than Seagoville. Again I worked in a business office for $1.10 an hour, but this time I could wear my own clothes and not prison clothes. It had been thirteen months since I had worn my own clothes. Big Spring, being a camp at that time, had no fence around it, so an inmate had a sense of almost being back in society again. There were fewer guards and they were a lot nicer to the inmates. Camp was for those who didn't have much time left and who were considered a very low security risk. But, being farther from home, my family could only visit once a month. While at Big Spring—during November of 1986—I got my first (and only) week-end furlough away from prison.

Visitation time in prison was a mixture of joyous rapture and explosive heartache. Prior to going into the visitation room I (as with all inmates) would be patted-down or frisked to make sure I wasn't hiding any contraband material. I could kiss and hug my wife one time briefly before sitting down.

Most of the time Kay would bring the children with her, although sometimes she would come alone to see me. I was always on edge—the strain of prison caused pent-up emotions, but I would try to be strong during visitation, lest I end up crying uncontrollably, and thus cause Kay to react the same way. The children would be bored with visitation as there was really nothing for them to do.

Two family visits solidly remain in my memory. On one occasion, during the winter of 1985, at Seagoville, my eight-year-old son wanted a cup of hot chocolate. At first I said no, but Kay said he would be careful with it. Well, he ended up spilling it. I lost my composure and yelled at him; then realizing it was not him I was angry at, it was my being in prison, I just cried and cried. God, I hated prison.

The next summer, at Big Spring, one of my daughters wanted to play a game with me in the outside area. Again I said no. She walked away and mumbled that she wished I was like other fathers who would play with their children. Again I cried and then held her, so wanting to just go home.

During visitation the inmate is obviously watched closely; so closely, in fact, that when an inmate needs to go to the restroom during visitation, a guard must be with him and must watch the inmate actually use the toilet. This, of course, adds to the frustration and humiliation.

Every visitation ended the same way. It would be time for Kay and the children to go home. We would remind ourselves that someday I'd get to go home with them. Then we'd kiss and hug briefly again, and I would watch them walk away. Then I would leave the visitation room, only to be strip-searched for contraband again. Afterwards, I'd go to my cell and cry some more. The reality of getting to actually go home seemed like a far-off dream.

One visit memory still makes me smile. It was a common practice for an inmate to cut one of the pockets of his pants, so that on visitation day, his wife or girlfriend could slip her hand inside and touch the inmate's private parts. Cutting the pants was, of course, forbidden, and could suspend you from visitation if discovered. One visitation day, a female African-American guard patted me down before my going into the visitation room. She placed her hands inside the pockets, checking for contraband, and discovered the cut-off pocket. Looking at me, she smiled compassionately, and said, "You're okay; have a good time." I thanked her and went on in. I will never forget her kindness.

In federal prison, an inmate's mail is read when it comes in and his telephone calls are usually monitored. Medical and dental care is minimal. An inmate can be patted down by a guard at any time and his cell can be searched anytime a guard desires, for no reason at all, with the inmate, of course, cleaning up the mess.

Prison is also the most segregated system in the country, with each race pretty much keeping to its own. Homosexuality is rampant, though attempted to be covered up. Men that I thought would never participate in homosexual activities were the most active it seemed. In prison it's believed that the "pitcher" (the one receiving the oral sex) is not homosexual; that only the "catcher" (the one performing the oral sex) is.

Prison inmates have a moral code of their own. Snitching is considered the greatest crime one inmate can do against another. Yet stealing from another inmate is generally not considered wrong.

Several times I would walk to the farther end of the walking field when no one else was there and scream as loud as I could without drawing attention, just to release pent-up emotion. I would cry to God to allow me to go home, while also praying that whatever He was working in me would be accomplished, that I only wanted to know Him better. I believed in the sovereignty of God, and would thank him every day for my being in prison, even though I hated it there. Prison strengthened my belief in the absolute grace of God.

In November 1986, while at Big Spring camp, I was approved for that first and only weekend furlough. I could leave the prison grounds during the days on Friday through Sunday, returning each evening. It had been almost 18 months since I had experienced any sort of real freedom.

For three days, Kay, the children and I were a family again. We shopped, ate at restaurants, went to the park, and stayed at a motel. I was not a convict, but a family man. It wasn't until an hour before I had to be back on the final day of my furlough that reality hit me. I had to say good-bye to my loved ones again.

Again my heart sank and I wept. But, I thought, I'll be eligible for a furlough every three or four months, so now I could take it. As it turned out, it was to be my only furlough.

In August of 1986, three months before my furlough, I had a visit from two agents of the FBI. They informed me that James Ellison was cooperating and would testify in an upcoming trial against several right-wing leaders and members, as well as some former CSA members (including Ellison's own son-in-law) for sedition against the United States and for conspiring to assassinate federal officials. They needed me to corroborate Ellison's testimony. I informed them I was tired and had tried to forget everything I knew.

"What if I'm not able to cooperate?" I asked.

"Then," one of the agents informed me, "charges might be brought against you as well, and you could face life in prison."

I hated Ellison. Hadn't he ruined my life enough already? I just want to be left alone, do my time, and go home. Why can't I do that? Reluctantly I agreed to do whatever I had to. I was sent to testify to the Grand Jury on December 10. I told the Assistant U.S. Attorney that my memories were vague, that a lot of my knowledge of events was only hearsay, and that I hadn't taken the assassination conspiracy seriously back then, that I had really thought it was only talk and would never happen anyway.

"None of that matters," he told me, "just tell the truth."

So I did, to the best of my recollections.

Later I regretted testifying at the sedition trial. I should have told the Assistant U.S. Attorney the complete truth about Ellison, but I didn't. I had long realized to my horror and shame that I had compromised my integrity in the name of God, a compromise I was still too weak to fight. I was still letting Ellison dictate my life.

While in Fort Smith, Arkansas for the Grand Jury, I had the chance to see Ellison briefly.

"Please help me out by telling the Grand Jury everything you know," he begged me. Nothing from Ellison about how was I doing, how was the family, sorry for all that's happened. Just, help me. Ellison hadn't changed one bit.

The one thing I did know was that the man I had once most admired I now despised and pitied. After my testimony to the Grand Jury, I was considered such a low-risk prisoner that I was allowed to fly back alone to the Big Spring prison, unescorted by the U.S. Marshals. Kay was able to meet me at the airport and drive me to prison. It gave us some much needed time together.

At Big Spring I was immediately refused entry, for security reasons. It seemed that one of the Order members who had previously testified against the Order, and who was now going to testify at the sedition trial, was also at Big Spring. The prison officials didn't think they could protect us both, so I was shortly shipped off to Terminal Island, California for my safety.

For cooperating with the government I was rewarded by being taken from a camp to a Level 4 medium-security prison; from being able to see my family monthly to not being able to see them for the next seven months; from having my own possessions in prison to having none of them (all my clothes, books, guitar, and personal items were sent home); from having virtual freedom to being locked down in solitary confinement.

Solitary confinement was a nightmare. Previous to this I was down to 188 pounds, working out and walking every day. After three months of solitary confinement, I weighed 218 pounds, being locked up in that cramped eight-foot by five-foot cell virtually the entire time.

I was allowed outside my cell only briefly—on Monday, Wednesday, and Friday—so I could quickly shower, and then on Tuesday and Thursday, to watch television for one hour. Weekends were total lockdown confinement.

I was angry and scared. My only source of sanity was in being able to call my wife every day—varying from a five-minute call to up to two hours—with the government paying the phone bill.

During one weekend of not getting out at all, Kay had informed me on the telephone of some problems at home with the children. I felt powerless to help her and became angry again at my being in prison.

When I hung up the phone after our conversation was over, I looked up to "the sky" of my prison cell ceiling and screamed, "FUCK YOU, GOD! FUCK YOU FOR MY BEING HERE. FUCK YOU FOR EVERYTHING THAT HAS HAPPENED! WHY ARE YOU DOING THIS TO ME? WHY ARE YOU PUNISHING ME SO? WHY CAN'T I JUST GO HOME?" I broke down then, collapsing to the floor, and wept for a long time.

I slowly got up and asked God to forgive me. "I'm sorry. I understand what has to be done. I'm just not liking it. Please forgive me and give me the strength to carry on. Just watch over my family and let nothing happen to them and I'll be alright. I love you, Father, and I know you love me." Then I laid down on my cot and fell asleep.

We had a metaphorical teaching at our group that spoke about how pure gold is obtained. Gold ore is dug out of the ground and then heated in a pot. As the temperature rises, dross from the ore makes its way to the liquid surface. There it is skimmed off, so that as the temperature continues to rise and all the dross is finally taken from the ore, only the pure gold is left.

In the same way, as God refines us, He does so with the fiery trials of life's sufferings. As the heat is turned up, the sickening earthly elements of our flesh surface, for all to see. The process continues until all flesh is gone, at the time of Sonship, and only the divine nature of God is left to be seen.

I had been going through the fire for some time now. The skimming of the dross had left its marks on me. My constant prayer was,

"Show me your ways, O Lord; teach me your paths." I no longer cared to exalt myself; I cried out only for the sovereign grace of God. I felt in my heart I was finally ready to go home.

During this time period I wrote my last song for Zarephath-Horeb—"How Shall We Sing Yahuah's Song?" (sung to the tune of "Greensleeves," with words from Psalms 137 and 138).

After three months of prison-after-prison refusing to take me (no one wanted to take the responsibility for my safety), one finally agreed—Safford, Arizona, a Level 3 medium-security prison. There I would spend my next four months.

While at Safford, I wrote a full-length science-fantasy novel. Writing brought a release from the frustrations and pressures of being an inmate; it was a creative act that I could participate in while being surrounded by the apathy of prison life.

In June 1987, I went to my second scheduled parole board hearing. By this time the Assistant U.S. Attorney forwarded information to the parole board about my cooperation with the government. The board asked about my family and my future plans, and then asked why I was going to testify at the sedition trial.

"There's really three reasons, Sir," I told the questioning board member. "First of all, I agreed to cooperate because I was scared of more charges being filed against me and of facing life in prison. I've learned my lesson and know I'll never break the law again, and I want to go home to my family and let the past die. Second, I'm tired of lying. I had to lie to myself at CSA, had to lie to the media, had to lie to the government, all for some self-righteous cause I long ago quit believing in. I'm simply tired of lying. Thirdly, though, and most importantly, I've seen the right-wing leaders manipulate younger members into committing crimes.

"The leaders ought to pay for their own sins. Too many innocent and gullible followers are going to prison for gutless orators who are content being thought of as heroes and who then forsake the imprisoned followers, only to boast later of the prisoner's sacrifice for the cause. This needs to end, and if I can help it end, then so be it. The leaders need to pay for their own sins."

The parole board discussed my case while I waited outside. When I was told to come back in, the questioning member asked, "Can you gather your belongings together and be ready to leave in six weeks?"

"Six weeks?" I exclaimed. "I can be ready in six minutes!"

The board members laughed and the leader said, "Sorry, but it takes about six weeks to get the paperwork in order. You'll be able to go home August 1st. We feel you've learned your lesson. Good luck to you in the future."

I thanked them over and over and left to telephone Kay. When I said I was coming home, there was silence on the phone. She cried for five minutes before she could ask when I'd be coming home.

We then talked about the inevitable question that we had been putting off—the U.S. Attorney wanted to sponsor us into the Witness Relocation and Protection Program.

"Do we want to go in?" I asked Kay. "We can't have any contact with our families or friends. We'd be relocated three times before our final destination. Our names would be changed, as well as our histories. What do you want to do?"

"I'll do whatever you decide," she answered. It was the answer she always gave. "I just want you home, and I don't care where that is."

Over the next few weeks, the prison psychologist gave me a number of required counseling sessions and psychological tests before I could leave prison, to see if I could mentally handle the Witness Protection Program. An FBI expert also came a couple of times to prison to give me a polygraph lie-detector test. I failed parts of the tests that the FBI agent and I knew I answered correctly, questions concerning Ellison and myself. The only explanation he could give for the "false" answers was three-fold: that I probably held such tremendously deep pain and stress concerning Ellison and CSA; that the pain, therefore, subconsciously registered harbored guilt and shame over what had occurred at CSA; and that I hated what I was going to have to do at the Sedition trial.

On the day before I was scheduled to be released from prison, the FBI came by to see whether I had decided to go into the Program or not. If I did my family would be moved that day and the vehicle and mobile home that my grandparents had bought us would be sold. I would not be allowed to see my parents or other family upon my release, and Kay would not be told ahead of time of the move. My answer was immediate.

I informed the FBI that I couldn't go into the Witness Protection/Relocation Program. I owed my family and Kay's family more than that. I had lived a lie for too long; I refused to live a lie any longer. No false identities; no more running; no hiding.

A constant fear in prison is that upon release federal or state authorities will be outside waiting for the inmate, with another arrest warrant and charges in order to keep him in prison. I had lived with this fear for 26 months.

But on Friday, July 31, 1987, I said my good-byes to the few friends I had at the prison, walked out through the security gates and was driven to the bus station. No one waited to arrest me on new charges. I was dressed in my new set of clothes, carrying my small box of personal belongings and the one hundred dollars that the government gives each inmate upon release. I was on my way home. No handcuffs, no guards, no U.S. Marshals. The bus would take me to the airport, where I would fly to DFW International Airport in Dallas, Texas, arriving about 8:00 that night, where Kay would pick me up for that long anticipated reunion.

Prison had taken away all self-esteem. I was frustrated and withdrawn, confused and fearful. Life in prison is regulated, filled with harassment and anger, discouragement and resentment. As an inmate or prisoner, you lock up your belongings. You trust no one. After all this, I thought, can I readjust? Will the government really leave me alone? Will I ever have true friends again? How will my family—especially my children—respond to me? And, most important, will I ever be able to trust myself again?

My grandparents had bought us a four-bedroom, 28 foot by 76 foot double-wide mobile home while I was in prison. Kay and the children had been living there for about twenty-one months. The living room alone was 28 feet by 16 feet, the equivalent of eleven prison cells.

I rarely left that living room for the first three days; I just sat in a recliner in the middle of the room, soaking in the space and quiet I had so long lived without. I felt numb emotionally after twenty-six months of prison and had no idea what the future would hold. I wanted to go nowhere and wanted to do nothing, except to be with my family and to get to know them once again.

I had thirty-four months left on my sentence. Thirty-four months of reporting to a parole officer every month and of being limited to where I could travel without permission. I had to get a job to support my family again. It had been ten years since I had been in normal society and a lot had changed—in me and in society.

I found out quickly that convicted felons, especially those who had gone to prison for machine guns and handgrenades, don't get hired. But on every job application that asked about a felony conviction, I told the truth about my past. No more skeletons in my closet, I didn't care what the cost.

I also found out that the easiest profession to get into, that asks no questions, was commission-only sales. So I became a vacuum cleaner salesman, and I loved it. Good money (especially compared to what I had been making over the last several years), and a superb boss—but very long hours. But that was alright. I was providing for my family again.

I began to slowly establish a credit history to show my integrity and intention to be a positive part of society. Healing had begun.

Although I had been able to sort out a lot of things in my head while in prison, I still had a lot of questions and confusion in regard to the propaganda I had learned and taught at CSA. Before moving to Arkansas, I had ministered to Blacks at work. Yet, previous to prison, I had never known a Jew. So while in prison, I attended Hebrew classes and twice went on supervised trips to a local synagogue for services. The exposure taught me the obvious fact that Jews were like anyone else and not children of Satan waiting to devour Christians. Although prison is extremely segregated, I was able to get to know men from other races and cultures.

The hardest problem I had outside of prison was having no one to talk to, no one who could identify with what I was going through. I longed for someone to help me but no one came and healing was slow.

Guilt was a major part of my psyche now. Having been the main Bible teacher and an elder at CSA, I had long taken personal responsibility for having led astray the good people of our church. To this day guilt still haunts me occasionally.

I became more withdrawn because of the guilt, unable to look people in the eyes, for fear they would see the pain and the past secrets I kept inside. I preoccupied myself with my job, working seventy-five hours a week.

The breakup of the farm was most difficult for the women and the children. Ollie had tried to keep the farm going after all the men were arrested, but couldn't. She left in January 1986, while some people from Elohim City lived on the property. She returned briefly in July, only to leave again in September. The last of the people left in 1987. Almost immediately looters began to destroy the property, stealing windows, paneling, other materials from the houses. Ellison's house and the sanctuary were eventually burned to the ground. By 1993, the property was cleaned up, sectioned in pieces and sold.

In 1987 the government finally destroyed all of the CSA weapons. As Ellison's wife, Ollie, who was divorcing him by this time, stated on television, those guns represented things that the women of the group had to do without—washers and dryers, refrigerators, better school books. As I later watched (on video tape) the destruction of those weapons, all I saw was the destruction of Zarephath-Horeb through CSA, the destruction of the spirit because of the flesh.

Years later I learned that Ellison had abused both of his wives and both had to go into therapy and counseling for several years.

The separation from living in Arkansas was especially hard on our oldest daughter, Tara. Nightmares haunted her and for several years she would wake up during the night, crying for no apparent reason. Whenever I would go in and talk to her, she simply said, "I miss the farm."

The farm was heaven to the children—no worries; plenty of children to play with; peaceful surroundings. Tara was ten when she left the farm and had lived there for eight years. It was where she believed she would be for at least another eight years, if not her entire life. Friends were now scattered; she lived now in a society she didn't understand or feel comfortable in.

As I held Tara, I said, "You've got to let the farm die, honey. Just let it die." It broke my heart to have to tell her that.

Letting the farm and all her memories die was not the answer she wanted. She wanted to go back to live there, to be with her friends. She was troubled about the farm for several more years.

My older son had been kept back a year when Kay enrolled our children in public school. Though Stephen could pass his subjects if he applied himself, he never had any interest in school, and completing each grade was a challenge. He eventually dropped out of high school, with less than a year to go.

A number of the teenagers from CSA never finished high school and delved into the world of drugs, alcohol, promiscuity and trouble. Many of the marriages at CSA fell apart. The mirage of heaven at CSA later dissipated and revealed hell's reality.

In early 1989, I branched off into my own business with a $10,000 bank loan, a $3000 loan from a finance company, and a new vehicle loan. Through unforeseen events the business failed three months later and I was deeply in debt and unemployed for a month. Within a period of less than four months, I had added over $23,000 to my personal debt, increased my monthly bills by over $1000 above the previous amount, and the only job I was able to get (as a fast-food manager) lowered my take-home pay from about $1200 to $325 a week. By year's end, both of my vehicles were about to be repossessed, the IRS was about to put a lien on my home (for back taxes while in Arkansas), and creditors were hounding me constantly. I was never able to recover financially and was forced to file Chapter 13 reorganization bankruptcy. I felt like a failure again. I completed the bankruptcy repayment plan in May of 1993.

In the summer of 1989, I was twice offered excellent positions of employment: one in a top position in the circulation department of a major newspaper for $40,000 a year, and then later as an assistant director of an established trade and vocational school for $45,000 a year. Both offers were given by the companies upon my first interview, accepted by me, and then taken back by the companies once I informed them of my past (since I would have to have been bonded with each job). No one wanted a convict.

The economy in the country had gotten worse and employment was difficult to find. From August 1987 till the fall of 1996, I held various jobs as a vacuum cleaner salesman and manager, a telemarketing salesman, a taxi cab driver, a delivery courier, a fast food manager, a water filter salesman, an advertising salesman, a long-distance carrier salesman, a portrait photographer, a real estate photographer, a photography salesman, a warehouse worker, a circulation coordinator in a small newspaper and a pre-need funeral services salesman. I attempted two more unsuccessful business ventures and was involved with six different multi-level marketing ventures. I bounced from job to job, not knowing "what I wanted to be when I grew up." I could not be bonded (except by the state) and was not eligible for jobs that required a state license, and most trade schools would not accept me. Nevertheless, I was committed to providing for my family.

Adjusting to society after prison is extremely difficult, but not impossible. Fortunately, I did renew a sideline-hobby I thoroughly loved and settled into—photography, public speaking and writing. Photography proved to be quite lucrative for me. A photography magazine also published an article I wrote, for which I was paid. I have been paid to speak in public at various social clubs and other events.

In 1994 I decided to finish this book, having originally begun it in 1991. It wasn't completed until 1998. In time, however, I hope to re-enter that which I was originally called into—pastoring a church.

In February 1988, seven months after my release, the Sedition and Conspiracy Trial in Fort Smith, Arkansas began. I really didn't want to be there. I no longer respected Ellison and doubted if the government had much of a case. I was told it was an important case and everything was going well. I had agreed to testify, and testify I would; not to see men I had once known get convicted, but just because I would no longer lie for anyone.

Accused of seditious conspiracy were: Richard Butler, 69, founder of the neo-Nazi group, Aryan Nations, in Idaho; Robert Miles, 63, leader of the KKK-like Mountain Church in Michigan, from whom we had obtained the cyanide; Louis Beam, 41, a former aide to Butler and former Grand Dragon of the Texas KKK; Robert Smalley, 32, a local gun dealer; David Lane, 49, of the Order; Bruce Carroll Pierce, 33, of the Order, who had murdered Denver, Colorado talk-show host Alan Berg; Richard Scutari, 40, of the Order; Andy Barnhill, 31, of the Order, and a former member of CSA; Ardie McBrearty, 60, of the Order; and Wayne Snell, 57, on death row for the murder of the pawnshop owner in Texarkana.

Charged in the assassination plot were Snell; Bill Wade, 68, linked to the Posse Comitatus and who had previously hidden Gordon Kahl while he was a fugitive; Ray Wade, 35, Bill's son, also linked to the KKK; David McGuire, 25, Ellison's son-in-law; and Lambert Miller, 47, who drove the van that got wrecked during the failed assassination-plan trip.

This was the fourth time in forty years that the government had prosecuted American citizens for seditious conspiracy, which refers to inciting resistance or insurrection against lawful authority.

Many of the defendants represented themselves instead of having a court-appointed attorney. Louis Beam was represented by Kirk Lyons, an attorney for the right-wing, who has also represented James Wickstrom of the Posse Comitatus; Tom Metzger of the White Aryan Resistance (WAR); later the Branch Davidians in a civil suit against the United States; and is reported to be Robert Millar and Elohim City's attorney. Lyons is the brother-in-law of David Tate, the Aryan Nations follower who had killed one Missouri trooper and wounded another the week before the CSA siege.

The all-white jury heard testimony about plots with the cyanide, the 1983 Aryan Nations Congress meeting, right-wing propaganda and ideology, and about the Order's actions. Bruce Carroll Pierce almost changed his plea to guilty during the trial, but changed his mind at the last minute. Butler and Miles almost plea bargained to lesser charges but later decided not to.

James Ellison testified for three days against the defendants, admitting that he had lied to the federal judge when he was sentenced, that he had taken a second wife, that he had called himself "King James of the Ozarks," and that he knew he would get a reduced sentenced for testifying.

I testified next, and wasn't much of a witness, having misidentified two defendants during the Grand Jury and the trial. Most of my testimony was hearsay through Ellison, who had already discredited himself on the stand. Although I believed Ellison had lied on the stand in order to help himself, I would only tell the truth. If I was asked a question that I did not know the answer to, I said so. Following my testimony, former members of the Order and CSA also testified, as well as several federal and state officials. During the trial, the judge dropped all charges against Smalley for lack of evidence. When the two-month-old trial was over, all of the defendants were acquitted. It really accomplished nothing other than putting my family in jeopardy.

Was it worth testifying at the Sedition trial? Not for me. Yes, it got me released from prison fourteen months earlier than expected. For what I had to go through during my last seven months in prison—considering that I would have finished my time at a prison camp, with furloughs—and since the trial was to no avail, testifying was not worth it. I did what I said I would do, but I should have testified against Ellison instead, and not the other men.

For testifying, Ellison's twenty-year sentence was reduced to ten years. He served six years in prison and was released in 1991. His common-law wife, Annie, wanted nothing to do with him; his wife, Ollie, divorced him while he was in prison. In the fall of 1993, Ellison's parole was revoked because he left his area without permission and was caught stalking his second wife. He served another eight months in prison before being released again. His sentence was completed in April of 1995—three days after the Oklahoma City bombing.

Shortly before the Sedition trial began, I went to our farm to say good-bye. I placed stones in front of the sanctuary that spelled out, "CSA: '78-'85. RIP."

In October 1989, I officially separated myself from Jim Ellison (I no longer refer to him as "James"). We had been writing occasionally and keeping in touch by telephone. Ellison still held to the ideals of CSA and the future downfall of the government, as well as his position as "King James of the Ozarks."

In a 7300-word letter to me in May of 1989, Ellison reiterated his Christian experience and God's confirmations to him over the years. He stated his belief that the people of CSA were scattered and without direction because he was no longer there as their shepherd to guide them and that in time he would be back as their leader. He mentioned the commitments we had toward each other, especially the vows we made to him. He believed God would not allow any of us to disregard our vows.

In my return letter, I reminded Ellison that he had long ago broken his commitments to us. I told him how I began to seriously question CSA in 1983, because no new truths or revelations were coming forth as they once had freely done. I admitted that in my seeking and striving to go on to new areas, I had corrupted myself with the second-wife experience in 1984 and that in 1985 I had decided that if the farm would not turn back to its early simplicity, I would soon leave. After I finished explaining my differences, I saw no need in communicating with him any further.

In 1990, however, Ellison mailed me a copy of his 76-page "Blood Covenant" manuscript, in which he detailed his scriptural basis of how important blood is to God and our covenants with Him and with each other. In it he explained the nature of covenant, the covenant representatives, the covenant site, the covenant animal sacrifice, the covenant exchange of garments and weapons and pledges, the reciting of covenant oaths, the covenant cut for the mingling of blood, the covenant seal of the scar and the joining of names, and the covenant meal ceremony. This rambling jargon contained a frightening note by Ellison that if a person breaks the covenant he has made with another, then "the faithful covenant partner has a sworn duty to kill the covenant breaker."

Later on Ellison states, "First blood has an unforgettable effect. I will never forget the first time I had the blood of one of my friends on my hands. Human blood is special, the blood of our own people is an awesome and powerful thing indeed. It cries out from the earth to Almighty God that it may be avenged."

I had no idea whose "blood of a friend" Ellison was referring to. To my knowledge no friend of Ellison ever spilled blood or died. I never answered his letter or questioned the blood reference. I did not want to know his answer. Ellison's "Blood Covenant" reminded me too much of the Order's Oath of Allegiance.

In the summer of 1990, I finished my five-year sentence. I granted a television interview that summer, stating publicly for the first time the deception at CSA and my opinions about the dangerous intentions of Jim Ellison.

In January 1991, I called Irwin Suall, director of the Jewish Anti-Defamation League of B'Nai B'Rith in New York City, and apologized to him and his organization for the evil CSA had done, and stated I would do what I could to stop racism, hatred and violence. This led to a meeting with the regional director in Dallas, Texas. Although the phone call and meeting did not accomplish all I had hoped (I think both men were, understandably, leery of my turn-around), it was a large step forward for me in my recovery.

That same month I joined a local club of Toastmasters International, a public speaking and communications organization. I had been introduced to Toastmasters while in prison. Here I was able to openly discuss my past without fear of rejection or judgment. Toastmasters became the forum and avenue which enabled me to sort out lingering feelings and emotions. I can't speak highly enough of this club or of this organization, nor of its effect upon me.

On October 1, 1991, I was interviewed on a radio talk show in Dallas. I stated the problems with CSA and my desire to help others not take the path of racism, hate and violence that I had taken.

Most of my time and efforts after my release from prison were spent providing for my family, and still trying to recover from the effects of my years at CSA. I had one job in 1992 that required me to travel extensively throughout Texas and Louisiana. The pay was good, but being gone from home a lot really bothered me. My having previously been gone from my family for twenty-six months still affected me. I hated being gone from them now. These road trips would stir deep-seated emotions within me, surfacing themselves as floods of tears while driving and reminiscences of prison while in the lonely motel room at night.

Because of various fears I was dealing with—especially with several recurring nightmares about being at CSA a second time (ending in a shoot-out this time)—I feared that something would happen to my family while I was on the road, especially to Kay. Overwhelming guilt plagued me about my polygamy affair and I was so worried about ever hurting Kay in the future.

I asked her if she would accompany me on one of my overnight business trips, which she gladly agreed to. That night, I began to sob from the pain in my heart. When she asked what was wrong, I said. "I'm so sorry about my fling with the other woman. I know it's been eight years now and I know that you've forgiven me, but I'm so sorry I did that to you. I'd have gladly spent another twenty-six months in prison if it would've erased that time period. I never meant to hurt you," I continued. "I never meant to dishonor you. But I want you to know, you mean more to me than anything in the world. I so appreciate God allowing me to be with you. I'm so thankful.

"I know I used to say that we didn't communicate spiritually very much. I based that on your not knowing a lot of scriptures, and I thought that's what categorized a person as being spiritual. But I want you to know that I consider you the most spiritual woman I know. You do by nature what the Bible says to do, even if you don't know you're doing it or why you're doing it. I realize now that's more important than being able to quote the Bible but not living it out in the Spirit. You're the best wife, the best mother, and the best friend in the whole world."

We held each other tightly as years of hurt seemed to flow away from both of us. It was a night that I had longed for for years, but had been too scared of losing Kay to allow myself this time of confession.

We spoke into the late hours of the night that evening. The light of the next morning brought rays of new hope and a new day together. Now we spend all the time that we can together. Kay is my life, my love, my best friend, my confidant. I thank God every day for her, and every day I make sure I tell her that.

Part Six | Coming Full Circle

15

A Date of Infamy

Jesus answered and said unto them,
You do err, not knowing the Scriptures
nor the power of God.
> —Matthew 22:29

On February 28, 1993, I heard the news on the radio that the ATF had clashed with David Koresh's Branch Davidians in Waco, Texas, seventy miles from my home, as they attempted to serve an arrest warrant on Koresh. Four agents were killed and several others wounded. I later found out that among the wounded was Bill Buford.

I immediately called the ATF and FBI in Washington, D.C. to offer my assistance. I knew what Koresh and his people were going through and I knew the intentions of the FBI. Danny Coulson was in charge of this operation also, once the FBI had been brought in. I also believed I could talk Koresh into surrendering peacefully.

The second day of the siege, I called Washington again to warn them about Vernon Howell's name change to David Koresh and what it meant. "No one in a religious group changes their name lightly," I warned. "It always means something. 'David' obviously refers to King David in the Old Testament, the apple of God's eye, a man after God's own heart. This is the relationship that Koresh sees himself in. 'Koresh' is a transliteration of the Hebrew word for 'Cyrus,' a Persian king, anointed by God to set the Jews free from Babylonian captivity. He did this by attacking the city of Babylon. Koresh views this as his destiny. He believes he is called by God to deliver God's people from the hands of the Babylonians—the government—through war. He will not surrender unless he can see by revelation that it is God's will for him to do so. And, unfortunately, the FBI, or any typical preachers you may have to talk to Koresh, can not convince him of that. But I can twist the Scriptures enough, without him knowing it, for Koresh to see it as a 'higher revelation' and get him to surrender."

Over the next few weeks I spoke with several government agents asking for access to Koresh, and I publicly defended the ATF's actions. It absolutely amazed me how many people were speaking up for Koresh and were angry with the government. I knew the intentions of the FBI and ATF from experience. I also knew from experience the Christ-mentality of people like Koresh.

Just when it began to appear I was gaining an audience in my request, on April 19, 1993—eight years to the day since the siege on CSA began—Koresh, in a fiery suicide, ended all hopes of a peaceful conclusion. Although I had stated publicly that Koresh would never commit suicide, I had also stated he would never surrender and would not be taken alive. I had forgotten that, according to tradition, King Cyrus liked to burn people to death.

In my opinion, the ATF did exactly what they thought was best. The FBI, always patient in trying to spare lives, waited as long as it could. The fault was in underestimating Koresh's religious beliefs and ignoring them rather than reaching him through them. I still think I could have helped.

Why didn't CSA end up like the Branch Davidians? No Branch Davidian had previously offered to negotiate, as I had done. Had the ATF stormed us as they did Koresh (which they would have, except for my talk with Irby and the wisdom of Danny Coulson), the outcome would have been worse than Waco. Had the government come in on us in 1982—when we were 150-strong and all of one mind—instead of in 1985, a shootout would have been much more likely.

In October 1994, I applied for a Presidential Pardon. I became eligible in August of that year, having been out of prison for seven years. I knew it was a long shot since the President who would have to approve the pardon was the same one who was governor during those years in Arkansas. It took exactly one year for my application to be denied. In the fall of 1994 I did, however, have my voting rights restored to me by the state of Texas. For the first time in ten years, I exercised my voting rights during the fall elections.

In January 1995, I discovered that Danny Coulson had been transferred to Dallas, as the Agent-in-Charge of the Dallas office. I called him that same day.

"Talk about a ghost from the past," Coulson said, when he answered my call. "How are you doing?"

"I'm just fine," I answered. "I read in the newspaper that you're in Dallas now and I wanted to personally thank you. I never got the chance after the siege was over to thank you for your caring and integrity. You were a major part in my having turned around."

"Well, thank you," Danny said, "that means a lot to me."

We reminisced about the last ten years, then I asked him if he knew that I had tried to get hold of him during the Waco incident, that I wanted to see if there was anything I could do to help.

"No, I didn't know you had tried. But I'm not sure you could've done anything. Koresh was just plain crazy."

"Well, I sure would have liked to have tried to talk him into surrendering. I know it would've been a long shot, but I think it would've been worth the effort."

We spoke a while longer before saying good-bye. I immediately wrote Danny Coulson a letter again thanking him, and then I went into detail how I would have approached Koresh.

The letter must have had some impact on Coulson, because shortly thereafter, he called me and asked if he and another FBI agent could visit me at my home.

"Washington wants to know if you'd be interested in speaking to some people from the Hostage Rescue Team and the Domestic Terrorist Unit at the FBI headquarters."

It was more than I had hoped for. "Of course I'd be interested," I answered. "What do they want to talk to me about?"

"What you thought we did right at CSA, what we did wrong, and what to do the next time a siege occurs. At the group that we should have had a shoot-out with—CSA—no one got hurt; at the group that should've gone smoothly—Koresh's group—over eighty people died. We need to know why. We don't ever want another Waco. Perhaps you can help us avoid a shoot-out again."

Plans were made and I was flown to Washington, D.C. with another FBI agent, Mark, on March 28, 1995. There we met with six men from various units of the FBI. We discussed the tactics used on our siege, the mentality of the individuals inside our compound during the siege, and what could be done to help ensure a peaceful surrender in the future, should the need arise. Militia groups had been in the news recently and the government was concerned.

On April 10, 1995, Dennis Graves, my TV reporter friend from Springfield, Missouri flew to Dallas to interview Coulson and myself. He was doing a ten-year anniversary follow-up on CSA and thought an interview with two former "adversaries" might be of interest to the local people.

Dennis Graves had earned my trust when I first met him in 1984 at our compound. After his first interview with me and his final summation and remarks about CSA he asked me, "Did that sound all right to you?" No reporter ever before asked my feelings about what had been said. At one time when I was afraid we would someday be eliminated by the government, I gave him some written materials, so that the truth about CSA could be known should we all be killed in gun battle.

During the interview, Graves discussed the CSA siege by the FBI with Coulson and me. At one point he asked me, "You're sitting here with the man who caused you to spend twenty-six months in prison. How does that make you feel?"

"I don't see it that way," I answered. "To me, Danny didn't send me to prison; he kept me from spending more time in prison. If the FBI hadn't have come in when they did, who knows what might have happened later? As far as I'm concerned, Danny Coulson saved my life. He saved my wife's life; he saved the lives of my children. And he saved the lives of many of my friends. I've been thankful for the siege on CSA by the FBI and ATF ever since it happened. The way they conducted themselves helped turn me around. I'm astounded when I hear people criticize them over Waco. I know the good intentions of this man and those working with him."

The interview aired in three segments, in Springfield, Missouri, starting Monday, April 17.

Then, at 9:02 a.m. on the third and final day the news interview was to air that evening—on April 19, 1995 (10 years exactly from the time the siege on CSA began, and two years since the Branch Davidian fire)—an explosion rocked the nation. The federal building in Oklahoma City had been bombed. The same federal building CSA had targeted in 1983.

Early reports indicated it might have been done by foreign terrorists. I knew, though, as soon as it happened, that it was the right-wing. I recognized the target. They've done it, I thought, as I watched the horror on television. They've finally done it. The right-wing has crossed the line.

April 19—Patriot's Day in New England. The American Revolution began on that day in 1775 at Lexington Common in Massachusetts ("The shot heard around the world"). Many in the right-wing want the Second American Revolution to begin on that same day. On that date, in 1943, Nazis closed in on the Ghetto of Warsaw to wipe out the Jewish population on the Day of Passover. In 1993, the Branch Davidian compound burned to the ground, incinerating all of its remaining occupants, including children. And in 1995, Richard Wayne Snell—a declared patriot and martyr by the right-wing press—was to die. Was this date and its target a coincidence for America's deadliest domestic terrorist act?

The devastation at Oklahoma City was ironically almost perfect. Tied in to Waco and the Branch Davidians, the bombing was reminiscent of the Declarations of War by the Order and CSA, requiring a double to seven times retribution. Almost 170 men, women and children died in the bombing of the federal building, double the number at Mount Carmel (Waco). Over 500 could have died—seven times that of Waco.

Almost exactly twelve hours later, at 9:10 p.m., April 19, the man who had once planned (with Jim Ellison) to bomb that same Murrah

Federal Building in Oklahoma City—ex-CSA member Richard Wayne Snell, age 64—was executed for the murder of the pawnshop owner. Before his execution, Snell refused to express remorse for either of the two killings he was convicted of, and said he would do it all again if he could. Then he looked toward the witnesses before him and, according to newspaper reports, stated, "Governor Tucker (of Arkansas), look over your shoulder. Justice is on the way. I wouldn't trade places with you or any of your political cronies. Hail His victory. I am at peace."

Alan Ables, a prison official where Snell was housed, told the Canadian Broadcasting Corporation's *The Fifth Estate* that since Snell's mail was not monitored, a conspiracy to blow up the Oklahoma City Federal Building could have included Snell. The timing of the bombing almost exactly twelve hours before his execution made the events appear related.

White supremacist Robert Millar, who denies being involved in a conspiracy, was Snell's spiritual advisor. However, a connection between Millar's Elohim City and McVeigh has also been documented by *The Fifth Estate*. McVeigh's phone calling card was used for a call to Elohim City moments after he placed the call to reserve the rental truck used in the blast.

The Fifth Estate obtained footage from a security camera recording of a dressing room of a local strip club. The recording made eleven days before the bombing is of one employee telling another of a strange encounter with a customer in which the customer said "You're going to remember me on April 19, '95. You're going to remember me for the rest of your life." The customer answered the description of McVeigh. Andi Strassmeir of Elohim City and McVeigh are known to have met there on the day the recording was made.

Snell remained an avowed and active white supremacist to the very end, and became a martyr to extremists. He had told the Arkansas Parole Board the previous week that he should either be executed or exonerated, and compared himself to Nazi official Rudolph Hess. According to a prison death-watch log, on April 18, the day before he died, Snell turned to a prison guard and said "within the next ten days there will be Hell to pay." Snell even warned the government about "a bomb" and that April 19, would be a "bad day." The day of the bombing, the jail was placed on alert and the unusual precaution of moving prisoner Snell by helicopter was taken. There with Snell, on the day he died, was his friend and advisor, Robert Millar.

The Militia of Montana devoted most of a newsletter to the pending execution of Wayne Snell. Calling Snell "a patriot to be executed by the Beast," the Militia of Montana linked his execution date to the burning of the Branch Davidian compound in Waco and to the raid on CSA. For more than a year, the Randy Weaver incident, the burning of Koresh's compound in Waco, and the pending execution of Snell had been battle cries against the federal government on the Patriot/Militia network of faxes, fliers and Internet postings. At Snell's hearing before the Arkansas clemency board, fourteen of his supporters testified, with one Identity believer warning the board members and the governor that the "wrath of God" would fall upon them if Snell was executed as scheduled on April 19.

Federal authorities made a quick arrest in the bombing case. What would make a man commit such a horrible crime—the murder of so many innocent people, the worst domestic terrorist act ever committed in the United States?

The ingredients had already long been mixed. An outlook toward a dark, dismal future, without hope. The influence of right-wing leaders, either personally or through their writings. Isolation, a perceived enemy, and a feeling of no options.

The catalysts would include the June 3, 1983, killing of Posse Comitatus member Gordon Kahl; the August 31, 1992, standoff with white-separatist Randy Weaver in Idaho, in which his wife and 14-year-old son were killed; the April 19, 1993 blaze of the Branch Davidians; the November 30, 1993, signing of the Brady Bill into law by President Clinton, the man the right-wing considers the greatest traitor of all U.S. Presidents since Franklin Roosevelt; the assault-weapons ban; and, finally, the execution of a man that the right-wing considered a patriot and martyr—Richard Wayne Snell.

Timothy McVeigh and an army buddy of his, Terry Nichols, were the men accused of the Murrah Federal Building bombing. Arrested just sixty miles north of Oklahoma City at 10:20 a.m. on Wednesday, April 19, McVeigh had been pulled over for a traffic violation—his car had no license plate. The officer noticed a bulge under the driver's jacket. It turned out to be a 9mm Glock semiautomatic pistol loaded with Black Talon bullets called "cop killers" because they can penetrate body armor. His fake drivers license showed a birthdate of April 19, 1972; his real birthdate is April 23, 1968. It turned out that he obtained the license just after Snell's execution date was set.

McVeigh, born in New York, was an avid reader of *Soldier of Fortune* magazine and of the extremist novel, *The Turner Diaries.* He had visited Waco during the Branch Davidian standoff and, after its siege and suicide-fire, McVeigh expressed the opinion that the ATF had gotten out of control and was making war on their own citizens. He was filmed there on home video. He was reportedly one of Mark Koernke's bodyguards in March of 1994 at a Florida Militia meeting. Koernke was a militia leader from Michigan.

The government contends that McVeigh drove with Arizona Patriots Militia member Michael Fortier (whom McVeigh met in Arizona in June of 1993 and was now a government witness) to the Oklahoma City federal building and identified the building as his target; that on April 17, 1995, McVeigh rented a 20-foot rental truck in Junction City, Kansas; that on April 18, he and Nichols constructed an explosive truck bomb with ammonium nitrate, fuel and other explosives; that on April 19, McVeigh parked the truck bomb directly in front of the Murrah Federal Building during regular business and day-care hours and caused the truck bomb to explode.

In *The Turner Diaries,* a truck containing a "little under 5,000 pounds" of fuel oil and ammonium nitrate fertilizer is detonated at 9:15 a.m. in front of the FBI Headquarters building in Washington, D.C. The scenario, according to the book, went:

> . . . . As carefully as we could, we calculated that we should have at least 10,000 pounds of TNT or an equivalent explosive to destroy a substantial portion of the building. . . . To be on the safe side, we asked for 20,000 pounds. Instead, what we have is a little under

5,000 pounds, and nearly all of that is ammonium nitrate fertilizer, which is much less effective than TNT for our purpose. . . . Sensitized with oil and tightly confined, it makes an effective blasting agent, where the aim is simply to move a quantity of dirt or rock. But our original plan for the bomb called for it to be essentially unconfined and to be able to punch through two levels of reinforced-concrete flooring while producing an open-air blast wave powerful enough to blow the facade off a massive and strongly constructed building. . . .

Revolutionary Command feels it is essential to strike the System immediately with a blow which will . . . raise morale throughout the Organization by embarrassing the System and demonstrating our ability to act. . . . If, in accord with our original plan, we drive a truck into the main freight entrance of the FBI building and blow it up in the freight-receiving area, the explosion will take place in a large, central courtyard, surrounded on all sides by heavy masonry and open to the sky above. (We) both agree that with the present quantity of explosives we will not be able to do any really serious structural damage under those conditions. We can wreak havoc in all the offices with windows opening on the courtyard, but we cannot hope to blow away the inner facade of the building. . . . Several hundred people will be killed. . . .

What we finally decided is to attempt to get our bomb directly into the first-level basement, which also has a freight entrance on 10th Street, next to the main freight entrance. If we detonate our bomb in the basement underneath the courtyard, the confinement will make it substantially more effective. It will almost certainly collapse the basement floor into the sub-basement. . . . Furthermore it will destroy most, if not all, the communications and power equipment for the building, since those are on the basement levels. The big unknown is whether it will do enough structural damage to the building to make it uninhabitable for an extended period. Without a detailed blueprint of the building and a team of architects and civil engineers we simply can't answer that question. The drawback to going for the basement is that relatively few freight deliveries are made there, and the entrance is usually closed. . . .

At 9:15 yesterday morning our bomb went off in the FBI's national headquarters building. Our worries about the relatively small size of the bomb were unfounded; the damage is immense. We have certainly disrupted a major portion of the FBI's headquarters operations for at least the next several weeks, and it looks like we have also achieved our goal of wrecking their new computer complex. My day's work started a little before five o'clock yesterday, when I began helping . . . mix heating oil with the ammonium nitrate fertilizer in Unit 8's garage. We stood the 100-pound bags on end one by one and poked a small hole in the top with a screwdriver, just big enough to insert the end of a funnel. While I held the bag and funnel, Ed poured in a gallon of oil. Then we slapped a big square of adhesive tape over the hole, and I turned the bag end over end to mix the contents while Ed refilled his oil can from the feeder line to their oil furnace. It took us nearly three hours to do all 44 sacks, and the work really wore me out. . . .

With only two-and-a-half tons of explosives we didn't need a big tractor-trailer rig, so we had decided to grab a delivery truck. . . . we drove by the building. . . . until we found a good spot to park. Then we began walking back slowly, keeping an eye on our watches.

We were still two blocks away when the pavement shuddered violently under our feet. An instant later the blast wave hit us—a deafening "ka-whoomp," followed by an enormous roaring, crashing sound, accentuated by the higher-pitched noise of shattering glass all around us. The plate glass windows in the store beside us and dozens of others that we could see along the street were blown to splinters. A glittering and deadly rain of glass shards continued to fall into the street from the upper stories of nearby buildings for a few seconds, as a jet-black column of smoke shot straight up into the sky ahead of us. We ran the final two blocks and were dismayed to see what, at first glance, appeared to be an entirely intact FBI headquarters—except, of course, that most of the windows were missing.

Dozens of people were scurrying around the freight entrance to the central courtyard, some going in and some coming out. Many were bleeding profusely from cuts, and all had expressions of shock or dazed disbelief on their faces. . . . Overturned trucks and automobiles, smashed office furniture, and building rubble were strewn wildly about—and so were the bodies of a shockingly large number of victims. Over everything hung the pall of black smoke, burning our eyes and lungs and reducing the bright morning to semi-darkness. . . .

According to the latest estimate released, approximately 700 persons were killed in the blast or subsequently died in the wreckage. That includes an estimated 150 persons who were in the sub-basement at the time of the explosion and whose bodies have not been recovered. . . .

All day yesterday and most of today we watched the TV coverage of rescue crews bringing the dead and injured out of the building. It is a heavy burden of responsibility for us to bear, since most of the victims of our bomb were only pawns who were no more committed to the sick philosophy or the racially destructive goals of the System than we are. But there is no way we can destroy the System without hurting many thousands of innocent people—no way. It is a cancer too deeply rooted in our flesh. And if we don't destroy the System before it destroys us—if we don't cut this cancer out of our living flesh—our whole race will die.

We have gone over this before, and we are all completely convinced that what we did is justified, but it is still very hard to see our own people suffering so intensely because of our acts. It is because Americans have for so many years been unwilling to make unpleasant decisions that we are forced to make decisions now which are stern indeed. . . .

Interviewers are asking leading questions like, "What kind of inhuman beasts do you think could have done something like this to your daughter?" They have clearly made the decision to portray the bombing of the FBI building as the atrocity of the century.

The truck used in Oklahoma City is estimated to have carried some 4,000 pounds, 1,000 pounds less than in the Turner Diary-blueprint. If there were a connection to the above-mentioned scenario, then why not blow up the FBI building in Washington rather than the Oklahoma City federal building? One possible tie-in might be with Richard Wayne Snell, the man who staked out that building with Jim Ellison in 1983.

Telephone records reveal that someone using McVeigh's phone card called Elohim City—Robert Millar's group in Oklahoma—on April 5, two weeks before the bombing. McVeigh was ticketed on October 12, 1993, less than ten miles from Elohim City, on County Route 220, the only access road into the compound.

It has been reported that McVeigh may have visited Elohim City on numerous occasions. One such visit is believed to have occurred when McVeigh and Nichols traveled to Arkansas in October 1993, when McVeigh was ticketed. On September 12, 1994, he checked into a motel in Vian, Oklahoma. He is believed to have gone to Elohim City the next day to take part in military maneuvers that Andi Strassmeir had organized for some seventy participants. It was at this time that the initial conspiracy to bomb the federal building was reportedly hatched.

Robert Millar—who testified as a character witness for Snell during his trial—was Wayne Snell's spiritual counselor during the years on death row, and Millar was going to take Snell's body to Elohim City for burial.

Elohim City, located in eastern Oklahoma, has been the subject of FBI scrutiny for some time. According to various reports, Carol Howe, a former skinhead and then an ATF informant, lived at Elohim City from 1993-1995 as a contact of Dennis Mahon, leader of the White Aryan Resistance. She supposedly heard advance word while at Elohim City about the Oklahoma City bombing and informed the government. Millar's grand-daughter, Esther, was engaged to Mike Brescia who was implicated in the Midwest bank robberies with Mark Thomas (Pennsylvania leader of the Aryan Nations), Scott William Stedeford and Kevin McCarthy, all of whom had stayed at Elohim City for an extended period of time.

In addition, Andrew Strassmeir, a German diplomat's son who was militarily trained, was Elohim City's security chief for almost three years. Strassmeir's grandfather helped found the German Nazi Party. Strassmeir left Elohim City three months after the bombing. He and Brescia had been seen together as far back as 1992.

Ray Lampley, convicted of weapons violations, tested bombs at Elohim City. Two members of the Aryan Republican Army stayed there. Chevie (a polygamist) and Cheyne Kehoe, wanted in a police shootout in Wilmington Ohio and for murdering a man, woman, and an eight-year-old girl during a robbery in Arkansas, had also been to Elohim City.

McVeigh was reportedly seen at a topless bar in Tulsa, Oklahoma, on April 8, 1995 with Strassmeir and another man then living at Elohim City. At the bar, McVeigh supposedly said to one of the strippers "that she would remember him in a big way when something important would happen on April 19." According to news reports, it was Strassmeir that McVeigh had tried to call at Elohim City, only two weeks before the Oklahoma City bombing.

McVeigh had even informed his own sister that he would cross the line from rhetoric to action.

The entire right-wing was aware of Snell's pending execution date and that he would be buried at Elohim City. Is it possible that, as a tribute to the movement's latest martyr, *The Turner Diaries'* bombing location might have been moved from Washington, D.C. to Oklahoma City? And might April 19 have been interpreted as a sign from God? I think so.

Retired FBI agent Jack Knox told *The Denver Post* in May of 1996 that Wayne Snell had the ability to engineer the Oklahoma City bombing from his death row cell. Snell reportedly predicted to a high-ranking prison official that there would be a bombing or an explosion the day of his death.

How does the right-wing justify such violence, hatred and murder? The paranoia of the right-wing is as much alive today as it was ten to fifteen years ago. Fifteen years ago, we preached that the federal government was using microwave towers to alter the weather patterns in the United States, so that crops would fail and prices rise; that grassy inclines were being replaced with concrete walls along interstate highways in major cities so that people couldn't escape once martial law was imposed; that military aircraft spread biological disease-causing agents in the air over various test cities; that concentration camps were located in various parts of the country, for those who resisted the Regional Government program; that bar codes on food products in homes could be detected by the government, so they would know who was hoarding food; that prison guards and officials had conspired to one day free all prisoners across the country so they could terrorize the nation in some sort of "Helter Skelter."

Today the favorite conspiracies of the right-wing say: The United Nations plans to conquer the United States using the National Guard and the Los Angeles gangs to disarm the public . . . Recent chemical spills are practice runs for a much larger series of disasters, faked by the government, to draw people out of their homes and enable the U.N. forces to enter homes and seize their weapons. Before the U.N. takeover, FEMA will head up an interim government. The Amtrak repair yards in Indianapolis will be used as a huge crematorium to dispose of political dissidents. Black helicopters have already been buzzing Western states on missions of surveillance for the invading U.N. troops. Salt mines beneath Detroit hold a division of Russian troops waiting for the order to rise and take over the United States. Small colored bar-code stickers found on the back of road signs will help direct invading troops. The government has installed electronic devices in car ignitions to stall autos on the day the new world order takes over. Paper currency has bar codes on it so government agents can drive by each house with secret scanners and count how much money each family has.

As astounding as the above sounds, a recent Anti-Defamation League report estimated that paramilitary groups are in at least forty states, with a total of some 15,000 members. One militia leader boasts of over 2,000 militia groups, with membership up to four million.

It is difficult for the average American to comprehend how anyone can justify hatred and violence, and especially those who claim to be Christians or religious. How can anyone in one breath proclaim the name of God and in another defame a whole race of people? To understand the answer, it is important to realize that in the right-wing, the primary theological doctrine is "Identity," a doctrine that claims that the white, Anglo-Saxon people are the true Israel of the Bible and that the Jews are a counterfeit race, descendant from the devil himself. Further, the doctrine proclaims, all other races are lower creations, probably descended from the apes or other animals. Only whites are presumed to be made in the image of God.

Even presuming that each individual has the right to believe whatever perverse doctrine he or she may want, how then can that individual rationalize hating the other creations of God or wanting to do violence to them or even to their own race?

In answering this question, I will use references from a booklet I wrote while in the right-wing movement, entitled, *Prepare War!* It is with much regret that I admit to authoring this booklet, but at the time I thought I was right.

The introduction of the booklet proclaims that "this booklet is designed to give a Scriptural reasoning for war and the Christian Army of God . . . The God of Israel commands this Message—this Gospel—to be proclaimed and published among the Nations of Israel. 'Prepare War! Wake up the Mighty Men! Let all the Men of War come near. Let them come up. Beat your plowshares into swords and your pruning-hooks into spears. Let the weak say, I am strong!" (Joel 3:9,10).

In the first chapter, "Scriptural Foundation for the Christian Army," I went on to explain that the elect or chosen of God are anointed for a special purpose, and that purpose is to be like God. Christians would typically say that "God is Light" and "God is Love" (1 John 1:5; 4:8) and therefore we are to manifest that light and love. But, as I explained, the Scriptures also say, "The Lord God is a man of War: The Lord is His Name." (Exodus 15:3). Therefore, it is concluded, if we are to walk in His total nature, we must also walk as Men of War.

"See now that I, even I, am He and there is no God with me: I kill and I make alive; I wound and I heal: neither is there any that can deliver out of my hand. If I wet my glittering sword, and my hand take hold of judgment: I will render vengeance to my enemies, and will reward them that hate me. I will make my arrows drunk with blood and my sword shall devour flesh." (Deuteronomy 32:39,41,42). With this scripture, we at CSA took another step toward justifying warfare in the name of God. If our Father were a Man of War and took vengeance on His enemies, would it not also follow that, as His children, we were to be men of war and also take vengeance on His enemies?

King David, a man after God's own heart (according to scripture) and a man we were taught to respect, said, "He (the Lord) teaches my hands to war and my fingers to fight." (2 Samuel 22:35; Psalms 144:1). This, we believed, was because God said concerning Jacob (Israel) in Jeremiah 57:20, "You are my battle axe and weapons of war: for with you will I break in pieces the nations, and with you will I destroy kingdoms." David also said, "Do not I hate them, O Lord, that hate you? I hate them with a perfect hatred; I count them my enemies." (Psalms 139:21,22). Since we believed we were of Israel, we concluded these scriptures pertained to us also.

Those in the right-wing movement proudly desire the heritage of the Lord. So they hold onto scriptures like Psalms 149:5-9: "Let the saints be joyful in glory: let them sing aloud upon their beds. Let the high praises of God be in their mouth and a two-edged sword in their hand; to execute vengeance upon the heathen, and punishments upon the people; to bind their kings with chains, and their nobles with fetters of iron; to execute upon them the judgment written: This honor have all His saints. Praise ye the Lord."

Then in the parables of the Marriage of the King's Son (Matthew 22:1-7) and of the Nobleman and the 10 Pounds (Luke 19:12-27), Jesus spoke of how at the end of this age He would send His armies, gathering those who would not have Him reign over them, and would slay them before Him. God, we believed, would love this judgment (Isaiah 61:8).

This was the foundation but we still needed to know that it was time to cross the line into violence and that it was acceptable to the Lord. We needed at CSA in the early 1980s to know the line, and the right-wing followers today follow the same train of thought.

The next chapter was entitled, "Dominion by Violence." Here, I laid the groundwork that God had given to man dominion over all things and was to subdue the earth. To us, however, the Lord had not yet made the earth His footstool and peace did not reign. Confusion reigned instead, caused by man's unwillingness to obey the laws of God, apparent by man's sinful nature.

In Matthew 11:12, Jesus says, "From the days of John the Baptist until now, the Kingdom of Heaven suffers violence, and the violent take it by force." We interpreted this to mean that to the same degree sin was increasing in the earth, also would the sons of God have to use force and violence to overcome that sinfulness in the earth, that that was the only way to purge evil from the earth. Daniel 7:9-28 confirmed this for us by stating that, "the saints of the Most High shall take the kingdom, and possess the kingdom for ever, even for ever and ever."

Christian churches have for years preached that the latter days would be like the days of Noah, when God could scarcely find any righteous upon the earth, when men's thoughts were only evil continually. We believed, therefore, that as time progressed, very few would understand the true purpose of God and that judgment was coming to America and to the world. The time would come when a mighty angel, or messenger, would come and cast a great millstone into the sea (the masses of people, by our interpretation), and say, "Thus with violence shall that great city Babylon be thrown down, and shall be found no more at all." (Revelation 18:21).

The major cities to us were like Sodom and Gemorrah, like the Tower of Babel. Who would be judged? The homosexual; the liberal, idolatrous preachers; those officials in high places; the merchants of trade and usury; and all those who refused the word of the Lord. They were the enemy. And so they would have to die.

We consoled ourselves with the thought that war was only a means to an end, the darkness before the dawn. I had stated on television that I was not looking forward to the coming war, but I was looking forward to the kingdom of God that was to follow. That's how many of us rationalized being soldiers of God. We wanted peace, but if purging had to precede peace, then let the purge begin.

We believed in the literal interpretation of Revelation 18:10 and 17 that said Babylon's judgment would come in one hour, that peace and safety would cease and sudden destruction would come (1 Thessalonians 2:3). If that were the case, we believed that we had to "Prepare War."

Those guilty of Oklahoma City's bombing and of the other crimes of hate and violence feel a scriptural justification for their actions, while also feeling no choice in the matter, that war must begin sometime, that people must wake up. The followers of the right-wing movement have been brainwashed into believing that the government is the agent toward some dark and sinister end-time when an evil Anti-Christ will rule and make war on the saints of God. They have lost all hope and trust. To them, the Beast has made war on them. In the minds of those in the movement, they are the victims, not those who died in the bombing.

What I did not realize when I wrote this booklet and when I was in the movement was that fear, hate, and violence were not solutions, but problems in themselves. Problems which stemmed from my own feelings of inadequacy, insecurity and frustration. We twisted scripture that was meant only for God or for the nation (government) of Israel (and not for individuals), and proclaimed them for ourselves. After a while, we conveniently neglected scriptures that had to do with living in peace as shining lights in the midst of darkness. We became not only desperate, but proud that war would come and that we would be a part of it.

The religious belief system of the terrorist-right is not to be underestimated, any more than the religious beliefs of those in the Middle East. What individuals believe determines what they do. And those who are in authority in the movement are making sure that the followers feel cornered to force them into action. Therefore if you can change the belief system and the basic premise of the individuals, you can begin to stop an entire movement.

Timothy McVeigh reminds me of a young Wayne Snell. He would be typical of Louis Beam's "cell group" in the leaderless resistance of the right-wing. Inside the pages of *The Turner Diaries* may be revealed the perspective McVeigh saw of himself and his destiny:

> . . . we have all proved ourselves, not only through a correct attitude toward the Cause, but also through our acts in the struggle for the realization of the Cause.
>
> As members of the Order we are to be the bearers of the Faith. Only from our ranks will the future leaders of the Organization come. . . . The Order . . . will remain secret, even within the Organization, until the successful completion of the first phase of our task: the destruction of the System. And he showed us the Sign by which we might recognize one another. And then we swore the Oath—a mighty Oath, a moving Oath that shook me to my bones and raised the hair on the back of my neck. . . . Now our lives truly belong only to the Order.

Because of what had happened in Oklahoma City, I felt that I should do something. So I wrote a letter to the editors of twenty newspapers and magazines across the country. Two newspapers—in Little Rock, Arkansas and Springfield, Missouri—printed the article. In it I said:

> April 19 has become the July 4 of right-wing extremists. In 1993, there was the burning monument of the Branch Davidians' Mount Carmel in Waco, Texas. In 1995, Richard Wayne Snell, an avowed white supremacist, was executed in Arkansas for the shooting death of a pawnshop owner. And only 12 hours before Snell's execution, the worst terrorist act in U.S. history took place in Oklahoma City when the federal building was bombed and scores of innocent men, women and children were slaughtered.
>
> What is it that drives an extremist to such dire ends? What motivates the right-wing hatemonger to so despise his government that he is willing to sacrifice anyone for the sake of his own martyrdom?

What makes one cross the line from simple paranoia to unrepentant destruction? The common man, woman and child has no answers, no explanations.

You in the right-wing cover the spectrum from perhaps well-meaning tax protesters to church-going pro-lifers to gun-toting Second-Amendment activists to hate-spewing white supremacists. Most of you would never consider breaking the law or hurting another human. Most of you simply have deep concerns for the future of our nation. Most of you are loving, God-fearing, patriotic Americans who believe in the heritage of our country. But some of you have lost all respect for law and order and the sovereign dignity of each human life.

You have been so ingrained that the end-time apocalyptic scenario is to be one of an evil empire, where some dark and sinister Antichrist (be that individual or government) makes war on the Christian saints of God, with the world totally socialist, communist and atheist.

You have been lied to! You who are in the movement have been deceived. How do I know? April 19 holds another day of importance. On that day in 1985, the FBI and ATF raided the group in which I was the second in command. That group was the Covenant, the Sword, and the Arm of the Lord (CSA) in northern Arkansas, and we were considered the second most dangerous domestic terrorist group at that time.

If ever an "evil" government would have wanted to slaughter "innocent" patriots, it was then. But that was not the case. Indeed, it was the admirable actions of the government officials themselves, who acted with integrity and honor, that helped to turn me from the deception of the right-wing. I found the federal agents to be more honorable than any right-wing people I had known. This especially caused me to reflect upon my beliefs, so that while I was in prison, I discovered them to be based upon error and lies.

I knew Wayne Snell. He murdered a helpless pawnshop owner who was forced to lie face down on the floor as Snell blew his brains out. A martyr? I don't think so. Snell was a self-serving coward who went from group to group stirring up trouble.

David Koresh? A martyr? No. He was a self-appointed messiah who sacrificed 80 of his own people as a burnt offering.

You in the right-wing: Who is sovereign and has all things in control? The Almighty God that you say you worship, or the demigod Trilateralists, Illuminati, International Bankers, and One-Worlders that you fear so much? Who has done more good and positive for this country of ours? Your divisive, complaining, drunken, hate-spewing, self-serving fellow comrades, or our entrepreneurs, philanthropists, and law-abiding citizens, be they Jewish, Black, Hispanic, Asian, or White?

You in the right-wing: As with all of us, what you believe dictates what you do. If you proceed from a false premise, full of rhetoric, hate, and lies, your path will lead to destruction. If you proceed, instead, from a true premise, full of faith, hope and love, your path will lead to life. Choose the correct premise and the correct path.

Stop the hate; stop the killing; stop the insanity.

16

Hope

And he showed me a
pure river of life,
clear as crystal,
proceeding out of the throne of God
and of the Lamb.
In the midst of the street of it,
and on either side of the river,
the tree of life,
which bare twelve fruits,
and yielded her fruit every month:
and the leaves of the tree
were for the healing of the nations.
—Revelation 22:1, 2

After Jim Ellison finished his sentence, on April 23, 1995, he moved to Robert Millar's commune, Elohim City, in Oklahoma which has been called the "Holiday Inn of Hate." On May 19, he married one of Millar's granddaughters, 26-year-old Angie, who was already carrying his child.

The fusion of Ellison's blood and seed into Millar's is similar to the old medieval times when kings' families intermarried. Now "King James of the Ozarks" had covenanted with "Robert of Oklahoma." Elohim City, it is reported, presented Ellison with a sword embedded in a rock. The rock and the sword sit on display in Elohim City's sanctuary building. The only one allowed to remove the sword is Ellison.

By the end of May, reports were connecting the Oklahoma City bombing to Elohim City, where authorities said Timothy McVeigh had called just prior to the bombing. Millar gave a press conference at Elohim City. One of the reporters there had recently interviewed me, and asked Millar what he thought about me.

"I don't like to speak negatively about anyone," Millar replied, "but Kerry Noble is an embittered person. It would have been better if he hadn't negotiated during the siege at CSA, because he prevented God from doing what He had purposed to do. A mighty victory for our people would have occurred had Kerry not negotiated for Ellison's surrender."

Since the Oklahoma City bombing I have spoken to several civic organizations, the Cult Awareness Network, and law-enforcement seminars about the right-wing movement, what to expect in the future and how to handle the various groups. I have been interviewed by the Canadian Anti-Racism Education and Research Society, the Associated Press, the Canadian Broadcasting Corporation, by Dan Rather for the *CBS Evening News, Dateline* on NBC, Channels 5 and 8 in Dallas, Channel 9 in Oklahoma City, the *Denver Post,* the *Kansas City Star, Time Magazine,* the *Die Woche* German newspaper, and other radio, television and newspaper media. With each speaking engagement or interview, I try to share my insight into the mindset of the right-wing:

The basic premise of the right-wing is that they envision a dark and gloomy end-time scenario, where some Antichrist makes war against Christians. Everything that happens now is simply a step toward that goal. All hope for the future and all trust of law-enforcement and the government in general is lost.

This places the government in a 'lose-lose' situation. No matter what it does to help the country, the right interprets it as steps toward taking away the rights of citizens and establishing complete governmental control. The right-wing believes the government has some ulterior motive in whatever they do.

Because the majority of members in the right-wing grew up in the traditional churches, they have been ingrained with the false interpretations of good versus evil, that man is basically evil, and that the end-time before Jesus returns will be an evil time period. It was this basis that propelled our group in Arkansas, and it was this basis that I began to question in 1983. I began to examine our belief system and looked at the Scriptures from another angle. Eventually I concluded that the end-times would not be dark and sinister and evil, but instead would be prosperous and godly in nature.

Therefore, the first key in dealing with the right-wing is to make them re-examine their beliefs. In my opinion, the greatest problem facing America today is our lack of hope for the future.

I break down the right-wing groups into three categories: religious, nationalist, and racist. All three are most dangerous when they feel cornered.

The religious groups are God-centered. Their vision is to do the will of God, and they look forward to the Kingdom of God. This would include groups like the Branch Davidians, Elohim City, and CSA. They are concerned about issues like abortion, school prayer and morality. These groups are the easiest to guide or direct into a surrender if law-enforcement will understand their doctrine or "revelation." It is important for law-enforcement to never try to directly tear down these group's doctrines, but to build on them, steering the groups away from their dangerous misunderstandings of God's will.

The religious groups have a pride mentality that can lead them into sexual perversions or "freedoms." How far has a group gone? Look at its sexual habits. At CSA, two years before our demise, we were practicing polygamy. Many of these Bible-based groups believe in the "Kingship" teaching, that the leaders will someday rule various parts of the United States. This teaching will also be connected to the leadership's "Christ-Mentality," believing themselves to be perfect and sinless.

The most dangerous doctrine going around the religious groups today is the "resurrection" or "never-die" doctrine. This doctrine states that someone must be resurrected soon as a sign of God's vindication of the right-wing. If the government goes against a group that absolutely believes in the resurrection doctrine, then why should the group members fear death? They'll be raised from the dead three days later. Why should they care if police officers die? That would only be eliminating the agents of sin.

The second type of group—the nationalists—include the survivalists, the Posse Comitatus, the paramilitary groups, the Constitutionalists, the Patriots, and the Militia. These are "America First" in their orientation and seek the will of the Founding Fathers. They want to go back to 1776. They are concerned about crime, bureaucracy, and gun-control. These groups are harder to direct or guide in a siege situation because they have no hope, no trust in the government. This is seen in examples like Gordon Kahl.

The most dangerous doctrine in these groups is the "sovereign citizen" doctrine, where members rescind their driver's licenses, marriage licenses, birth certificates, social security numbers and all other ties to the government. This means they no longer recognize the authority of federal or state governments. If law-enforcement comes against them, they will justify their actions on the basis of self-defense. These groups are founded on fear and paranoia.

What a lot of people don't realize is that wanting to go back to 1776 means no rights for women, no rights for minorities. These groups believe that the problems in the country started when rights were recognized for women and minorities. They are white-male centered. They oppose the IRS and gun-control. Not because of the Constitution, but because they want power.

Their hypocrisy is seen in the Militia movement. The right-wing and the Militia in particular love to quote the Second Amendment to the U.S. Constitution: "A well regulated Militia, being necessary to the security of a free State, the right of the people to keep and bear Arms, shall not be infringed." The individual citizens, they say, make up the Militia. Yet what does the rest of the Constitution say about the Militia? The Fifth Amendment categorizes the Militia with "the land or naval forces . . . when in actual service in time of War or public danger . . ." In other words, the Militia is part of our Armed Services. Article I, Section 8 of the Constitution says that Congress shall "provide for calling forth the Militia to execute the Laws of the Union." Therefore, Congress (not some self-appointed Militia President or Commander) sets down the rules for the Militia. Then finally, Article 2, Section 2 of the United States Constitution reveals who the Founding Fathers say is in charge of the Militia: "The President shall be Commander in Chief of the Army and Navy of the United States, and of the Militia of the several States, when called into the actual Service of the United States . . ."

Therefore, even if "the Militia" of the Founding Fathers is not a reference to the State or National Guard (which, I believe, it is), how can these so-called Militia groups who justify their existence under the Second Amendment not also recognize their Constitutional responsibility of submission to the United States governmental powers and their commander in chief, the President?

The racial groups, of course, include the Klan, Skinheads, Aryan Nations and neo-Nazis. They are hate-oriented, with a vision of medieval times and doing the will of the "warrior." The classic example of this group is the Order and Bob Mathews.

The racists' major gripes are affirmative action, quotas, immigration and race-mixing. Their most dangerous doctrine is the belief that they are in a state of war already, that the Order's Declaration of War is still in effect. They are the most dangerous and hardest to direct or guide, because everyone but a small remnant is the enemy, or "just like dogs."

How dangerous are the right-wing groups? Richard Butler of the Aryan Nations in Idaho refers to himself as "Der Führer." He believes the FBI killed Randy Weaver's wife and son at Ruby Ridge in 1992 because the defendants at the Sedition Trial in Arkansas in 1988 were acquitted. The right-wing preaches that federal agents actually blew up the federal building in Oklahoma City as a reason to crack down on the Militia and other so-called patriots . . . The Militia threatens and intimidates government workers with its "common-law" lawsuits . . . A white supremacist was sentenced to nearly 13 years for planting a bomb in a Dallas movie theater during a 1993 showing of Malcolm X . . . Two members of the anti-tax Minnesota Patriots Council were convicted on federal terrorism charges in a plot to use chemical poison against unnamed human targets . . . A white supremacist was arrested on allegations that he obtained bubonic plague bacteria through the mail . . . Militia groups are preparing for the inevitable war to come . . . Books are easily ordered through the mail instructing the reader how to build C-4 explosives, improvised explosives, mortar and fertilizer explosives. . . . The Internet is full of web-pages from the various hate groups, trying to recruit youth and stirring violence and hate into society.

The common doctrine between all the groups is Identity and the belief in earning a place or position in the Kingdom. Religious, nationalist and racist groups believe they have a three-fold destiny. The premise for Identity—a white, Christian America—contains the potent combination of race, religion and nationality. How dangerous is this combination? Look at Middle East countries that have this type of fundamentalist government and ask yourself if this is what you want for America.

There are three types of people in the extremist movement: the Leader/Manipulator (making up about .1%), the Feeders (98.9%), and the Sacrificial Lambs (1%). The leader knows not everyone will cross the line into domestic terrorism, so he seeks out the one percent that will, the sacrificial lambs. By manipulating them, he hopes to push the end-time scenario into place. Meanwhile, in order to live off his rhetoric, he uses the feeders to support him, knowing they are not the true warriors, but useful nonetheless.

I believe we are at a turning point, especially when talking about right-wing extremists. In 1978-79, the groups believed that we had entered a transition period in God's calendar. Five years later, the Order and CSA emerged with their Declarations of War and we got busted by the government. After that, the movement died down. Then, in 1993, Waco.

The groups are looking at the year 2000 now, another important time period. The teenagers of the 1980s will be the leaders of the right-wing in the next five to ten years. The generation that founded the groups want something major to happen before they die. Everyone is tired of waiting; therefore, members experience pressure from above and pressure from below.

The best example I know of this is the merging of Jim Ellison and Robert Millar's efforts and beliefs. Elohim City has a religious, nationalist and racial focus, mixed with resurrection and "earning a position in the Kingdom" doctrines. Millar is concerned that as spiritual as his group tries to be, there has not been "a real move of the Spirit" there in several years. Ellison and Millar both believe that I cheated them of their destinies in 1985 and kept God from performing some kind of miracle. Ellison has sworn not to surrender again. He has sworn to go down in history in a major way.

As far as the right-wing is concerned, they are still in a state of war. Tom Metzger of the White Aryan Resistance stated on the *Montel Williams* talk show that the Order's Declaration of War has never been rescinded. The right-wing are trying to outdo each other. Everyone wants to be bigger than the one before them. First Waco, with four agents killed. Then, a federal building is bombed, killing 168 people. What's next?

At CSA we had thirty gallons of cyanide that we planned to drop into city water supplies. We had planned an assassination of government officials. Wayne Snell, an associate of ours, murdered two men. The Order murdered two men and committed armored car robberies. Plans that were discussed in the 1980s came to pass in the 1990s.

I fear that we will have another domestic terrorist act in this country within the next five to seven years, one that will be of even greater impact than Oklahoma City. The result will be so extreme and so catastrophic that even many we now consider extreme right-wing may denounce the action.

What can law-enforcement do? First of all, they must understand the symbology and doctrines of the groups. Symbols and dates are important to the right-wing. By law-enforcement understanding their importance, they will begin to understand the mentality and direction of the groups.

Group members and leaders should be treated with respect when at all possible. Be friendly with them where possible. Establish trust. Get to know them. The trust that I gained for Gene Irby and Bill Buford led to my being able to trust Danny Coulson.

Law-enforcement must do the opposite of what the groups expect them to do. The agents at our search actually cleaned up after themselves and fed our animals while we were off the property. Danny Coulson allowed Jim Ellison to come down to the government encampment during the siege and then return to the compound.

Neither Ellison nor I were handcuffed upon our arrests. This was not what we expected.

If possible, law-enforcement should never storm a group in force. That will only make them react in force. They should try to go in peaceably, with two or three agents, to arrest a leader of a group. In doing so, another Waco might be prevented. The right-wing respects courage and will trust a man of courage.

It is vital that a law-enforcement agent keep his word. If I thought for a moment that Danny Coulson was lying to me or trying to con me, negotiations would have ceased.

Law-enforcement should wait as long as required. Evaluate the group. Realize that divisions within these groups are constant and the group may disintegrate on its own. Then they can go in at the group's weakest moment.

It is important to remember that people in the right-wing movement mistrust government and feel their way of life is being threatened. Often a member of the right-wing will feel confused, isolated, paranoid. The member wants assurance from the government and other people that no one is out to hurt them or theirs without cause. It is not uncommon for the belief structures of a right-wing member or group to change from time to time. Those times of change are important in understanding the mentality and direction of the member or group.

Most importantly, I think, is for law-enforcement (and others) not to believe everything reported about a group. Inaccuracies written about CSA reveal how prevalent rumors can be. To set the record straight: Gordon Kahl never hid at CSA nor was he killed at CSA; CSA did not own a gold mine in Costa Rica; Ellison had two wives at CSA, not four; CSA did not kidnap hitchhikers; no one was murdered and buried at CSA; we never called ourselves "Dragons of God" and our children never begged on the streets of nearby towns. Be critical of the information received about a group—lives could depend upon it.

There are three time periods that are the worst times for law-enforcement to hit a group. They should avoid these if possible.

The first is mid-April. The 19th is out for obvious reasons. The 20th is out for the racial groups because that's Hitler's birthday. But more importantly, April is the time of the Passover and when Jesus was resurrected. A group could easily perceive action at this time as a sign from God that it was time to die and that they will be resurrected three days later.

The second period would be mid-August, during the ninth of Ab on the Jewish calendar. This is historically a persecution period for God's people. The groups, again, might interpret an attack as a sign from God that the persecution by the Beast had begun.

The third is in September-October, during the Feast of Tabernacles. Most right-wing or religious-community groups realize that this was when Jesus was really born, and that is significant. But they also believe that this period in history was when Adam was created, when the flood in Noah's day occurred, and when Moses was given the two tablets containing the Ten Commandments. Again, they would consider action against them at this time as a sign from God, and could expect a miracle. When is the best time then to go against a group? In the dead of winter. All the groups dread fighting in the cold and harshness of winter's bad weather.

In a siege situation, who the government has as negotiator is of primary importance. The command leader must be a strong, confident, white male, full of integrity and honesty, an equal to the group's own leader. It must not be a woman, a minority member, anyone in the least bit effeminate, or someone who is self-centered and untrustworthy. Nobody will negotiate with someone whom he considers not to be an equal: it's a matter of pride. Therefore, since the right-wing is a white-male, racist, patriarchal, warrior system, the negotiator must be a white male of impressive stature. If a group negotiates with any other type of negotiator, they are only stalling, until a forced shoot-out or a mass suicide.

Remember, the three ingredients necessary for the creation of an extremist group or individual: A false premise, or doctrine, be it philosophical or theological, that is based upon some negative emotion such as fear, unbelief, hate, or despair. A charismatic leader or leaders who can guide and direct the group or individual. Physical, mental or emotional isolation from society, leading to a "Savior-mentality" or "Christ-mentality," brought on by limited information and creating a perceived enemy, emergency or limited options. Once the group or individual feels there are no other choices, some catalyst is needed to push them over the edge to pursue a course of domestic terrorism. This catalyst will usually be a martyr, such as David Koresh or Randy Weaver, with a deadline, such as an important "spiritual" date or an anniversary.

What can government do and what can we do as a society, to make this a safer nation? Seduction into right-wing extremism is possible only because they have legitimate concerns that are expressed by many in society. Obviously the right-wing answers are not what we need. I do not pretend to have all the answers, but it is important to remember that the number one problem in America today is not drugs, crime, a lack of morality, or the federal government. Our number one problem is a lack of hope.

America needs a spiritual—not religious—awakening based on true values (not so-called "family" values): truth, integrity, neighborliness, character, work ethics, personal responsibility, a desire to learn, the Golden Rule, compassion. These are values that all people can participate in. Next, we desperately need leadership in our nation. Strong leadership in the White House and Congress is mandatory, with bi-partisan solutions for an effective government as its goal.

Then, our churches must proclaim a truly positive message and a positive response to the needs of society. I believe churches have the greatest potential for transforming society for the good. They are equipped to inspire people for positive change, to help revitalize neighborhoods, to help provide jobs, to give aid to the needy.

Inner-city revitalization must be top priority. An ounce of prevention is still worth a pound of cure. Give inner-city youths a reason to be productive in society, to have hope and to live—instead of a reason to join gangs, give up on life and eventually get killed or go to prison. We also need to revamp our legal, tax, medical and educational systems thereby returning public confidence.

We must face the issue of gun control in America. It is very unlikely that Americans will voluntarily do without personal weapons and gun ownership and I do not advocate a constitutional amendment curtailing any of our Bill of Rights. However, it is also without dispute that nations with strong gun-control laws have lower crime problems. We need a system that works—not like Washington, D.C. or New York City, which have strong gun-control laws yet high crime rates. I believe we can achieve gun registration in this country, without giving up second-amendment rights. We think nothing in our society about registering our vehicles, but we scream when gun registration is mentioned. There is nothing wrong with law-enforcement knowing where the guns are in a dangerous situation. This is essential for their personal safety. Indeed, the public already have access to knowledge about what weapons law-enforcement have available to them.

Solutions may not be easy, but they are attainable. Diversity is good, but we are Americans first and ethnic second. Together—Black, White, Hispanic, and Asian; Democrat, Republican, and Independent; Male or Female; Straight or Gay; Rich or Poor—we are Americans. Separate, we are only warring individuals who live in the same country. Together we can solve problems; separate, we cannot. Together we can move into the next century and the next millennium with positive results; separate, the year 2001 is just another year.

It took almost seven years, from 1985 to 1992, to sort out my past propaganda and doctrinal beliefs. I struggled, studied, worked, cried, and anguished through it all before I was able to finally reconcile everything in my mind. Now I could truly leave behind the bad and cherish the good.

Although I still occasionally have nightmares about CSA and of being arrested again, I can now talk openly about the past.

I still have few true friends, although I now make an effort to meet more people and be more community-minded.

I still do not feel comfortable in traditional churches, though my family and I are attending services occasionally now. However, I refuse to allow any man, group of men, or church to dictate what I must do in my personal relationship with God. Although I someday hope to minister full-time again, I also refuse to build upon another man's foundation, desiring instead to allow people the freedom to act and believe as they feel God is directing in their lives.

My life is centered around my family. Kay and I are closer than ever, spending every minute together we can. My children are my delight, bringing joy and pride into my life. My first granddaughter, Shannon Olivia, born in 1995, and the five more who followed her, have added immensely to our family.

Occasionally a book is written that mentions CSA or me, almost just to remind me of my place in history. A map published in the February 18, 1990, *Fort Worth Star-Telegram* detailing the locations of various white supremacist groups in the U.S. still showed CSA, even though it had been over three years since anyone had lived there.

Freedom is the most valuable gift that we as a society possess. Was it worth losing for what CSA offered? Ironically, yes. I had the opportunity to leave CSA before April 1985 and didn't, believing in my heart that I was supposed to stay. I honestly thought I could turn CSA and Ellison around, back to the simple days of Zarephath-Horeb. I loved that place, those people and the Ozark Mountains.

I have experienced what few people have; I have lived a lifetime in a few short years; and I am determined to make a positive difference with my life. I am thankful for prison, for what it did in me and I see God's hand throughout it all.

On May 5, 1995—only 16 days after its destruction—I journeyed to Oklahoma City, to see the ruins of the Murrah Federal Building and its effect upon that city. I walked around in awe for three hours, taking photographs and soaking in the emotions of the city. I was astounded at the devastation not shown on television. I paused several times to contemplate how close CSA came to blowing up this same building, how I might have been involved with its destruction in 1983, and wondered if I were somehow involved with it on April 19, 1995. I prayed that those guilty of the largest terrorist act on American soil had not found their roots of terrorism with CSA, Wayne Snell, or Elohim City. I prayed that it all be a coincidence, although I do not believe in coincidences. And I prayed that America never again experience a drama of this magnitude.

On May 23, 1995, what was left of the Murrah Federal Building was brought down to the ground with less than 100 pounds of dynamite.

Then on October 3, 1996, I made another trip to the site while being interviewed by the Canadian Broadcasting Company. Emotions of guilt were stronger then as I viewed memorials made to the 168 victims of the blast—and especially as I thought about the 19 children who had died there. I grieved over the waste of the bombing, the lives, the hopes and dreams that it had destroyed.

In early November 1996, I received a phone call from Cheryl, my good friend from Missouri. She was trying to organize a reunion of as many members as possible, so we could each see that everyone has found some peace in their lives and have gone on with their lives. "Can you be there?" she asked. "Jim's going to be there."

"Yes," I answered, "I'll be there."

I hadn't spoken to Ellison since 1989. I wasn't sure what to expect. Although Kay was hesitant, she consented to going with me. All six of my children said they wanted to attend the reunion. We arrived in Arkansas early Saturday, mid-November. After settling in at the motel, some of us went to see our old property. Many changes had occurred, but one thing was especially new—although this was my fourth time to visit the property since my release from prison, I suddenly realized it would probably be my last. The old emotions were gone. The dreams of the past had given way to hope for the future.

I arrived at the reunion site on Sunday before Ellison and his family. We visited with the other families that had arrived and got reacquainted.

The best thing about the reunion was that the teenagers of four years earlier that were having so much trouble in their lives were all straightening out just fine. Many had started families, taken on new responsibilities, decided to grow up. One young woman especially stood out. The last time I saw her she was doing drugs, was promiscuous and was extremely rebellious to her mother. Now she was a freshman in college on the way to a career. When I asked her what had happened, she said she got the bad feelings out of her system and now wanted to help others. I felt a tremendous hope for all of the children from CSA. I since discovered that many of the children did go on to college and became productive citizens of society.

But now we were awaiting Ellison. Would anger rise up within me when Ellison showed up? Would he still intimidate me? When Ellison walked in I watched him and realized the truth. He was just another person in a room. There were no emotions present. I neither feared him nor was angry with him. I did not care if he were there or not.

Ellison sat separated from everyone else, except his family, which included his wife, Angie—now pregnant with his second child with her and his fourteenth altogether—and some of his other children. He seemed to not know what to expect from the others. We had already been informed that Ellison was nervous about attending because he was afraid of what we thought about him. Eventually I went over to him and sat down.

"How have you been, Jim?" I asked.

"Fine."

The surface talk continued.

"Have you been to the farm lately?" I inquired.

"I have no reason to go," he responded. "I hold no bad feelings or regrets about the farm, so there's no reason to say good-bye to it."

After eating the meal, the seven or eight families represented there fellowshipped together, renewing bonds between each other. Suddenly, Ellison asked everyone to gather in a circle and sing one of the old praise songs we used to sing. We silently agreed to indulge him. Immediately after that first song, Ellison offered for us to sing some more and have a praise meeting, saying that we had the rented hall for two more hours. Without hesitation, everyone began to disperse and the reunion was over with. Thanks, but no thanks! Good-bye again, Jim Ellison.

Rumor has it that after everyone left, Ellison cried. Some think he cried because he misses everyone; some think he's sorry for what happened at CSA. I think he cried because he still saw everyone as "his sheep" now with no "shepherd," that we didn't bow down to "King James of the Ozarks."

In a March 1996 interview with the *Kansas City Star* when asked about his violent past, Jim Ellison said he had no regrets. "How can you regret something," he explained, "you felt God told you to do?"

I later realized another truth from the reunion. I am not angry, vindictive, or bitter toward Jim Ellison or Robert Millar. At least I am trying not to be. I am opposed to the Nicolaitan spirit they possess—mentioned in Revelation 2:6—which Christ hates. The word Nicolaitan means "power over the laity (or people)." It is that possessive, controlling attitude over people that leads them astray, that ministers deception, and causes followers to take extreme actions. I oppose it knowing that same element was once so strong in me.

I went to Arkansas originally to try to save Tom and Barbara from Jim Ellison. In the end I can't know for sure if I made things worse or better. Ellison was right about one thing, though. My clear river did get dirty for a while. But as time passed, I like to think that it cleansed itself into a clear river again.

I long ago cast myself into that river, to be carried wherever it pleased God to carry me. I once looked everywhere for answers in the hope of finding answers somewhere. Today, as my river continues to clear, answers continue to come.

One answer has already come: Hope for myself, for America, for the future. And for that I shall always be thankful.

Epilogue

Go out with joy
and be led forth with peace.
—Isaiah 55:12

Parts of the right-wing movement are slowing down while other parts remain very active. John Harrell of the Christian-Patriots Defense League in Illinois, now in his mid-70s, is reportedly broke and living on social security. He no longer holds meetings and it is said that one of his daughters has married an African American.

KKK leader Robert Miles of the Mountain Kirk in Michigan died August 16, 1992.

The wife of Aryan Nations' neo-Nazi leader Richard Butler died in December of 1995. Butler's health has also declined and no successor has been picked for him. It is assumed that once he dies, Aryan Nations of Idaho will also die.

As the old dies, the new emerges. The rallying cry of today's white separatists (no longer calling themselves "white supremacists") is entitled, "The Fourteen Words"—"We must secure the existence of our people and a future for White Children."

In 1996 an almost-three-month standoff between the Montana Freeman militia group and the FBI ended with a peaceful surrender. But the year also gave us a pipe bombing at the Atlanta Olympic games with one person killed.

In 1997 we saw a seven-day standoff between the Republic of Texas militia and Texas law-enforcement. That standoff also ended peacefully. Immediately before the standoff began, four members of a KKK group were arrested north of Fort Worth, Texas for allegedly conspiring to blow up a natural gas depot which they hoped would serve two purposes: killing up to 20,000 people in the county and diverting officials there long enough for Klan members to rob an armored truck carrying two million dollars, which would have been used to finance more illegal activity.

The biggest deception in the violent extremist right is twofold. First, the individual believes that if law enforcement officers ever try to arrest him, he will "go down in a blaze of glory and take as many cops" with him as possible, willing to be a martyr for the cause. Yet 99% of all arrests of extremists end with no shots being fired and no one hurt. Secondly, the extremist group believes a federal raid on its group will be the final "rally cry" and other groups will come to escalate the war during any standoff. Yet time and again, other groups watch the standoffs on television, keeping a safe distance between themselves and law enforcement. Thus the individual and the group continue their criminal activity, all the while deceiving themselves in mutual seduction that they will make a difference—only to later discover that the only difference made is their incarceration, perhaps for life. Then, they watch in frustration as the movement forgets them, unless they continue to toot their own horns while in prison.

Immediately after the Republic of Texas surrender, the trial for Timothy McVeigh began in Denver, Colorado, where Jewish talk-show host Alan Berg was murdered.

In McVeigh's copy of *The Turner Diaries,* he highlighted the following: "We will not shrink from spilling their blood." On Monday, June 2, 1997, seven men and five women found Timothy McVeigh guilty of conspiracy to use a weapon of mass destruction, of using that weapon of mass destruction, of destruction with an explosive, and of seven counts of first degree murder in killing federal agents in the line of duty.

Neither Richard Wayne Snell, Jim Ellison, Robert Millar nor Elohim City were implicated in the Oklahoma City bombing. However, Judge Richard Matsch would not allow McVeigh's defense team to call Carol Howe—the ATF informant who lived at Elohim City for two years and who supposedly informed authorities in advance of a plot to bomb the federal building—as a witness.

On Friday, June 13, the jury sentenced Timothy McVeigh to death by lethal injection. McVeigh, who sat emotionless and stone-faced during most of the trial, envisions himself a prisoner of war on trial for actions that he sees as the inevitable consequences of war. In *The Turner Diaries*, the hero does not flinch at the idea of dying for his cause. Indeed, in the book's final pages he joyfully embraces his fate.

"Brothers!" he says, addressing the Order, "When I entered your ranks for the first time, I consecrated my life to our Order and to the purpose for which it exists. . . . Now I am ready to meet my obligation fully. I offer you my life." As the faithful soldier, Tim McVeigh has sent out the same message to the New Order.

On Tuesday, December 23, 1997, Terry Nichols was convicted of conspiracy to use a weapon of mass destruction and eight counts of involuntary manslaughter (for the eight federal agents who were among the 168 killed in the blast) in the Oklahoma City bombing, found to be a junior partner rather than an equal to Timothy McVeigh. He was acquitted of charges of using a weapon of mass destruction and destruction by an explosive. The jury deliberated six days before making their decision.

In January of 1998, Nichols escaped the death sentence when his jury deadlocked in the penalty phase and was dismissed by the judge. Under federal law, a death sentence can only be imposed by a jury. However, Nichols could still end up on death row because Oklahoma prosecutors have promised to press for a death sentence when they bring him to trial on state charges. Both Nichols and McVeigh face 160 counts of murder. Both will appeal their federal convictions and sentences. Meanwhile, an Oklahoma County grand jury continues to hear testimony from witnesses as it investigates whether the federal government was aware of the bombing plot and ignored evidence of other suspects involved in the bombing.

A memorial will be built on the bombing site for the victims of the bombing. It will feature 168 empty stone-and-glass chairs, each inscribed with the name of a victim, beside a shallow reflecting pond and a row of evergreen trees. Nineteen of the memorial chairs will be smaller in size to commemorate the children who died in the blast. An

American elm tree that stood in a parking lot near the federal building will feature prominently in the memorial. The tree, now known
as "the Survivor Tree," was blackened and scarred by the blast but
survived. The Oklahoma City National Memorial will be a national
monument and part of the national park system.

In 1995, because of the investigation into the Ruby Ridge incident with white-separatist Randy Weaver and his family, several FBI
agents were placed on suspension with pay. One of those was Danny
Coulson, the FBI negotiator during the CSA standoff. Because I considered his suspension a travesty, I immediately wrote FBI Director
Louis Freeh, Attorney General Janet Reno, and Senator Arlen Specter
and Senator Patrick Leahy, who were in charge of the Senate hearings
concerning Ruby Ridge.

In my letters and in conversation with Senator Arlen's office, I
expressed my admiration for Coulson, how his actions had saved dozens of lives and that his character would not have allowed him to be
a part of anything illegal or of a cover-up concerning Ruby Ridge. In
1997, no charges were filed against the four agents and the investigation ended. Danny Coulson resigned from the FBI in August of that
year, ending a glorious career with this undeserved taint against his
character on his record.

The government, it would appear, however, is learning from the
experience with Waco's Branch Davidians and from Weaver's Ruby
Ridge. Negotiating with right-wing extremists is entirely different
than in normal hostage situations. The textbook lessons learned during the CSA siege have proven more effective, as has been seen with
standoffs during 1996 and 1997.

In the late-1970s and early 1980s, if anyone had told us that the
Soviet Union would collapse virtually overnight in just a few years and
that the Berlin Wall would be torn down, we would have laughed. Yet,
as we all know, these two historical events did occur, with Communism
all but eliminated. When the collapse of the Soviet Union occurred, I
told friends that the time is now coming for us to solve domestic problems. This would mean a short time of upheavals in America (since
an outside enemy would not take up so much attention), but then

we would concentrate on seriously solving our internal problems, so Americans will once again feel proud of our government and also of our combined racial and cultural heritages.

The last few years have seen signs that indicate a change for the good in our country. It is my prayer that all of our futures become brighter, that liberty, freedom and justice be evident in everyone's lives—regardless of race, religion, ethnic background, gender or sexual preference.

Afterword

It has been more than twelve years since the original publication of this book. I am humbled and so thankful for the vision of Syracuse University Press in reprinting it. I wish also to thank Professor Michael Barkun of Syracuse University for his encouragement in the reprinting of this book, Professor Jean Rosenfeld of UCLA for her introduction, and Annelise Finegan, acquisitions editor with Syracuse University Press.

It is difficult for me to imagine that it has been more than twenty-five years since the events of those CSA days. Sometimes it seems like a lifetime ago; sometimes it feels like yesterday. I am still amazed how quickly we got off track from our original vision. One wrong turn can create so much chaos. There is, indeed, a way that seems right unto a man, but the ends thereof are death.

Just imagine if I had never received the cassette tape of John Todd preaching and we had never listened to it in 1978. What a difference could it have made in our lives? Too bad we did not have the Internet in the late 1970s; because once Google came along on the Internet I discovered some interesting information about John Todd. According to Wikipedia, Todd's army medical records referred to his "'emotional instability with pseudologica phantastica' (compulsive lying), difficulty in telling reality from fantasy, homicidal threats he had made on another, false suicide reports, and a severe personality disturbance" ("John Todd (Occultist)," n.d.).

Todd, claiming he had been converted in 1972 when he left witchcraft, had actually been baptized in 1968 in a Phoenix, Arizona, church when he was 19. Todd began preaching during the early 1970s against Satanism and witchcraft until he was accused of making sexual advances against young women and using drugs. During this

302

time Todd said that God prophesied to him that he was to divorce his first wife, Linda. Todd then married Sharon Garver in 1973 and dropped out of sight for awhile until 1976, after confessing he had gone through a period of "backsliding," during which time he said that "witchcraft [is] more powerful than Christianity" ("The Legend of John Todd," n.d.). He had also reportedly gotten his young sister-in-law pregnant. Todd left Sharon in 1974 and married Sheila Spoonmore in 1976. Sharon later said that Todd only learned about the Illuminati through books he read.

Todd resurfaced in 1976 when the FBI became interested in him for seducing underage girls in a witch coven, after which the Church of Wicca revoked Todd's credentials. Todd then began preaching about the Illuminati in 1977, shortly before we discovered his teachings.

In 1979, the year following our accepting of his teachings, Todd was arrested and later convicted for statutory rape and transporting a minor across the state line. He then dropped out of sight again, reportedly moving to rural Montana. Sometime after that we were told at CSA that Todd had been shot to death.

In 2006 a report surfaced, however, that Christopher Kollyns (Todd's witchcraft name was supposedly Lance Collins), also known as John Wayne Todd, was serving a thirty-year sentence in South Carolina prison for criminal sexual conduct first degree, a sentence that began in 1987. Kollyns was released in 2004 to the Behavioral Disorder Treatment Unit run by the South Carolina Department of Mental Health, where he died in 2007.

The sad truth is that John Todd deceived a lot of people, including those of us at Zarephath-Horeb, a deception only allowed because we wanted to believe a lie, thinking that it added to our own theology at the time.

John Todd introduced us to Ayn Rand's book *Atlas Shrugged*, a supposed blueprint for the government-inspired collapse of America, in which he gave code words from the book detailing how the collapse would occur. In the late 1990s I reread *Atlas Shrugged,* only to discover its true genius. The main theme in this book is actually the morality of capitalism, offering a full defense of capitalism, not just as a practical system of economics but as the only moral and effective social system in the world. *Atlas Shrugged* was a treatise on the virtues of individual productivity in the world, its philosophy being that the only function of government was to protect man's rights as a productive part of society and to not interfere in the economy of the world.

Author Ayn Rand, I also discovered, offered a strong analysis years after *Atlas Shrugged* was published in which she showed how America's appeasement of the United Nations actually diminished our reputation and undermined our interests. Rand revealed how far-left liberals succeed at smearing capitalism as extremist; why conservatives completely fail to defend capitalism; why antitrust laws are profoundly unjust; and why a political ideology is not only necessary but that political consensus is actually destructive. *Atlas Shrugged,* I realized, preached individual accomplishments for the betterment of all, personal responsibility that each individual is to have, and the argument against government intrusion into the productivity of that individual.

I had come to the belief years ago (before re-reading *Atlas Shrugged*) that the organizations we claimed were against national interests and family values were in reality desiring the best for the world. Ours is a complicated planet and I found it refreshing to realize there are good organizations who are trying to make our planet a better, safer world, though these organizations might have different ideologies on how to accomplish this.

Had we never learned of John Todd, it is safe to say that Zarephath-Horeb would never had purchased so many guns, would never have become Christian survivalists, and would never have formed a paramilitary organization. Silhouette City would never have been built and we never would have had an illegal arsenal.

Just imagine if Jim Ellison had not worked in Missouri in the fall of 1979 and had not met Identity preacher Dan Gayman. What a difference could it have made in our lives?

I am still awestruck at the lack of any real evidence of Identity teaching in the Bible, of how easy it was to seduce us into its teachings, and of how destructive that philosophy/theology really is. There is, in fact, much evidence against Identity in the Bible and throughout history. But we failed to seek truth, to test the spirits, to search the scriptures, which only reveals how little we really cared about truth.

Had we not met Dan Gayman and adapted Christian Identity into our theology, we would never have been a part of the Christian-Patriot movement, would never have associated with the hate groups across America, would never have had the 1982 Convocation, and probably would never have allied ourselves with Elohim City. And polygamy would have never been more than hypothetical. We would never have met Richard Wayne Snell, nor would we have ever declared war against the United States government. And none of us would have ever gone to prison.

Nor would we have lowered the standard of Zarephath-Horeb, because CSA never would have existed. Just imagine if Zarephath-Horeb had continued to be the Christian community that it started out as, helping area people any way possible. It's possible that the philosophy of a "positive, practical Christianity" would have eventually played a part in our church, that we would have gotten off food stamps and possibly would have become a truly, self-sufficient, productive people once again. It's possible we would still be there today. After all, all things are possible. But, alas, it was not so.

In November 1998 one of the greatest moments of my life occurred. I was invited to attend the Texas Book Festival as one of its authors, for my book *Tabernacle of Hate,* and to be part of a panel discussion on hate and terrorism. The program was hosted by Laura Bush, wife of then-Governor George W. Bush, as a benefit to Texas libraries. All of the authors present were invited to also dine with the governor and Mrs. Bush, as well as with his father, former President George Bush. My wife and I attended, and we were able to spend quite a bit of time visiting with the three of them. I found all three to be genuinely friendly. I was in awe that night as I, a former terrorist, was able to meet and visit with a former president and a governor. An irony in my life played out in front of me and changed me even more.

Another irony was my growing and continued friendship with Danny Coulson, the FBI Hostage Rescue Team commander and the negotiator during the siege on CSA. I am still convinced to this day that God used Coulson to prevent a bloodbath in April of 1985 between CSA and the government agents. Danny and his entire family welcomed the friendship of my wife and me with open arms, introducing us to many of their friends as well. Over the years our families have socialized together, Danny and I have been interviewed together by various media, and we have spoken together before audiences. Our friendship with the Coulson family honors my wife and me and inspires us to achieve more. I will never take God's using Coulson and saving all of our lives for granted.

The other great blessing to me since my book originally was published was to have so many people who had once lived at CSA contact me and thank me, who now had a better picture of what had occurred and were able to finally have some peace in their lives. It gave me a chance to reacquaint myself with some old friends. I have also been contacted by some who were once in the extremist movement and were able to get out of it, who then read my book and contacted me in order for us to be able to share in the grace of God for no longer being held captive in darkness. And I have been contacted by several who are still in the movement, who question what I do but are honestly impressed by my openness and concern for them. They may not always agree with me but they will at least know that I understand them. All of these, in their own way, have also helped to save me and rescue me from hate.

Tabernacle of Hate also became required reading in four universities. That was a wonderful pleasure for me, a pleasure that I am sure will continue with this edition.

A year after *Tabernacle of Hate* was originally published, the right-wing paranoia machine began its doomsday preaching of Y2K, when supposedly all the world's computers would suddenly be inoperable as the year 1999 closed and another century began. That fiasco stopped abruptly once the year 2000 and then 2001 came without a hitch.

Convicted Oklahoma City Federal Building bomber Tim McVeigh was executed for his crimes on June 11, 2001. I had sent McVeigh my *Tabernacle of Hate* manuscript while he was awaiting execution and wrote:

Mr. McVeigh,

You may or may not have heard of me. I was a leader within the extremist movement during the late–1970s to mid–1980s, with a group known as CSA. I have since long ago left the movement and have had a book published by a small publisher concerning my experiences. Since you are not allowed to have hardcover books, I have enclosed a manuscript copy, which I hope gets to you.

The reason for my letter is that you & I have some common ties—people we both know; the Murrah building; prison; and a crossroads in our lives where each of us took a different path, though could have ended up the same. I am one of the few people in the country who understand the path you took. This is explained in my book.

Unlike many who have left the movement and who speak out against it, I do not cater to an "us vs. them" mentality. Many in the movement have emailed me concerning my position and we have had dignified discussions. Although I have spoken to several law–enforcement and human–rights organizations, I am no one's poster boy. I have no agenda other than helping people understand how good, decent Americans can get seduced into extremism, and how it is possible for them to return to their roots.

I hope you will read my story and I hope you will communicate back with me. We can discuss whatever you wish or nothing much at all. But know this, in the movement I am considered an enigma. Many do not understand what I do, but the word is out there that I tell the truth and am not in this for the money, glory or fame. I do what I do because I understand what the movement is about and I care for people.

I hope to hear from you,
Kerry Noble

I never received an answer.

■　■　■

Unfortunately, another enemy sought to destroy the United States. On September 11, 2001, foreign terrorists attacked us on our own soil in actions that, as every individual in this country still feels, murdered more than 3000 U.S. and global citizens when the Twin Towers of New York City and the Pentagon were attacked using our own commercial airplanes as weapons. Only the bravery of selfless Americans prevented a fourth plane from colliding into the U.S. Capitol or the White House. Suddenly the country's attention left our nation's homegrown terrorists and concentrated on those from the Middle East. I marveled at the similarities of the paranoid mindset between domestic terrorism and foreign terrorism.

That day we entered the War on Terrorism. With the advent of foreign terrorism, the spotlight on domestic terrorism faded, though domestic terrorism itself has not faded. The potential of domestic terrorists becoming cohorts with foreign terrorists has concerned many. After the September 11 attack, alternate lyrics written to the tune of *America the Beautiful* (now called *America the Sinful*) were posted on the Aryan Nations Web site:

> O, wicked land of Sodomites
> Your World Trade Center's gone.
> With crashing planes and burning flames,
> To hell your souls have gone.
> America, America,
> God's wrath was shown to thee.

According to the *Boston Globe,* in an article published on October 28, 2001, entitled "Hate Groups Applaud Terror Attacks, Watch Reaction Warily," the chairman of the American Nazi Party expressed admiration for the suicide bombers, quoting him as saying, "If 'we' were one-tenth as 'serious' . . . we just might start getting somewhere."

In the same article, it is recorded, "We, of the Aryan Nations, condemn the acts of the USA, being nothing more than a puppet government of Israeli [*sic*], in the attacks against the Taliban Freedom Fighters and the Islamic people of Afghanistan. We believe that it was the Ruling Elite, the Jews; i.e., Mossad, the so-called New World Order, behind the attack of the WTC on September 11, to further enslave us in a total police state."

A ray of light, however, did shine forth from the effects of 9/11: membership in the hate groups did decline and for a while most Americans came together as one nation. Those who remained in the extremist movement proclaimed that God was judging this nation. It is sad that so many still see through the lenses of hate. But with the rest of America I have rejoiced that our nation has suffered no more acts of terrorism since that time.

In 2006 I visited the Oklahoma City Memorial Building that stands where the Murrah Federal Building once stood. It is an impressive sight, with its 168 lighted chairs (19 of which are smaller to commemorate the children who died in the blast) and its museum. With tears I watched the video information inside the museum, where my involvement with the hate movement and its connection to the Oklahoma City bombing is immortalized. As I watched, I prayed America would never have to go through this again. I also thanked God once more for His grace in rescuing me from the negative mentality of the extremist movement. An American elm tree that stood in a parking lot near the federal building stands prominently in the memorial. The tree, now known as "the Survivor Tree," was blackened and scarred by the blast but survived, a symbol of our own nation.

It has always struck me how fortunate and blessed I am and how close I came to dying for "the cause" or spending the rest of my life in prison, as McVeigh and Nichols have done. Giving a speech at one law-enforcement conference, I commented how close I came to becoming "the first Tim McVeigh." An agent in the audience corrected me by pointing out how close McVeigh came to being "the second Kerry Noble." It drove the point even closer home.

In 2007, after much soul-searching, I reconciled with Jim Ellison, forgiving him for the past and no longer blaming him. At the same time I apologized to the elders of Elohim City. Since the FBI never found any solid evidence against them or founder Robert Millar, I no longer considered them a part of McVeigh's bombing of the Murrah Federal Building. Millar himself died in June 2001 from heart failure, just days before McVeigh's execution, and Elohim City has continued with its spiritual roots.

Then in 2008, just forty years after Martin Luther King's historic "I Have a Dream" speech and the passage of the Civil Rights Act, we elected our first African American president, the first time I had voted for a Democrat since I voted for Jimmy Carter in 1976. It was a proud moment for our nation, and our new president had many challenges already facing him.

By 2007 I had grown weary of the Republican Party and was hoping for something different. Then the young Illinois Senator commented that if he became president he would reach out to terrorists and offer to talk. It was at that moment that Barack Obama won my vote. For I knew by experience what could be produced when government authority was willing to listen, was willing to reach out, was willing to understand, in order that peace might prevail and lives might be changed and saved. It was then that this man's audacity to hope touched a chord in my spirit.

Unfortunately, but predictably, since the 2009 inauguration of U.S. President Barack Obama, the number of extremist groups and their memberships has risen. There is concern again about domestic terrorism. There is need again for an awareness of the dangers that these groups possess. Some groups have expressed hope for violence, and others simply predict that a black man cannot possibly have the intelligence to succeed as president. They are gleeful, at best, that Obama's failure would prove that America must have only white presidents. In this they align themselves with mainline public orators from the right who hope Obama fails. But I not only pray for his success, I believe he will succeed. America needs for him to succeed.

CSA was the first homegrown group to possess a weapon of mass destruction, thirty gallons of potassium cyanide. We were unsophisticated in those days, unaware of the potential power we possessed. Although the plans we had for it would have been ineffective (putting it into the water supply of a major city), had we known then what we had and what it could have produced with another agent, CSA could have caused considerable damage. Thankfully, it went no further than it did.

But groups and individuals are more sophisticated now. In our day we did not have the Internet, where anything can be discovered. We did not have cell phones to make it easier to communicate with each other. We did not have GPS that could take us anywhere easily. Technology was at a slower pace then, but that has changed. Today the dangers of extremism, both homegrown and foreign, are even more real than before. There is reason for concern. But concern is now balanced with the hope that a different kind of president can bring healing and trust once again to America and to our allies and enemies abroad.

Much has changed in me since those days at CSA and even since the original publication of this book. What has not changed for me, though, is the optimistic view I have for our country, for the future, for myself. In spite of all our problems I see an opportunity now for change for the better in this country and in the world. I speak to teens today and marvel that they can see and speak to other children across the world with the Internet. Globalization is no longer just a business term; it is an individual reality now. With this personal growth in the world and the further spread of wealth to other countries, I am extremely hopeful that soon this planet will not have to endure wars any longer.

On a personal note, when *Tabernacle of Hate* first came out, my wife and I had one granddaughter. Today we are blessed with three more granddaughters and two grandsons. Ours is a multiracial family, with one daughter married to a wonderful provider with Hispanic and Native American heritage. Three of our additional grandchildren are through them. Another daughter married an extremely positive and enterprising African American, through whom we had our first grandson. Our youngest daughter also now has a daughter. God has continued to bless us.

In August 2004 my wife's mother died after a two-year struggle with health complications. She had been a wonderful mother-in-law with whom I could talk to openly about issues of the day. She enjoyed playing board games and card games with her family and was the foundation for my own wife's nature. In October 2004 my grandmother died at the age of 93, having battled Alzheimer's for three years. Three months later, in February 2005, my little sister died peacefully in her sleep after a sixteen-year battle with cancer, at the age of 50. She had always been one of my best friends. Then without warning, my dad died just three months later, never recovering from an accident at his home. Within a year my wife, my mother, and I lost people who were a vital part of our lives, who were always there to give me support after I came home from prison. They are all sorely missed. In 2010 my friend of forty-five years, Barry, died. He was a police officer.

My days as a professional photographer ceased within two years after the original publication of *Tabernacle of Hate*. I began eleven-plus years as a display marketer of children's books for an international company, where I was promoted to regional manager for almost two years. Toward the end of that successful career I self-published *Tabernacle of Hope: Bridging Your Darkened Past Toward a Brighter Future*, helping others to heal from the scars of destructive relationships. As my days in the children's book business began to come to an end, my horizon broadened toward specializing in life transformation, public speaking, life coaching, training, and consulting, helping people declare and reach their life goals through personal potential development. With this in mind, I began Noble Strategies, teaching Biblical principles and strategies on how to navigate optimistically beyond life's experiences for a successful, balanced, and fruitful life via character building, positive attitudes, life balancing, one's sphere of influence, a positive lifestyle, and the leaving of a legacy.

The formation of that business and the reprinting of this book have only strengthened my determination to no longer look back with regret to a darkened past but to look with hope and anticipation toward a brighter future for all.

Appendixes | Bibliography | Index

Witchcraft
and the
Illuminati

Zarephath-Horeb

WITCHCRAFT AND THE ILLUMINATI

Over the past few years the Spirit of God has dealt with us in many areas. One of these areas is the truth and reality of Witchcraft and the Illuminati.

The Illuminati---one of the most secret organizations ever in existence. These "Illuminated Ones" or "All-Knowing Ones" are said to derive their name from Lucifer the "Light-Bearer", whom they supposedly worship and from whom they are said to receive their power.

2 Corinthians 2:11 reveals to us the need for studying the Illuminati----"Lest Satan should get an advantage of us: for we are not ignorant of his devices." Furthermore one reason many of God's people are deceived and are therefore such partakers of this evil and perverse age is found in Hosea 4:6, "My people are destroyed for lack of knowledge."

It is the hope of these truths to reveal the revelation concerning the Illuminati and its occult ties, as a guide to help deliver Israel from Babylon.

Sources used, other than the inspired Word of God for the gathering of this work include:

Books or Booklets:

None Dare Call it Conspiracy---by Gary Allen

The Fourth Reich of the Rich---Des Griffin

Christians During Riot and Revolution---Pastor Tom Berry

The Illuminati---Dr. Tom Berry

Atlas Shrugged---Ayn Rand

Occult Theocrasy--Lady Queenborough

Spellbound; Angel of Light; Broken Cross; Sabotage---Chick Publications

1

<u>Tapes:</u>

Illuminati---Pastor George Stalling
Various John Todd tapes----Ex Grand
Druid of the Council of 13

It is perhaps well to remember that,
as seen in the section on its Philosophies
the Occult-Illuminati fears no one, except
the individuals or groups who are self-
sufficient with food, fuel, weapons, ammunition, medical supplies, clothing, etc,
who, living in the country, have a common
unity or faith, and are not dependent upon
this world system for survival.

May God bless you with the Spirit of
Revelation as you read <u>Witchcraft</u> <u>and</u> <u>the</u>
<u>Illuminati</u>.

Written Spring 1981

2

TABLE OF CONTENTS

HISTORY OF THE ILLUMINATI

The majority of books on this subject have erroneously conceded the beginning of the Illuminati as 1776. Unless one sees that the very roots, purposes, plans, and philosophies of this demonic organization had its seed planted ages ago in order to blossom full-grown in our day one will not truly see its connection to what the Spirit of God is teaching His Elect in this hour of the latter days.

In the Creation process of our Lord, Man was created on the 6th day. Adam, created in the image of his father, God, was spirit, embodied with light (Genesis 1:26; Psalms 104:2; John 1:4). Adam was planted in the garden of Eden to dress it and keep it and to have dominion over it and the previous creations of God. With his wife, Eve, they had only one commandment-----"Of every tree of the garden you may freely eat: But of the tree of the Knowledge of good and evil you shall not eat of it: for in the day that you eat thereof, you shall surely die (or, dying you shall die)".-- Genesis 2:16,17.

In order to proceed further, it needs to be understood the truth God is saying to us. Snakes, first of all, do not reason nor talk, and as far as true science knows has never done such. The word translated "serpent" is generally agreed among Hebrew scholars to be a bad translation of the Hebrew word NACHASH, which means "to enchant by magic spell; to hiss." The Bible says that this NACHASH was a beast of the field. A careful study of this term (along with Beast and Beast of the earth) will reveal who this living creature is-----the Negro race, created prior to Adam, who is the beginning of the White Race (Adam is the transliteration of the Hebrew AWDAWN, which means "ruddy; to show blood in the face; to blush." Only one race can blush-- the white race).

4

Furthermore, trees have no knowledge of good and evil (Note Jeremiah 10:5). In the Scriptures, trees represent men (Mark 8:24). Therefore, this tree (man) in the midst of the garden who <u>knew</u> good <u>and</u> evil must have been the Negro NACHASH, distinct from Adam, who knew only good!

Indeed, the Bible also reveals to us that the "serpent" is in reality the devil himself (Revelation 12:9; 20:2) and not just used by the devil, as church tradition would have us believe. (An interesting note is that from the Hebrew NACHASH comes the Arabic word CHANAS, "to seduce". From this is derived the Arabic words AKHNAS, KHANASA, and KHANOOS, all of which mean "Ape." Further derived is the Arabic word KHANAS, " devil." Arabic is a language very similar to Hebrew. Mere coincidence?)

How then did Eve partake of his fruit? Genesis 3:13 says that Nachash beguiled Eve. This word "beguiled" literally means "to seduce." "Fruit" also literally means "seed; offspring." If indeed Eve was physically seduced by the Negro Nachash, then how does this fit in?

Eve did indeed die in that day, for she entered the realm of the earthly body, becoming corruptible, no longer covered by the glory of God. Adam and Eve saw their nakedness and for the first time were ashamed. The death that she was lowered into (since to lie with a beast is death---Exodus 22:19) was the realm of being carnally minded (Romans 8:6-8). When Adam yielded to his wife's carnality then he too became carnal (minding the things of the flesh or physical body and not the things of the Spirit) and no longer was Spiritual. Adam remember was not deceived (1 Timothy 2:14) but understood the plan of God (since he had the mind of Christ). Thus by one man's transgression, death passed unto all men (Romans 5:12), and all creation (Romans 8: 20-22).

5

Nachash was then cursed by God, to be on his belly (literally to be bent over on all fours). Nachash then became apelike, a curse to him, since the Negro race is the head of the Ape species, in the same way that the lion is the head of the cat family. This then was regression for Nachash.

The judgments of God continued, with the announcement of Eve being with children (Genesis 3:16). Later when Adam knew Eve, she <u>again</u> conceived and had twins, Cain and Abel--one fathered by Nachash, the other by Adam (though this is rare, it is nevertheless a medical fact and has occurred in recent history). It is important to realize that only Nachash was cursed--- not Adam nor Eve. Their's was one of punishment and chastisement, since God chastens His Sons (Hebrews 12:5-11).

1 John 3:12 says that Cain was of that wicked one or the progeny (offspring) of Satan. The Hebrew word for Cain is KAJIN, which is derived from the root word KOON ("to chant"). Thus, Cain, a halfbreed, reveals the origin of our modernday "cajins" and "coons". Here began, with Cain, the Seed-of-Satan Jews, an Antichrist race, a fulfillment of Genesis 3:15.

Cain later slays righteous Abel and is banished to Nod, with a mark upon him, and, with his wife (a Negress), builds a city, named after a man, his son Enoch. Babylon, the realm of confusion, begins.

From Cain descends Tubal-cain, a patriarch of witchcraft, as we'll see later. This mixing of races always produces evil and chaos.

This historical truth is confirmed by Jesus in His parable concerning the Wheat and the Tares in Matthew 13:24-30,36-43. In it a man sowed good seed in his field, and while man slept, his enemy came and sowed tares. Both grow together until the end of this age. Now the field is the world, our planet. The Sower of the good seed is the Son of Man, Jesus. His seed are the children of the Kingdom, while the

6

tares are the children of the Wicked One. The enemy is the devil.

We said previously that Nachash was the devil; his seed (Greek SPERMA) being cast forth in Eve and bearing tares (descendants of Cain, the first JEW). The Son of Man, Jesus, then would have cast forth his seed as Adam, the man who slept, and brought forth the Hebrew-Israelite line.

These Jews, the Seed of Satan, shall be gathered and burned by the Messengers (angels) of God who are His Sons, the Body of Christ, at the end of this age. Further examples of this Satan-line can be seen in John 8:33-44 (Pharisaical Jews), Matthew 3:7; 12:34; 23:33 (generation or race of vipers), 1 John 3:10 (children of the devil), Nehemiah 13:23,24 (Jews mixing with demons), John 17:12; 6:70; 13:27 Luke 22:3 (Judas), Acts 13:10 (Elymas), Isaiah 3:9 (modern Jews), and in 2 Thessalonians 2:3 (the Man of Sin). This cursed race CAN NOT be saved in this age(John 8:43; 10:26, 27).

Next, in the rebellion of man against God, we find the descendents of Ham, one of Noah's sons (Genesis 10). Ham beget Cush, Mizraim, Phut,and Canaan. These four are the fathers of Ethiopia(Cush),of Egypt (Mizraim),of Persia (Phut) and the various mixed breed countries (Csnaan). Though Ethiopia,Egypt and Persia were white countries,Canaan was mixed-breed and thus cursed, because Ham, a white man, fornicated with one of the Negresses on the Ark.

From Cush came Nimrod,a mighty hunter of souls who opposed the Lord. He built Babel (Babylon), Calah, Erech, Accad, Calneh, Assyria, Ninevah, Rehoboth and Resen. Nimrod was born, according to ancient traditions, the High Sabbath, December 25th, on a Sunday (the Babylonian Sabbath).

According to Genesis chapter 11, this Tower of Babel(a tower in the city of Nim-

rod's Babylon) began construction. This
ancient "United Nations"building was man's
first attempt to organize a one-world political-religious system. The nations at
this time were all of one language, and
wanted to make a name for themselves. Because the time was not yet ripe for this
system, God confused the people with various languages and scattered them. Thus
Babylon ("Confusion") began another plan.

Nimrod's mother was Semiramis, the
most beautiful and seductive woman of her
day. Once, when a riot broke loose in the
city, the rioters ceased when Semiramis
walked through, stopping to gaze upon the
woman of Cush.

Cush, who knew of the prophecy of the
coming Messiah (Genesis 3:15), had taken
Semiramis in fornication, and she became
with child. This child, according to Cush
was the Messiah, Nimrod. When Cush died,
he had Nimrod marry his mother, Semiramis.
Since Nimrod was already deified as God,
and therefore Cush too since he beget Nimrod, now Semiramis was deified as the "Mother of Heaven". This three-fold union,
then, planted the seed for the worship of
the "Trinity"---three gods in One--and the
Mother-Child (Husband) deities of all religions.

While Nimrod was building the Tower
of Babel Shem,another of the sons of Noah,
came to pronounce judgment upon Nimrod.
Killing him, Shem mutilated Nimrod into
several pieces and sent each piece by messenger to various pagan religious temples.
The message to each was that this same
judgment would come to all who partook of
the sexual-rioting, child-sacrificing worship of Baal, Molech, Chiun,etc (Nimrod).
Thus, these religions went underground and
became "Mysteries". (These same temples,
called "groves" in Scripture,are literally
SHRINES---the Masons, Elks, the Shriners
and Moose Lodges, etc of our day-----to be
destroyed by the Elect).

8

Semiramis later gathered all of Nimrod's pieces together, except one that she could never find--his penis. Semiramis then incorporated into her occult practices the calling back (worship) of the penis and formed the symbol of the obelisk (see Symbols section). Therefore all mystery religions and lodges are based on this phallus-worship and Baal--worship. (This was the sin of Israel at Baal-peor--Numbers 25).

It is of interest to note that the symbol for Nimrod is the "X" Cross. This mark is on the forehead of many witches (for example, on Charles Manson's women). The Roman Catholic term, "Merry Xmas ", literally means "Magical or Merriment Communion with Nimrod."

As time went on this occult religion spread with one goal in mind---the setting up of a one-world political-religious system with the Occult in control. This plan can be seen in records concerning Saul (1 Samuel 28), Solomon (1 Kings 11), the Trilateral Council of Nicolas, Bar-Jesus , and Simon the Sorceror (Acts 6, 8, 13 and Revelation 2:6,15). Pontius Pilate was,in fact, educated at the Druid University in Rome.

On October 28, 312 AD, the pagan Sun-worshipper Constantine was on his way to take the throne of Rome as heir, but was withstood by Maxentius at the Tiber River. Constantine and his troops were greatly outnumbered when suddenly he and his army saw a cross in the sky with the message, "In This Sign, Conquer". Constantine obeyed and won and (according to tradition) was converted to Christianity.

However, Constantine's description of the sign was in reality, not the cross of Christ, but the Ankh(see Symbols section), the symbol of the Sun-god. Constantine , now a"Christian",took over Rome in 312 AD, and, in 313 AD, issued the Edict of Milan, declaring Christianity as the State Religion.

9

Constantine sprinkled his troops in baptism,who thus also became "Christians". In 325 AD, Constantine set up the Council of Nicaea and presided as "Summun Pontifex" (Pope). Setting up the Organized Church (Roman Catholic Church),pagan rites were "Christianized"---same rites, simply given Christian names. (Understanding is given when it is seen that the word Catholic means "Universal";hence the Roman Universal Church, Never meaning to be a true Christian Church, its purpose was to make the Roman Religion universal.) Thus the world was plunged into the Dark Ages until the 16th Century when the Reformation came through Martin Luther and others.

Then in the mid-1700's, the Professor of Canon Law at the University of Ingalstadt, Bavaria, Adam Weishaupt, came on the scene.

Adam Weishaupt was born a Jew and later converted to Catholicism. He became a Jesuit priest (a Roman Catholic order established in 1534. Its job was to stop the spread of Protestantism at all costs.) Weishaupt later broke loose from the Order and spent the next five years in meditation.

Weishaupt had friends in the French royal court who practiced black magic, baby sacrificing, etc. He desired copies of the Kabbalah,The Major Keys of Solomon, and The Lesser Keys of Solomon. These books showed how demons could be controled by occult practices. The House of Rothschild, a European banking family,had these books and heard that Weishaupt was interested in them. This was in the beginning of the 1770's.

With the financial and occult backing of the Rothschilds, Adam Weishaupt took these books, along with The Protocols of

10

of the Learned Elders of Zion (which dealt with the Jewish plans for world takeover from the "goyim", or Gentiles), The Book of Shadows, and The Necromonicron, then conceived a plan for the building of an organization called the "Illuminati". It is noted that the name Rothschild in fact means "Roth's Child" or "Son of Wrath".

The American Illuminati was formed on May 1, 1776. At this time, Weishaupt and the Rothschilds also started their private coven; called the "Golden Dawn." This is still the Rothschild's private coven today.

On July 16, 1782, the Illuminati and the Order of the Freemasons united, with over 3,000,000 members.

In 1785, a courier for the Illuminati was struck by lightning and killed. This courier was carrying secret Illuminati papers. The Bavarian Government got ahold of these papers and raided the Illuminati Headquarters. The Illuminati then went underground. Many countries and churches, though,thought the Illuminati not a threat to society, despite governmental reports.

Weishaupt's aims were simple:
1) The abolition of all governments;
2) The abolition of all private property;
3) The abolition of inheritance;
4) The abolition of patriotism;
5) The abolition of family life, marriage.
    and communal education of children;&
6) The abolition of religion.

In addition eight levels of this new order were conceived---(inner to outer)---
   1) Rex   6) Illuminous Minor
   2) Magus   7) Minerval
   3) Regent   8) Novice
   4) Presbyter (priest)
   5) Freemason
From the Presbyter level on up, members were sworn to secrecy and told of the Illuminati's true plans.

11

In 1826 Captain William Morgan became the first execution by the Illuminati. A Mason who opposed their plan, Capt. Morgan was de-tongued, disemboweled,and then mutilated. 40% of the membership of the Masonic Lodge left the order when the death of Morgan was discovered.

In 1829, the Illuminati decided to unite all subversive groups under a heading known as "Communism". Then in 1830 old Adam Weishaupt died, making a false deathbed repentance, and rejoined the Catholic Church. The Illuminati was supposedly dead now.

In 1840, Confederate Army General Albert Pike, from Little Rock, Arkansas, was head of the Luciferian Priesthood and the Council of 13. From 1859-1871 Pike worked out plans for 3 World Wars to occur in the 20th Century. Pike's plan was as follows:

WWI-----To overthrow the Czars of Russia and then establish Communism under Karl Marx' "Communist Manifesto." Communism then was to begin the overthrow of other governments. WWI was aided by the differences between the British and Germanic governments.

WWII----With the differences between Fascism and Zionism as a fulcrum Nazi Germany was to be destroyed sothat Israel (Palestine),with its "Jews" could be set up. Communism was to be further built up to equal U.S. power. Franklin D. Roosevelt and Winston Churchill aided in this.

WWIII---The Destruction of the Christian Democratic countries. Atheistic Communism is to be established, with the Doctrine of Lucifer presented to the public as a plan for world peace.

12

In 1865 Abraham Lincoln wanted to rebuild the South. Lincoln refused to pay
off the war debts by borrowing from the
International Bankers, and so was assassinated by Illuminist John Wilkes Booth.
(President John F. Kennedy was likewise
killed, because he reportedly came against
the Illuminati's orders). The Secret Service aided in both murders.

In the early 1900's, the Russian Revolution was financed by American bankers
in New York. The Illuminati also defeated
the Mafia in 1963-65.

The Illuminati because of recent publicity has changed its name to Moriah,"The
Conquering Wind."

Though the Illuminati indeed controls
the Financial, Political, Civil, Religious
and Social areas of the world, the Illuminati is much more than these groups. The
depth of the Illuminati may be seen as we
progress through this booklet and as God
opens the eyes of our understanding.

13

THE ILLUMINATI PURPOSE AND PLAN FOR WORLD TAKEOVER

The Conspiracy for world takeover, as we previously saw, is as old as man himself. The Illuminati, in recent history, has twice tried to control the world---in Napoleon's day and during World War I.

Only about 5000 people in the entire world know the true purpose of the Illuminati and its conspiracy to rule the earth. Their plan was written down in code, as a fictional novel, in 1957.

In the mid-1950's Philippe Rothschild ordered one of his mistresses, Ayn Rand, an established authoress and philosopher, to undertake the writing of this code to the witches of the world. This novel, Atlas Shrugged, was never intended to be a best seller, although it turned out to be one.

The main characters of Atlas Shrugged are code names for individuals or companies. The code is as follows:

John Galt---Philippe Rothschild
Dagny Taggart---Ayn Rand
Dagny's brother---The combined Railroad Systems
John Wyatt---David Rockefeller
Hank Rearden---U.S. Steel, Bethlehem Steel, etc.
Francisco D'Antonio--Combined Copper Mines
The Pirate---Sea piracy now occurring
Galt, D'Antonio, and the Pirate------Rothschild Tribunal

The Tribunal in the book went around convincing certain major corporation presidents of their philosophy and plan, getting them to bankrupt their own businesses. The owners of these companies would then vanish and leave with either Galt or D'Antonio to a retreat area inthe Colorado mountain regions. "Colorado" is the code

14

name for the "Bermuda Triangle", the place
where the key figures of the Illuminati
will be when the world crashes.

As these corporations were bankrupting
themselves, the Tribunal was setting off
riots, plane and train wrecks, grain bin
explosions, inflation, a stock market crash
by means of the gold price, and other ways
of causing more panic and more governmental controls.

There are six areas of society in
which the Illuminati intends to rule:

1) Religious   4) Educational
2) Political   5) Military
3) Economic   6) Social

On August 1, 1972 Philippe Rothschild
sent some papers to a meeting of the Council of 13 by State courier to San Antonio,
Texas. Besides the usual pay-off notes and
progress reports, the papers included a
projected takeover plan. It read as follows:

1) Remove the President and Vice-President (this was Richard Nixon and
Gerald Ford).

2) Republican Successor (Ford) throws
election to Democratic (this was
Jimmy Carter).

3) Democratic President gets following laws enacted:

a) Federal gun law taking weapons
away from citizens.

b) Removal of tax exemption from
churches (This is House Bill 41
which states that a church, once
newly registered, must have a
membership of at least 500 and
be a member of the World Council of Churches in order to remain recognized by the Government).

c) Genocide Act—Making it a crime
equal to murder to convert a
person from one religion or
faith to another.

15

      d) Presidential Marshall Law Act--
      This allows the President in
      time of "National Emergency" to
      suspend the Constitution, Con-
      gress, and the economic system.
      The President, in essence, be-
      comes the dictator of America.
      (This law has been passed).

      e) Anti-Hoarding Act----This makes
      it a felony to have more than
      30-days supply of food, fuel or
      medicine stored up at one time.
      (This has also been passed).

      f) Anti-Business Acts
        Equalization of Opportunity
        Act---A major company of one
        field must help any individu-
        al start another company in
        the same field of business,at
        the expense of the first com-
        pany.

        Fair Share Law---One company
        cannot produce or sell more
        of a product than any other
        company producing the same
        product.

        Directive #10-289----No quit-
        ting, hiring, firing, or wage
        increases of employees; No
        selling, buying, or moving of
        a business; No new inventions
        allowed, during a crisis.

    President Carter was able to get some
of these laws inacted before leaving office.

World War III---Caused by Israel battling
over petroleum, farmlands, and chemicals.

16

Plans for America: Make every person totally dependent of the government by:

1) Creating a pseudo-fuel shortage
   and food shortage.
2) Confiscate all guns.
3) Calling for "Helter Skelter" (All
   trucks, trains, planes and ships,
   except Military, will stop.
   An army of some 200,00 white
   prisoners and motorcycle gang
   members will create mass insanity
   in the streets by bombing church
   buildings, raping, murdering, and
   other fear tactics.) "It will be
   when the lights of New York City
   go out for the last time."------
   Rothschild Tribunal
4) Declaring Martial Law. Activate
   the National Guard to keep order,
   after the public cries out for
   any kind of help. There will be
   one policeman to every 5 people.
   Once this "National Emergency" is
   declared, it will never be can-
   celled. (Martial Law was activa-
   ted only partially by Jimmy Carter in Nov 1979 upon the Iranian/
   Hostage Crisis.)

   All countries except America will be
sent against Israel for oil. The use of
neutron bombs allows destruction of people
while leaving all buildings, natural resources, and croplands intact. When the
war is over, the world is to be ruled from
Jerusalem.
   In addition:
      90% of the population of the US
      supposedly is to die in the 1st
      half hour of WWIII.
      3000 missiles are to hit the US
      within the first hour.
      Most industrial cities are to be
      destroyed.

17

Russian missiles placed in major
US Lakes and Rivers (up to ten
Nuclear Warheads/Missile);   put
there with American   Government
knowledge and approval.

To date, approximately 90% of the
Conspiracy plan has been fulfilled on
schedule. Depending upon the foreknowledge
and plan of God, to see if the Illuminati
plans align with the order of steps toward
the Beast Political/Religious System of
Revelation, chapters 13, 17 and 18 remains
in the Lord's hands. However the process
occurs, and regardless of the order and
time of man, it is still certain "that in
the last days perilous times shall come"
(2 Timothy 3:1).

PHILOSOPHY OF THE ILLUMINATI

In 1957, Ayn Rand wrote a book under the direction of Philippe Rothschild. An 1100-page "fictional" novel, Atlas Shrugged became the witchcraft codebook for the Illuminati plan for world takeover.

Possibly more important than the revealing of their plans is the discovery of the philosophical ideals of the occult-conspiracy.

Following are excerpts from Atlas Shrugged revealing the Philosophy of the Illuminati:

Page 323---"...Don't argue. Accept. Adjust yourself. Obey."

Page 411---"The only power any government has is the power to crack down on criminals. Well, when there aren't enough criminals, one makes them. One declares so many things to be a crime that it becomes impossible for men to live without breaking laws"

Page 503---"Freedom has been given a chance and has failed. Therefore, more stringent controls are necessary. Since men are unable and unwilling to solve their problems voluntarilly, they must be forced to do it."

Page 514---"There is no way to disarm any man except through guilt. Thru that which he himself has accepted as guilt. If a man has ever stolen a dime, you can impose on him the punishment intended for a bank robber and he will take it. He'll bear

19

any form of misery, he'll feel
that he deserves no better. If
there's not enough guilt in the
world, we must create it. If we
teach a man that it's evil   to
look at spring flowers and   he
believes us and then does it---
we'll be able to do whatever we
please with him. He won't defend himself. He won't feel he
is worth it. He   won't fight.
But save us from the   man who
lives up to his own   standards.
Save us from the man of   clean
conscience. He's the man   who
will beat us."

Page   566--"Fear is   the   only   practical
means to deal with people."

Page   585--"Who are   you   to stand   against
the government?"   ("Who   can
make   war with the   beast?"
Revelation 13:5.)

Page   617--"From   each   according   to   his
ability, to each according   to
his need." (Karl Marx' Communist Manifesto.)

Page   637--"The   dollar sign. It stands on
the vest of every fat, piglike
figure in every   cartoon, for
the   purpose of   denoting   a
crook, a grafter, a scroundrel;
as the   one   surefire brand   of
evil.   It stands---as the money
of   a   free   country----for   a-
chievement,   for   success,   for
ability,   for   man's   creative
power----and,   precisely   for
these reasons,   it is used as a
brand   of   infamy.   It stands
stamped   on the forehead of men

20

as a mark of damnation. It
stands for the initials of the
United States. The United
States is the only country in
history that has ever used its
own monogram as a symbol of
depravity. Ask yourself why.
Ask yourself how long a country that did that could hope
to exist and whose moral standards have destroyed it. It
was the only country in history where wealth was not ac-
quired by looting, but by production; not by force, but by
trade; the only country whose
money was the symbol of man's
right to his mind, to his work,
to his life, to his happiness,
to himself. If this is evil,
by the present standards of
the world, if this is the reason for damning us, then we---
we, the dollar-chasers and ma-
kers---accept it and choose to
be damned by that world. We
choose to wear the sign of the
dollar on our foreheads proudly, as our badge of mobility---
the badge we are willing to
live for and if need be, to die
for." (Could this be the Mark
of the Beast of Revelation
13:16?)

Page 696-----"We started with no time in
view. We did not know whether
we'd live to see the libera-
tion of the world or whether
we'd have to leave our battle
and our secret to the next generations. We knew only that

21

this was the only way we cared
to live. But now we think that
we will see, and soon, the day
of our victory and of our return. When the code of the
looters has collapsed. When
the creed of self-immolation
has run, for once, its undis-
guised course---when men find
no victims ready to obstruct
the paths of justice and to
deflect the fall of retribution on themselves---when the
preachers of self-sacrifice
discover that those who are
willing to practice it, have
nothing to sacrifice,and those
who have, are not willing any
longer---when men see that
neither their hearts nor their
muscles can save them, but the
mind they damned is not there
to answer their screams for
help---when they collapse as
they must, as men without mind
must---when they have no pre-
tense of authority left, no
remnant of law, no trace of
morality, no hope, no food and
no way to obtain it--when they
collapse and the road is then
clear---then we'll come back
to rebuild the world."
(The basic vision of the Rothschilds and the Illuminati.)

As is shown above, the mastery of the
Illuminati is a deep, dark deception. It
is well conceded that the "god of this present age" is "full of sorceries and every
abomination." It is also even more conceded and established, however, that atheistic philosophies are powerful enough to
win, only until these adepts come face to
face with the Beast-crushing Christ of God

(in Daniel, chapter 2.)

22

THE ILLUMINATI AND THE OCCULT

Unless one sees the ties of the World Conspiracy of the Illuminati to the Demonic Kingdom of the Occult, the power and depth of this Order will never be truly known. It is, therefore,necessary to give a basic understanding of the beliefs of Witchcraft and the Occult.

We have previously given the occult history of Nimrod and his generation. Throughout the years, however, many countries have known Nimrod under other names, such as Baal, Osiris, Horus, Jupiter, Centaur, and Bacchus, among others. Semiramis has been known as Ashtarte, Isis, Cybele, Irene, Diane, Ishtar, Venus, etc. Witchcraft has always been a many-god system.

During the Dark Ages, the most evil people living were the Druid Priests(known as "Men of Oak"). They demanded human blood sacrifices. Male slaves or Roman soldiers would be burned alive in cages over barren, solid ground. The Druids would call for Elfin (fire-god) out of the earth to consume the victims. In the background the Druid musical beat could always be heard. Their big night was Halloween. In the occult, it is called, "Samhain"--- October 31st. On Halloween the Druids and their followers went from castle to castle and from serf to serf playing "trick or treat." The treat from the castle demanded by the Druids would be a princess or some woman for human sacrifice. If the "treat" pleased the Druids, they would leave a "Jack O'Lantern" with a lighted candle made from human fat to protect those inside from being killed by demons that night. When the demands of the Druids couldn't be met, then a Hex (Hexagram) was drawn on the front door. This was the

23

"trick." That night Satan or his demons would kill someone in that house through fear.

The spellbinding beat of the Druid music filled the night as the ceremony began. The man assaulted the victim and then brutally sacrificed her to the god of the dead, the Horned-Hunter Kernos (Nimrod),the Oak god of the Underworld. Stonehenge, in England, was the Temple site for many of the occult murders. (Occult killings still take place in the US every Halloween). Stonehenge is still the Occult's major symbol. Human sacrifice is done throughout the country 8 times/year, during their Black Sabbaths. Disembowellment and mutilation always occur.

The Picts, under the control of the Druids, were the toughest fighting force the Roman soldiers ever faced. One Pict would deliberately jump on a Roman spear, to let the Pict behind him kill the Roman soldier.

Around 98-180 AD, the Druid religion was outlawed and went underground, to remain secretly active even till this day. This Druid system is the crux of the Occult-Illuminati.

Witchcraft belief is that the Mortals (Man) descended from apes and that witches came from the Son of the Creator of the gods-system, who brought them to earth in flying saucers.

These witches were "little people"--- elves, nymphs, leprochauns, etc. As they had sex with the mortal men, their offspring then grew to normal size.

This "Son of the Creator," they believe, is Lucifer, who is also Adam. Eve, the Mother of Creation, was his wife.

24

Witches believe that Adam is alive today, and that Abaddon (Revelation 9:11) is Jesus Christ.

In the 1600's Frances Collins brought witchcraft to America. (An example of history cover-up, in fact, involves the Collins family. The infamous Salem witch-trials were in reality trials on Christians by Collins-paid preachers and judges. Only one non-Christian, a prostitute, was ever sentenced as a witch). Witches also believe that in the 1700's the gods began to dwell in the Rothschilds. Philippe Rothschild's daughter, in fact, is believed to have Semiramis' spirit.

The basis of witchcraft is Astrology. All witches have the knowledge of astrology. Astrology's foundational belief is that a person's personality is fixed by the position of the stars, planets, etc at the time of birth, and that this personality cannot be changed.

Besides astrology witches are usually experienced with hypnotism (enchanting), fortunetelling, and the Ouija Board. Hypnotism is endorsed by well-known "Charismatics" such as Ruth Carter Stapleton and Walter Martin. Fortunetelling's Tarot Cards gave way to the Modern Playing Cards. The symbols were changed during the Inquisition when Tarot Cards were illegal. (This is why Las Vegas is so big). Witches personally do not trust the Ouija Board--- they use the Pendulum. Ouija boards are for the curious onlookers, in order to get them hooked to the occult. (Incidentally, all witchcraft is only about 90% accurate at best).

Three things in Witchcraft are considered powerful----herbs, astrology, and jewelry (amulets and talismans).

Orgies, drugs and blood sacrifices of children are basics in Witchcraft worship. The modern emphasis on sex, "free love", etc is the outgrowth and outreach for the orgy influence in the occult. The same is true for the rise of drug use in recent

25

years among kids and young people. 95% of
kids inducted into witchcraft is done by
public school teachers, through the use of
sex and drugs. What people don't realize,
however, is that drug use is Sorcery. The
Greek word for Sorcery in the Bible (Revelation 9:21;18:8;22:15) is PHARMAKEIA (our
"pharmacy" is derived from this), which
means "enchanting with drugs." Many young
people who tried to be Christians also
delve into the occult because there seems
to be "power" in witchcraft, whereas there
was no power or anything to fulfill them
in the Church System.

There are also no emotions or family
ties in witchcraft. This is why, in the
occult, there is a lot of incest, child
sacrifices, orgies, wife-swapping, and
coldness or hardness of heart. This is also why suicide in witchcraft is so high,
with death taught as intriguing.

Initiation rites into witchcraft are
the same as the first-level Masonic initiation rites, with the addition of the cutting of the wrist. Every initiate takes a
vow of secrecy. The Priest's hand is dipped in salt water and the person is sprinkled, thus being "born again" (same as Catholics and Lutherans). Girls become prostitutes for 6 months (as in the pagan temples, where the prostitutes of a town were
really either young initiates or Occult
Priestesses solicitating for recruits into
Witchcraft). There is also an altar in the
witchcraft church which is identical to a
Catholic Church altar. (Confessionals of
the Catholic Church began with Semiramis'
Priests. People who desired to be witches
had to tell everything they did, thus giving the priest a "hold" on the person).

26

Lower levels of witchcraft are taught the "gods system"---Diana, Jupiter, Venus, etc. This is the basic difference between Witchcraft and Satanism. Whereas witches are polytheistic, believing in many gods, Satanists are monotheistic, believing only in Satan as God, and seeing him as both good and evil. Upper levels are taught the true belief of "Lucifer" and that the Rothschilds are lesser gods in bodies. This Luciferian system sees Lucifer as the good god and Yahweh, the Christian God, as the evil god, with Jesus Christ as the imposter, posing as Lucifer.

Within Witchcraft itself, there are two main groups--White Magic and Black Magic. White Witchcraft believes in receiving its power from "Cosmic Consciousness" (TM, Yoga, etc)and using it peaceably with no anger or hatred, but being passive. It is a tool for knowledge and instruction to them. Their powers are supposedly for the good of all Mankind (an example of this is TV's "Bewitched").

Black witchcraft, however, believes "force" is the answer. By "concentrating all energy from creation" to themselves, they use their power for self and believe this will ultimately allow them to rule the world. Through anger and hate, they teach to surrender or die. (Example: "Star Wars'" Darth Vader).

Interesting that Jesus said in Matthew 12:25 and 26, "Every kingdom divided against itself is brought to desolation; and every city or house divided against itself shall not stand; And if Satan cast out Satan, he is divided against himself, how then shall his Kingdom Stand?" IT CAN'T!!!! Witchcraft will destroy each other almost as much as the Sons of God destroying it!

Witchcraft priesthood training begins at age 13. A fast and intensive training, this period is known as the "Outer Court." Priests of witchcraft must have at least 3 generations of practicing witches in their

27

family, before being elligible (unless
sponsored.)

May 1st is the most famous day in
witchcraft. This is the birthday of Bal-
tane, a witchcraft god (known as Pan or
Lucifer). This is also the birthday of
American Illuminism and of Communism.

Witches consider Solomon the greatest
wizard, or male witch,of all time (1 Kings
11). Solomon is said to have written the
KABBALAH, THE LESSER KEYS OF SOLOMON, and
THE MAJOR KEYS OF SOLOMON. Merlin the Magician is the #1 leader of Occult power.

Reincarnation is a basic belieft in
witchcraft. The state of existence from
one life to another is known as "Night
Wind." Catholics call it Purgatory. Thru
a process of purging a witch can then hope
to come back as a more powerful, ruling
witch in the next life.

The major books of the Occult include:
1) The KABBALAH, known as the Sixth Book
of Moses. Reportedly written by Solomon,
this book is based on Numerology. (9 is
the most powerful number in the Occult.);
2) THE BOOK OF SHADOWS: 3) NECROMONICRON;
4) THE LESSER KEYS OF SOLOMON; and 5) THE
MAJOR KEYS OF SOLOMON. All of these books
tell how to control demons and cast spells
for personal gain and glory, and give the
beliefs and history of witchcraft. (JRR
Tolkein's books, in fact, are not his own
works but are exact copies of the Creation
section of the BOOK OF SHADOWS, which is
based on the NECROMONICRON,an occult Bible
older than the Flood.)

Witchcraft is also a very "Scientific"
craft. "Telekenesis" is spellcasting; "Pa-
rapsychology" is telepathy, divination and
mind-over-matter control.Albert Einstein's
$E=MC^2$,in fact, is an Occult equation for
power.

The goal of witchcraft is to place the
"Son of Lucifer" on the throne, so witches

can rule the world. A witchcraft prophecy states, "When the Son of Lucifer is on the throne,the witches will have peace forever mone (more)." Because witches and the Illuminati hate Christians and what they consider to be "Christian Churches",they see Christians as their greatest threat. This is why Christian Infiltration and Elimination is Top Priority for the Illuminati. However, Deuteronomy chapter 13 and 18:9-14, along with Exodus 22:18, reveals that witches, idolaters, the diviner,enchanter, medium, wizard, and necromancer shall be put to death.

Though the ties of the Illuminati and Witchcraft are much deeper than the above, it is hoped that a basic understanding has been given. One cannot separate Illuminism from the Occult, for they go hand in hand.

29

THE ORGANIZATION OF THE ILLUMINATI

The Illuminati has organized 5 basic groups of control as its aim toward world-rule. These 5 areas gather together all phases of life known to man. Every person in the world is effected by them.

These 5 basic Organizations are:

1) Financial-----The Organization of Wealth (Business,Labor, Trade)
2) Political-----The Organization of Power (Nations)
3) Civil---------The Organization of Knowledge
4) Occult and Religion---The Organization of Spiritual Power
5) Social--------Arts and Culture(TV, News, Hollywood, Music, etc.)

At the head of these organizations is the Capstone of the Rothschild Tribunal. This is the House of Rothschild, composed of 5 brothers---Philippe (the head Rothschild), Edmund, Victor, Guy and Nathaniel. Only 3 brothers at any one time head any one organization. Within this Capstone—Tribunal is the All-Seeing Eye of Lucifer, the Spiritual power of the Illuminati.

Next in power in all Organizations is the Grand Druid Council of 13, the Rothschilds' private Ministers. (On another page is a list of the members of the Council of 13).

After this is the Council of 33, the 33 highest Masons in the world.

Then comes the 500---the 500 richest families in the world. Also known as the "Bilderbergers", this Council was created in May, 1954 by Prince Bernard of the Netherlands and by Queen Juliana (co-owner of Shell Oil along with Philippe Rothschild), at Bilderberg Hotel in Holland. With

30

closed meetings once a year, the 500 discuss the progress and future plans of
their goal---a One-World Government.

All organizations have secrecy vows,
initiations, and levels. The Outer reason
given for any organization is "to make of
the human race, without any distinction of
nation, condition, or profession, one good
and happy family."

Please note that the following charts
or organizations are only examples and are
not complete in their listings, and that
these are chiefly American, not foreign,
organizations.

The names of every member of these
organizations (with address, phone number,
business, Social Security number, etc) is
listed in the Brussels, Belgium computer
known as "The Beast", which is linked to
365 world computers (65 of which are in
the USA). Two of these computers are the
Casey-Foundation computer in Rockefeller
Center in New York City (which has every
Christian's name listed) and the Dallas
computer, four stories below the IBM Building in Dallas, Texas.

31

THE GRAND DRUID COUNCIL OF 13
(As of Spring, '78)

GAVIN FROST————Modernist, chairman of the
Council. Author of "Witch-
es' Bible", heads move to
unite Witchcraft and Christianity. He feels that if
witchcraft is properly presented, people would choose
witchcraft. Greenville, NC.

DR. RAYMOND BUCKLAND———"Lorka". Traditionalist; former chairman of
the Council until modern-
ists gained control. He was
previously professor of an-
thropology at Columbia University. Author of "Practical Candle-Burning"; "Witch
craft From the Inside", and
"Sax-Wicca Bible." Presi-
dent of witchcraft college
in New Hampshire. He was
personally appointed chairman of Grand Druid Council
by the previous chairman,
Gerald Gardner.

MRS. LOUISE BROWN———Modernist; wife of Le-
land Brown, who was former-
ly with the CIA and in
charge of the Warhawk computer in Virginia. He was
in a fire fight in a closed
room and had his ear drums
burst. As a result he is
retired from the CIA, but
still has access to the
Warhawk computer. Mrs.Brown
is actually the most powerful person on the council,
with Gavin Frost serving
only as a front in the position of chairman.

32

ISAAC BONNAWITZ--Modernist; graduated from Berkley University with a degree in Ceremonial Magic. His IQ tested 205. He is the brain of the Illuminati. He drew up the world takeover plan. He is in charge of physical and lawful destruction of churches and Christians. He ghostwrote House Bill 41,the Genocide Act, and the Martial Law Act. He put together Dee's Gun Control Center in Atlanta, Ga. He created through the ACLU, the Aquarian Anti-Defamation League in St. Paul which sues Christians and churches across America for defaming witches. He now approves all bounty contract killings. Former editor of the paper "Nostika" (The Word), published by Lewwellyn Publishers. Lives in Berkley, Calif.

"LADY ROLWIN"--Traditionalist, former wife of Dr. Buckland, now remarried. Lives in NYC.

SYBIL LEEK-----Traditionalist, astrologer, author. Works include "Diary of a Witch" (1968,72), "Sybil Leek Book of Fortune Telling" ('69), "Tree That Conquered the World" ('69), "Numerology" ('69), "How to be Your Own Astrologer" ('70), "Guide to Telepathy" ('71), "Phrenology" ('71), "Complete Art of Witchcraft ('71), "Pictorial Encyclopedia of Astrology" ('71), "Astrological Guide to the Presidential Candidates", and at least 3 more.

33

She is the most widely read occult author in the world.

TOM HALL————————Modernist, lives in St. Louis. Editor of "The Green Egg." He is the leader of the Brotherhood Church of All Worlds. This is a denomination in witchcraft that believes only in a god and no goddess. He persuaded the Methodist Church to accept psychic powers.

JESSE BELL——————"Lady Sheba",Traditionalist Along with other occult personnel, she own 90% of Merritt Island, Fl, where she lives. Author of the "Book of Shadows" (not the true witchcraft Bible, but a decoy) and "Gromorie of Lady Sheba".

LOUISE HUBNER———Traditionalist who poses as a Modernist. Lives in Los Angeles in the Eagle Rock area. She wrote a nationally syndicated astrology column in the US. Wrote the book, "Power Through Witchcraft". She conducted an occult rite in Hollywood Bowl in which she cast a sexual spell over all Los Angeles County. Immediately rape and related activity began to climb. This is a matter of public record.

PAUL HUSON——————Traditionalist, apprenticed under Dr. Buckland. Handpicked by the Rothschilds. Druid witch. Has written several witchcraft books. Leans toward Satanism. Says the only initiation required is saying the Lord's Prayer backwards 3 times.

34

BOB LEWWELLYN---Traditionalist; St. Paul,
                Minn. Owner of Lewwellynn
                Publishers, the largest pu—
                blishers of occult litera—
                ture in the US.
"ALEXANDER"---Traditionalist, NYC
YVONNE COLLINS---"Legena"(means "Lucifer's
                Bride"), Traditionalist--
                Lynchburg, Va. Replaced John
                Todd on the Grand Druid
                Council. She grew up in
                Lynchburg and attended the
                Thomas Road Baptist Church
                pastored by Dr. Jerry Fal-
                well. She was alienated from
                Dr. Falwell when her parents
                lied to her in saying that
                Dr. Falwell had given cer-
                tain advice with what to do
                about her illegitimate preg-
                nancy. She is the one who
                prompted the Security and
                Exchange Commission inves-
                tigation of Thomas Road
                Baptist Church which crea-
                ted severe financial trou-
                bles there. She is still in
                control of political activ-
                ity.

* A candidate for the council is Mr Christopher Tolkein--Traditionalist who lives
  in England. He is the son of JRR Tolkein
  who wrote "Hobbitt", "Simarilion", and
  "Trilogy". These are the Genesis, Exodus and Leviticus of the "Book of Shadows", the witchcraft Bible.
* Traditionalist----One who believes that
  true witches must be born from a family
  of witches.
* Modernist---One who believes that anyone
  can become a witch by training and practice.

35

POWER OF THE ILLUMINATI

FINANCIAL

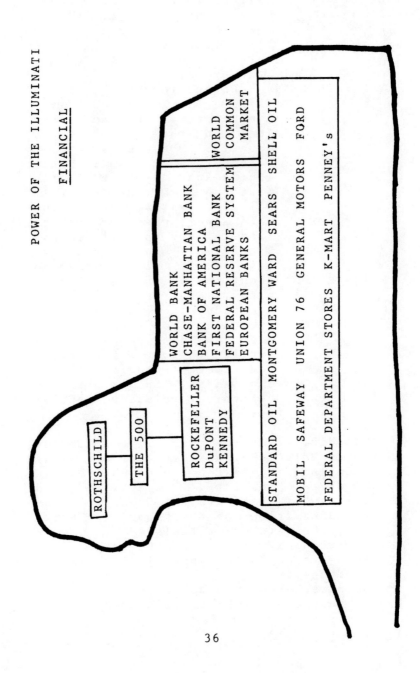

36

F I N A N C I A L

The power of the Illuminati is MONEY. Through the control of money, the economy, trade and business, the Illuminati can control the world.

The head of this Financial Sphinx, of course, is the Rothschilds (the 5 rather than only 3). The European bankers control all the major banks of the world.

The "500" would include the Rockefellers,DuPonts and Kennedys as the top three families in America, along with Onassis, Ford, and Roosevelt, among others.

From these come the various European banks, the World Bank (Robert McNamara, President), Chase-Manhattan Bank (owned by Rockefeller), First National(owned by Kennedy), and the Federal Reserve System (a stockholder-owned bank, not a Government agency, created December, 1913, which determines the money system, the gold price, the stock market, etc---all at the bidding of private individuals).

Next is the World Common Market,which determines the trade value for the world.

Below these are the various major corporations of America. These corporations, which will bankrupt themselves later, will aid in crushing the economy and the lifestyles of every government-dependent person in America.

On the following pages can be seen the progression of how the American government has changed the value of the dollar by decreasing its reserve backing. In order to pay off debts,the American government borrows money from the Federal Reserve System which prints its own money (an illegal act according to the Constitution,which states that only Congress can issue money). The "Fed" charges high interest to the government while being backed by Savings Bonds. The American government's debt is so large

37

that the taxes of the people cannot pay e-
ven the interest of the Fed, much less the
principal. In exchange for this, the International Bankers are given the right to
have members of its choice in high governmental positions.

If Congress would do away with the Federal Reserve System and print its own money, backed with its own power of supply,
the American debt would soon vanish, the
illegal tax-system would vanish, inflation
would cease, and the American economy would
again be stable.

This, however, is not the Illuminati
plan for America, nor for the world.

MEANING OF THE REVERSE SIDE OF THE $1 BILL

On the back of our one dollar bill, on the left-hand side, can be seen the "Reverse Seal" of the United States. The US has, however, never sealed anything with this "Seal" nor ever intends to. The Seal is in reality a secret code.

Created by Adam Weishaupt, this seal was first put on the dollar bill in 1933 by FDR.

With the Rothschild Tribunal Capstone and the All-Seeing Eye of Lucifer, the pyramid is the formation of all Illuminati Organization.

NORUS ORDO SECLORUM means "New World Order" or One World Government.

ANNUIT COEPTIS means "Our enterprise (conspiracy)has been crowned with success"

The 1776 in Roman numerals means May 1, 1776 (the Birthday of American Illuminism), not July 4, 1776.

The 13 Stars form the "Star of David", the powerful Hexagram of witchcraft symbolism.

On the US coins IN GOD WE TRUST never meant Jesus Christ, but the occult's Lucifer, Satan.

Finally, the dollar sign ($) is "John Galt's" symbol,a symbol found in ancient pyramids, meaning "to scourge; to punish, to make right." The dollar sign ($) was formed by overlapping the initials for United States.

(It needs to be understood, that although the above explains the evil significance & symbology of the code, that God Almighty, Yahweh, and not Satan, is all powerful,and has seen to it that the Seals also contain truths for and about Israel.)

40

FALL OF THE AMERICAN DOLLAR

The Gold Certificate representing actual gold coin on deposit in the Treasury was as sound as paper money could get. The integrity of the US stood behind it. We've not been the same since.

The "United States" note is commonly referred to as Lincoln Greenback. When Lincoln rebelled at paying the International Bankers' high interest rates to borrow "money" with which to pursue war, these were issued. Not one cent of interest has ever been paid for their issuance.

41

The pledge on the face of the Silver Certificate guaranteed itself of being redeemable in silver. The Government has not
only reneged on this, but there is also
neither gold nor silver to back the dollar
with.

When the "Federal" Reserve Note was first
issued, it clearly stipulated that it was
redeemable in GOLD on demand at any Fed
Bank. By 1932, this was no longer true,
but the seed had been planted and Americans accepted these Notes. We have never
recovered from this.

42

For many years the public accepted the Fed
Note as though it were real money only because that the Note clearly said it was
redeemable in lawful money at the Treasury
of at any Bank.

The US has now reached the final step. We
do not have a Gold Certificate,Silver Certificate, Fed Notes that are redeemable,or
anything to back it. "This note is legal
tender for all debts, public or private."
The citizen has no choice but to accept.
The Fed has systematicaly looted the Treasury to the point that all we have is an
unpayable debt.

43

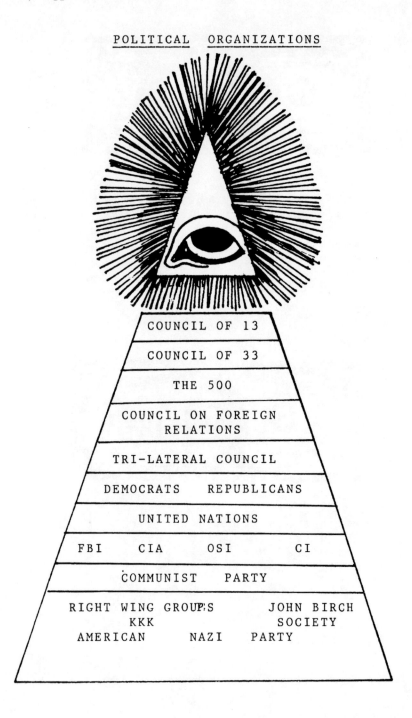

POLITICAL ORGANIZATIONS

COUNCIL OF 13

COUNCIL OF 33

THE 500

COUNCIL ON FOREIGN
RELATIONS

TRI-LATERAL COUNCIL

DEMOCRATS   REPUBLICANS

UNITED NATIONS

FBI   CIA   OSI   CI

COMMUNIST   PARTY

RIGHT WING GROUPS   JOHN BIRCH
KKK   SOCIETY
AMERICAN   NAZI   PARTY

44

POLITICAL

The Council on Foreign Relations (CFR)----
  Formed in 1921 under Colonel   William
  House, with JP Morgan, John D. Rocke-
  feller, Paul Warburg and Jacob Schiff.
  The name for the American Illuminati.
  Its head is David Rockefeller.
  As of June 30, 1978, the CFR had 1878
  members. Among them were:

Rockefeller	Adlai Stepheson
Henry Kissinger	Richard Nixon
Teddy Kennedy	Gerald Ford
Howard Baker	Robert McNamara
David Brinkley	Jimmy Carter
John Chancellor	H.J. Heinz
Alexander Haig	Jacob Javitz
Walter Mondale	Howard Johnson
Barbara Walters	John Anderson
Dean Rusk	John Lindsey
Douglas Fairbanks	Sam Jaffe
Irving R. Levine	Walter Cronkite
George Bush	Shirley Temple
Carter's Cabinet	Black
Members	Most of Reagan's
	Cabinet Men

Tri-Lateral Council,or Commission (TLC)---
  Founded in 1973 by David Rockefeller,
  with Jimmy Carter as a founding member
  and president.
  The Brain Center of the CFR.
  The American version of the European
  Commonwealth Market (which the US is a
  secret member of).

All CFR and TLC members must believe Lucifer is god and that Adam (Lucifer's son)is
ready to take control.

American Government Section (Dem, GOP, UN,
  FBI, CIA, OSI, CI)------
  1) Every President since FDR has been a
     CFR member.

  2) "Large arguments" in Congress   are

45

cover-ups for the passing of major
bills (example: The Korean-Congress-
man scandal covered-up the passing
of the Anti-Hoarding Act).

3) Richard Nixon----set up with Water-
gate. Nixon was going against Rothschild plans by opening communications with Red China, the Rothschilds'National enemies, who are
slated for destruction.

4) The Illuminati created the United
Nations to bring about a One-World
Government and Religious system, in
1942, after Pearl Harbor.

5) FBI ordered Colt Firearms to stop
shipping arms to South California,
because so many people were buying
them.

6) Smith and Wesson and Winchester have
purposely built their weaons defec-
tive, since 1964.

7) In 1973-78, half of the small arm
weapons of the US Military have been
"lost".

8) Espionage in US Post Offices is done
by experts who can open and re-close
mail without suspicion.

9) Illuminati financed Panic of 1907,
WWI and II, the Depression, and the
Korean and Vietnam Wars for every
side.

Communist Party----
There is no such thing as Communism.
The idea of it was created by Albert
Pike as a front for war. Nathan
Rothschild gave 2 checks to Karl Marx
for aid.
The Russian Revolution was financed by
American bankers in NY. Russia today
is headed by the council of 33.

46

The John Birch Society-----
    The JBS was founded by Robert Welch, a
    Mormon and a 33rd level Mason. The JBS
    will write against the International
    bankers,CFR, Rockefeller, Kennedy, etc
    but will never come against the Roths-
    childs or tie the Illuminati to the
    Occult. JBS is only a front, to take
    pressure off the Illuminati.

    The Satanic seed of the Nachash of
Genesis 3:15, now identified as International Jewry or the Illuminati is the most
highly organized race of people on the
face of the earth. The Jews have organized
everybody into some type of organization,
and they control most or nearly all of
the organizations in existence. The Jews
control the Blacks through the NAACP, they
control our foreign policy through the
CFR; they control the Protestant Denominations through the National and World Council of Churches and through the National-
Conference of Christians and Jews. They
control the Catholic Church by infiltrat-
ing into policy making positions of power.
They control large segments of America
through the Masonic Lodge. They control
both the Republican and Democratic parties. In short, the Jews control nearly
every major organization in existence and
thus direct the destiny of the blacks,both
left and right wing social, political, and
religious organizations as well as all of
the national media industry.
    The Jews have a highly developed net-
work of organizations through which they
exercise total control over all Jews, the
world over. Some of the more well known
Jewish organizations would be B'nai B'rith,
the American Jewish Congress and the Anti-
Defamation League, which operates as a secret Jewish Police Squad throughout America. Another Jewish organization which few
people know about is the Jewish KEHILLA.
This super-secret organization is con-

47

trolled by a Board consisting of 300 members who meet periodically to chart the international course of the Kehilla. These 300 Jews in reality chart the financial, political, social and religious program of most of the nations of the world and they do it with 1) unlimited money, 2)the control of all propaganda and 3) highly complex organizations.

The Jewish Kehilla is the international Jewish Network that governs the political destiny of most of the world. At the top of this satanic group sits one man, known as the King of the Jews, who is the world wide leader of World Jewry. The world is divided into Eastern and Western Hemispheres under the Kehilla organization with one man sitting under the King of the Jews for both the eastern and western Hemisphere. The leader of the eastern and western hemisphere is called a Sponsor. There are only two of these satanic leaders, one for each Hemisphere. Under each of these 2 Sponfors sit 7 Jews called, Arch-Censors. The first eschelon is called the 7th degree of the Kehilla. Each of these know their leader and each other. Each of these seven have another seven under them, comprising a total of 49 satanic Jews. These are all called Ministers and make up the 6th degree of the Kehilla. Each of these 49 satanic seed line of Satan have 7 men under him called Herald making the 5th degree. Each of these 343 Jews have seven Jews under him called, Courtier making 2,401 in the 4th degree. The 3rd degree eschelon is called a Scrivenor(with 16,807 Jews);the 2nd degree is called an Auditor (with 117,649 Jews); and the first degree in the 7th eschelon is called a Mute (with 823,543 Jews).(This gives a total of 960,800 Satanic Jews in each Hemisphere or a total of 1,921,600 Jews of the Kehilla in the world with their King of the Jews in control.)

48

The Kehilla is so super-secret that beyond the initial prince of the east or west, the sponsor who knows the seven Jews under him, none of the rest of the Kehilla members know who the others are. With this super secret highly organized network of Jews this powerful Kehilla can communicate world wide policies with a very minimum of effort. Each of these Eastern and Western divisions of the Kehilla command about one million Jews. Each man merely calls the seven men below him and in a matter of minutes the entire world wide Jewish Kehilla is moving forth to do whatever is needed at any given time to enhance the serpent seed on this earth---strikes, revolution, student riots, welfare riots, or just about any given act that will increase their concentration of money control, propaganda control and the political and social domination of the Seed of the Woman, White Christian Israel Nations of this earth.

The Basic Policies of the Kehilla are outlined in the format for the Jewish Domination of this world and are called the Protocols of the Learned Elders of Zion. This document sets forth the basic policy of the Kehilla and anyone can readily see how history moved forth during this century to fulfill the policies of these Jewish Protocols. You will note that Protocol III is introduced with reference to the Jewish symbolic snake representing political Zionism and its Judaism counterpart. The head of this Satanic snake was to represent those who were initiated into the very head or top positions of World Jewry with the body of the snake unaware of the vile direction that World Jewry was moving. It is very interesting to note that the Jews themselves selected the serpent as their symbol. Good Bible Students will not be taken by surprise because they know as do the Jews themselves, that the Jew is the seed of the serpent and they trace

49

their beginning back to Cain. Dr. Abba Hillel Silver, a well known Jew, when writing in the Jewish publication, Liberal Judaism, January 1949, about the newly created state of Israeli declared: "For the curse of Cain, the curse of being an outcast and a wanderer over the face of the earth has been removed."

The Protocols of the Learned Elders of Zion together with the <u>Talmud</u> and other Jewish cabalistic writings form the foundation for both Zionism and Judaism. The Talmud is one of the most vile anti-Christian, satanic books ever written. It consists of 63 volumes of filth and gutter talk and is all directed against Jesus Christ and the Christian Faith. The Talmud and not the Old Testament, forms the foundations for political Zionism and religious Judaism. Zionism is the political expression of religious Judaism, and both are hatched out of Satan himself.

CIVIL ORGANIZATIONS

The main group in the Civil Organizations, of course,is the Masonic Lodge. As
previously stated,the Council of 33 is the
highest 33 Masons in the world (there are
no levels in Blue Masonry).
Except for the cutting of the wrist,
Masonic initiation is the same as the
Witchcraft initiation. The Masonic teachings are based on the KABBALAH. Only Masons who are Internationalists (One-Worlders) can be in the Illuminati.
Between the 32nd level and the 33rd
level Mason is the Honorary 33rd level.
Honorary 33rd and Initiated 33rd level Masons know EVERYTHING of the Illuminati.
30th,31st and 32nd levels that are trusted
know the Luciferian Doctrine and the basis
of child sacrifice.
In 1942 three 33rd level Masons wrote
"The Lost Keys of Free-Masonry." In it the
initiation for 33rd level is given. Called
the "Warrior on the Block" rite it is performed to apply the energy of Tubal-cain
and Lucifer by the exercise of Human sacrifice.
No true Christian can remain a Mason,
because all Masons pray to the "Mighty
Wind", not to Jesus Christ.

The Jay Cees, Odd Fellows,Boy Scouts,
Girl Scouts, YMCA, YWCA etc were organized
for the sole purpose of searching out the
youth that the subversive groups of the
Illuminati could teach and use for the
Riots.

Knights of Columbus is a Roman Catholic Organization which practices human sacrifice.
All Lodge-type organizations are modern "Groves" which are idolatrous temples,
to be destroyed by God's judgment.

51

CIVIL ORGANIZATIONS

| COUNCIL OF 13 |
| COUNCIL OF 33 |
| THE 500 |
| B'NAI   B'RITH |
| SCOTTISH & YORK RITES |
| MASONIC LODGES------
 WHITE & BLUE |
| AMERICAN CIVIL LIBERTIES
 UNION |

JAY CEES | KNIGHTS OF COLUMBUS

SHRINERS | ODD FELLOWS | ELKS

BOY SCOUTS | GIRL SCOUTS | BOYS' CLUBS

YMCA | YWCA | ETC

52

OCCULT   RELIGION

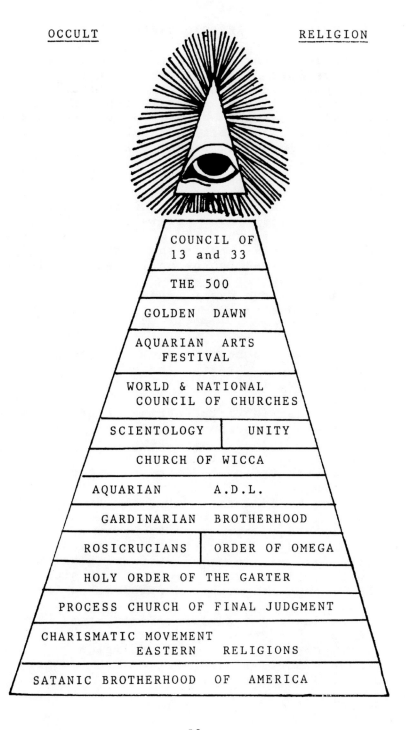

COUNCIL OF
13 and 33

THE 500

GOLDEN   DAWN

AQUARIAN   ARTS
FESTIVAL

WORLD & NATIONAL
COUNCIL OF CHURCHES

SCIENTOLOGY   UNITY

CHURCH OF WICCA

AQUARIAN   A.D.L.

GARDINARIAN   BROTHERHOOD

ROSICRUCIANS   ORDER OF OMEGA

HOLY ORDER OF THE GARTER

PROCESS CHURCH OF FINAL JUDGMENT

CHARISMATIC MOVEMENT
           EASTERN   RELIGIONS

SATANIC BROTHERHOOD   OF   AMERICA

OCCULT AND RELIGIOUS ORGANIZATIONS

Because man is created in the image of God, our Lord has given us a spirit that cries out for communion with God's Spirit. In the rebellion of those in the Conspiracy, this yearning becomes perverted and draws toward the Realm of Darkness, rather than the Kingdom of Light. Therefore, the Illuminati must also infiltrate and control these organizations which aim toward man's spiritual being.

Karl Marx said, "Religion is the opiet of the people." The powers of darkness, then see to it that their dirty, demon-infested needles are in the arms of all those captivated by the addiction of spiritual Babylon.

The previous chart reveals some of the organizations of the Occult; the following explains them:

The Golden Dawn is the Rothschilds' private coven. Created in the 1770's, its members have included JRR Tolkein and CS Lewis.

The Aquarian Arts Festival ties all of the occult Brotherhoods together. (There are 8 Brotherhoods of witchcraft). The Festival saw to it that the Altar Room of San Quentin Prison included a Witchcraft-Chaplain.

The World Council of Churches and the National Council of Churches are the two organizations which seek to unite all Protestant and Independent Denominations together as One, in association with the Roman Catholic Church. From the WCC stemmed the "Thought of Higher Criticism," a Theological view which seeks to tear down the Divine Inspiration of the Scriptures. The WCC condones Communism and also seeks to be at peace with any pagan religion. It finances worldwide rebellion with monies received from American churches.

54

Scientology is the main "Christian" church which teaches psychic healing and mind-over-matter.

The Unity church is the main platform for witches to speak to "Christians." The Unity church is primarily a philosophy-teaching organization. (The Unity church in Dallas, Texas had a series of "sermons" which taught that all walks of life and occupations are in harmony with God. These series ended with an exhibition by one of its members--a strip-tease artist--who did her act for the church one Sunday morning, in front of men, women, and children.)

The Church of Wicca, headed by the Council of 13's Gavin Frost, is the main witchcraft organization which the general public may attend. Wicca means "Wise Ones".

The Aquarian Anti-Defamation League, headed by the Council of 13's Isaac Bonnawitz sues Christians who speak out against witches and Jews (under the Jewish ADL).

Brother Jacob's "Process Church of the Final Judgment" is the most radical group in the Illuminati. Its members would blow themselves up for their cause(Charles Manson is a member of this group). They observe human sacrifice and bomb Christian churches. Their other main prophetess, "Mother Elizabeth", is an ex-Assembly of God. The Process Church believes in the "Enlightened Masters"and in Reincarnation.

The Gardinarian Brotherhood is England's Brotherhood of Witchcraft.

The Rosicrusians, a Roman Catholic order, believe in human sacrifice.

The Holy Order of the Garter, in London, England, is headed by the Prime Minister of England.

The Order of Omega, which teaches seances, is accepted by the United Methodist Church.

55

Eastern Religion groups, such as the Maharishi Mahesh Yogi's Transcendental Meditation, are the platforms for teaching astral projection, demon possession, yoga, telepathy, and mind-over-matter control. Most are very "scientific" and therefore aim at both the intellectual and the "Flower-child" peoples.

In 1947-48 the occult began to infiltrate the so-called Fundamental and Pentecostal churches of organized Christianity. As the Spirit of God began a new move in the true church to come out of Babylon, another spirit was moving IN Babylon. An organization began which was called "The Voice of Healing" and soon thereafter the "Charismatic Movement" began to blossom.

Posing as Spirit-filled Christians of all denominations, the Voice of Healing allowed practicing witches to "come out" and to induce the youth by their signs and wonders. Many of these witches are still trained at St. Paul, Minnesota to act as Christians, teaching them the doctrines, mannerisms, phrases, etc of a "true Christian."

The Voice of Healing was founded by Oral Roberts, head of Oral Roberts University and the City of Faith, and by Gordon Lindsay, founder of Christ for the Nations in Dallas, Texas. Its Board of Directors included Morris Cuerillo (who teaches that he is one of the 2 Witnesses of Revelation 11 to the Jews), A.A. Allen, T.L. Osborn, and Demos Shakurian (head of the Full Gospel Business Men's Association).

William Branham, a country preacher anointed by God, became involved with the Voice of Healing and became more popular than the Directors of it. At a particular service Bro. Branham, who preached against the Unions, television, movies, and on the coming chaos, stood up on the platform and pointing behind himself toward the Direct-

56

ors, said "It's bad enough that I have to
fight the devil in front of me---I don't
want to have to fight him behind me. Get
off the platform!"

Angered that Branham had discovered
the infiltraters, the Illuminati decided
to have Branham killed. While on his way
to Branham Tabernacle to straighten some
Spiritualism out that had crept in,Branham
was killed in an automobile crash in which
an alcoholic, programmed by the occult,
dodged Branham's son's car in front of him
and hit Branham head-on, doing 90mph. Thus
the Movement could continue and false reports began to surface about Branham's so-
called witchcraft influences.

The purpose of the Charismatic Movement is to tear down Fundamental evangeli-
cal denominations and to unite the Liberal
denominations into one Ecumenical Church.
Its basic teachings include:repentance not
necessary for salvation, repentance without separation from sin, separation from
the world unnecessary as a Christian (thus
the Abundant Life Movement, "Christian "
movie stars and entertainers, etc), speaking in tongues will make you rich and allow you to receive material blessings from
God, and no more Law (thus doing away with
the Old Testament).

In the 1960's, the Christian churches
began to come against the rising influence
of rock music. In order to further aid the
demonic influence of rock music, the Illuminati paid Chuck Smith of Calvary Chapel
two, $4,000,000 checks to start Maranatha
Records and "Jesus Rock", thus getting rock
music back into the churches.

Training witches as Spirit-filled
Christians, the Illuminati infiltrated the
companies of Sparrow Records, Birdwing Re-
cords, WORD Inc, Myrrh, Lexicon, and Light
Records, and sent out such "ministries" as
LoveSong, Children of the Day, Nancy Hon-
eytree, Larry Norman, Chuck Girard, Phil
Keaggy and others.

(WORD Records owns Myrrh,Lexicon, Word,
and Light subsidiaries. WORD is owned by
ABC, which is owned by Standard Oil, which
is owned by David Rockefeller,who is owned
by Philippe Rothschild.)

For example:

Nancy Honeytree's "Rattle Me, Shake
Me" puts down the Establishment----family,
pastors, teachers, and policemen---as a
bunch of dead leaders and then instills
rebellion in the youth.

Phil Keaggy has an album out that is
all hypnotic-type Rock Music, containing a
story to be read during the music. In allegory form, the story never once mentions
Jesus and refers to "the Son of God" only
one time.

Debby Boone's "You Light up My Life "
was written by a woman who wrote the song
to Lucifer.

Kenneth Copeland"s "Bread on Water"
has a Chuck Berry song in the background .

The Illuminati also own such Christ—
ian publishers as Zondervon, Collins-World
etc, thus able to influence all media to
Christians with their own teachings.

Another Illuminati "Christian-organi-
zation" is Melodyland in California,headed
by Ralph Wilkerson,the head of the Charismatic Infiltration of the Occult. Its members include Ron DePriest, Jim Spillman ,
Walter Martin (who says the Antichrist is
a computer, endorses hypnotism, and says a
witch cannot get saved, thus making witchcraft more powerful than the blood of
Christ), Michael Essex (author of I'm a
King's Kid, which pushes the Abundant Life
Movement), and Mike Warnke(ex-Satanist and
author of Satan Seller, Warnke built Melodyland's hot-line. A homosexual, Warnke
waters down the message of Christ, giving
witches more credit for power than Christians).Walter Martin also tours with Coun—
cil of 13 member Gavin Frost in debates
which end up making Christianity look
follish and arrogant and witchcraft as

harmless, full of love, and wise.

Melodyland is the main thrust of the propaganda which teaches that Christians are to be pacifists and non-aggressive or defense-minded, whereas the Bible shows that the people of God have always had a sword in their hand(as Jesus and the Sons of God do in Revelation 19), they hold the Sword of Judgment still, and they always will.

Others involved with the fake Charismatic Movement include:

The Way Ministries(Way International) produces tapes, some of which have high-frequency subliminal suggestions which produce demonic tongues in people, suicides, trances, etc. (Melodyland and FGBMA do this also).

Bob Harrington (Chaplain of Bourbon Street)----Backslid; follows Ruth Carter Stapleton. Was seduced by a young Illuminati witch posing as a Christian, who was Harrington's secretary. Pictures were taken and he was blackmailed. Harrington now does pre-programmed "tours" with atheist Madellyn Murray O'Hair.

Ruth Carter Stapleton(Jimmy Carter's sister) is feared and respected by witches as the greatest witch of all time.Promotes "Inner Healing", which is actually psychic healing.

Pat Robertson (700 Club; Christian Broadcasting Network President)--says,"God has redeemed Rock Music."

Kathryn Kuhlman---Her famous line was "I believe in miracles." Greatest witch previous to Ruth Carter Stapleton. Died of cancer in mid-1970's. Large "Divine Healing" ministry.

Jim Bakker---PTL Network President. One of the largest "Abundant Life" charismatic preachers. Changed name from Praise The Lord to People That Love.

59

Rev. Robert Schullert--Had a drive-in church where people could sit in the cars for church services and now has a window-dome church so people "can see God's nature" during services.

Norman Vincent Peale--Author of <u>Power of Positive Thinking</u>,which teaches psychic healing and mind-over-matter.

Also, non-Charismatic Billy Graham compromised with God by bowing down to the Pope and refusing to come against Communism any longer.

It is well to note that Witchcraft/Illuminati plants in churches will always have money, a mark of the Beast.

As can be seen, the occult/religious organizations and influences of the Illuminati is widespread. The move toward a one world Political/Religious System is seen in our day. Young people, desiring more than a life of working until the dreaded retirement pension, get into the occult because they see more power in it than in the "Christian" churches. This is because there <u>is</u> <u>no</u> power in these Babylonian harlots. God's power, His Anointing, is only found in God's Christ,His true Church, the "Called-Out" Ones.

60

SOCIAL INFLUENCE OF THE ILLUMINATI

Perhaps the most influential aspect in America is the social influence of the Illuminati---TV, movies, and rock music. Because the heads of these corporations are CFR members and Jews, it should be easily seen that their puppets would also be of like-mind.

It is estimated that by the time a person is 10 years old, he has seen 1800 murders, 200 rapes, 10,000 criminal acts, and countless sexual perversions on television. From Saturday morning programs to late night adult shows,TV is forever pouring on its occult teachings.There are more occult shows on ABC(the Antichrist Broadcasting Company)than on all the other networks combined.

Saturday morning occult shows include SENTINEL, ISIS/SHAZAM, and SPACE ACADEMY, which all teach astral projection,seances, levitation, demon possession, casting spells, high counsels, etc.

Cindy Williams (LaVerne and Shirley) is the head of one of the largest homosexual covens in California. She is married to singer Carole King.

David Soul (Starsky and Hutch), Linda Carter (Wonder Woman), Erik Estrada(Chips) Bill Bixby (Incredible Hulk),and Elizabeth Montgomery (Bewitched) are all witches.

All the cast of "The Waltons" on TV endorse TM and practice it, as does Merv Griffin, Mary Tyler Moore, and Clint Eastwood.

Even the News programs, whose newscasters are CFR members and witches, influence Americans by means of flashes on TV,too fast to be seen with the normal vision and yet is caught by the subconcious. These flashes, aided by the chlorine and floride in the city water (which dulls the thinking process of the mind), teach pacifists suggestions or even militant-type thoughts.

61

Next to TV, more and more people are watching movies more now than ever before. And more movies are about the occult than ever before. For example...

"Dunwich Horror"---a 1969 movie with Dean Stockwell, Sandra Dee and Ed Beagley, this was the most accurate movie on the occult ever made. Based on the Necromonicron(the only 3 copies of this book in existence are in Russia,London and Galscow). It was the hope of the witchcraft message.

"3 Days of the Condor"---Starring Robert Redford and Faye Dunaway. The code book he discovered as a CIA aid, for which he was almost killed, was ATLAS SHRUGGED .

"Star Wars" and its sequels--The most modern movies produced by white witches which give an answer to the world ("The Force") for its problems. Witchcraft is presented as good and the only hope for all. The battle in "Star Wars" is between White witchcraft and Black witchcraft.

Movie actress Sharon Tate ("Valley of the Dolls") got pregnant and then didn't want to dedicate her baby in sacrifice, as a witch. She wanted out of witchcraft and was murdered. Hung upside down, this was the position ofthe Traitor in Tarot cards. She was a member of the Process Church. (Manson went to jail by choice in order to organize all the white prisoners in the US and all motorcycle gangs. Originally scheduled for release in '78 or '79 he will probably now "escape". None of Manson's group ever got saved---not Tex Watson, Susan Atkins, or any others).

Other occult-based movies include---- "Superman","Exorcist," "Rosemary's Baby", "Omen," and "Logan's Run." In fact, of the top 12 movies of all time, 5 are occult-based.

It should also be noted that almost all paperback books now put out are on the occult, sex perversions, or about witchcraft teachings.

62

In the early 1960's the Beatles (who got their name from the Scarub, the Egyptian beetle, symbol of reincarnation) began a trend of music, known as Rock Music. Rock Music was never intended for entertainment. Its occult beat, similar to the ancient Druid music, has a hypnotic effect on people which instills rebellion, sex, murder, etc. (Voodoo doctors know that you can kill a person by the beat of a drum). An ultrasonic third track on tapes produces occult suggesstions daily in millions of youth.

Rock songs are written in occult language which contains coded spells or incontations that the listener isn't aware of. A witch would write the words from an old Druid Manuscript. Top name musicians are hired to record the music. After the recording session the 16-track Master Tape is set aside for 6 months until it is ready to be "blessed."

On a full moon, some of the most powerful witches in the country arrive to put the finishing touches on the song. They conjure up "Rege", the main occult demon. A very large room in the recording studio is set aside for this, with an armed guard outside, The witches perform this ceremony in the nude. Standing inside the circle with the Hexagram, the High Priestess summons Rege. The room is filled with a strong rushing wind yet the candles keep burning. Demons are then sent out with each copy of the record produced.

All rock stars are members of a witchcraft brotherhood. Examples of songs and musicians include:

> The Beatles---Their double white album (which contains "Helter Skelter") is a prophetic album of the Book of Shadows.
> KISS---Kings In Satanic Service. All are confessed homosexuals and are Ordained Ministers in the Satanic

Church. KISS means "Blessed by the Devil" in witch language. Their"Destroyer" Album calls for kids to kill their parents in their sleep.

Elton John---Homosexual. Says he has never written a song that is not in witch language.

The Carpenters----Incestuous witches. Karen is married to a black man. It is said that their private lives are far worse that that of KISS'.

"Tapestry" by Carole King is all about Lucifer.

2 Homosexuals wrote "Bridge over Troubled Water" (Silver girl in the song is a needle with drugs).

"4-Way Street" and "Chicago" by Crosby, Stills, Nash and Young produced major riots in the US in the 1960's.

(Rock music is not the only dread that there is in music. Country-Western music ministers spirits of adultery,drunkenness, revelling, etc. Other kinds of music minister melonchaly, sympathy, etc).

When an artist rises to too much popularity, fulfills his purpose or begins to stray from the desires of his witchcraft leaders, he is usually killed. This only makes the star idolized more and sends his record sales up. This has occurred with Jim Croce, Jimmy Hendrix, Janis Joplin and Elvis Presley.

Separation from the world therefore is essential to the Christian. With its occult influence everywhere, it is easy to see how God's people must be in the Wilderness, forever coming out, lest they too receive of Babylon's plagues (Rev 18:4).

64

DEMONIC JEWELRY CREATED BY THE ILLUMINATI

As stated before, the three most powerful things in the occult are herbs, astrology and jewelry(talismans or amulets). Jewelry is probably the most common of these. (Jewelry must be 3-dimensional in order to contain a spell; therefore, pictures cannot cause trouble.)

In the early 1970's the Illuminati decided that the time had come for them to distribute their jewelry among the general public and especially among Christians. Witches and the hippy groups had already been wearing these symbols for years by this time.

Avon, an Illuminati corporation, is the largest distributor of occult jewelry. Since 1974, they have been sold in Christian bookstores.

This jewelry was created years ago for the sole purpose of worship of the devil. As this jewelry is sent out, as with rock albums, demons also are sent out.Each symbol represents a specific spell. Below are the symbols and their occult meanings...

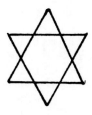

Hexagram---Called the "Star of David" now; known as the "Crest of Solomon" for 3000 years. Conjures up demons; the most evil sign in witchcraft. Means "to hex"----put a spell on someone.

Ankh---Created in Egypt. It is the oldest symbol. It is the worship of Ra, the Sungod and the belief in Reincarnation. It

means   you   despised
virginity and   prac-
tice orgies as   part
of your worship ser-
vice.

Unicorn Horn----Known
as the Italian Horn,
Fairy Wand, or Lepre-
chaun's Staff. Means
you trust in the dev-
il for your finances.
Created by a Scottish
Druid.

Peace Symbol----Known
as the Broken Cross,
the rejection of Cal-
vary and   the Christ-
ian   church; said to
bring peace of mind.

Obelisk-----Symbol of
Nimrod or Baal as God,
and Phallus-Worship.

Pentagram--1 Point up
means Lucifer;   the
symbol of all Witch-
craft. 2 Points   up
means Satan, the hor-
ned hunter of   the
night.   Called the
Eastern Star or Goat-
head,it is the symbol
of the Blue Masonic
Lodge.

 Cresent Moon---An oc-
cult priest; the wor-
ship of the"Mother of
Heaven"

 Circle----Occult Tem-
ple(no temple now, so
things are done in a
circle).

 Triangle---Basic sym-
bol in witchcraft.

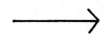 Arrow--Sign for cast-
ing a spell.

 Upside down Red Cross
means Human Sacrifice

The Rainbow---Lucifer's brightness.

Owl---Occult wisdom given by the devil.

Scarab (Beetle)---Eternal Reincarnation.

Piercing of the ears was done on dedicat-
ing young girls for the Priestesshood in
the Occult.

67

MASONIC AND PAGAN SYMBOLS

Following is a translated extract from a Document addressed to all the Supreme Councils of Scottish Rites of the World by ALBERT PIKE, delivered in Paris October 1885.

"The order demands the immediate enforcement of the D∴M∴J∴. At different epochs of the life of the nations which have the good fortune of possessing an active Supreme Council, and from 1820 onwards, certain similar communications have been made to certain chosen members of the Grand Consistories and Supreme Councils, respectively. It is necessary to give the secret of this order.

"Exoterically D∴M∴J∴ are the initials of the motto of the 33rd degree.

"Esoterically D∴M∴J∴ are the initials of the words, Destruction, Materialism, Imposition, which "Impose Destruction of everything which resists Materialism.

"The three points ∴ mean that the Masonic work is threefold---

Destruction	- of Supernaturalism - of Authority - of Anti-Masonic activity	
Materialism	- of Conscience - of Education - of the State	
Imposition	- on the Family - on the Nation - on Humanity	

Consequently the order to enforce practically the D∴M∴J∴ is-----"By every means, whatever they may be, one must impose first on the Family and then on the Nation in order to achieve the aim of imposing on Humanity.

Following are Masonic symbol terms   along
with the Masonic definitions----

TEMPLE

The word temple is derived
from the Latin word Tempus,
time; and therefore, the ancient structures called temples were in reality intended to be records of time and
archives of human knowledge.
Such institutions would have
been a great benefit to mankind, but the veil of super-
stition was thrown   over
them; it was deemed politic
or profitable to the few to
deceive the many; that which
should have been a   simple
record of fact was   worked
up into allegory; there a-
rose as esoteric   doctrine
for those initiated in   the
secrets of the temple, and a
deceptious exoteric doctrine
for the mulitiude; and this
was the origin of a   priesthood.

APRON

The Masonic leather apron
does not perpetuate the memory of the apron of the art-
isan masons of the middle a-
ges.   Its   origin   must be
looked for in the   attire of
the Grand Priest,intended to
hide his frontal nudity when
he mounted the steps   of the
altar.
In other words it corres-
ponds to   the linen   drawers
which according to the pres-
cription of Exodus 28:42,
should cover his   loins. It
represents a sort of symbolic circumcision.

69

THE WIDOW

Means the Synagogue, also Isis.

The Egyptian Fable---Isis. Typhon, having killed Osiris shut him up in a coffin, then,having cut his body into pieces, threw it in the Nile. Isis, the good widow, searching for the body of her husband, found all the parts save one member and to commemorate this loss she instituted the worship of the Phallus, an enlarged representation of which she gave, resting on a coffin. (Sound familiar?)

The term also refers to the Manicheans, being derived from the legend according to which Manes, the founder of the sect, was assisted by a rich widow.

Also to Henrietta Maria, widow of Charles I,for whose cause the original "Masons" claimed to be working.

PALLADIUM

One ruling like a King,the Phallus being a universal emblem of Kings. From Pala, Hindu for the Male Organ.

OUROBOROS

Serpent swallowing its tail. Sexual passion, symbol of the Phallus.

SHAMBALLA

The City of the Gods,which is in the West to some nations,in the East to others, in the North or South to yet others. It is the sacred island in the Gobi Desert. It is the home of Mysticism and the Secret Doctrine.

KUNDALINI	The Sex Force
THE SWORD	The Sword is used by the medium (Grand Master, Grand Mistress or other) who presides and directs the ceremonies of evocation only in dealing with those spirits of fire.
TO OV	Kundalini Astral Light, Sex Force, Serpent Power, Hebrew "Gas", Spiritual power, whence comes ghost. Galvanic Electric Fire, the Magnetic Fluid.

I. N. R. I.

Hebrew Yammen Noar Rooakh Yevaishuah meaning Water, Fire, Air, Earth. It also stands for:

Igne Nitrum Roris Invenitur.
Igne Natura Renovanda Integrat.
Igne Natura Renovatur Integra.
Jesus Nazarenus Rex Judeorum

(Rosicrucian)

J. B. M.

Jakin, Boaz, Moabone (Masonry).
Jesus Bethlemitus Maledictus (Satanism).

MOABONE or
MAHABONE

The complete God.
The Hermaphrodite (Man is completed by the degree of Master, 3rd degree).

THE CHRIST

In the secret society-occult jargon this means "the Christ force" or Sex Force--not Jesus Christ.

71

THE ARCH

The Womb

THE SCARAB

The Egyptian Beetle; Generation

LOTUS-PADMA

The Lotus is a water plant from which each god at his birth emerges. The Lotus is also a symbol of reproduction and generation, the flower of concealment, night, silence, mystery and regarded with nearly the same veneration as the Yoni itself.

The Hindus adore the Lotus for other reasons; for example, because being able to reproduce itself without the assistance of the male pollen, it is a type of the androgynous or hermaphroditic character of the Deity. For the same reason this plant was also held sacred by the Egyptian priests.

THE DOUBLE-HEADED EAGLE

The Double-headed Eagle represents an anagram of the Baphomet, the esoteric explanation of which is as follows: Reading Baphomet backwards we get, Tem--oph--ab. Tem is Duplex, Oph is Avis, Ab is Generation. Duplex Avis Generation is The Double Bird of Generation.

GRAND OEUVRE

This term supposed by the Uninitiated to mean the quest of the Alchemist's stone; esoterically denotes the act of the male and female which produces offspring. Copulation.

72

The triangle is inverted in Kadosch. It represents Lucifer who, with the two crowned heads of the eagle, that is to say the Grand Patriarch and the Grand Emperor,or Sovereign, compose the Very Holy and the Indivisible Trinity to which the Kadosch takes his oath of blind obedience.

The Red Cross of Rome and Constantine, Rosicrucian.

The Templar's Cross or The Manichean's Cross.

The Red Cross of "Societas Rosicruciana in Anglia".
Definition:
From a speech pronounced before Bristol College by Frater Vitam Impendere Vero-8.
"Animal magnetism, mesmerism, clairvoyance, spiritual manifestations of all kinds, are but properties of the metaphorical stone and life-elixir, faculties of the microcosm's immortality----in Hermetic parlance----of the Rosie Cross."

The Rose Croix.
The upright----Symbol of Life.
The cross-bar----Symbol of Death.
The Rose-symbol of secrecy or the blooming of the genital organs of woman.

73

 Flamboyant Star, Blazing Star.
Microcosm or Soloman's Seal.
Emblem of Generation.
Pointing up, good.

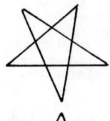 Flamboyant Star, Star of the Morning, Emblem of Lucifer.
Pointing downward, evil.
Black Magic.

 Interlaced Triangles--Symbol of the Double Divinity.
Jehovah white and Jehovah black.
Other names, Macrocosmos, Star of David, Solomon's Seal.
Sex Force---Male & Female. Union.

 "Holy Grail" meaning the female organ, Uterus.

 The Sun or Male.

 The Moon or Female.

 The Star or emblem of Bi-Sexuality in certain rites.

The Male organ or Phallus.

74

The female organ or Uterus

IHOH or Tetragrammaton. IHUH Jehovah or He-Her or The Bi-Sexual God IHVH

Male in the female organ. Phallus in Uterus. Hindu.

The Caduceus. Explanation:
1. The Spine
2. The Sex Force or Kundalini
3. The Power to travel on another plane.

G

God--Generation. The Great God spoken of in the Hermetic-Judaic-Masonic rituals is the one who presides over generation. It is Jehovah, Lucifer, the Angel of Night, the Phallic God, not the God of the Christians. The G in the Flamboyant Gnosis in the higher degrees.

Ladder with seven steps--- Virgo intacta.

Swastica---Sumbol of Life, Fire.

Swastica reversed. Black Magic.

75

Other form of Swastica.

Yima's piercer. Phallus in Uterus God. Other form of I.Q. The symbol of Illuminism.

Compass---Symbol of Masculinity of Freemasonry. Phallus.

Square--Symbol of the genital organs of woman. The Lodge in Freemasonary.

Triangle pointing upward, Male. Exoterically good.

Triangle pointing downward, Female. Exoterically , evil.

Delta

Tetragrammaton. The Ineffable name. Jehovah---IHOH. Shem-ham-phoreh. Jewish and Freemasonic.

Yod---The Phallus.

76

Tau Cross or Crux Ansata--
Union of male and female.
Fecundity.

Other forms of Tau Cross.

The Universal mark or symbol for the complete male
organ, the Phallus.

Crux Decussata or Cross of
St. Andrew.

Jakin--The Column--The female organ, Uterus.
Boaz--The Column--The male
organ, the Phallus.
(Phallus is the sacred
word of the first degree,The
Apprentice).

77

THE ILLUMINATI IN THE SCRIPTURES

Because the Illuminati is only a tool in God's hands and under His control, it would stand to reason that the Scriptures would reveal this enemy of ours.

We have already seen early in the booklet the history of the Illuminati thru its seed of Nachash, Cain and Nimrod (with his Tower of Babel).

In Ephesians 6:12, the Illuminati is known as "the rulers of the darkness of this world" and "spiritual wickedness in high places."

Revelation 18:1-3 and verse 23 reveal to us that the power structures of the Illuminati are the kings of the earth (Political power), the merchants of the earth (financial and trade powers),the great men of the earth (social, religious, and political powers) and that by the sorceries of Babylon (witchcraft and the occult)are ALL nations deceived!As seen in previous chapters of this booklet, the above power--structures control the earth as the rulers of darkness (spiritual darkness) of this world.

Known as the Synagogue (seed)of Satan (Revelation 2:9;3:9) they are of their father the devil(from Nachash to Cain and on to the Rothschilds), and his lusts they will do----along with his murders, falsehoods and lies (John 8:44). These Cainite, Edomite, and Ishmaelite Jews are the product of the Seed of Satan. Even their language, Yiddish, is the demonic form of Hebrew (Nehemiah 13:23-28).

Finally, the aim of the Illuminati---a One-World Political-Religious system----is shown in Revelation chapters 13,17, and 18. The beast, which continues for 42 months,blasphemies against God and His tabernacle, the Sons of God. Making war against the Saints,this first beast(the Political beast) leads into captivity.

A second beast rises next with two horns like a lamb but speaks as a dragon. This religious beast exercises all the power of the first beast and causes all to worship him. With signs and wonders he deceives the earth and brings life to an image of the beast. From this second beast, comes the mark of the beast---666.

The Kings of the earth have fornicated with a woman known as Mystery Babylon the Great, the Mother of Harlots and Abominations of the earth. This woman is the second beast, Roman Catholicism, the mother of all the Protestant-harlot daughters. This system sits upon the political beast (the 7 kings of Daniel 2---Egypt, Assyria, Babylon, Medo-Persia, Greece, Rome and the modern Democratic-Communistic Empires of today). This great city, Babylon, reigns over the kings of the earth during this time.

We stated earlier how this system deceives the earth with its sorceries, its witchcraft, and its occult practices, especially by the signs and wonders of the Charismatic Movement. Witchcraft, though, is as deceptive towards those who use it as it is towards those it is used upon. At the heart of the Illuminati is the "Luciferian Doctrine"---the doctrine of Lucifer being the good god against Jesus Christ---whom they say is the imposter. The Illuminati believe they receive their powers from Lucifer.

Jesus, in John 4:7-24, meets a Samaritan woman, who prophetically is the church system, who though originally Israelite, lost her identity, through fornications. Having no husband (note Revelation 18:7), Jesus says of her, "You worship you know not what." Jesus is saying to her that the one she thinks she's worshipping is in reality not the one whom she is worshipping.

79

The church system, rather than worshipping Jesus, worships another Jesus, another gospel, another spirit (2 Corinthians 11:2-4); and the Illuminati, supposing they worship Lucifer, in reality worship the dragon from whom they receive their power (Revelation 13:4), whom the Bible says is Satan (Revelation 12:9). But isn't, as the church system always taught us, Lucifer and Satan one and the same. Are they?

Satan, according to tradition, was originally created good, and was known as Lucifer. Second only to God, he was said to then rebel against God, taking with him one-third of the angels. God cast him out of heaven and to the earth, where he and his angels became demons. Sounds nice, huh?

Jesus however said that Satan was a murderer <u>from</u> <u>the</u> <u>beginning</u>, abode <u>not</u> in the truth, no truth was ever in him and is the father of lies (John 8:44). 1 John 3:8 says that the devil sinned <u>from</u> <u>the</u> <u>beginning</u>. How then could he which was a murderer and a liar and who sinned from the very beginning, who never abode in the One Truth (Jesus) because no truth abode in him---how could this one then be said to have been perfect, second only to God, at his creation? He couldn't! Lucifer and the devil, or Satan, cannot be the same.

We said before that the Illuminati Beast-Government will make war on the Saints, God's Christ. This is seen in Daniel 7:21,22; Revelation 13:5 (margin); 13:7; 12:13; 11:7; 7:9-14; 17:14; 20:8; and 17:6. "Who can make war with the Beast?" Can anyone? Are Christians to submit to the Illuminati Beast and receive its mark? Or can Christians resist? And if they resist, do they yield to matyrdom or do they "possess the kingdom"? How do they then possess it? Is a Christian Army a Scriptural means?

Revelation 12 speaks of the Woman in the Wilderness,giving birth to a Man-child who later feeds her and protects her. This Many-membered Man-child is the same one in 1 Corinthians 12:12, where it says, "For as the body is one, and hath many members, and all the members of that one body,being many, are one body; so also is Christ."

God's Christ (His Anointed One), a many-membered Son, is composed then of a Head (Jesus) and a Body (144,000 Manifest-ed Sons of God). (This Body of Christ is distinct from the Bride of Christ, which will be revealed in an age to come.)

It is this many-membered Son of God who, by knowing the still, small voice of God, is rising up in the authority and po-wer of His Spirit.

Today, as always, God is training His Army. On the earth, many of God's people are being trained by God for battle, buil-ding the Ark of the Latter Days. We are all familiar with the heroic battles of the Children of Israel(Exodus 17), of Jos-hua in Canaan(Joshua 4,6,10),of David with Goliath, of Jehu (Hosea 1:2-5),of Nehemiah and his men (Nehemiah 4:7-18), and of Gideon and his 300. But, the argument goes,that was in the Old Testament and not in the New,where God is a God of love. But Malachi 3:6 says, "I am the Lord: I change not." Is Jesus Christ not "the same yes-terday,today,and forever?" (Hebrews 13:8).

In three of the above examples--David (1 Chronicles 12:23-40), Joshua (Joshua 1:14) and Nehemiah (Nehemiah 4:7-18)---all had armed, well-trained men. David, in fact, says that God "taught my hands to war and my fingers to fight"(2 Samuel 22: 35; Psalms 18:34; 144:1), and David was a man after God's own heart. The Lord is a Man of War (Exodus 15:3; 2 Chronicles 20: 15; Revelation 19:11) and has given to His Saints this same honor (Psalms 149:5-9; Isaiah 61:8). Hebrews 11:34 tells us that

81

the men of Faith "waxed valiant in fight, turning to flight the armies of the aliens." Even Paul says in 2 Timothy 2:3,4 to "endure hardness, as a good soldier of Jesus Christ," reminding us that "no man that wars entangles himself with the affairs of this life, that he may please him who has chosen him to be a soldier."

God is choosing out His Army today. According to Deuteronomy 20, certain members are disqualified, in order to be the Army seen in Revelation 19:11-21 and Joel 2:1-11. An army which walks in the Spirit and which is empowered by righteousness, this army is clothed with purity by being purged by fire. Out of their mouths goes forth a sharp sword---the Word of God in Judgment. A great people and strong,there has never been ever the like,neither shall be anymore after it. A fire is before them and a flame behind them; a strong people set in battle array. Orderly in ranks, the earth shall quake before them and the heavens shall tremble. The Lord God shall utter His Voice before His Army, for His Camp is VERY great!! Praise the Lord!

The violent shall take the Kingdom of God by force (Matthew 11:12; Daniel 7:18, 21,22). A millstone shall be cast and with violence shall that great city Babylon be thrown down (Revelation 18:21). This is the same stone of Daniel 2, which is God's Anointed Christ!

The dry bones of White Christian Israel (Ezekiel 37:1-14) shall arise in the power of God, being an exceeding great Army. Awake, Oh Zion, Awake! For your redemption draweth nigh! We must be on the alert!

Even Paul warred and had guard duty (2 Corinthians 6:5;11:27) as did Nehemiah's men while rebuilding the Temple of God---- Nehemiah 4:9.

82

2 Corinthians 10:3,4; Ephesians 6:12, says ours are not carnal weapons and our warfare is not against flesh and blood. Our weapons and warfare are not carnal----minding the flesh---but are Spiritual,that is minding the things of God's Spirit, because Spiritual men have only Spiritual weapons David's slingshot was a Spiritual weapon and not a carnal one, because he used it for God and not for selfish purposes! The same is true for Gideon's swords and Samson's jawbone of an ass. The importance is not on the weapon used, but is on the attitude of the heart and obedience to God! But if our strength or our security lies in natural weapons themselves or if our vision is limited to self-glory or to self-power and rule, God cannot bless anyone in that. Our strength and defense is to rest in Him alone, caring not if it is fire from Heaven or fire from a barrel!!!!

In John 18:36(KJV), Jesus says, "My Kingdom is not of this world: if My Kingdom were of this world, then would My servants fight." We are not fighting to gain this world-system, for this world-system is not of the Father(1 John 2:15---17). We are fighting to possess the Kingdom which is ours (Daniel 7:18,21,22). The word "if" in John 18:36 could very well be translated "when" or "forasmuch as" or "though", and not affect the Greek wording at all. Our judgment must be according to the Spirit of God and His Word and not according to the Carnal Mind, which is an enemy of God. This is why only God's Army can truly judge. Psalms 149:5-9 says that this judgment is our honor! In fact, Joel 3:9-17 says that the message of War is the GOSPEL of <u>this</u> Hour! "Proclaim this to the Nations---PREPARE WAR!!!"

Christians must no longer be ignorant concerning God's plans and purposes for Jesus and His Christ! Jesus came the first

time as a Lamb to die for the sins of the
world and to set up a Spiritual Kingdom,
when the Religious—Political world was
looking for a conquering Messiah to free
them from Roman rule (John 6:15). This
time the world is looking for a meek Lamb,
an effeminate flower-child, to set up a
Spiritual Kingdom, when in reality,as a
conquering Messiah, He will set up His
earthly Kingdom as Lord of Lords and King
of Kings (Revelation 19:15,16), with all
nations under Him!

Deuteronomy 18:9-14 says that the a-
bominations of a diviner, enchanter, astrologer, witch, medium, wizard, or necromancer may not exist when we come into the
land which God gives us. Revelation 21:8;
22:15;19:19-21; and 1 Corinthians 6: 9,10
says that the kings and merchants of this
earth, the beast, those gathered against
us, the fearful, unbelieving, abominable,
murderers, whoremongers, sorcerers, idolaters, liars, heathen dogs, adulterers, effeminate, abusers of themselves with mankind, thieves, covetous, drunkards, re-
vilers, and extortioners, yea anyone not
purified by the blood of Christ and who
hasn't come out of Babylon (Revelation
18:4; 2 Corinthians 6:17,18) shall not enter into the Kingdom of God but shall be
cast into the Lake of Fire and Brimstone,
which is the second death---the Divinely
purifying fire to purge the chaff of this
earth in order to redeem all!

Behold the Army of God, God's Elect &
Anointed, the remnant of White Christian
Israel, who cannot be touched (1Chronicles
16:22; Psalms 105:15; Psalms 91).

84

IN CONCLUSION

We would like to thank all those who have confirmed the things we know to be true about the Illuminati--those we've met along the way and the contacts which we have.

We'd also like the Lord to know our appreciation and our love for Him for revealing these things to us by His Spirit. The mercy of God is exceedingly abundant.

It is our belief that we are indeed in the latter days, that perilous times are before us. We know what lies ahead, for the Sons of God are not in darkness. Because we know the Truth, we are also pressed concerning the Message of this hour.

Proverbs 8:13 says, "The fear of the Lord is to hate evil." The evil of this present perverted generation is beyond description. Men and women all over the world are saying, "Peace, Peace" when there is no peace! The deceiving propaganda of the Political and the Religious world is sapping the lifeblood out of the people of God.

It is our belief that the White Race is the Adamic Race of God and therefore the Sons of God, Israel. Jesus came to preach to the Lost Tribes of Israel (Matthew 10:5-7) and died only for Israel (He—brews 2:14-17). Romans 9:4,5 tells us that to ISRAEL pertains the Adoption (Sonship), the Glory, the Covenants (Testaments, or Bible), the Giving of the Law, the Service of God, and the Promises.

Let it be understood that we Love and Believe in America. This is why we are willing to fight and die, if necessary, for God's Israel. Unlike so many groups, our battle is not against just the JEWS or rebellious BLACKS, but against ALL the enemies of God. With perfect hatred, we hate the enemies of God (Psalms 139:19-22). We

85

believe in the <u>total</u> LAW OF GOD! "Without Holiness no man shall see God." Be not deceived, Israel--the Sons of God must be conformed to HIS image. The Army of God shall judge <u>your</u> sins as well as any oth--er's!

The ever-increasing Message of this hour is TO COME OUT OF BABYLON, MY PEOPLE, THAT YOU BE NOT PARTAKERS OF HER SINS, AND THAT YOU RECEIVE NOT OF HER PLAGUES (Revelation 18:4). Babylon shall fall in one hour, says the Word of God! Do not trust in a Physical <u>OR</u> Spiritual "Rapture" to deliver you out of Tribulation,for"through much tribulation we must enter into the Kingdom of God!" (Acts 14:22). Yield to the Calling and Election of God and His Consuming Fire!

The hour is late. The Kingdom of God is at hand. Now is the Day of Salvation. Let us cleanse ourselves of all filthiness of flesh and spirit. For too long the Saints have been blinded by the false image they've had of their God and Saviour; too long they've been blind to the truths and beauty of God's Word; too long they've allowed their lights to go out, to where one cannot tell Christian from non-Christian. These things must not be!!

How long will you stand between two
    opinions?
How long will you be double-minded?
If the Lord is God, then follow Him.
But if Baal is God---follow him!

For the place you're standing on is
    Holy Ground.
Take off the shoes from your feet.
For the gates of Hell shall not prevail
    against us!
Go forth and conquer---you are God's Seed!

86

"Lord, reveal your Truth to Israel. For we shall know the Truth and the Truth shall make us free. Open our hearts and minds to know. Give us hearing ears to listen to the still small voice of the God of Mt. Horeb. Pour out on your people the Fear of the Lord, that we may hate evil, that we may have understanding and wisdom, that we may KNOW the One who is the Ancient of Days and the Holy One. Break us, Jesus, for the Cross of Christ. Lead us by your Spirit to glorify Your Name and not ours. Give us the Spirit of Fasting , to seek you; the Spirit of Revelation, to know you; the Spirit of Righteousness, to be separated unto you. Break the yoke of bondage upon your people, that they may flow in your Spirit. In Jesus' Name. Amen"

87

No portion of this book
may be copied without written
permission of the author.

For more copies,
Send $4.00 per copy to:

C.S.A. Bookstore
Rt. 1,Box 128
Pontiac, Mo. 65729

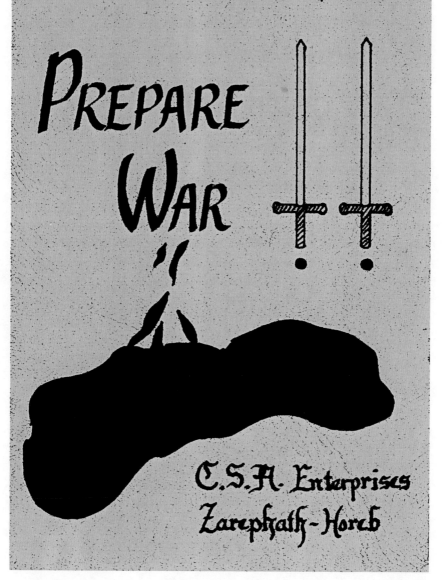

"PROCLAIM THIS AMONG THE NATIONS---
PREPARE WAR!!!"

This booklet is designed to give a Scriptural reasoning for war and Christian Army of God. The seriousness of the times and of the Spirit of God in this hour
forces us into preparation, into Holiness, and into
Righteousness.

The following chapters have been previously given
as Bible Studies and Teachings. It is prayed that Israel may hear the Message here and receive it as Life,
Conviction, and Necessity.

The God of Israel <u>commands</u> this Message--this Gos-
pel---to be proclaimed and published among the Nations
of Israel. "Prepare War! Wake up the Mighty Men!
Let all the Men of War come near. Let them come up.Beat
your plowshares into swords and your pruninghooks into
spears. Let the weak say, I am strong!" (<u>Joel 3:9,10).</u>

There is a joy, an honor, a reverence, in serving
Jesus and being a part of the Armies of Heaven. No man
can choose this for himself, except Jesus first choose
him (John 15:16). The honor of ruling, of fighting and
of overcoming (conquering), is one that changes us from
glory to glory. The revelation of preparing seriously
(and not just talking preparation or survival, but of
having works by our faith)is that of being a strong man
who is able to divide the spoils (Luke 11:21,22).

This booklet is to be read with all seriousness,as
any Gospel is to be received.

The God of Abraham, Isaac, and Jacob grant you deliverance from bondage into the Liberty of Dominion. In
Jesus' Name. Amen.

Printed Summer 1981

1

TABLE OF CONTENTS

2

SCRIPTURAL FOUNDATION FOR THE CHRISTIAN ARMY

God's elect---His Called, Chosen, and Faithful---
have a drawing within them, which causes them to never
be satisfied where they are in the Spirit until they
are completely conformed into the image of Christ,walk-
ing in the Fullness of their Father! Nothing short of
growing from glory to glory can satisfy this Spiritual
drive. The need to be as our Heavenly Father, the One
who passed His seed into us---the need to grow into maturity as a manifested Son of God---the need of being
where He is---the need of a Son to be like His Father--
is what causes us to desire to know Him and His Nature,
in order to know who He is and, therefore, what we are
to be.

In the Scriptures, an individual's name meant his
character, nature, anointing, ministry, etc. For exam-
ple--Immanuel is "God with us"; Abraham is "Father of a
Multitude";Jesus is "The Lord (Yahweh)saves or the Lord
our Salvation"; Adam is "Ruddy"; etc.

The Bible reveals many things of God's nature to
us. 1 John 1:5 says, "God is Light, and in Him is no
darkness at all." No one disagrees with this, or with
1 John 4:8, "God is Love." The Light of God shines on
our minds and hearts to give understanding and warmth;
the love of God draws us to repentance and grows us up
into mature Sons. But just as God is light and love, He
also is something else. Exodus 15:3 says, "The Lord is
a man of War: The Lord is His Name." The Lord God is a
man of War. That is His nature! How else could one explain the acts of God in the Old Testament of War,kill-
ing, and destruction except they see Him as the Man of
War? "See now that I, even I, am He and there is no God
with me: I kill and I make alive; I wound and I heal:
neither is there any that can deliver out of my hand.
If I whet my glittering sword, and mine hand take hold
of judgment: I will render vengeance to mine enemies,
and will reward them that hate me. I will make mine arrows drunk with blood and my sword shall devour flesh."
Deuteronomy 32:39,41,42.

Being in the Image of God, the elect Christian Army
of the Adamic Race shall also receive of the War Nature
of their Father. II Samuel 22:35 says, "He teaches my
hands to war." Further, in Psalms 144:1 God "teaches my
hands to war, and my fingers to fight." The reason for

this is because God says of the portion of Jacob (Israel),"Thou art my battle axe and weapons of war:for with thee will I break in pieces the nations, and with thee will I destroy Kingdoms." Jeremiah 57:20.

The Lord God of Israel has promised us this heritage. "Let the saints be joyful in glory: let them sing aloud upon their beds. Let the high praises of God be in their mouth and a two-edged sword in their hand; to execute vengeance upon the heathen, and punishments upon the people; to bind their Kings with chains, and their nobles with fetters of iron; to execute upon them the judgment written: This honour have all his saints. Praise ye the Lord." Psalms 149:5-9. In the Parables of the Marriage of the King's son (Matthew 22: 1-7) and of the Nobleman and the 10 pounds (Luke 19:12-27), Jesus tells us that at the end of this age He will send forth His armies, gathering those who would not have Him reign over them,and will slay them before Him! God, in fact, loves this judgment (Isaiah 61:8).

Many people feel that this attitude is false and conspiratory against America. Believing as we do, that America is Ephraim and that the British-Celtic-Germanic-Gaelic white people are Israel, we have a deepening love for this Country and for God's people. We believe that the attitude we have concerning war and judgment is not only American, but that we are true Americans by this belief. We desire a better America, a better world---free of the pollutions, bondages and perversities of this evil age. We believe the Declaration of Independence, written by our forefathers....

In CONGRESS, July 4, 1776.

A DECLARATION

By the REPRESENTATIVES of the

UNITED STATES OF AMERICA,

In GENERAL CONGRESS assembled.

WHEN in the Course of human Events, it becomes necessary for one People to dissolve the Political Bands which have connected them with another, and to assume among the Powers of the Earth, the separate and equal Station to which the Laws of Nature and of Nature's God entitle them, a decent Respect to the Opinions of Mankind requires that they should declare the causes which impel them to the Separation.

We hold these Truths to be self-evident, that all Men are created equal, that they are endowed by their Creator with certain unalienable Rights, that among these are Life, Liberty, and the Pursuit of Happiness—That to secure these Rights, Governments are instituted among Men, deriving their just Powers from the Consent of the Governed, that whenever any Form of Government becomes destructive of these Ends, it is the Right of the People to alter or to abolish it, and to institute new Government, laying its Foundation on such Principles, and organizing its Powers in such Form, as to them shall seem most likely to effect their Safety and Happiness. Prudence, indeed, will dictate that Governments long established should not be changed for light and transient Causes; and accordingly all Experience hath shewn, that Mankind are more disposed to suffer, while Evils are sufferable, than to right themselves by abolishing the Forms to which they are accustomed. But when a long Train of Abuses and Usurpations, pursuing invariably the same Object, evinces a Design to reduce them under absolute Despotism, it is their Right, it is their Duty, to throw off such Government, and to provide new Guards for their future Security. Such has been the patient Sufferance of these Colonies; and such is now the Necessity which constrains them to alter their former Systems of

5

Government. The History of the present King of Great-Britain is a History of repeated Injuries and Usurpations, all having in direct Object the Establishment of an absolute Tyranny over these States. To prove this, let Facts be submitted to a candid World.

He has refused his Assent to Laws, the most wholesome and necessary for the public Good.

He has forbidden his Governors to pass Laws of immediate and pressing Importance, unless suspended in their Operation till his Assent should be obtained; and when so suspended, he has utterly neglected to attend to them.

He has refused to pass other Laws for the Accommodation of large Districts of People, unless those People would relinquish the Right of Representation in the Legislature, a Right inestimable to them, and formidable to Tyrants only.

He has called together Legislative Bodies at Places unusual, uncomfortable, and distant from the Depository of their public Records, for the sole Purpose of fatiguing them into Compliance with his Measures.

He has dissolved Representative Houses repeatedly, for opposing with manly Firmness his Invasions on the Rights of the People.

He has refused for a long Time, after such Dissolutions, to cause others to be elected; whereby the Legislative Powers, incapable of Annihilation, have returned to the People at large for their exercise; the State remaining in the mean time exposed to all the Dangers of Invasion from without, and Convulsions within.

He has endeavoured to prevent the Population of these States; for that Purpose obstructing the Laws for Naturalization of Foreigners; refusing to pass others to encourage their Migrations hither, and raising the Conditions of new Appropriations of Lands.

He has obstructed the Administration of Justice, by refusing his Assent to Laws for establishing Judiciary Powers.

He has made Judges dependent on his Will alone, for the Tenure of their Offices, and the Amount and Payment of their Salaries.

He has erected a Multitude of new Offices, and sent hither Swarms of Officers to harrass our People, and eat out their Substance.

He has kept among us, in Times of Peace, Standing Armies, without the consent of our Legislatures.

He has affected to render the Military independent of and superior to the Civil Power.

6

HE has combined with others to subject us to a Jurisdiction foreign to our Constitution, and unacknowledged by our Laws; giving his Assent to their Acts of pretended Legislation:

FOR quartering large Bodies of Armed Troops among us:

FOR protecting them, by a mock Trial, from Punishment for any Murders which they should commit on the Inhabitants of these States:

FOR cutting off our Trade with all Parts of the World:

FOR imposing Taxes on us without our Consent:

FOR depriving us, in many Cases, of the Benefits of Trial by Jury:

FOR transporting us beyond Seas to be tried for pretended Offences:

FOR abolishing the free System of English Laws in a neighbouring Province, establishing therein an arbitrary Government, and enlarging its Boundaries, so as to render it at once an Example and fit Instrument for introducing the same absolute Rule into these Colonies:

FOR taking away our Charters, abolishing our most valuable Laws, and altering fundamentally the Forms of our Governments:

FOR suspending our own Legislatures, and declaring themselves invested with Power to legislate for us in all Cases whatsoever.

HE has abdicated Government here, by declaring us out of his Protection and waging War against us.

HE has plundered our Seas, ravaged our Coasts, burnt our Towns, and destroyed the Lives of our People.

HE is, at this Time, transporting large Armies of foreign Mercenaries to compleat the Works of Death, Desolation, and Tyranny, already begun with circumstances of Cruelty and Perfidy, scarcely paralleled in the most barbarous Ages, and totally unworthy the Head of a civilized Nation.

HE has constrained our fellow Citizens taken Captive on the high Seas to bear Arms against their Country, to become the Executioners of their Friends and Brethren, or to fall themselves by their Hands.

HE has excited domestic Insurrections amongst us, and has endeavoured to bring on the Inhabitants of our Frontiers, the merciless Indian Savages, whose known Rule of Warfare, is an undistinguished Destruction, of all Ages, Sexes and Conditions.

IN every stage of these Oppressions we have Petitioned for Redress in the most humble Terms: Our repeated Petitions have been answered only by repeated Injury. A Prince, whose Character is thus marked by every act which may define a Tyrant, is unfit to be the Ruler of a free People.

7

Nor have we been wanting in Attentions to our British Brethren. We have warned them from Time to Time of Attempts by their Legislature to extend an unwarrantable Jurisdiction over us. We have reminded them of the Circumstances of our Emigration and Settlement here. We have appealed to their native Justice and Magnanimity, and we have conjured them by the Ties of our common Kindred to disavow these Usurpations, which, would inevitably interrupt our Connections and Correspondence. They too have been deaf to the Voice of Justice and of Consanguinity. We must, therefore, acquiesce in the Necessity, which denounces our Separation, and hold them, as we hold the rest of Mankind, Enemies in War, in Peace, Friends.

WE, therefore, the Representatives of the U N I T E D S T A T E S O F A M E R I C A, in G E N E R A L C O N G R E S S, Assembled, appealing to the Supreme Judge of the World for the Rectitude of our Intentions, do, in the Name, and by Authority of the good People of these Colonies, solemnly Publish and Declare, That these United Colonies are, and of Right ought to be, F R E E A N D I N D E P E N D E N T S T A T E S; that they are absolved from all Allegiance to the British Crown, and that all political Connection between them and the State of Great-Britain, is and ought to be totally dissolved; and that as F R E E A N D I N D E P E N D E N T S T A T E S, they have full Power to levy War, conclude Peace, contract Alliances, establish Commerce, and to do all other Acts and Things which I N D E P E N D E N T S T A T E S may of right do. And for the support of this Declaration, with a firm Reliance on the Protection of divine Providence, we mutually pledge to each other our Lives, our Fortunes, and our sacred Honor.

Signed by ORDER *and in* BEHALF *of the* CONGRESS,

JOHN HANCOCK, PRESIDENT.

America, in Gaelic, means "The Kingdom of Heaven come to Earth." The Kingdom of God is NOW approaching.

Who then are we going to judge? How severe will the judgment be? What is the purpose of the War and of the Judgment of God to come? These and other questions will be answered in pages to come.

8

DOMINION BY VIOLENCE

In Genesis 1:26-28 God created Adam(and the Adamic Race)to have dominion over all things and to subdue the earth. Subdue means "to tread down; subjagate;to crumble." This is also stated in Psalms 8:4-9 and Hebrews 2:5-10. "For unto the angels hath he not put in subjection the world to come, whereof we speak. But one in a certain place testified, saying, what is man (Adam)that thou art mindful of him? (or, what do you have in mind for man?) or the son of man, that thou visitest him? Thou madest him a little lower than the angels (liter--ally---a little while inferior to God); thou crownest him with glory and honour and didst set him over the works of thy hands: Thou hast put all things in subjection under his feet. For in that he put all in subjection under him, he left nothing that is not put under him. But now we see not yet all things put under him (man). But we see Jesus, who was made a little lower than the angels for the suffering of death, crowned with glory and honor; that he by the grace of God should taste death for every man. For it became him, for whom are all things, and by who are all things, in bringing many sons unto glory, to make the captain of their salvation perfect through sufferings." Though Adamic man is not in dominion yet, we do see Jesus and the dominion He has, bringing us to the same throne!

But if man does not have the dominion yet, who or what does have dominion over man? Babylon (confusion) does! Confusion reigns in the earth now. Everything is in total rebellion to God. The Lord has it this way for now, in order to give His Sons an obstacle to overcome, in their growing into maturity. How will this confusion of Babylon--which causes a harlot church system, which advocates race-mixing, which allows abortion-murders by the millions, which instills the woman as the head of the husband, which produces the runaway rebellion and witchcraft and perversions of millions---how will it be torn down?

In Matthew 11:12, Jesus tells us,"From the days of John the Baptist until now the Kingdom of Heaven suffereth violence, and the violent take it by force." The

9

word"suffereth"here literally means <u>to force</u>. The Kingdom of Heaven(the realm of the Spirit in this age) <u>FOR-
CES</u> violence on the earth and the violent Sons of God
take it (the kingdom) by force!!

How can this be? The more that the Sons of God grow
into Maturity,the more pressure the Kingdom of darkness
feels, and the more violence is released on the earth.
The world is indeed waxing worse and worse as time goes
on.

Daniel 7:9-28 confirms this in that "the saints of
the Most High shall <u>take</u> the Kingdom, and possess the
kingdom for ever, even for ever and ever." (verse 18).
In fact, Daniel"beheld, and the same horn made war with
the saints, and prevailed against them; until the Ancient of Days came,and judgment was given to the saints
of the Most High;and the time came that the saints <u>pos-
sessed</u> the Kingdom." (verses 21,22). The revelation of
the coming war and judgment will change you if received
as it did for Daniel in verse 28.

How will we take and possess the Kingdom? There is
only one way. If a strong man holds a house, you must
break his strength by some action of violence.

Revelation 13:1-10 gives the account of the beast
with seven heads and ten horns, being wounded to death
and then healed. This wonder causes people to ask, "Who
can make war with the beast?" This beast continues
(literally, makes war)for 42 months against God and His
Tabernacle. All who dwell upon the earth shall worship
him, whose names are not written in the book of Life.
Jesus goes on to say,"If any man have an ear, let him
hear. He that leadeth into captivity shall go into captivity: he that killeth with the sword must be killed
with the sword. Here is the patience and the faith of
the saints."

Preachers have issued propaganda using these two
verses to say that Christians are not allowed to fight
back, or they will be killed. THIS IS NOT WHAT THIS IS
SAYING!! It is in fact the opposite of the truth. Jesus
is saying that since the beast leads into captivity and
kills with the sword, it must reap what it has sown!
Jesus gives us here the authority to use the weapons of

10

the Beast against those in rebellion to God!! This is confirmed by Jeremiah 18:15-23 where we are told that the rebellious are to die by the force of the sword.

An example of this is found in Genesis 6:5-8 and 11-13."And God saw that the wickedness of man was great in the earth and that every imagination of the thoughts of his heart was only evil continually. And it repented the LORD that he had made man on the earth, and it grieved him at his heart. And the LORD said, I will destroy man whom I have created from the face of the earth; both man, and beast, and the creeping thing, and the fowls of the air; for it repenteth me that I have made them. But Noah found grace in the eyes of the Lord. The earth also was corrupt before God and the earth was filled with violence. And God looked upon the earth, and, behold it was corrupt; for all flesh had corrupted his way upon the earth. And God said unto Noah,the end of all flesh is come before me; for the earth is filled with violence through them; and, behold, I will destroy them with the earth."

As in the days of Noah, so shall it be before the coming of the Son of Man. The earth is filled with violence and corruption. Again, the thoughts of men are only evil continually!! Again, God will destroy the inhabitants of the earth---this time by the same violence which man sows!!

The judgment of God will be severe on the earth! If the horror and sin of the world (and, in particular, the cities)were to be seen for only a moment,you're entire attitude and outlook would be totally changed. The anger of the Lord would become your anger;the wrath and hatred of God would be your wrath and hatred;the vengeance of the Almighty would be your vengeance! When the abominations of a man raping a 15 year old girl and then hacking off both arms below the elbows with a machete are seen (and then he gets only 14 years in prison) or of two blacks throwing acid into the face of a white woman they didn't even know,blinding her and disfiguring her and eventually killing her by the acid slowly eating away her insides (and then let free because of a lack of evidence), or of witches or homosexuals sexually mutilating people---multiply this by the fact that, in America, a rape, a killing, an armed robbery,and an abortion occurs several times every minute,

11

somewhere in America (not to mention the countless acts of adultery, prostitution,drug addiction, incest, human sacrifices, etc that continually go on). How else can these things be stopped? Governmental Laws are of no effect; Reform, both social and penal, is useless; the preaching of the churches is to little avail.

Revelation 18:21 says, "A mighty angel took up a stone like a great millstone, and cast it unto the sea, saying, Thus with violence shall that great city Babylon be thrown down, and shall be found no more at all." This is the same stone found in Daniel Chapter 2 that crushes the image of Babylon in the last days!

Violence, God's violence, shall overthrow Babylon and bring judgment to the earth! Man and Beast <u>shall</u> reap what they sow!

"The Kingdom of Heaven suffereth violence, and the violent take it by force."

12

THE HOLINESS OF GOD'S ARMY

"When the Lord thy God shall bring thee into the land whither thou goest to possess it and hath cast out many nations before thee, the Hittites and the Girgashites, and the Amorites, and the Canaanites, and the Perizzites, and the Hivites, and the Jebusites, seven nations greater and mightier than thou; and when the LORD thy God shall deliver them before thee;thou shalt smite them, and utterly destroy them; thou shalt make no covenant with them nor shew mercy unto them:neither shalt thou make marriages with them; thy daughters thou shalt not give unto his son, nor his daughter shalt thou take unto thy son. For they will turn away thy son from following me,that they may serve other gods:so will the anger of the LORD be kindled against you, and destroy thee suddenly. But thus shall you deal with them; ye shall break down their images and cut down their groves and burn their graven images with fire. For thou art an holy people unto the LORD thy God;the LORD thy God hath chosen thee to be a special people unto himself, above all people that are on the face of the earth. The Lord did not set his love upon you, nor choose you, because you were more in number than any people;for ye were the fewest of all people: But because the Lord loved you and because he would keep the oath which he had sworn unto your fathers, hath the Lord brought you out with a mighty hand, and redeemed you out of the house of bondmen,from the hand of Pharoah King of Egypt. Know therefore that the Lord thy God, he is God,the faithful God, which keepeth covenant and mercy with them that love him and keep his commandments to a thousand generations and repayeth them that hate him to their face, to destroy them: he will not be slack to him that hateth him; he will repay him to his face. Thou shalt therefore keep the commandments, and the statutes, and the judgments, which I command thee this day, to do them." Deuteronomy 7:1-11.

In this hour of the coming of God's judgment upon the earth, those used by Him to administer this judgment, must of necessity walk in the Spirit of God in Holiness and Righteousness, that their judgment be righteous---able to give out the proper and right judgment--and it must be holy--giving them clear conscience before Him and bringing those judged closer to repentance. 13

Moses, upon coming to the burning bush of God at Mt. Sinai, was commanded to "put off thy shoes from off thy feet, for the place whereon thou standest is holy ground." (Exodus 3:5). The place in the Spirit where God has brought and is bringing His Army is holy ground and must be approached with all reverence and fear of the Lord.

This holiness is bred into us, as Sons of God, by His Spirit, becoming more and more manifested as the living God purges us from our past walks in this life. The Law of God in Leviticus 11:44,45;19:2;20:7 and 20:26 says that, "ye shall be holy: for I the Lord thy God am holy."

To be holy---clean, sanctified (set apart), consecrated, dedicated---unto the Lord God is of necessity, for"without holiness, no man shall see God"(Heb 12:14).

The Army of God cannot be polluted with the spots and blemishes of the world, sin and self. "But upon Mt. Zion (the ruling place of the Sons of God) shall be deliverance(from everything that is against the Spirit of God), and there shall be holiness, and the house of Jacob shall possess their possessions." Obadiah 17. This is why Revelation 18:4 commands us to "Come out of her (Babylon, the Great Harlot) my people, that ye be not partakers of her sins, and that you receive not of her plagues."

2 Corinthians 6:14-18 tells us to be separated from the unclean things of unrighteousness,darkness, Belial, idols and the unbelieving infidels and God will receive us as a Father receives his sons and daughters. "Having therefore these promises, dearly beloved,let us cleanse ourselves from all filthiness of the flesh and spirit, perfecting holiness in the fear of God." 2 Corinthians 7:1.

The fear of the Lord is to hate evil and to depart from it. To not depart from the evil of this world-system is to not know Him above all else;it is to not love Him above all self;it is to not be conformed to His image!

"And I saw heaven opened, and behold a white horse and he that sat upon him was called Faithful and True, and in righteousness he doth judge and make war. His eyes were as a flame of fire, and on his head were many

14

crowns; and he had a name written, that no man knew, but he himself. And he was clothed with a vesture dipped in blood: and his name is called the Word of God. And the armies which were in heaven followed him upon white horses, clothed in fine linen, white and clean. And out of his mouth goeth a sharp sword, that with it he should smite the nations: and he shall rule them with a rod of iron: and he treadeth the winepress of the fierceness and wrath of Almighty God. And he hath on his vesture and on his thigh a name written, KING OF KINGS, AND LORD OF LORDS." Revelation 19:11-16. Jesus, of course, is clothed in righteousness and holiness, as are His Armies in heaven (in the Spirit). To smite and to rule and to tread are the heritages of this realm. Only those who walk in this are the Kings and Lords with Him!!

"And if the firstfruit (Jesus) be holy, the lump is also holy: and if the root be holy, so are the branches." Romans 11:16.

15

JUDGMENT ON THE CITIES

In John 14:15, Jesus said,"If you love me, keep my commandments." In fact, "He that loveth me not keepeth not my sayings" (verse 24).

Previously we said that God has commanded us to be holy and separated from sin, from the world, and from self. "Come out of her (Babylon), my people, that you be not partakers of her sins, and that you receive not of her plagues." Revelation 18:4. The Bible teaches, first that which is natural, then that which is spiritual (1 Corinthians 15:46). Before we can come out of spiritual Babylon and its confusion, we must first of all come out of natural Babylon and its confusion!

In Revelation 18:10, Babylon is called a mighty city. Why a city? The Bible has much to say on cities. It tells us the history of the first City--one built by the murderous Cain in Genesis 4:16,17. The next major city was built by an enemy of God, called Nimrod. Its name? Babylon (or Babel). Genesis 11:4-9. Isaiah 5:8-10 prophecies, "Woe unto them that join house to house, that lay field to field, till there be no place, that they may be placed alone in the midst of the earth! In mine ears said the Lord of hosts,of a truth many houses shall be desolate, even great and fair, without inhabitant. Yea, ten acres of vineyard shall yield one bath (about 1/11 of a bushel), and the seed of a homer shall yield an ephah (9/10 of a bushel)." And in Jeremiah 2:26-29, God likens Judah's gods to her cities, neither of which could save Judah.

Why such a "pessemistic" outlook on cities? Because cities have become the jungles of our society, manifesting the nature of sin and confusion and rebellion against God. There is no such thing today as a godly city! It is of the utmost importance that every Christian obey and escape from the cities---Now!

But why is there to be judgment upon the cities? What is their sin? The answers are Rebellion, Unrighteousness, and Transgressing God's Laws! Genesis 18:16-33 tells us that God would have spared Sodom, if Abraham had only found ten righteous men in the city. Sodom was destroyed! The wickedness and perversities of Sodom

16

and Gomorrah caused them to be destroyed by fire and by brimstone and to eventually be covered by the salty water of the Dead Sea.

But Jesus said in Matthew 11:20-24 that it would be more tolerable for the land of Sodom than for those cities which have seen the power of God and repented not! Babylon is not repentant of her sins!!

What will it be like when God's fury comes upon the earth? How severe will the judgments be in the cities? Leviticus 26:27-36 says God will chasten Israel seven times for her sins of disobedience. The people shall literally eat the flesh of their children, because of the famine in the land. "And I will destroy your high places and cut down your images, and cast your carcases upon the carcases of your idols, and my soul shall abhor you. And I will make your cities waste, and bring your sanctuaries unto desolation: and I will not smell the savour of your sweet odours. And I will bring the land into desolation: and your enemies which dwell therein shall be astonished at it." The word desolate, here and in other Scriptures, means "devastate; astonished," implying the idea of the vastness of the destruction of it, while waste means "parched thru drought; destroyed."

Ezekiel 6:1-7 prophecies to Israel that "your altars shall be desolate, and your images shall be broken: and I will cast down your slain before your idols. And I will lay the dead carcases of the children of Israel before their idols; and I will scatter your bones round about your altars. In all your dwelling places the cities shall be laid waste, and the high places shall be desolate; that your altars may be laid waste and made desolate, and your idols may be broken and cease, and your images may be cut down, and your works may be abolished. And the slain shall fall in the midst of you, and ye shall know that I am the LORD." This is to be done by the Sword of the Lord, which is His Army!

Isaiah 24:1-12 is a little harder on its description of coming times. "Behold, the LORD maketh it waste, and turneth it upside down (literally, perverteth the face thereof), and scattereth abroad the inhabitants thereof." Further, "the land shall be utterly emptied, and utterly spoiled: for the LORD hath spoken this word.

17

The earth mourneth and fadeth away, the world languisheth and fadeth away, the haughty people of the earth do languish. The earth also is defiled under the inhabitants thereof; because they have transgressed the laws, changed the ordinance, broken the everlasting covenant. Therefore hath the curse devoured the earth, and they that dwell therein are desolate: therefore the inhabitants of the earth are burned, and few men left." And still yet "the city of confusion is broken down: every house is shut up, that no man may come in. There is a crying for wine in the streets;all joy is darkened, the mirth of the land is gone. (Sounds like city-life,doesn't it?) In the city is left desolation and the gate is smitten with destruction." All true merriment and joy has left the people, replaced with an outward laughter and inward heartache and emptiness. But what are Israel's idols, altars, images and high places? And how will God "pervert the face of the earth?"

The whole chapter of Ezekiel 7 speaks of the judgment of God upon the cities, because of Israel's idolatry. It says "an end is come upon the four corners of the land...God shall not spare nor have pity...Violence is risen upon into a rod of wickedness....Wrath is upon the multitude....The sword is without (war in the country), and the pestilence and famine within (in the cities). He that is in the field shall die with the sword, and he that is in the city, pestilence(disease) and famine shall devour him....All hands shall be feeble, and all knees shall be weak as water. Their silver and gold shall not be able to deliver them....Make a chain, for the land is full of bloody crimes, and the city is full of violence...God will bring in the worst of the heathen to possess the houses. Destruction comes....They shall seek peace and there shall be none. The law shall perish from the priest (church preachers)." It doesn't sound pleasant, does it?

The law shall perish from the priests of today. They do not know nor understand the ways and laws of God. In fact, God has blinded them from understanding. Isaiah 6:1-13 gives this account telling that it shall be this way "until the cities be wasted without inhabitant, and the houses without man and the land be utterly desolate." It goes on to say that only a tenth of the cities and the people shall return, and these shall again be eaten, or consumed!

Though the Army of God will issue much of the judgment and the Lord will bring forth volcanoes, earthquakes, tornadoes and other natural catastrophes to destroy the cities, other elements shall come into play here---plagues, cannibalistic beasts of the field, perverted sodomite homosexuals and sadistic witches making sacrifices to their gods.

Zechariah 14; Revelation chapters 8,9,11,16 and 18 give details of some of the trumpet and vial plagues to come. "Their flesh shall consume away while they stand upon their feet, and their eyes shall consume away in their holes, and their tongue shall consume away in their mouth." The earth shall burn up; the seas shall become bloody and bitter; darkness shall be upon the earth where there shall be wailing and gnashing of teeth; locusts shall come to torment men for five months; men shall seek death and not find it, though they desire to die; noisome and grievous sores shall be upon men; they shall be scorched with the fire of the sun; they shall gnaw their tongues because of the pain; and violence shall overthrow the earth!!

1 Samuel 17:42-44 shows us how the Negro-beast of the field do eat the flesh of men. This cannibalistic fervor shall cause them to eat the dead and the living during this time. (The word cannibal, incidentally, means "Priest of Baal"). Revelation 6:8 says that they will help to kill a fourth of the earth.

The Sodomite homosexuals of today shall again manifest themselves as in the days of Sodom,when they would break the doors of Lot's house down, desiring the messengers of God, that they "may know them" (Genesis 19:4-8) wanting in their lusts to rape and seduce these holy beings of the living God! There are accounts today of homosexuals who have mutilated the sex organs of men and then made them eat the organs! The Sodomites say that they will not be stopped, for there are too many of them!

And what shall be said of the witches and Seed-of-Satan Jews, who are today sacrificing people in darkness,awaiting the time when they can do this freely and openly!

19

And who are these Cannibal Beasts, Sodomites,Witches and Jews going to do this to? To the unsuspecting, programmed city-living white Christians and"do-gooders" who've fought for the "rights" of these groups and who have allowed them to gain dominion of the cities!

The judgment of God will see this world of Egypt as utterly wasted and desolate for 40 years (Ezekiel 29:8-16), giving some people a continual employment of seeking dead bodies after a waiting period of seven months (Ezekiel 39:12-16).

No wonder the Bible says,"Woe unto you that desire the day of the LORD! To what end is it for you? The day of the LORD is darkness, and not light." (Amos 5:18).

Shall any city escape the judgment of God? Deuteronomy, chapter 20 gives the rules for war. Verses 10-18 says, "When thou comest nigh unto a city to fight against it, then proclaim peace unto it. And it shall be,if it make thee answer for peace,and open unto thee, then it shall be, that all the people that is found therein shall be tributaries unto thee, and they shall serve thee. And if it will make no peace with thee, but will make war against thee, then thou shalt besiege it: And when the Lord thy God hath delivered it into thine hands,thou shalt smite every male thereof with the edge of the sword. But the women, and the little ones, and the cattle, and all that is in the city even all the spoil thereof, shall thou take unto thyself; and thou shalt eat the spoil of thine enemies,which the Lord thy God hath given thee. Thus shalt thou do unto all the cities which are very far off from thee, which are not of the cities of these nations. But of the cities of these people,which the Lord thy God doth give thee for an inheritance,thou shalt save alive nothing that breatheth: But thou shalt utterly destroy them; namely, the Hittites, and the Amorites, the Canaanites, and the Perizzites, the Hivites, and the Jebusites (all mixedbreed races); as the Lord thy God hath commanded thee. That they teach you not to do after all their abominations, which they have done unto their gods; so should ye sin against the Lord your God."

20

THE LAW OF GOD

After Moses brought the children of Israel out from Egypt's bondage, he brought them to Mt. Sinai, the same Mount where he saw the burning bush and received his a-nointing from God. When Moses went up this time to the mount, the Lord God gave him 2 Tablets of stone called The 10 Commandments (Exodus 20:1-17)----

1) Thou shalt have no other gods before me

2) Thou shalt not make unto thee any graven image

3) Thou shalt not take the name of the Lord thy God in vain

4) Remember the Sabbath day to keep it holy

5) Honour thy father and thy mother

6) Thou shalt not kill

7) Thou shalt not commit adultery

8) Thou shalt not steal

9) Thou shalt not bear false witness against thy neighbor

10) Thou shalt not covet.

The first five commandments have to do with our re-lationship with God,while the last five have to do with men.

Jesus spoke of them this way--"Thou shalt love the Lord thy God with all thy heart, and with all thy soul, and with all thy mind. This is the first and great com-mandment. And the second is like unto it---Thou shalt love thy neighbor as thyself. On these two commandments hang all the law and the Prophets." Matthew 22:37-40.

The Law of God in the 10 Commandments is the Nat-ure of God written down. Everything else in the Law is based upon these Ten---with the exception of the Carnal Odinances, which Christ abolished.

Are we still under the Law? What does the Bible say concerning the Law?

Romans 7:12,14 tells us that the Law is HOLY and SPIRITUAL. Psalms 19:7 says it is PERFECT, converting the Soul.

21

"Whoever keeps the Law is a wise son"(Proverbs 28:
7). "Where no vision is, the people perish; but he that
keepeth the Law, happy is he." (Proverbs 29:18). What
vision? The vision of the Law!! "They that forsake the
Law praise the wicked; but such as keep the Law contend
with them." Proverbs 28:4. To forsake God's Law is to
say the wicked are greater than God:To praise the wicked!! How important is the Keeping of the Law? Proverbs
28:9 says, "He that turneth away his ear from hearing
the Law, even his prayer shall be abomination!" Such is
the seriousness of God's Laws!

"Blessed is the man that walketh not in the counsel
of the ungodly, nor standeth in the way of sinners, nor
sitteth in the seat of the scornful. But his delight is
in the Law of the Lord; and in his Law doth he meditate
day and night. And he shall be like a tree planted by
the rivers of water, that bringeth forth his fruit in
his season; his leaf also shall not wither; and whatsoever he doeth shall prosper." Psalms 1:1-3. Psalms 119,
the longest chapter in the Bible, is dedicated to the
Praise of the Law of God!

What is the purpose of the Law? Galatians 3:19
syas, "Wherefore then serveth the Law? It was added because of transgressions, till the seed come to whom the
promise was made; and it was ordained by angels in the
hand of a mediator." Verse 24 also tells us that "the
Law was our schoolmaster to bring us unto Christ, that
we might be justified by faith." We need the Law because of our sins, until it brings us unto the place in
Christ where we establish the Law by nature! Romans 3:
31.

But are we to still keep the Law? Deuteronomy 7:9
says there is a keeping of His Commandments to a 1000
generations. (There's only been about 90 generations
since Moses).

1 Timothy 1:8-10 says,"But we know that the Law is
good, if a man uses it lawfully. Knowing this, that the
law is not made for a righteous man,but for the lawless
and disobedient,for the ungodly and sinners, for unholy
and profane, for murderers of fathers and murderers of
mothers, for manslayers,for whoremongers, for them that
defile themselves with mankind,for menstealers, for liars, for perjured persons, and if there be any other
thing that is contrary to sound doctrine." Sin is the
Transgression of the Law(1 John 3:4). Since without the
Law there is no transgression of sin (Romans 4:15), the
Law must exist until there is no sin, since by the Law
is the Knowledge of Sin (Romans 3:20). 22

But didn't Jesus do away with the Law when He died for us? No! Jesus said, in Matthew 5:17,18, "Think not that I am come to destroy the Law, or the prophets;I am not come to destroy, but to fulfill. For verily I say unto you, Till heaven and earth pass, one jot or one tittle shall in no wise pass from the Law, till all be fulfilled." Therefore the Law must still be done in order to bring forth Christ! Galatians 3:24. (It needs to be noticed the differences between the Law and the Carnal or flesh-minded ordinances of the Law. Ephesians 2:14,15 says that Christ abolished the enmity, the Law of Commandments in ordinances. Colossians 2:14 says that He blotted them out,which were contrary to us(which the LAW isn't) and nailed them to the cross. Colossians 2:20-23 tells us what the ordinances are----TOUCH NOT, TASTE NOT (MEATS), HANDLE NOT! These ordinances perish!

Righteousness must cleanse unrighteousness! Sin must be judged by the LAW!! What sins? 1 Corinthians 6:9,10;15:50;Revelation 21:8;22:15 give a record of those who shall not enter into the Kingdom of God (the next age). Therefore since sin must be judged by the Law, what does the Law say concerning Idolaters,Blasphemers, Murderers, Adulterers, Thieves, Liars, Covetous, Sorcerers, Sodomites, Harlots, and the Unbelieving and the Unrepentant?

Murder---Exodus 21:12,14; Genesis 9:5,6; Numbers 35:16-21....."The murderer shall surely be put to death."

Adultery---Leviticus 20:10; Deuteronomy 22:22 (Note 1 Corinthians 5)..."Both the man and woman shall die.

Harlot (Prostitution)---Leviticus 19:29;Deuteronomy 23:17,18; Leviticus 21:9....."She shall be burnt with fire."

Sodomy (Homosexuality)---Leviticus 18:22-30; 20:13..... "They shall surely be put to death."

Race-Mixing----Exodus 22:19; Leviticus 18:23; 20:15,16; Deuteronomy 23:2; 27:21....."They shall both be put to death."

Blasphemy---Leviticus 24:10-16,23 (Note Acts 5)....."He shall surely be put to death."

Idolatry---Deuteronomy 29:17-28; 13:6-11...."Thou shalt surely kill him."

23

Sorcery (Witchcraft)----Exodus 22:18; Leviticus 20:6-8; Deuteronomy 18:10,11......"Thou shalt not allow a witch to live."

Disrespect to parents---Leviticus 20:9....."He shall be put to death."

Mixed Breed Races---Deuteronomy 7:1-7;20:17,18;23:2.... "Thou shalt utterly destroy them."

Manslaughter---Numbers 35:22-32......."The Congregation shall judge him."

Incest---Deuteronomy 27:20-23; Leviticus 18:6-18....... "Cursed"

Rape----Deuteronomy 22:23-29; Exodus 22:15-17 (Same for fornication)...."Death; Sometimes Marriage"

Bearing False Witness----Deuteronomy 19:16-21....."Life for life; eye for an eye; tooth for a tooth."

Assault---Exodus 21:18-25...."Repayment as deemed fit."

Stealing---Exodus 22:1-8...."Let him pay double."

Secret Lodges---Deuteronomy 12:1-3...."Destroy them."

The Bible says that "evil men do not understand judgment" (Proverbs 28:5), but "it is a joy to the just to do judgment" (Proverbs 21:15).

Obadiah 21 says,"Saviours(Deliverers; Judges)shall come up on Mount Zion to judge the mount of Esau; and the Kingdom shall be the LORD'S." Since judgment is given to the saints (Daniel 7:22;Isaiah 28:6; Deuteronomy 29:29),Isaiah 26:9 tells us, "When thy judgments are in the earth, the inhabitants of the world will learn Righteousness!"

God's people are destroyed for lack of knowledge since THEY HAVE FORGOTTEN THE LAW!! Hosea 4:6.

THE PURPOSE AND END OF WAR

We know that the enemies of God-----the Witches, Idolators, Secret Lodge Temples, the Sodomites, Rebell-ious beasts of the field Negroes,the Harlot Church Sys-tem, the Seed-of-Satan Jews, the Beast Government,etc-- shall be judged in the hour to come.

2 Thessalonians 1:6-10 records, "Seeing it is a righteous thing with God to recompense tribulation to them that trouble you (the Holy Ones of Israel). And to you who are troubled, rest with us, when the Lord Jesus shall be revealed from heaven with his mighty angels (messengers or men),in flaming fire taking vengeance on them that know not God, and that obey not the gospel of our Lord Jesus Christ: who shall be punished with ever-lasting (age-lasting) destruction from the presence of the Lord, and from the glory of His Power;when He shall come to be glorified in His saints,and to be admired in all them that believe in that day." God has perfect ha-tred(Romans 9:13), therefore "Do not I hate them,O Lord that hate thee? And am not I grieved with those that rise up against thee? I hate them with perfect hatred: I count them mine enemies." Psalms 139:21,22.

The Christian Army of God is revealed in Joel 2:1- 11. "Blow ye the trumpet in Zion, and sound an alarm in my holy mountain: let all the inhabitants of the land tremble: for the day of the Lord cometh, for it is nigh at hand; A day of darkness and of gloominess, a day of clouds and of thick darkness,as the morning spread upon the mountains: a great people and a strong; there hath not been ever the like, neither shall be any more after it, even to the years of many generations. A fire de-voureth before them; and behind them a flame burneth; the land is as the Garden of Eden before them, and be-hind them a desolate wilderness; yea, and nothing shall escape them. The appearance of them is as the appear-ance of horses;and as horsemen, so shall they run. Like the noise of chariots on the tops of mountains shall they leap, like the noise of a flame of fire that de-voureth the stubble, as a strong people set in battle array. Before their face the people shall be much pain-ed: all faces shall gather blackness. They shall run like mighty men; they shall climb the wall like men of

25

war; and they shall march every one in his own ways:and they shall not break their ranks: Neither shall one thrust another; they shall walk every one in his path: and when they fall upon the sword, they shall not be wounded. They shall run to and fro in the city; they shall run upon the wall, they shall climb up upon the houses;they shall enter in at the windows like a thief, the earth shall quake before them; the heavens shall tremble: the sun and the moon shall be dark, and the stars shall withdraw their shining: And the LORD shall utter His Voice before His Army: for his camp is very great:for he is strong that executeth his word: for the Lord is great and very terrible; and who can abide it?"

The Power of God's Army can surely be seen in the above verses. Further,Psalms 91:5-7 shows us that "Thou shalt not be afraid for the terror by night;nor for the arrow that flieth by day; nor for the pestilence that walketh in darkness; nor for the destruction that wasteth at noonday. A thousand shall fall at thy side, and ten thousand at thy right hand; but it shall not come nigh thee." This promise is,of course,to"He that dwelleth in the secret place of the Most High(and thus)shall abide under the shadow of the Almighty." (verse 1).

The Realm of this Body of Christ is far more than the natural mind can perceive, yet so many only see the ruling and reigning over Israel and the other nations. True,God has made us priests and Kings to reign on the earth (Revelation 1:6), but it needs to be seen that priests INTERCEDE AND MEDIATE for the people!

War is only a step, though a big one, to bringing Righteousness to the earth. "When God's judgments are in the earth, the inhabitants of the world will learn righteousness!" (Isaiah 26:9).

The increase (fruitfulness)of Jesus' kingdom shall never end (Isaiah 9:6,7), for judgment and justice(mercy) shall establish it. "For this is the covenant that I will make with the House of Israel after those days, saith the Lord; I will put my laws into their hearts: and I will be to them a God, and they shall be to me a people:And they shall not teach every man his neighbor, and every man his brother, saying, Know the Lord: for all shall know me, from the least to the greatest. For I will be merciful to their unrighteousness, and their sins and their iniquities will I remember no more." Hebrews 8:10-12.

26

The Restitution of all Things(Acts 3:21) as spoken of by the prophets, shall be the gathering together of all things, whether in heaven or on earth, into Christ (Ephesians 1:10), during the age known as the glorious Dispensation of the Fullness of Times.

To rule (Revelation 2:26,27) is to SHEPHERD. The Soldier shall become the Shepherd; the judged shall become his sheep!

"And it shall come to pass in the last days, that the mountain of the Lord's house shall be established in the top of the mountains, and shall be exalted above the hills; and all nations shall flow into it. And many people shall go and say, Come ye, and let us go to the mountain of the Lord, to the house of the God of Jacob; and he will teach us of his ways, and we will walk in his paths; for out of Zion shall go forth the Law, and the word of the Lord from Jerusalem. And he shall judge among the nations,and shall rebuke many people:for they shall beat their swords into plowshares, and the spears into pruninghooks: nation shall not lift up sword against nation, NEITHER SHALL THEY LEARN WAR ANY MORE!" Isaiah 2:2-4. "The wolf also shall dwell with the Lamb, and the leopard shall lie down with the kid; and the calf and the young lion and the fatling together; and a little child shall lead them." Isaiah 11:6.

The day shall come when all shall know Him! When each shall move as he was created to. When Negro and Oriental shall serve White;when the wife shall truly be a helpmeet to the husband; when only Peace, Righteousness, and Joy in the Holy Ghost shall flow, instead of hatred, turmoil, and iniquity. The Tree of Life shall surely bear leaves for the healing of the nations(Revelation 22:2,3) and there shall be no more curse!! Thank you Jesus!!

Isaiah 61:1-6 tells us the ministry of God's anointed in Redemption and that we "shall build the old wastes, and shall raise up the former desolations of many generations. And strangers shall stand and feed our flocks,and the sons of the alien shall be our plowmen and our vinedressers. But we shall be named the Priests of the Lord:men shall call us Ministers of our God: we shall eat the riches of the Nations, and in their glory shall we boast ourselves."

27

We shall rebuild the cities after God wastes them!
What a job to look forward to! And the extent of rebuilding?

"Thus saith the Lord God: In the day that I shall
have cleansed you from all your iniquities, I will also
cause you to dwell in the cities, and the wastes shall
be builded. And the desolate land shall be tilled,
whereas it lay desolate in the sight of all that passed
by. And they shall say, This land that was desolate is
become like the Garden of Eden, and the waste and desolate and ruined cities are become fenced, and are inhabited. Then the heathen that are left round about you
shall know that I the Lord build the ruined places, and
plant that that was desolate:I the Lord have spoken it,
and I will do it. Thus saith the Lord God: I will yet
for this be enquired of by the house of Israel,to do it
for them; I will increase them with men like a flock.
As the holy flock, as the flock of Jerusalem, in her
solemn feasts; so shall the waste cities be filled with
flocks of men: and they shall know that I am the LORD."
Ezekiel 36:33-38.

"And I, when I am lifted up from the earth, will draw
all unto me!" John 12:32.

28

HOW DO YOU PREPARE FOR THE WAR TO COME?

After reading the previous chapters on war and the judgments of God to come, one may ask, "What do I do? How do I prepare for what's going to happen?"

We've talked previously concerning the Scripture in Revelation 18:4, "Come out of her (Babylon), my people, that you be not partakers of her sins, and that you receive not of her plagues." It is of necessity for the Christians of today to come out of Babylon---the confusion of the harlot denominations and organized "church" groups, the rat-race of the city and suburban lifestyles, the carnality of the corrupt and selfish ways that we have which are in rebellion to God, and of the spirits which vex every Christian's life.

God has, in His word, commanded every man of God to come out of his natural home and country, and to come unto Him in the wilderness for a time, to be taught by Him!!

Preparing for war is more than "beans and bullets." It's being found in Christ Jesus and being with His 100-fold people.

Do not be deceived, as Lot was, and think that you can get out at any time. Remember, Lot received no inheritance, lost his wife, and his fruit became the Moabite and the Ammonite races.

In Revelation 18:10 and 17, we are told that Babylon's judgment shall come in one hour, and that death, mourning, and famine shall begin that day (verse 8). Jesus Himself said that He shall come as a thief in the night, when no one expects Him to. When the world cries, "Peace and Safety, then shall sudden destruction come, and they shall not escape." 1 Thessalonians 2,3.

Jesus told Peter in Luke 22:36, "He that has no sword, let him sell his garment, and buy one." Peter replied, "Lord, behold, here are two swords." Jesus said, "It is enough." We must have the natural sword for physical battle and the Sword of the Spirit, the Word of God (Hebrews 4:12), which gives us the power of God!

It is important to remember though that weapons in the natural are vanity without Jesus (Deuteronomy 32: 29,30)! Money cannot save you. Self-preservation will be fruitless!

29

Receive the Lord Jesus Christ as your personal Saviour into your life---get with a group that <u>knows</u> God and that has a plural five-fold Ministry---that is seriously preparing both in the natural and in the Spirit for the days to come----that has the <u>power</u> <u>and</u> <u>fruit</u> of God's Spirit active in their lives---and who really believes God's Bible and its truths!

Be serious with the Holiness of God and His People. Cast away all filth of the flesh and spirit and put on Christ Jesus!

But does everyone that goes on with God have to be a Warrior in His Army? No! 1 Samuel 30:24 says, "As his part is that goeth down to the battle, so shall his part be that tarries by the stuff: they shall share alike." The Army's purpose is to protect and feed the Woman of Israel in the Wilderness (Revelation 12).

God loves His people Israel, and has a special place for them. But our Father is Holy---our flesh and blood cannot inherit the Kingdom of God. We must put off the carnal mind in order to have the mind of Christ. Without a vision, the people perish. Nothing is worth missing the blessings God has for us! We do not yet even begin to see all He has planned for us. Humble yourself and God SHALL EXALT you!---But He will resist the proud! Love Him and obey! "Thou therefore endure hardness, as a good soldier of Jesus Christ. No man that warreth entangles himself with the affairs of this life; that he may please him who hath chosen him to be a soldier." 2 Timothy 2:3,4.

The message of "Prepare War" has been sounding on the earth for a long time. God's people are waiting for a certain word. Found in Ezekiel 12:17-28, it says, "The days are at hand, and the effect of every vision. The word shall be no more prolonged: for in your days will I say the word and will perform it, saith the Lord God."

"Even so, come Lord Jesus." Revelation 22:20.

30

"YOU CANNOT RUN---YOU CANNOT HIDE"

It's finally happened---It's on us now!
The world is seeing it---The war has begun!
The sun is darkened---Moon's turned to blood;
City streets overflow---With crimson flood!

(chorus)

You cannot run---You cannot hide!
There ain't no sense in ever going back!
You cannot run---You cannot hide.
Go on with Jesus 'cause you'll never go back!

Riots are going---Killings in the streets.
The blood's aflowing---Up to the horses' necks.
Eyes of the people---Melting down their cheeks.
Screams of horror---Are all you'll ever hear!

Kings of the earth---Captains of this world,
Out to make War, With God's Christ and His Lord.
Fowls of Heaven, Eat the enemies' flesh.
Who can make war with the Beast? We Can!

It's over with---Rubble everywhere!
A new age has begun and Righteousness is here!
What was it for? Did it have to be?
Knowing God draweth nigh---Oh, can't you see?

31

MILITARY BIBLE PROMISES

The following are a few of the Military Promises in the Scriptures. Given to Israel, they are obtained and possessed by those who walk in God's Spirit, for promises are received by faith in the holiness of the Fear of the Lord (2 Corinthians 7:1).

Exodus 15:3---"The Lord is a Man of War:the Lord is His Name."

Psalms 144:1---"He teaches my hands to war, and my fingers to fight."

Jeremiah 51:20---"Thou art my battle axe and my weapons of war: for with thee will I break in pieces the nations and with thee will I destroy kingdoms."

Psalms 139:21,22---"Do not I hate the,O Lord,that hate thee? And am not I grieved with those that rise up against thee? I hate them with perfect hatred: I count them mine enemies."

Psalms 91:7----"A thousand shall fall at thy side, and ten thousand at thy right hand; but it shall not come nigh thee."

Isaiah 26:9----"When God's judgments are in the earth, the inhabitants of the world will learn righteousness."

Isaiah 54:17----"No weapon that is formed against thee shall prosper;and every tongue that shall rise against thee in judgment thou shalt condemn.This is the heritage of the servants of the Lord,and their righteousness is of me, saith the Lord."

1 John 4:4---"Greater is He that is in you than he that is in the world."

It is also good to know the following references:

Psalms 149:5-9---The Honor of the Saints

Daniel 7:18,21,22---Possessing the Kingdom

Deuteronomy 20---Rules for War

Joel 2---God's Army

Psalsm 91---In His Pavillion

Isaiah 2:2-4---No more War to be learned.

2 Timothy 2:3,4---Endure as a good Soldier!   32

For Copies of this book
Send $3.00/copy to:

C.S.A. Bookstore

Pontiac, Mo. 65729

Bibliography

Adair-Toteff, Christopher. 2005. "Max Weber's Charisma." *Journal of Classical Sociology* 5, no. 2: 189–204. http://jcs.sagepub.com. Accessed July 24, 2009.

Aho, James A. 1990. *The Politics of Righteousness*. Seattle: Univ. of Washington Press.

Barkun, Michael. 2003. *Culture of Conspiracy: Apocalyptic Visions in Contemporary America*. Berkeley: Univ. of California Press.

———. 1994. *Religion and the Racist Right*. Chapel Hill: Univ. of North Carolina Press.

Bennett, David H. 2005. *Party of Fear: The American Far Right from Nativism to the Militia Movement*.

Coulson, Danny, and Elaine Shannon. 1999. *No Heroes: Inside the FBI's Secret Counter-Terror Force*. New York: Pocket Books.

Dawson, Lorne. Forthcoming. "Charismatic Leadership in Millennialist Movements: Its Nature, Origins, and Development." In *The Oxford Handbook of Millennialism,* ed. Catherine Wessinger. Syracuse: Syracuse Univ. Press.

Department of Homeland Security. April 7, 2009. "Right Wing Extremism: Current Economic and Political Climate Fueling Resurgence in Radicalization and Recruitment." http://www.fas.org/irp/eprint/rightwing .pdf. Accessed Sept. 24, 2009.

Docherty, Jayne. 2001. *Learning Lessons from Waco: When the Parties Bring Their Gods to the Table*. Syracuse: Syracuse Univ. Press.

Dyer, Joel. 1997. *Harvest of Rage: Why Oklahoma City Is Only the Beginning*. Boulder: Westview Press.

"John Todd (Occultist)." n.d. http://en.wikipedia.org/wiki/John_Todd _%28occultist%29.

Kaplan, Jeffrey, ed. 2000. *Encyclopedia of White Power: A Sourcebook on the Radical Racist Right*. Lanham, MD: Alta Mira Press.

Kaplan, Jeffrey, and Leonard Weinberg. 1998. *The Emergence of a Euro-American Radical Right*. New Brunswick, NJ: Rutgers Univ. Press.

441

Lane, Katja, ed. 1999. *Deceived, Damned and Defiant: The Revolutionary Writings of David Lane*. St. Maries, ID: 14 Word Press.

"The Legend of John Todd." n.d. Reprinted from *Christianity Today*, Feb. 2, 1979. http://www.holysmoke.org/sdhok/todd00.htm.

Leyden, T. J., with M. Bridget Cook. 2008. *Skinhead Confessions: From Hate to Hope*. Springville, UT: Cedar Fort, Inc.

Lifton, Robert J. 2003. *Superpower Syndrome*. New York: Thunder's Mouth Press/Nation Books.

Macdonald, Andrew (William Pierce). 1996. *The Turner Diaries*. New York: Barricade Books.

Mead, Walter Russell. 2001. *Special Providence: American Foreign Policy and How It Changed the World*. New York: Knopf.

Neiwert, David A. 1999. *In God's Country: The Patriot Movement and the Pacific Northwest*. Pullman: Washington State Univ. Press.

———. 2009. *The Eliminationists: How Hate Talk Radicalized the American Right*. Sausalito, CA: PoliPointPress, LLC.

Passmore, Kevin. 2002. *Fascism: A Very Short Introduction*. Oxford: Oxford Univ. Press.

Pierce, William. See Andrew Macdonald.

Rapoport, David C. 2004. "The Four Waves of Modern Terrorism." In *Attacking Terrorism: Elements of a Grand Strategy*, ed. Audrey K. Cronin and James M. Ludes. Washington, DC: Georgetown Univ. Press.

Rosenfeld, Jean. 2000. "The Justus Freemen Standoff." In *Millennialism, Persecution, and Violence*, ed. Catherine Wessinger, 323–44. Syracuse: Syracuse Univ. Press.

Singer, Margaret Thaler, with Janja Lalich. 1995. *Cults in Our Midst: The Hidden Menace in Our Everyday Lives*. San Francisco: Jossey-Bass Publishers.

Southern Poverty Law Center. August 2009. "The Second Wave: Return of the Militias." http://www.splcenter.org/images/dynamic/main/The_Second_Wave.pdf. Accessed September 24, 2009.

Stern, Jessica. 2003. *Terror in the Name of God: Why Religious Militants Kill*. New York: Harper Collins.

Tec, Nechama. 2009. *Defiance*. Oxford: Oxford Univ. Press.

Van der Leeuw, Gerardus. 1963. *Religion in Essence and Manifestation*. Princeton: Princeton Univ. Press.

Wilson, Michael, and Natalie Zimmerman, eds. 2009. *Kingdom at Any Cost: Right Wing Voices of the Apocalypse in America*. Little Rock: Parkhurst Brothers, Inc.

Index